The Economics of Knowledge, Innovation and Systemic Technology Policy

There is wide consensus on the importance of knowledge for economic growth and local development patterns. This book proposes a view of knowledge as a collective, systemic and evolutionary process that enables agents and social systems to overcome the challenges of the limits to growth. It brings together new conceptual and empirical contributions, analysing the relationship between demand and supply factors and the rate and direction of technological change. It also examines the different elements that compose innovation systems.

The Economics of Knowledge, Innovation and Systemic Technology Policy provides the background for the development of an integrated framework for the analysis of systemic policy instruments and their mutual interaction with the socio-political and economic conditions of the surrounding environment.

These aspects have long been neglected in innovation policy, as policy-makers, academics and the business community have mostly emphasized the benefits of supply-side strategies. However, a better understanding of innovation policies grafted on a complexity-based approach calls for the appreciation of the mutual interactions between both supply and demand aspects, and it is likely to improve the actual design of policy measures.

This book will help readers to understand the foundations and workings of demand-driven innovation policies by stressing the importance of competent and smart demand.

Francesco Crespi is Associate Professor at the Department of Economics of Roma Tre University, and Research Associate at the Bureau of Research on Innovation, Complexity and Knowledge (BRICK), Collegio Carlo Alberto, Italy.

Francesco Quatraro is Associate Professor at the Department of Economics and Statistics of University of Torino, and Research Associate at the Bureau of Research on Innovation, Complexity and Knowledge (BRICK), Collegio Carlo Alberto, Italy and at the GREDEG, University of Nice Sophia Antipolis, France.

Routledge studies in global competition
Edited by
John Cantwell
Rutgers, the State University of New Jersey, USA
and
David Mowery
University of California, Berkeley, USA

The Economics of Knowledge, Innovation and Systemic Technology Policy

Edited by
Francesco Crespi and
Francesco Quatraro

Routledge
Taylor & Francis Group

LONDON AND NEW YORK

First published 2015
by Routledge
2 Park Square, Milton Park, Abingdon, Oxon OX14 4RN

and by Routledge
52 Vanderbilt Avenue, New York, NY 10017

First issued in paperback 2020

Routledge is an imprint of the Taylor & Francis Group, an informa business

British Library Cataloguing in Publication Data
A catalogue record for this book is available from the British Library

Library of Congress Cataloging-in-Publication Data
The economics of knowledge, innovation and systemic technology policy /
edited by Francesco Crespi and Francesco Quatraro.
   pages cm
   Includes bibliographical references and index.
   1. Knowledge management–Economic aspects–Europe.
   2. Technological innovations–Economic aspects–Europe.
   I. Crespi, Francesco. II. Quatraro, Francesco.
   HD30.2.E264 2015
   338.94'06–dc23   2014046462

ISBN 13: 978-0-367-66882-2 (pbk)
ISBN 13: 978-0-415-70301-7 (hbk)

Typeset in Times New Roman
by Wearset Ltd, Boldon, Tyne and Wear

Contents

Figures

Tables

Contributors

Cristiano Antonelli, Department of Economics, University of Turin and BRICK Collegio Carlo Alberto.

Pierre-Alexandre Balland, Urban and Regional Research Centre Utrecht (URU).

Federico Biagi, JRC-IPTS European Commission, University of Padua and SDA Bocconi.

Susana Borrás, Copenhagen Business School.

Ron Boschma, Lund University – CIRCLE.

Davide Consoli, INGENIO (CSIC-UPV), Valencia (Spain).

Riccardo Crescenzi, Department of Geography and Environment & SERC, London School of Economics, Rossi Doria Centre for Economic and Social Research, Roma Tre University, Italy.

Francesco Crespi, Associate Professor at the Department of Economics of Roma Tre University, and Research Associate at the Bureau of Research on Innovation, Complexity and Knowledge (BRICK), Collegio Carlo Alberto, Italy.

Charles Edquist, Lund University – CIRCLE.

Amnon Frenkel, Samuel Neaman Institute for Advanced Studies in Science and Technology Technion – Israel Institute of Technology.

Luisa Gagliardi, Department of Geography and Environment, London School of Economics, Centre for Regional Economics, Transports and Tourism (CERTeT), Bocconi University, Italy.

Agnieszka Gehringer, Department of Economics, University of Göttingen.

Jens Horbach, University of Applied Sciences Augsburg.

Dieter Kogler, University College Dublin.

Jackie Krafft, University of Nice Sophia Antipolis, CNRS-GREDEG.

Sorin M.S. Krammer, University of Groningen, Faculty of Economics and Business, Department of Global Economics and Management.

Shlomo Maital, Samuel Neaman Institute for Advanced Studies in Science and Technology Technion – Israel Institute of Technology.

Alberto Marzucchi, Department of International Economics, Institutions and Development (DISEIS), Catholic University of Milan, Italy.

Cristian Matti, INGENIO (CSIC-UPV), Valencia, Spain.

Sandro Montresor, Faculty of Economics and Law, Kore University of Enna, Italy.

Marco Percoco, Department of Policy Analysis and Public Management, Università Bocconi.

Andreas Pyka, University of Hohenheim, Economics Institute, Wollgrasweg 23, D-70599 Stuttgart, Germany.

Francesco Quatraro, Associate Professor at the Department of Economics and Statistics of University of Torino. Research Associate at the Bureau of Research on Innovation, Complexity and Knowledge (BRICK), Collegio Carlo Alberto, Italy and at the GREDEG CNRS, University of Nice Sophia Antipolis, France.

Jacques-Laurent Ravix, University of Nice Sophia Antipolis, CNRS-GREDEG.

Verónica Robert, Universidad Nacional de General Sarmiento.

Pier Paolo Saviotti, INRA-GAEL, Université Pierre Mendès-France, BP 47, 38040 Grenoble, France. GREDEG CNRS, Sophia Antipolis, Valbonne, France; Eindhoven Centre for Innovation Studies (ECIS), School of Innovation Sciences, Eindhoven University of Technology, P.O. Box 513, NL-5600MB Eindhoven, The Netherlands; Temporary Research Fellow, Institute of Advanced Studies (IAS), Durham University, Durham, UK.

Jurai Stančík, JRC-IPTS European Commission.

Gabriel Yoguel, Universidad Nacional de General Sarmiento.

1 Knowledge, innovation and the different dimensions of systemic technology policy

Francesco Crespi and Francesco Quatraro

1 Introduction

Knowledge and innovation are increasingly recognized as being among the main ingredients to boost the competitiveness of countries and regions. In this perspective, the effectiveness of the policy instruments aimed at promoting the generation of new technologies plays a crucial role as a way to open up new growth paths.

The starting idea of this book is that the complex and distributed character of scientific and technological knowledge asks for an in-depth analysis of the different but complementary and strongly interrelated drivers of the generation of new ideas.

The importance of technological knowledge to economic processes has been recognized relatively late by scholars in economics. Nowadays, despite the variety of approaches to the issue, the consensus is basically unanimous on the boosting effects that the creation of new technological knowledge may have on economic performances.

The mechanisms by which knowledge can affect the performances of firms, regions and nations are manifold. New knowledge can be embodied in new and more effective machineries, or it can contribute to improve the design of the production process. This increases firms' productivity. A new technology can be at the core of the development of a new product, which allows a firm to enter new markets or to improve its position in its usual market. This paves the way to new growth paths. Knowledge creation generates important spillovers at the local level, which are likely to benefit innovation dynamics of firms settled in a specific area. When new knowledge stems out of a radical discontinuity in the technological paradigm, spillovers are more likely to be exploited by new entrants than by incumbents, fostering the entrepreneurial process. These dynamics can also yield positive dynamics on employment and job creation in the long run, by stimulating self-enforcing growth processes.[1]

Once the role of innovation in economic processes and the existence of a variety of mechanisms that lead to the generation of new knowledge are recognized, the relevance of setting a multi-dimensional system of policy instruments to activate and foster the different sources of innovation dynamics can be properly appreciated. Hence, as it will be clarified in the next sections of this chapter, the structure of the book is conceived as to show how the peculiar characteristics of knowledge call for an integrated system of policies to foster its generation and diffusion that takes into account all actors (including the public sector itself) and all forces involved in these processes along with their interactions.

2 Modes of knowledge production: from linearity to complexity

The increasing evidence about innovation dynamics has stimulated a wide body of literature dealing with the very mechanisms by which technological knowledge is generated, diffused and exploited. By looking at the evolution of the theoretical approaches to technological knowledge in the economics of innovation, one may identify three main turning points, which are also featured by coherent empirical approaches (Krafft and Quatraro, 2011; Quatraro, 2012).

The former explicit attempt to model the production of scientific knowledge dates back to the 1940s. Vannevar Bush's report to the US president was dominated by a vision of knowledge accumulation as an outcome of a linear process like this one: science precedes technology development, which then comes to be adopted by firms, and finally affects production efficiency. This has long been the main reference text to students of science and technology, as Kline and Rosenberg's critique to this representation came only in the 1980s (Bush, 1945; Kline and Rosenberg, 1986; Balconi *et al.*, 2010). The empirical counterpart to such a theoretical approach can be found in Zvi Griliches' 1979 paper, in which he proposed the famous extended production function. In this article, Griliches provides a formalization of the concept of knowledge capital stock, which is modelled by applying permanent inventory method to calculate the knowledge stock starting from R&D expenditures. It is clear that the application of lag generating functions to investments measures so as to get a stock implies an underlying sequential process that starts with R&D investments to yield a proxy of cumulated knowledge that in turn is supposed to show some effects on economic performances.

In the late 1980s and early 1990s, some scholars of science and technology started criticizing the linear model, by proposing an alternative view basically drawing upon systemic models of innovation based upon the interaction among different and yet complementary institutions involved in the complex business of knowledge production (Kline and Rosenberg, 1986; Gibbons *et al.*, 1994). Moreover, the analysis of knowledge as a factor in an extended production function became an object of criticism. Actually, it was just a way for economists to preserve the basic microeconomic assumptions about production sets out of which firms take their profit-maximizing choice. However, such approach assumes the existence of a separate R&D sector that is partly responsible for the change in the production technology, and hence for the shift of the production function (Nelson, 1980). On the contrary, science and technology are far from being sharply differentiated and it is not possible to identify a one-to-one mapping from science to public institutions or from applied technology to private business firms. Different kinds of organizations take part in the process of knowledge production, like firms, research labs and universities (Nelson, 1982, 1986). This set of arguments has been on the whole well received in the literature dealing with knowledge production function (KPF), which has been articulated both at the firm and at the regional level.[2] Knowledge is no longer the mere result of cumulated R&D spending subject to decreasing returns. The knowledge production function provides a mapping from knowledge inputs to knowledge outputs, so as to accommodate the idea that knowledge is the result of the interaction of a number of complementary inputs provided by different research institutions.

The development of the knowledge production approach inevitably leaves a basic question as to what the micro-founded mechanisms are underlying knowledge production. In this respect, the interest in the cognitive mechanisms leading to production of new technological knowledge has recently emerged in the field of economics of innovation. This strand of analysis has moved from key concepts brought forward by Schumpeter (1912, 1942), who proposed to view innovation as the outcome of a recombination process. Most innovations brought about in the economic system stem from the combinations of existing elements in new and previously untried ways. Such innovations appear to be mainly incremental. Radical innovations stem instead from the combination of existing components with brand new ones.

The contributions by Weitzman (1996, 1998) represent the former, and very impressive, attempt to draw upon such assumptions. His recombinant growth approach provides a sophisticated analytical framework grafting a micro-founded theory of knowledge production within an endogenous growth model. The production of knowledge is seen as the outcome of an intentional effort aimed at reconfiguring existing knowledge within a genuine cumulative perspective. However, there is no particular focus on the constraints that the combination of different ideas may represent, especially when these ideas are technologically distant. The only limiting factor seems to be the bounded processing capacity of economic agents.

The recombinant knowledge approach is based on the following assumptions. The creation of new knowledge is represented as a search process across a set of alternative components that can be combined with one another. However, within this framework, a crucial role is played by the cognitive mechanisms underlying the search process aimed at exploring the knowledge space so as to identify the pieces that might possibly be combined together. The set of potentially combinable pieces turns out to be a subset of the whole knowledge space. Search is supposed to be local rather than global, while the degree of localness appears to be the outcome of cognitive, social and technological influences. The ability to engage in a search process within spaces that are distant from the original starting point is likely to generate breakthroughs stemming from the combination of brand new components (Nightingale, 1998; Fleming, 2001).

Recombination occurs only after agents have put much effort into searching within the knowledge space. This strand of literature posits that knowledge so obtained is complex, meaning that it comprises many elements that interact richly (Simon, 1966; Kauffman, 1993). This has paved the way to an increasing number of empirical works based on the NK model proposed by Kauffman (Kauffman and Levin, 1987), according to which the search process is conducted across a rugged landscape, where pieces of knowledge are located and which provides the context within which technologies interact.

Such a framework clearly has the merit to push the economic discussion about technological knowledge beyond the conventional vision, considering it as a sort of black box. It sheds light on the possibility to further qualify knowledge and provides a former and innovative link between knowledge and complexity. However, the notion of complexity used therein seems to be constrained to a generic definition of an object the elements of which are characterized by a high degree of interaction. The degree of complexity of the system is considered as exogenous, defined ex ante. As an implication, the empirical effort does not go beyond the count of classes and of patents assigned to classes.

The viewpoint of endogenous complexity makes the analysis of knowledge dynamics particularly appealing and challenging. Knowledge can indeed be represented as an emergent property stemming from multi-layered complex dynamics. Knowledge is indeed the result of a collective effort of individuals who interact with one another, sharing their bits of knowledge by means of intentional acts of communication (Antonelli, 2008; Saviotti, 2007). The structure of the network of relationships amongst innovating agents represents, therefore, a crucial factor able to shape the ultimate outcome of knowledge production processes. Collective knowledge so produced stems from the combination of bits of knowledge dispersed among innovating agents. Creativity refers to the ability of agents to combine these small bits of knowledge so as to produce an original piece of technological knowledge. This in turn may be thought about as a collection of bits of knowledge linked to one another. The knowledge base of a firm can therefore be imagined as a network in which the nodes are the small bits of knowledge and the links represent their actual combination in specific tokens. Knowledge in this sense turns out to be an emergent property of complex dynamics featuring the interdependent elements of the system, i.e. the bits of knowledge.

This is a consequence of the collective character of knowledge production, which provides further richness to its dynamics. Such a complex system may be represented as a network, the nodes of which are the smaller units of knowledge, while the edges stand for their actual combination. Hence the knowledge base is characterized by a structure with its own architecture. Learning dynamics and absorptive capacity represent a channel through which the topology of knowledge structure affects search behaviour at the level of agents' networks. Indeed, agents move across the technology landscape in regions that are quite close to the area of their actual competences.

The empirical efforts related to the endogenous complexity of the knowledge base are based on the exploitation of patent data, but try and use the rich information provided therein. In particular, technological classes are used to investigate the patterns by which they are combined into patent documents and to calculate some key indicators, such as: variety, which points to the differentiation of knowledge; cognitive distance, which can be defined as the distance between the present knowledge base of a firm or a sector and the external knowledge which is the object of the search; and knowledge coherence, which is related to the extent to which the technologies combined together are complementary to one another (Krafft *et al.*, 2014).

3 Knowledge complexity and the systemic approach to innovation technology policy

The recognition of the peculiar characteristics of knowledge and of the complex mechanisms related to the generation and diffusions of innovation has relevant implications for innovation and technology policies. In this respect, a systemic approach appears to be necessary to be adopted in innovation studies and, more specifically, in the analysis and design of innovation policy (Borrás and Edquist, Chapter 14 of this book). As private innovative efforts, technological and institutional capabilities and different public support policies should be accounted for in an integrated manner, the systemic approach suggests analysing the patterns of production and diffusion of innovations by adopting a complex framework of research. This means that private activities, public policies and consumers' behaviour dynamically co-evolve and define development pathways (Saviotti and Pyka, Chapter 2 in this book).

In this context, a key role in the production and absorption of technological knowledge is played by the existing innovation system as a whole, represented by the industrial, institutional and social framework and the associated physical and knowledge infrastructures (Breschi *et al.*, 2000; Crescenzi, Gagliardi and Percoco, Chapter 8 in this book). Moreover, the systemic perspective allows for the recognition of the important interrelations and complementarities between technological and market forces and different policy instruments (Edquist, 2005; Smits *et al.*, 2010). In this context, both demand and supply forces should be taken into account. In particular, the stock of knowledge and the improvement of technological capabilities through research and development (R&D) activities are found to be very important for production and diffusion innovation at both the micro and the macro levels. In parallel, the extent of market demand and the level of prices have been considered as relevant market incentives to innovative activities (Schmookler, 1966; Mowery and Rosenberg, 1979).

The systemic approach to innovation and technology policy also allows the shortcomings to be overcome of the standard normative economic theory of innovation policy in guiding policy-makers in the design and implementation of effective policy tools (Crespi and Quatraro, 2013). The traditional foundations of innovation policy relates to the correction of market failures by changing the incentives of private sector agents. Market failures may also limit the generation of new technologies because of the public good nature of knowledge and the related problems of appropriability (Nelson, 1959; Arrow, 1962). However, a growing body of economic literature suggests that traditional economic approaches are inappropriate for dealing with the dynamics of structural and adaptive changes in economic systems (Rammel and van der Bergh, 2003), while highlighting the potential of evolutionary economics to interpret the process of economic development and innovation policies (Metcalfe, 1995). According to these contributions, an evolutionary foundation of innovation and technology policies should account for concepts such as adaptive behaviour, policy learning, policy interactions, diversity, path-dependence and lock-in processes. When the generation of new knowledge is conceived as a complex evolutionary process distributed in a system of different agents whose behaviour and interactions are governed both by market forces and by non-market institutions (Metcalfe and Ramlogan, 2005), it clearly appears that agents' interactions and the institutions governing them determine the innovative performance of the system. Hence, in this framework, the coordination problems arising from these interactive behaviours importantly affect the performance of policy action. In this respect, the systemic framework opens up a new perspective for policy-making as it shifts the policy perspective from a top-down view to a network steering approach (Bleda and del Rio, 2013). Moreover, policy-making emerges as part of and subject to system failures, entailing a process of adaptive and learning policy-making, thus acknowledging the challenges of state intervention in a context of economic and policy complexity (Metcalfe, 1995).

This shift is exemplified by the increasing interest in the concept of 'policy mix' (Flanagan *et al.*, 2011). According to this literature, policy instruments must be combined into mixes in ways that address the complex problems related to the generation and diffusion of new technologies. In particular, the choice of instruments is a crucial decision regarding the formulation of policy design as it has to consider their individual characteristics, their potential complementarities and the trade-offs between different policies in relation to the specific policy portfolio adopted (Borrás and Edquist, Chapter 14 of this book).

4 The structure of the volume

With reference to the issues outlined, this book brings together new conceptual and empirical contributions, to provide new insights to the different elements that make up innovation systems, and to enrich the analytical and empirical foundations of systemic public policies for the creation and diffusion of new knowledge. Most of the ideas and results proposed in this book benefited from the discussions developed within the context of the EU-funded project PICK-ME, which focused on the complex nature of knowledge generation and the policy implications for its governance.

By acknowledging the inherent complexity of innovation dynamics, this approach provides relevant insights to the development of an integrated framework analysing innovation as an emergent process where strong interrelations and complementarities exist between technological and market forces and between different policy instruments.

The papers included in this book focus on a limited set of issues but contribute to improving the characterization of innovation dynamics in order to provide the basis for the design of policy measures and at emphasizing how innovation takes place in organized contexts characterized by qualified interactions among heterogeneous and creative agents.

The structure of the book follows this perspective as it includes a first part where the proposed contributions provide new elements for the analysis of the often neglected relationship between demand and innovation, offering an integrated framework based on a view of knowledge as a collective, systemic and evolutionary process, engendered by generative relations that enable agents and social systems to overcome the challenges of the limits to growth. The first two chapters approach this issue from a theoretical perspective, while the third one offers an analysis on how demand can trigger innovation grounded on practical examples.

In particular, Chapter 2 by Pyka and Saviotti argues that innovation could not have contributed to economic development unless a demand for the goods and services created by innovation existed. They explore the conditions required for such a demand to exist and suggest that the process which gave rise to the observed path of economic development was the co-evolution of demand and innovation. Furthermore, they explore how the co-evolution of demand and innovation changed the capitalist economic system and analyse the possible impact of economic policies on the above co-evolutionary process.

The analysis of the relationship between demand and innovation is further explored from a symmetric perspective by the contribution of Antonelli and Gehringer in Chapter 3, which analyses the role of demand in pulling innovative activities, suggesting that the lack of consensus in assessing the effects of demand pulling is caused by the fact that the demand assumed to be able to exercise positive influence was generic. In this respect, they advance the hypothesis that demand needs to be competent and, moreover, it needs to be involved in user–producer interactions in order to effectively pull an innovative outcome.

The demand-pull hypothesis is finally addressed in Chapter 4 by Frenkel and Maital, who focused on demand-driven innovation by presenting seven key principles of market-based innovation, and then illustrating them with a series of 18 stories or case studies about market-based demand-driven innovation. In their chapter, they attempt to reveal the key success factors in demand-driven innovation suggesting the importance of creativity, not only in developing new products but also in the way they are driven by real, proven needs established through intimate contact with customers.

The second part of the book is devoted to the analysis of some specific but relevant aspects of innovation activities looked at from a supply-side perspective.

The first two contributions of this part of the book look at firms' strategies and performances. More specifically, the contribution by Stančík and Biagi in

Chapter 5, using data from the *Industrial Scoreboard* from 2002 to 2010, looks at the R&D intensity gap between companies based in the EU and companies based in its major competitors. They show that EU firms are less R&D intensive than US, Japanese or Asian Tiger firms. This gap is found to be mainly due to different sectoral compositions, with EU companies relatively more specialized in sectors with low or medium-to-low R&D intensity. Chapter 6, by Krafft and Ravix, offers instead a review of the analytical and empirical contributions that led to identifying the shareholder value model as being in the best position to promote better efficiency at the firm level. Moreover, they discuss the implications of this model in terms of firms' innovation performances. Finally, the chapter addresses this issue by looking at two major financial crises which have probably contributed to changing strategies and policy orientations.

The other two chapters in this part look at the geographical-social systems into which innovation activities are embedded. In particular, the contribution by Boschma, Balland and Dieter Kogler in Chapter 7 illustrates how basic concepts of evolutionary economic geography, such as firm heterogeneity, proximity and path dependence, can be fruitfully applied to the study of the geography of inter-firm knowledge spillovers. They argue that firms develop firm-specific routines, which makes it hard for them to connect with and learn from other firms. Knowledge spills over across firms now and then, and the proximity of a firm to other firms on various dimensions (such as geographical, social and cognitive proximity) may be a conditioning factor in this respect. In addition, they account for self-producing, path-dependent processes in which knowledge dynamics are grounded in and build on pre-existing knowledge and previously formed network ties. Their findings on the knowledge spillover networks of biotech firms analysed by means of inter-organizational citation patterns suggest that that an evolutionary perspective on the spatial dynamics of inter-firm knowledge spillovers is very different from a knowledge production framework that is commonly applied in the knowledge spillover literature.

Finally in this part, Chapter 8 by Crescenzi, Gagliardi and Percoco looks at social capital as propensity towards civicness and pro-social behaviour that facilitates the circulation of non-redundant knowledge among otherwise disconnected groups. Their quantitative analysis of the innovative performance of Italian provinces shows that social capital is an important predictor of innovative performance after controlling for 'traditional' knowledge inputs (R&D and human capital). They identify clear causal links between social capital and innovation, suggesting that social norms play an important role in shaping the incentives for knowledge generation, circulation and accumulation.

The former two parts of the book evidenced how different interacting forces shape innovation performances, which can be qualified as emergent properties of the system into which they take place. In this respect, the last part of the book provides contributions on different dimensions of policy actions for fuelling the dynamics of knowledge generation and diffusion in a complex systemic framework. This part is opened by a chapter from Robert and Yoguel, which explores the implications of complexity theory for the design of innovation and technology policies. In Chapter 9, the authors discuss the general idea of complexity from a trans-disciplinary perspective by suggesting an integrative ontology identifying the main dimensions of complexity. They examine the backgrounds of the idea of complexity which can be found throughout economics history in two main traditions. The first one, made up by Smith–Marshall–Schumpeter–Hayek–Knight, is focused on coordination problems and the links between this and economic change. The second path, from Smith to Myrdal and Hirschman, via Marshall, Young, Schumpeter and Kaldor, is concerned with transformation and divergence issues. They analyse how the main dimensions of the ontology of complexity reflects different dimensions of complexity of innovation policies.

The subsequent four chapters offer some specific analysis that qualifies the complexity of policy intervention for sustaining innovation activities. In particular, Chapter 10 by Marzucchi and Montresor proposes and applies an original multi-dimensional evaluation of the additionality of innovation policy, which takes into account its multi-level nature. The input, output and behavioural additionality effects of innovation policies (multi-dimension) are jointly investigated, at the national and regional level (multi-level). An empirical application is carried out for Italy and Spain. Through a propensity score matching estimation of the average treatment effect on the treated, they show that the two multi-level systems of policies appear quite different, both in the extent to which their additionality affects the different dimensions and in the extent to which it does it at the two levels of government. Regional policies are found to miss input additionality in both countries, while they show output additionality in Spain only, where they are also able to spur innovative behaviours of funded firms. National policies show output additionality in both countries, but in terms of different variables in Spain (product innovations) than in Italy (process innovations).

Chapter 11 by Krammer examines the linkages between different elements of STI systems and economic competitiveness, as depicted by export performance. As a case study, the author focuses on a laggard EU economy (Bulgaria) and employed several quantitative and qualitative analyses. The results suggest that Bulgarian export competitiveness relies heavily on low-tech and low value-added products with limited potential for future growth and sophistication. Modest STI performance, lack of strong incentives and financial means, low R&D investments and failure to adapt faster to market demands all contribute to a low-tech dominated export basket with limited possibilities for future growth. Subsequently, Krammer proposes a mix of 'standard' and 'systemic' policy measures for Bulgaria to tackle these issues and highlights how considerable efforts from all STI actors are needed to build well-harmonized, long-term policies.

Considering the increasing academic and policy concern on the issues related to the emergence and diffusion of environmental technologies and of the co-evolving socio-economic, institutional and policy contexts (Borghesi *et al.*, 2013), the subsequent two chapters are specifically devoted to this aspect. More specifically, Chapter 12 by Consoli and Matti outlines the intertwining of techno-logical, industrial and institutional developments that allowed Spain to become an active pole of innovation and growth in the wind energy sector. They provide an analysis of the policy mix related to the development of this new sector in the search for market deployment and technology development, by highlighting the role of synergies in a multi-level and multi-sectoral context.

The interactions between innovation and environmental policies for the gen-eration and diffusion of environmental technologies are analysed further in Chapter 13 by Horbach, who summarizes the main determinants of eco-innovations from a theoretical perspective and reviews the recent empirical liter-ature on the drivers of eco-innovation aimed at deriving some common 'stylized facts', with a particular emphasis on the role of environmental policy for the realization of eco-innovations. In this context, a thorough discussion of the prob-lems of measuring the impacts of environmental policy on eco-innovation and the different approaches to find empirical evidence for the Porter hypothesis is also carried out.

Finally, the overall discussion on the multi-dimensional and systemic charac-ter of innovation policy is systematized in Chapter 14 by Borrás and Edquist, who study the role of knowledge production (especially R&D activities) in the innovation process from an innovation system perspective. In particular, they examine how governments and public agencies in different countries and at dif-ferent times have actually approached the issue of building, maintaining and using knowledge production in their innovation systems. Moreover, they examine the critical and most important issues at stake from the point of view of innovation policy, looking in particular at the unresolved tensions and systemic unbalances related to knowledge production. Finally, the chapter elaborates on a set of overall criteria for the selection and design of relevant policy instruments and addresses those tensions and unbalances and suggests that innovation policy should develop a portfolio approach to the public investment in R&D and know-ledge production.

Notes

1 There is a large body of literature on these aspects. Key contributions are those by Griliches (1979, 1984), Acs *et al.* (2009) and Birch (1979).
2 See Antonelli and Colombelli (2013) for a critical discussion of the concept. See Acs *et al.* (2002) and Fritsch (2002) for the use of KPF in regional analyses.

References

Acs, Z.J., Anselin, L. and Varga, A. (2002). Patents and innovation counts as measures of regional production of new knowledge. *Research Policy*, 31, 1069–1085.
Acs, Z.J., Braunerhjelm, P., Audretsch, D.B. and Carlsson B. (2009). The knowledge spillover theory of entrepreneurship. *Small Business Economics*, 32, 15–30.
Antonelli, C. (2008). *Localized technological change: Towards the economics of com-plexity*. London: Routledge.

Antonelli, C. and Colombelli, A. (2013). Knowledge cumulability and complementarity in the knowledge generation function. LEI&BRICK Working Paper (03/2013), Department of Economics, University of Torino.

Arrow, K. (1962). Economic welfare and the allocation of resources for invention. In: Nelson, R.R. (ed.), *The rate and direction of inventive activity*. Princeton: Princeton University Press.

Balconi, M., Brusoni, S. and Orsenigo, L. (2010). In defense of the linear model: An essay. *Research Policy*, 39, 1–13.

Birch, D. (1979). *The job generation process*. Cambridge MA: MIT Press.

Bleda, M. and del Rio, P. (2013). The market failure and the systemic failure rationales in technological innovation systems. *Research Policy*, 42, 1039–1052.

Borghesi, S., Costantini, V., Crespi, F. and Mazzanti, M. (2013). Environmental innovation and socio-economic dynamics in institutional and policy contexts. *Journal of Evolutionary Economics*, 23(2), 241–245.

Breschi, S., Malerba, F. and Orsenigo, L. (2000). Technological regimes and Schumpeterian patterns of innovation. *Economic Journal*, 110, 388–410.

Bush, V. (1945). *Science the endless frontier. Report to the president*. Washington DC: United States Government Printing Office.

Crespi, F. and Quatraro, F. (2013). Systemic technology policies: Issues and instruments. *Technological Forecasting and Social Change*, 80, 1447–1449.

Edquist, C. (2005). Systems of innovation: Perspectives and challenges. In: Fagerberg, J., Mowery, D., and Nelson, R. (eds), *Oxford Handbook of Innovation*. Oxford: Oxford University Press, Oxford.

Flanagan, K., Uyarra, E. and Laranja, M. (2011). Reconceptualising the 'policy mix' for innovation. *Research Policy*, 40(5), 702–713.

Fleming, L. (2001). Recombinant uncertainty in technological search. *Management Science*, 47, 117–132.

Fritsch, M. (2002). Measuring the quality of regional innovation systems: A knowledge production function approach. *International Review of Regional Science*, 25, 86–101.

Gibbons, M., Limoges, C., Nowtny, H, Schwartzman, S., Scott, P. and Trow, M. (1994). *The new production of knowledge: The dynamics of science and research in contemporary societies*. London: Sage.

Griliches, Z. (1979). Issues in assessing the contribution of research and development to productivity growth. *The Bell Journal of Economics*, 10(1), 92–116.

Griliches, Z. (ed.) (1984). *R&D, patents and productivity*. Chicago: The University of Chicago Press.

Kauffmann, S. (1993). *Origins of order: Self-organization and selection in evolution*. Oxford: Oxford University Press.

Kauffman, S. and Levin, S. (1987). Towards a general theory of adaptive walks on rugged landscapes. *Journal of Theoretical Biology*, 128(1), 11–45.

Kline, S.J. and Rosenberg, N. (1986). An overview on innovation. In: Landau, R. and Rosenberg, N. (eds), *The positive sum strategy*. Washington DC: National Academy Press.

Krafft, J. and Quatraro, F. (2011). The dynamics of technological knowledge: From linearity to recombination. In: Antonelli, C. (ed.), *Handbook on the economic complexity of technological change*. Cheltenham: Edward Elgar.

Krafft, J., Quatraro, F. and Saviotti, P.P. (2014). The dynamics of knowledge-intensive sectors' knowledge base: evidence from biotechnology and telecommunications. *Industry & Innovation*, 21(3), 215–242.

Metcalfe J.S. (1995). Foundations of technology policy – equilibrium and evolutionary perspectives. In: Stoneman, P., Dasgupta, P. and Nelson, R. (eds), *Handbook in the economics of innovation*. London: Blackwell.

Metcalfe, J.S. and Ramlogan, R. (2005). Limits to the economy of knowledge and knowledge of the economy. *Futures*, 37, 655–674.

Mowery, D. and Rosenberg, N. (1979). The influence of market demand upon innovation: A critical review of some recent empirical studies. *Research Policy*, 8, 102–153.

Nelson, R.R. (1959). The simple economics of basic scientific research. *Journal of Political Economy*, 67, 323–348.

Nelson, R.R. (1980). Production sets, technological knowledge, and R&D: Fragile and overworked constructs for the analysis of productivity growth. *American Economic Review*, 70, 62–67.

Nelson, R.R. (1982). The role of knowledge in R&D efficiency. *Quarterly Journal of Economics*, 97, 453–470.

Nelson, R.R. (1986). Institutions supporting technical advance in industry. *American Economic Review*, 76, 186–189.

Nightingale, P. (1998). A cognitive model of innovation. *Research Policy*, 27, 689–709.

Quatraro, F. (2012). *The economics of structural change in knowledge*. London, Routledge.

Rammel, C. and van der Bergh, J.C.J.M. (2003). Evolutionary policies for sustainable development: Adaptive flexibility and risk minimising. *Ecological Economics*, 47, 121–133.

Saviotti, P.P. (2007). On the dynamics of generation and utilisation of knowledge: The local character of knowledge. *Structural Change and Economic Dynamics*, 18, 387–408.

Schmookler, J. (1966). *Invention and economic growth*. Cambridge MA: Harvard University Press.

Schumpeter, J. (1912). *The theory of economic development*. Cambridge MA: Harvard University Press.

Schumpeter, J. (1942). *Capitalism, socialism and democracy*. New York: Harper and Row.

Simon, H. (1966). *The sciences of the artificial*. Cambridge MA: MIT Press.

Smits, R., Kuhlmann, S. and Shapira, P. (2010). *The theory and practice of innovation policy: An international research handbook*. Cheltenham: Edward Elgar.

Weitzman, M.L. (1996). Hybridizing growth theory. *American Economic Review*, 86, 207–212.

Weitzman, M.L. (1998). Recombinant growth. *Quarterly Journal of Economics*, 113, 331–360.

Part I

Knowledge, innovation and the demand side

2   On the co-evolution of innovation and demand

Some policy implications

Pier Paolo Saviotti and Andreas Pyka

1 Introduction

The main objective of this chapter is to establish that innovation could not have contributed to economic development unless a demand for the goods and services created by innovation existed. We explore the conditions required for such a demand to exist and argue that the process which gave rise to the observed path of economic development was the co-evolution of demand and innovation. Furthermore, we explore how the co-evolution of demand and innovation changed the capitalist economic system from one in which most people could afford only bare necessities to one in which most people have a highly and increasingly varied pattern of consumption, including a growing proportion of items which cannot be judged necessities, and which are of higher quality than in the past. Finally, we study the possible impact of economic policies on the above co-evolutionary process. We carry out these explorations by means of an extension of our TEVECON model of economic development, which is described in the following part of the chapter.

2 Conceptual background

2.1 Co-evolution and economic development

The concept of co-evolution has recently been used in the innovation literature to analyze the co-evolution of technologies and institutions. In this section, we make a brief reference to this literature and propose a more general concept of co-evolution. Technologies cannot develop in an institutional vacuum but need appropriate institutions (Nelson, 1994). Such institutions are required to support the collective interests of a new technology and of the corresponding industry, to lobby the industry, to regulate it, to establish intellectual property rights, to create the required infrastructures, etc. Examples of such co-evolution are mass production in the United States car industry, the emergence of synthetic dyes in Germany (Murmann, 2003) and biotechnology in the USA (Nelson, 2008).

   The need for new institutions becomes evident when new technologies emerge. There are even institutions which might be appropriate at a level of aggregation higher than that of an individual industry. For example, a set of interconnected technologies sharing common resources could require a set of institutions appropriate to the whole set. Perez (1983) used the related concept of techno-economic paradigm to encompass a technological paradigm (Dosi, 1982) and the institutions appropriate to it. She maintained that the creation of the appropriate institutions was likely to be a longer and more complex process than the initial creation of a given technology, or technologies, corresponding to a given technological paradigm. Other scholars stressed that a country which had been successful in creating a given set of technologies and the appropriate institutions might be unable to do the same for a subsequent set of technologies. Veblen (1915) had already remarked how British industry, which was very successful in the early part of the industrial revolution, could not adopt the institutions appropriate to the new technologies that Germany developed much more successfully. Lazonick (1990) maintained that the organization of work and the institutions for training labor which had underpinned the successful development of Britain in the late eighteenth and early nineteenth century became a handicap in the twentieth century. At a higher level of generality, Polanyi (1944) maintained that capitalism would require the creation of institutions which were capable of compensating for the harsh if efficient nature of capitalist societies.

A more general interpretation of the concept of co-evolution can be proposed at a system level. A system is constituted by different and interacting components. Co-evolution exists when two different components (C_1 and C_2) interact in such a way that changes in one of them, say C_1, affect C_2 and that changes in C_2 affect C_1. Typically, for co-evolution to exist this relationship of mutual interaction must last for several periods, giving rise to a sustained feedback loop.

The dynamics we can imagine for an economic system consists of the early emergence of an innovation in a pre-institutional form, that is, without institutions specific to the new technology. This would be followed by the creation of institutions which, for example, would provide the rules for the new technology to be used for the advantage of society at large avoiding as much as possible negative side effects, and of infrastructures which would allow the market for the new technology to grow. A clear example is given by cars and roads: the scope for cars has been considerably enhanced by the construction of roads. Thus, the more the new technology develops, the more the appropriate institutions need to grow, giving rise to a feedback loop which would slow down only when the market(s) for the new technology were completely saturated.

The type of co-evolution we are going to be concerned with in this paper is between innovation and demand. Thus, it would be the co-evolution of two different economic variables, mutually influencing each other during the course of economic development. In TEVECON, this co-evolutionary process occurs because sectoral search activities, which increase with sectoral demand, affect output price, quality and differentiation, which in turn affect demand. A positive feedback loop can be established which can give rise to a faster growth of both demand and innovation than would have been possible if the two variables had not been influencing each other. In this sense co-evolution works as autocatalysis (Nicolis and Prigogine, 1989) by using the output of one stage of the process as the input of the following stage.

2.2 Trajectories and patterns of economic development

Models of economic development need to be able to explain patterns of long-run development and growth. Here long run is intended to indicate a period such as the one from the industrial revolution to the present. Focusing on such a period requires an understanding of the broad features which occurred in it. First, we had the emergence of the manufacturing industry. Second, within manufacturing there was a progressive differentiation, beginning with sectors such as textiles, energy (steam engine), railways, steel and following with chemicals, electricity, cars, planes, etc. During this process, the manufacturing industry became increasingly differentiated, with newer sectors co-existing with older ones. Third, the employment share of services overtook that of manufacturing.

Any model of economic development that is in principle capable of interpreting events which occurred since the industrial revolution needs to explain why such structural change occurred. The fundamental ingredient which gives rise to growth and development in our work is innovation. The emergence of innovations is due to search activities, which provide the knowledge required to create and modify innovations. Innovations affect economic development because entrepreneurs fund new firms to exploit the outcomes of search activities and because consumers and users purchase the products and services embodying such innovations. In this process, the economic system becomes increasingly differentiated. The addition of new sectors to the economic system not only contributes to structural change but to a structural change occurring in a particular direction, that of increasing differentiation.

The above processes can be described in terms of three trajectories and of two periods.

Trajectory 1: The efficiency of productive processes increases during the course of economic development. Here efficiency must be understood as the ratio of the inputs used to the output produced, when the type of output remains *constant*.

Trajectory 2: The output variety of the economic system increases in the course of time. Here such variety is measured by the number of distinguishable sectors, where a sector is defined as the set of firms producing a common although highly differentiated output.

Trajectory 3: The output quality and internal differentiation of existing sectors increases in the course of time after their creation. This means that if during the period of observation the type of output changes, what we will observe is a combination of growing productive efficiency and of quality change.

From now on, we will use the term variety as synonymous with diversity, although the two are in principle not identical. Such variety can exist at the intersectoral as well as at the intra-sectoral level. Thus, two sectors will produce completely different types of output while one sector will produce a diversified output. In the literature, these two types are often described as vertical and horizontal differentiation, respectively. Such long-run trajectories do not emerge separately but exist due to a complex pattern of interactions within the economic system.

These trajectories occur at a level of aggregation higher than that of an individual industrial sector or a technology. Such ratio can be calculated in value or in volume terms. Growing productive efficiency is the oldest and, until the industrial revolution, the most developed of the three trajectories. For example, the efficiency of food production increased with the transition from hunters and gatherers to settled agriculture (Diamond, 1997). However, any such increases in productive efficiency were very slow and not necessarily cumulative. Productive efficiency started growing in a cumulative fashion only after the beginning of the industrial revolution (Maddison, 2007). Simple recent examples of this trajectory can be found in the falling number of workers required to produce a unit of output in the steel, chemicals or car industries. Of course, these are just examples and the phenomenon is far more general. Growing productive efficiency is certainly one of the factors which contributed to economic growth since the industrial revolution. However, the observed patterns of economic development could not have been produced by growing productive efficiency alone. In this case, we would produce today Ford Model T-like cars with much smaller quantities of all the inputs required. As even the most casual observer would have noticed, today's cars are not only produced much more efficiently than those of the early twentieth century but they are also of a much higher quality. Hence, growing productive efficiency and growing output quality were combined in the patterns of economic development which we can observe today.

During the industrial revolution, output differentiation (trajectory 2) was very limited. At the beginning, it occurred mostly at the level of capital goods (new textile and engineering equipment, railways equipment, etc.) and only considerably later at the level of consumer goods. The increasing internal differentiation and output quality of consumer goods and durables started increasing during the nineteenth century and in particular after the beginning of the twentieth century. Growing output variety can be observed at the inter-sector level. A clear example of this is the large number of completely new sectors which emerged during the twentieth century, such as cars, aircraft, television, computers, telecommunications, etc. All of these not only constituted completely new sectors but underwent a very high degree of internal differentiation.

These three trajectories are not independent. None of them could have taken place alone without the other two. Thus, a continuous increase in productive efficiency, if not accompanied by the emergence of new sectors and by their internal differentiation and rising quality, could have led the economic system to a bottleneck in which all demanded output could have been produced by a declining proportion of the labor force (Pasinetti, 1981). Such a bottleneck, determined by the imbalance between continuously increasing productive efficiency and saturating demand, could have been overcome by the emergence of new sectors

(Pasinetti, 1981). While the assumption of demand saturation and the neglect of the internal differentiation of sectors limited the possible generalization of Pasinetti's approach, we have shown (Pyka and Saviotti, 2012) that both the emergence of new sectors and their increasing quality and internal differentiation provided additional scope for further growth and allowed its continuation in the long run. In this context, full demand saturation is unlikely to occur within any sector as long as new sectors keep being created (Saviotti and Pyka, 2010). Furthermore, both the emergence of new sectors and their growing quality and internal differentiation can compensate the diminishing capability to create employment of incumbent and maturing sectors.

In the previous sections, we described the period from the industrial revolution to the present as the transition from necessities to imaginary worlds. This description emphasizes that, until the end of the nineteenth century, most people, even in countries which were for the standards of the time relatively rich, could not purchase anything but bare necessities. All throughout the nineteenth century, British working-class households spent about 90 percent of their income on food, clothing and housing. Only during the twentieth century, and in particular after the 1930s, did the share of income spent on the above three categories start to falling (Hobsbawm, 1968, diagrams 45 and 46). By the 1950s, the share of necessities fell to about 60 percent, leaving about 40 percent to be spent on other, presumably higher, goods and services. The compression of the combined expenditure on necessities (trajectory 1) created the disposable income required to buy the new goods and services which were gradually being created. Starting from the beginning of the twentieth century, new goods and services emerged (trajectory 2) and their quality and differentiation increased constantly (trajectory 3). This combination of trajectories contributed to a mechanism which allowed the capitalist economic system to create growing wealth for most of the population of industrialized countries.

2.3 TEVECON

2.3.1 Modeling philosophy

Our model, which we call TEVECON, can be considered an agent-based model (ABM) for a number of reasons. First, it is not an analytical model in the same sense as the more orthodox models, because it lacks *closure conditions*. The most important of such conditions is the presence of general equilibrium. Our model has an endogenously varying number of sectors, and thus an endogenously variable composition. In these circumstances, as Kaldor (1957) had already well understood, there can be no general equilibrium. However, we do have sectoral equilibrium in the form of a feedback mechanism ensuring that demand does not deviate too much from supply. Also, TEVECON agents are not optimizers but only improvers possessing bounded rationality (Pyka and Fagiolo 2007), since learning mechanisms (mainly learning by searching) play a central role in TEVECON.

TEVECON has a number of agents, but sometimes they are implicitly or lightly represented only. The central agents of TEVECON are sectors, defined as the collection of firms producing a unique though highly differentiated type of output. Firms are present and one of the most important modeling outcomes of TEVECON is the evolution of the number of firms in time. Although reduced, such a presentation of firms gives rise to the very interesting prediction of the existence of an industry life cycle (ILC) under a very wide range of conditions. However, the representation of firms can be considerably expanded by including firm characteristics, internal structure and distributional properties. An agent that is present only implicitly is the Schumpeterian entrepreneur, who is creating new firms by exploiting important innovations induced by the expectation of a temporary monopoly. The role of the entrepreneur is extremely important in TEVECON but its representation at the moment is reduced to the action of opening up new sectors. Thus, the central agents of TEVECON are industrial sectors as previously defined.

Another important feature of ABMs is the reconstruction of the macroeconomic states of the system from its microeconomic ones (Pyka and Fagiolo, 2007). In this sense, TEVECON is best defined as providing aggregation from micro to meso and from meso to macro. Firms (micro) are aggregated to sectors (meso) and sectors are aggregated to the macroeconomic state of the system. In the present version of the model, the meso to macro aggregation is better specified than the micro to meso one.

Sectors are very considerably heterogeneous in TEVECON. They can differ on a very large number of dimensions, such as expected market size, technological opportunity, investment patterns, wage rates, etc. Furthermore, TEVECON satisfies most of the conditions required to be considered an evolving complex system (ECS) (Pyka and Fagiolo, 2007, p. 474) since it is a highly interactive model in which new interactions are continuously being introduced between existing variables. One such interaction that was present from the very early versions of the model is that between search activities and demand, where there is a feedback mechanism from rising demand to rising search activities to further rising demand in following periods. More such interactions are continuously being introduced. Again, these interactions contribute to the emergence of complex properties out of repeated interactions among simple entities (Kirman, 1998).

TEVECON shows endogenous and persistent novelty (Pyka and Fagiolo, 2007, p. 475). It is non-stationary in the sense that its composition is continuously changing. New sectors produce outputs that are qualitatively different from the pre-existing ones. This means that in principle the outputs of different sectors should not be substitutable. In reality, our model includes two types of competition, intra- and inter-sector. The latter exists if different sectors produce comparable services out of non-comparable internal structures (Saviotti and Metcalfe, 1984; Saviotti, 1996). Thus, the qualitative difference lies mostly in the internal structure of sectoral outputs and in the sector's knowledge base.

As a consequence of the above, TEVECON shows "true dynamics" (Pyka and Fagiolo, 2007, p. 475). Some form of dynamics is present in orthodox models simply because they include equations which show the time paths of the system. This form of dynamics does not take into account qualitative change and is not affected by the emergence of new entities. One of the most important differences between evolutionary models and ABMs on the one hand and orthodox models on the other hand is the emergence of new entities, qualitatively different from pre-existing ones. The true dynamics, which is more difficult to represent and yet vital in understanding the long-run evolution of the economic system, is the one including qualitative change.

If the above considerations allow us to consider TEVECON an ABM, we can still situate it within the wide range of modeling techniques which are in principle compatible with the ABM definition. TEVECON bears a close similarity to dynamical systems since its basic framework is constituted by a set of simultaneous difference equations. Although complete closure conditions such as general equilibrium are absent, the equations used are in most cases similar or identical to those which are used in orthodox analytical models. Given the absence of closure and the nature of the equations involved, TEVECON cannot be analytically solved but needs to be simulated. Thus, amongst all ABM modeling techniques, TEVECON could be described as having a partly analytical, not entirely computational, structure but needing simulation to find solutions. This gives TEVECON both advantages and disadvantages. With respect to orthodox analytical models, it has the advantage of allowing us to include a greater number of variables and interactions while having a greater similarity to orthodox analytical models than purely computational ABMs. TEVECON's disadvantage with respect to purely computational ABMs is its lower adaptability to model institutions and policies.

2.3.2   The model

In TEVECON, the economic system is composed of an endogenously variable number of sectors. The emergence of new sectors is due to the dynamics of the incumbent ones and the main source of economic growth consists in the emergence of new sectors. Each sector is created on the basis of an important, pervasive, innovation taken up by entrepreneurs who start new companies and thereby provide the basis for a new industry. The innovation creating the sector gives rise to an adjustment gap AG_i, a variable intended to capture the size of the potential market established by the innovation. However, this market is initially empty because neither the production capacity nor a structured demand for the new products exists. Both the production capacity and the evolution of the demand will take place during a (possibly long) period of time, by means of a gradual interaction of producers and users. Thus, the adjustment gap measures the extent to which the market is far from saturation. When the market becomes saturated, the adjustment gap is reduced to zero or to a small and constant value. The adjustment gap is very large right after the creation of the sector, and later it decreases gradually, although not continuously. It is in fact possible for the adjustment gap to grow during certain periods if innovations, following the one creating the sector, improve either the performance of the product or the efficiency with which it is produced, or both.

Each sector has a dynamics given by the entry and exit of new firms. Schumpeterian entrepreneurs create new firms to exploit a pervasive innovation induced by the expectation of a temporary monopoly. The following bandwagon of imitators raises the intensity of competition and gradually eliminates any further inducement to enter. Thus, the once innovative sector is transformed into a part of the circular flow (Schumpeter, 1912) or into one additional routine of the economic system. This happens when the incumbent sector saturates, a condition which in TEVECON is attained when the adjustment gap AG_i becomes zero or reaches a very low and constant value (Saviotti and Pyka, 2004a, 2008). The saturation of incumbent sectors induces entrepreneurs to search for new niches which could subsequently become new markets. The dynamics briefly outlined above provides a mechanism for the endogenous generation of new sectors, which allows the process of economic development to continue in the long run.

A very important role is played in TEVECON by search activities, a general analogue of R&D (Nelson and Winter, 1982). Search activities can be defined as all the activities which try to better understand our external environment and which can provide the basis for the emergence of new routines. Thus, search activities are the source of new innovations and we can expect a positive relationship between the resources allocated to such activities and the rate of creation of innovations. In TEVECON, the resources allocated to search activities are expected to increase with accumulated demand (Eq. 1):

$$SE_i^t = SE^0 + k_4^i \cdot [1 - \exp(-k_5 \cdot Dacc_i^t)] \qquad (1)$$

The combination of the emergence of new sectors and of their increasing quality and internal differentiation leads to an increasing differentiation of the economic system during the process of development. However, this combination can occur in many different proportions, giving rise to many development paths. The analysis of the paths is one of the objectives of the present paper. A more detailed description of our TEVECON model can be found in Pyka and Saviotti (2011) and in previous papers (Saviotti and Pyka, 2004a, 2004b, 2008).

Here we describe an extension of our TEVECON model having two objectives. First we want to study the co-evolution of demand and innovation in the process of economic development; second, we want to study the effect of output variety and of output quality and differentiation on economic development paths. Most existing models of growth, including the endogenous growth ones (Aghion and Howitt, 1992; Romer, 1990, Grossman and Helpman, 2001), are supply based and they pay no attention to demand. However, innovation would not have had any impact on economic development if the products embodying specific innovations had not been purchased by consumers and users. Even evolutionary economics, which owed its origin to the difficulties encountered when attempting to use neoclassical economic theory to explain the nature and impact of innovation on economic development, is predominantly concerned with the supply side. On the other hand, models which focus on demand tend to stress structural change and to belong to a neo-Keynesian approach (Kaldor, 1957; Pasinetti, 1981; Aoki and Yoshikawa 2002). Recently, a growing attention has been paid to demand in models of economic growth, both orthodox (Murphy *et al.*, 1989; Matsuyama, 2002; Foellmi and Zweimuller, 2006) and evolutionary (Bianchi, 1998; Andersen, 2001, 2007; Aversi *et al.*, 1999; Metcalfe, 2001; Saviotti, 2001; Witt, 2001; Ciarli *et al.*, 2010). A recent paper by Nelson and Consoli (2010) makes the brave attempt to sketch a broad outline of such a demand theory. They explore the use of routines by consumers to guide their choices. In this approach, the mechanisms whereby routines are constructed are of crucial importance. In demand, as in supply, innovation creates uncertainty. Thus, consumers' knowledge is not just likely to be imperfect but to become more so when new types of goods and services completely unknown to them are introduced into the economic system. Especially at the beginning of the life cycle of the emerging goods and services, very few consumers are likely to be able to overcome this uncertainty. In fact, in these circumstances, consumers can be expected to act as innovators but to require a threshold level of human capital to do that (Saviotti, 2001).

With respect to these papers, ours differs on a number of aspects. First, this paper is part of a research program, the initial objective of which was to prove that economic development has occurred by means of a growing differentiation of the economic system. This objective placed our model not only within evolutionary economics but also with the research tradition of structural change. Furthermore, from the very beginning, we were interested in long-range patterns of economic development. The relationship between demand and innovation was always present in our model as the potential imbalance between saturating demand and continuously growing productive efficiency (Pasinetti, 1981). However, the specification of demand changed considerably in subsequent versions of TEVECON by first incorporating product quality and differentiation (Saviotti and Pyka, 2008) and becoming for the first time fully endogenous in this paper. The distinguishing features are:

- It does not share most of the assumptions of orthodox models, such as general equilibrium or optimizing behavior, but it only considers economic agents as potential improvers engaged in learning activities.
- The type of structural change that is at the center of the process of economic development leads to a growing output variety of the economic system. Thus, there is in TEVECON an arrow of time continuously raising the differentiation of the economic system. Interestingly, this feature of TEVECON finds a growing validation in recent empirical work (Acemoglu and Zilibotti, 1997; Imbs and Warcziag, 2003; Saviotti and Frenken, 2008; De Benedictis *et al.*, 2009).

- The mechanism whereby disposable income is created is closely related to the growing differentiation of the economic system.
- The growing product quality and differentiation within each sector contributes together with growing output variety to the compensation of the falling ability of mature sectors to create employment.

None of these features is present in the orthodox models referred to above. Furthermore, some of the objectives of the papers referred to above are similar to those of our paper, but they differ in a number of ways. Murphy *et al.* (1989; from now on MSV) rescue the theory of the big push put forward by Rosenstein-Rodan (1943) in the 1950s by developing a multi-sectoral model in which simultaneous investment in the different sectors of the economy can lead to growth even if no sector individually breaks even. The contribution of simultaneous investment to growth comes from the pecuniary externalities generated by each sector, which increase purchasing power in all sectors. Moreover, growth occurs by each sector shifting from constant returns to scale in cottage industry to increasing returns to scale in factory production. In this sense, for MSV it is a change in process technology which gives rise to growth while, in TEVECON, it is the emergence of new sectors which differ for the type of output they produce. Thus, in MSV neither the type of output of sectors nor the direction in which structural change can be expected to vary – for example, towards growing output variety – are defined. On the other hand, we find similarities in the ways in which MSV and our paper deal with demand: in both cases, it is the income generated by the investment in industrialization (MSV) or in the emergence of new sectors (TEVECON) which creates the required demand.

With Matsuyama (2002), we share the interest for a similar transition. What we call the transition from necessities to imaginary worlds and the closely related one from low to high quality are very similar to Matsuyama's rise of mass consumption societies. However, with respect to Matsuyama our model differs for (i) the types of learning mechanisms: different types of search activities (fundamental and sectoral in TEVECON) compared to only learning by doing in Matsuyama; (ii) the specification of preferences: non-homothetic for Matsuyama, differing for consumers' propensity to move up or down a hierarchical ladder of goods or services in TEVECON; (iii) the impact of income distribution on development, which is present in Matsuyama and so far not in our model. As for MSV, Matsuyama does not characterize the outputs of different sectors, and only allows them to be gradually adopted by different sections of the consumer population as the effect of learning by doing reduces the output cost of each sector, making it affordable for larger and larger sections of the consumer population. Thus, Matsuyama includes a form of co-evolution (he talks about two-way causality) and a mechanism which is very similar to our trajectory 1 (growing productive efficiency). However, he has neither any direction of structural change (trajectory 2, growing output variety) nor that of growing output quality and differentiation (trajectory 3).

Foellmi and Zweimuller (2006; from now on FZ) use non-homothetic preferences, hierarchically ordered goods, and investigate the effect of income distribution on growth. Their paper differs from Matsuyama (2002; from now on M) for its learning mechanism – learning by doing in M and industrial R&D in FZ – and from MSV due to their claim to apply a more general nature of a preference system and also due to the more dynamical character of their model.

All the three above papers investigate the effect of income distribution on growth but they reach different and sometimes opposing conclusions. For example, FZ find that falling income inequality reduces growth for MSV whereas it increases growth for FZ.

In summary, our paper is part of a research program, of which one of the most important objectives is to investigate the process of progressive differentiation which accompanies, and we maintain partly determines, economic development. None of the above papers shares this objective. The extent of differentiation is given. Change occurs by a transition in process technology (MSV), by learning by doing (M) or by industrial R&D technology (FZ). Given this difference in objective, TEVECON is the only model in which the number of sectors is endogenously variable, thus stressing the direction of structural change. From the very beginning, the interaction between demand and supply has been at the center of TEVECON in the form of the imbalance between saturating demand and continuously increasing productive efficiency. Aoki and Yoshikawa (2002) share part of this approach. Yet our specification of the co-evolution of demand and innovation has been completed only in recent versions of TEVECON by including disposable income in the sectoral demand function. The goods and services of TEVECON are hierarchically ordered, but what determines the order is the action of entrepreneurs creating new sectors in the expectation of a temporary monopoly. Consumers do not have the ability to anticipate the emergence or nature of future sectors but react to their existence by purchasing their goods and services to the extent that their disposable income and preferences allow them to do so. In particular, the preferences of our consumers differ for their propensity to reduce or discard the consumption of older goods and services to start consuming new ones. With respect to MSV, M and FZ, we do not include in our analysis income distribution but only calculate the average disposable income available for the consumption of new goods and services. The creation of such depends on the growing productive efficiency of older sectors (trajectory 1) and on the income created by the investment in the new sectors.

A further modeling approach which deserves to be discussed for both its similarities and differences with respect to TEVECON is that of Amendola and Gaffard (1998; from now on AG). AG share with TEVECON the out-of-equilibrium nature of the model and their emphasis on qualitative change. They include an interesting discussion of the nature of money but on the whole the sources of disequilibrium and the representation of technology are very different from TEVECON. For example, while they talk about qualitative change, they do not take into account the non-comparable nature of the product and process technologies which emerge in the course of economic development.

The comparison of ours and of the above papers shows that each of these models investigates different aspects of the economic system and thus they are not strictly comparable. Within this set of models, the specificities of ours are that: (i) it is much "lighter" in terms of its assumptions than orthodox models since it does not include closure conditions such as general equilibrium or optimizing behavior; (ii) it has a particular representation of structural change as leading to a growing output variety; (iii) it has an explicit analysis of the co-evolution of innovation and demand; (iv) it has an explicit representation of product quality and differentiation; (v) it has a more complete representation of search activities, including both fundamental research and sectoral applied research.

The previous references explored the mechanisms of creation of demand in relation to innovation at a microeconomic level. In this paper, we are more concerned with the joint dynamics of innovation and demand at a meso-economic level of aggregation. Two conditions are required in order for demand for new products or services to emerge:

i   Consumers must have a disposable income which allows them to purchase the new goods and services.
ii   Consumers must have or develop preferences which make them value positively the new goods or services.

Here the term disposable income must be understood to be the residual income, left over in a given period, after all the types of consumption of previous periods have been satisfied. A demand function had been introduced into TEVECON in a previous paper (Saviotti and Pyka, 2008). However, the demand function we used in that paper depended on output quality, on output differentiation and on price but not on income. This had the effect of overstating demand since high-quality products are always preferred to low-quality products irrespective of the consumer purchasing power. In this paper, we use a demand function (Eq. 2) which depends on disposable income and on preferences in addition to product price, quality and differentiation.

$$D_i^t = k_{pref,i} \cdot D_i^0 \cdot D_{Disp,i} \frac{Y_i \cdot \Delta Y_i}{p_i} \tag{2}$$

where

D_i^t = demand for product i at time t
Y_i = services supplied by the product, measuring product quality
ΔY_i = range of services supplied by the product, measuring product differentiation
p_i = product price
$D_{Disp,i}$ = disposable income which can be allocated to purchase product i
$k_{pref,i}$ = parameter representing preferences

We calculate $D_{Disp,i}$ as the difference between the total income and the income required to satisfy the types of consumption of previous periods in period t.

The co-evolution of innovation and demand

To study how different preference systems can affect the time path of demand and of economic development, we represent three very simplified preference systems which we call progressive, conservative and random. We realize that in a real economic system, preference systems of these different types would be distributed within a consumer population and that they would not be immutable. Consumers can learn and change their preferences in the course of time. Our main objective here is simply to show that consumer preferences can affect directly demand and indirectly the macroeconomic growth performance of the economic system.

Consumers with a progressive preference system value more highly new goods and services than older ones. Consumers with a conservative preference system value more highly old goods and services than newer ones. Consumers with a random preference system will have preferences randomly distributed amongst the outputs of different sectors, old and new. These three preference systems are represented as three different parameters in the demand equation (1). $k_{pref,i}$ is a parameter which is constant for each sector in the course of time but can vary between different sectors. The three preference systems are then represented as follows:

Progressive preference system: $k_{pref,i+1} > k_{pref,i}$

Conservative preference system: $k_{pref,i+1} < k_{pref,i}$

Random preference system: $k_{pref,i+1} >< k_{pref,i}$

The second objective of the paper consisted of comparing the economic development paths which would be obtained when product quality (i) remained unchanged or (ii) increased during the life cycle of each sector in TEVECON. This objective is attained by modifying the values of the parameters k_{14}–k_{17} linking search activities to product quality and differentiation (Eqs 3, 4)

$$Y_i^t = \frac{1}{1 + \exp(k_{14} - k_{15} SE_i^t)} \tag{3}$$

$$\Delta Y_i^t = \frac{1}{1 + \exp(k_{16} - k_{17} SE_i^t)} \tag{4}$$

When these parameters have extremely low values, product quality and differentiation remain virtually constant during the evolution of the respective sectors. Values of the parameters k_{14}–k_{17} are varied by giving them extremely low values in the low-quality (LQ) scenario and considerably higher values in the high-quality (HQ) scenario. Thus, in the LQ scenario, the saturation of each sector is attained much more rapidly due to the absence of quality change in sectoral outputs. In other words, in the LQ scenario market saturation occurs only by volume (Saviotti *et al.*, 2007). On the other hand, in the HQ scenario market saturation can occur much later, giving rise to longer industry life cycles (ILC) because the market can still expand after volume saturation has been attained by moving towards products of higher quality and thus of higher value.

By recalling that according to equation 1 search activities increase with accumulated demand and by combining equation 1 with equations 3 and 4, we can realize that search activities depend on demand and demand depends on search activities. This is the basis for the co-evolution of innovation and demand. The co-evolutionary loop is completed by equation 2, according to which demand is not only affected by three variables which are themselves affected by search activities (Y_i, ΔY_i and p_i) but also by the presence of a disposable income which can be used to purchase new goods and services.

Human capital is created by investment in education, which gives rise to an education capital stock (CS_{edi}), which in turn determines the quality h_i of human capital (Eq. 5). The parameter k_{ed} represents the effectiveness with which the investment in education is transformed into human capital. Hence, k_{ed} represents the quality of educational institutions in forming human capital. Overall human capital is obtained by multiplying sectoral labor by the quality h_i of human capital (Eq. 6).

$$h_i^t = k_{ed} \cdot CS_{edi}^t \tag{5}$$

$$HC_i^t = labour_i^t \cdot h_i^t \tag{6}$$

Bearing in mind that sectoral output depends on human capital, we can realize that the time path of output depends on investment in education and on the effectiveness with which educational institutions improve the quality of human capital. Furthermore, the intensity of production is determined by the parameter k_{HQ} (see Eq. 7). Equation 7 also shows that human capital in a given period depends on investment in previous periods, which itself depends on output in previous periods. In turn, future output is affected by present human capital. Here we see some more examples of the co-evolutionary patterns included in TEVECON.

$$Q_i^t = Q^0 + \gamma \cdot (1 + \alpha_{ci}^t) \cdot (1 - \exp(-k_{11} \cdot SE_i^t - k_{cspq1} \cdot CSphysical_i^t - k_{11} \cdot HC_i^t) \tag{7}$$

Q_i^t: = sectoral output
γ: = scaling parameter
α_{ci}^t: = production adjustment

Wages depend on labor productivity and on a parameter, k_{wages} (Eq. 8). The parameter k_{wages} leads to an increase or a decrease in wages at equivalent labor productivity. Thus, it could reflect the presence of particularly powerful labor unions, which would tend to raise it, or of reforms in the labor market, which could reduce it. We expect that at equivalent labor productivity a low value of k_{wages} increases the competitiveness of a sector or of a country.

$$wages_i^t = w_i^0 + k_{wages} \cdot \frac{Q_i^t \cdot P_i^t}{labour_i^t} \tag{7}$$

2.4 Disposable income for new sectors

Our calculations show that, under a wide range of circumstances, a disposable income can be created for new sectors, thus allowing consumers to purchase their output (Figure 2.1).

Further, we can observe that while to purchase the output of sector 2 a reduction of the expenditures on sector 1 is required, such a sacrifice is not necessary for subsequent sectors. The development of the economic system manages to create enough resources in the system to allow consumers to purchase the new goods and services. The mechanisms by means of which such increasing purchasing power is created are related to the three trajectories described above. First, the growing productive efficiency in incumbent sectors (trajectory 1) reduces the cost of those sectors' goods and services and creates a surplus which can be used to fund the search activities and the investment required to produce the new goods and services. Second, the previous investment creates income for the labor employed in the production of the new goods and services. Third, as the average revenues of the population increase, the possibility to make higher quality, more expensive and mo   29re profitable goods and services emerge. To the extent that such new goods and services fit consumers' preferences, they will create new markets or enlarge existing ones. Thus, the growing quality and differentiation of goods and services (trajectory 3) together with the emergence of new sectors (trajectory 2) can compensate the falling ability of incumbent sectors to create employment and enable growth to continue in the long run. While this conclusion expands the range of possible growth mechanisms, in

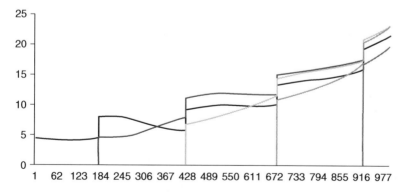

Figure 2.1   Effect of product quality on the disposable income created in the economic system (source: own elaboration).

relatively wealthy economic systems, it also introduces a source of uncertainty. In fact, compensation can occur only if the innovations required to create new sectors are available when the saturation of pre-existing ones occurs. While this has been assumed so far in TEVECON, there is no guarantee that in a real economic system this will always occur.

2.5 Preferences

The existence of an adequate disposable income is a necessary condition for consumers to be able to purchase the new goods and services which are created by innovation. However, consumers will do that only if they have an adequate set of preferences. In this section, we study how the three different preference systems we suggested in the previous section can affect the time path of demand and of economic development. We realize that that these representations of a preference system are an approximation. However, we consider that such an approximation is sufficient for our main objective here, which is to show that consumer preferences can affect directly demand and indirectly the macroeconomic growth performance of the economic system.

   In different experiments, we vary the degree of progressiveness or of conservativeness of our consumers by changing the Δk_{pref} between sectors i and $i+1$. Thus, a large and positive Δk_{pref} between sectors i and $i+1$ indicate strongly progressive consumers while a smaller but still positive Δk_{pref} indicate mildly progressive consumers. Likewise, a large and negative Δk_{pref} between sectors i and $i+1$ indicate strongly conservative consumers while a smaller negative Δk_{pref} indicate mildly conservative consumers. The results of these experiments are summarized in Figures 2.2 and 2.3 by plotting the straight lines which give the rate of growth of income (Figure 2.2) and of employment (Figure 2.3). Such

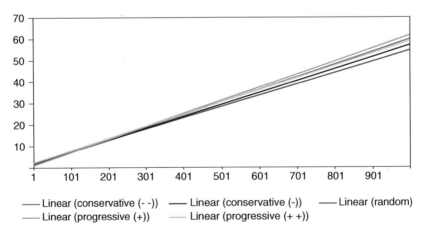

Figure 2.2 Influence of the different preference systems on the rate of growth of income (source: own elaboration).

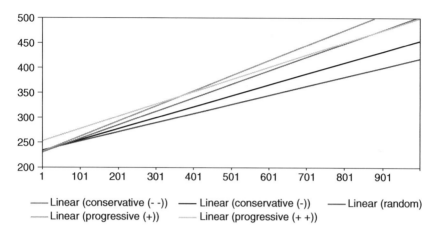

Figure 2.3 Influence of the different preference systems on the rate of growth of employment (source: own elaboration).

straight lines are the best linear fit for the income and employment curves and their slopes give us the rate of growth of income (RIG) and the rate of growth of employment (REG), respectively (see Saviotti and Pyka, 2008).

These results show that both REG and RIG increase when preferences pass from conservative to neutral to progressive. However, as more preferences become more and more progressive, both REG and RIG start falling, indicating the presence of a non-linear relationship between preferences on the one hand and employment or income on the other hand. Such non-linearity can be explained because the change from conservative to neutral to progressive preferences implies a transfer of resources from the purchase of old goods and services to that of emerging ones. While a moderate transfer can accelerate the emergence of new sectors, an excessive one can depress the demand for older goods and services and thereby reduce the overall growth of employment and of income.

The results of sections 2.4 and 2.5 show that (i) disposable income for new goods and services can be created by a combination of trajectories 1, 2 and 3, corresponding to the growing productive efficiency in incumbent sectors (trajectory 1), to the emergence of new sectors (trajectory 2) and to the growing quality and differentiation of goods and services (trajectory 3); (ii) consumer preferences can affect the macroeconomic performance of the economic system. We now pass to the second objective of this paper.

2.6 On the balance between the emergence of new sectors and the growing quality and differentiation of existing ones

To study this problem, we define a set of parameter values which seem to give the type of regular pattern of development we had detected in previous papers.

In other words, we started from a situation in which new sectors were regularly created and where the aggregate rates of growth of employment and of outcome were positive. We called this set of parameters our standard scenario. We then carried out a large number of experiments in which we vary the parameters which seem more likely to affect the formation of wages and of human capital and two variables that, according to our previous analysis, can be expected to have a considerable impact on the observed economic development path. The results of the experiments are presented in Figures 2.9 and 2.10 later in this chapter. In this paper, we summarize the results by means of a more synthetic representation, such as those given in Figures 2.11 and 2.12. On the other hand, Table A.2.1 in the appendix lists the parameter sets used in our experiments on the rate of growth of income and on the rate of growth of employment.

Although many combinations of the emergence of new sectors and of the growing quality and differentiation of goods and services can be envisaged, we can in principle expect such different combinations to give rise to different development paths. To explore the relative impact of the emergence of new sectors and of the growing quality and differentiation of goods and services, we simulate two development scenarios, called high quality (HQ) and low quality (LQ), respectively. These scenarios are obtained by giving different values to the parameters k_{14}–k_{17} of equations 3 and 4. These parameters determine the extent of product quality and differentiation corresponding to a given level of search activities. The LQ scenario is obtained by giving the parameters k_{15} and k_{17} values so low that product quality and differentiation are almost constant during the ILC of the sector. The HQ scenario is obtained by giving the same parameters considerably higher values. The results of this simulation show that the HQ and LQ scenarios give rise to very different development paths. The comparison HQ-LQ was explored by means of both micro and macroeconomic variables. In the LQ scenario, demand, human capital, wages and output remain substantially static or even declining, while they increase in the HQ scenario (Figure 2.4a, b and c).

At an aggregate level:

- Disposable income grows faster in the low-quality case with respect to the high-quality case (Figure 2.5).
- Employment growth is always faster in the low-quality case with respect to the high-quality case (Figure 2.7).
- The rate of creation of new sectors is higher in the low-quality case with respect to the high-quality case (Figures 2.6 and 2.7)
- The rate of income growth (RIG) of the HQ scenario is initially lower but it overtakes that for the LQ scenario at a later time (Figure 2.6). We can also notice that RIG slows down in the course of economic development for the LQ scenario while it accelerates for the HQ scenario.

The above results can be explained as follows: Constant wages and constant human capital limit the scope for income growth in the LQ case. The absence of

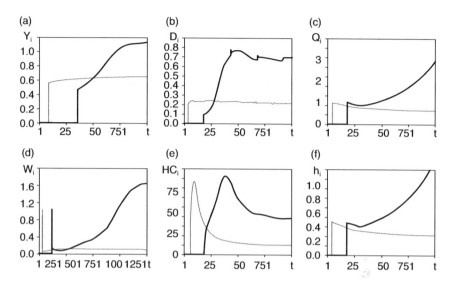

Figure 2.4 (a) Product quality, as measured by the services supplied by a product (Y_i) in the low-quality (thin curve) or high-quality (bold curve) case (source: own elaboration). (b) Effect of product quality on sectoral demand (source: own elaboration). (c) Effect of product quality on sectoral output (source: own elaboration). (d) Effect of product quality on sectoral wages (source: own elaboration). (e) Effect of product quality on the quantity of human capital used in a sector (source: own elaboration). (f) Effect of product quality on the quality of human capital used in a sector (source: own elaboration).

increases in quality and in sectoral differentiation, in the LQ case, lead to shorter industry life cycles (ILC) and to a higher rate of creation of new sectors. Since the rate of employment growth (REG) is higher in the early phases of an ILC, the aggregate REG is higher for the LQ than for the HQ scenario, although such higher REG is obtained at the expense of lower wages, lower demand and lower human capital.

Initially, the higher REG leads to a higher RIG for the LQ scenario. However, the rising wages and demand lead to a RIG which is not constant but increases in the course of economic development for the HQ scenario. The self-accelerating and self-limiting shapes of the RIG curves for HQ and LQ scenarios can be understood because, in the former case, an increase in demand leads to an increase in search activities, which in turn leads to an increase in output quality and differentiation, which is finally translated into an increase in demand. This feedback loop is considerably weakened in the LQ scenario because in this case search activities have a negligible impact on output quality and differentiation.

To interpret the previous results, we note that empirical observations show that product differentiation started considerably after the beginning of the industrial revolution, probably towards the end of the nineteenth century, and initially

(a)

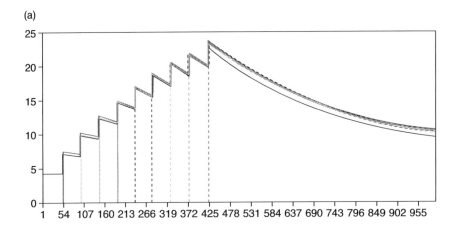

(b)

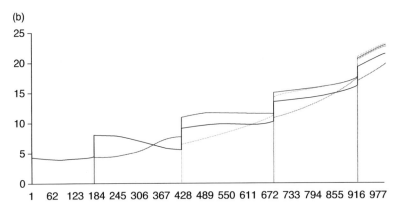

Figure 2.5 Effect of product quality on the disposable income created in the economic system for the low-quality case (a) and for the high-quality case (b) (source: own elaboration).

only in relatively rich countries. Such transition proceeded by liberating a growing proportion of household income from necessities and thus making room for the purchase of new goods and services which were not necessary in the physical sense in which food or shelter are (see Hobsbawm, 1968, diagrams 45 and 46). Rather than being necessities, the result of adaptation to the external environment in which human beings live, the new goods and services shape the external environment in ways which were not necessary and along a development path which was not necessarily unique. Thus, we described the evolution of the capitalist economic system as the transition from necessities to imaginary worlds. This transition could be interpreted as the result of a continuous, linear progress which constantly improves human welfare. We think that such an interpretation would be rather simplistic. We are more interested in

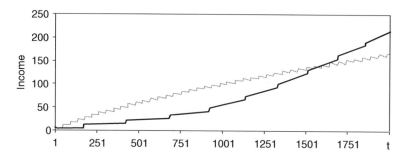

Figure 2.6 Effect of product quality on the aggregate rate of income growth (LQ light curve, HQ bold curve); the vertical line indicates the time required for HQ income to catch up with and to overtake LQ income, which we call ICUT (source: own elaboration).

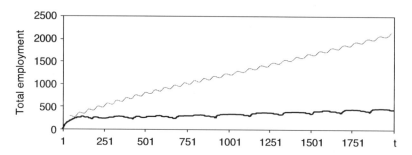

Figure 2.7 Effect of product quality on the aggregate rate of employment growth (LQ light curve, HQ bold curve) (source: own elaboration).

understanding how the mechanisms which we explore in this paper, however oversimplified, could provide us with an explanation of how the capitalist economic system managed to survive since the industrial revolution by profoundly transforming itself. Every economic system, however successful at the time it is created, brings in itself the seeds of its own destruction. Such destruction need not necessarily occur if the economic system manages to transform itself enough.

The development mechanism we hypothesize began with the saturation of the markets for necessities, attained during the early part of the industrial revolution due to the growth of productive efficiency which occurred in that period. In turn, that saturation is likely to have induced efforts by producers to avoid it by opening new markets or by enlarging existing ones. Assuming that new technologies potentially giving rise to new markets could be created, as they were, the markets themselves would not come into being unless a large enough percentage of the population had the required purchasing power. A mechanism which could give rise to the coordinated emergence of production capabilities and of purchasing power is the following:

- The production of some of the new goods and services and the rising quality and differentiation of existing ones required higher levels of competencies and of human capital.
- Such higher competencies required training and education.
- Better educated workers had to be paid higher wages.
- New jobs were created in the training and education system.
- The new jobs and higher wages created the disposable income required to purchase the new goods and higher quality goods and services.

The combination of the above steps gave rise to a virtuous circle which could continue expanding the economic system as long as technologies and demand could co-evolve. This co-evolution allowed the capitalist economic system to escape the development trap which Marx and other critics of capitalism had foreseen. Of course, we think that the mechanism previously described is only a component of an overall repertoire. The capitalist economic system cannot have been saved only by an ever-increasing shopping frenzy of new and more luxurious goods and services. Social innovations in pensions, unemployment benefits, health care, etc. are likely to have co-evolved together with the mechanism described above to allow the capitalist economic system to transform and adapt. Thus, the real co-evolution included more mechanisms and steps than the ones we described above. However, we think our exercise is useful because it provides an analytical approach to the explanation of long-range transitions in economic systems. The addition of further components to the co-evolutionary process described above can be envisaged without substantial modifications of our approach.

Let us observe that the transition from low- to high-quality goods and services, henceforth (LQ→HQ) transition, is not identical to that from necessities to imaginary worlds. The former is from an economic system dominated by trajectories 1 and 2 to one dominated by transition 1, 2 and 3, while the latter is from an economic development dominated predominantly by trajectory 1 for consumer goods but with trajectory 2 occurring in capital goods. In its present state, TEVECON cannot accurately distinguish between consumer and capital goods. In spite of these differences, the transition (LQ→HQ) is very similar to that from necessities to imaginary worlds, especially for what concerns the emergence of higher quality and internally differentiated goods and services. Thus, the study of the (LQ→HQ) transition can help us understand the mechanisms of capitalist economic development.

The analysis we carried out shows that long-range processes of economic development cannot be explained only by the increasing productive efficiency, or even by the increasing output quality, of a constant set of activities, but that they intrinsically involve a very high degree of structural change. In this context, structural change not only means the changing weight of different sectors but also other changes in the composition of the economic system, with the inclusion of completely new institutions and organizations and of their interactions. Structural change becomes more important for the explanation of processes of economic development the longer the time horizon chosen.

We now describe a set of policy-relevant experiments carried out with TEVECON.

3 Policy experiments

In these experiments, we explore the effects of changes in a number of TEVECON parameters on some aspects of the process of economic development. In particular, we focus on the role of human capital and of wages. According to the above-described mechanisms, we can expect that both human capital and wages had to increase to allow the economic system to generate the higher quality goods and services and the income required to purchase them. Thus, we chose to modify some parameters which affect these two variables. First, we hypothesized that at least in some types of economic activities there could be a barrier in human capital. In these activities, only human capital above this barrier could be employed. Second, we hypothesized that the weight of human capital in the production function could affect economic development processes. Third, we expected wages to affect economic development processes. In TEVECON, wages are proportional to labor productivity according to a parameter k_w, henceforth called the wage parameter. Accordingly, in our experiments, we vary the barrier in human capital, the weight of human capital in the production function and the wage parameter. We start by varying one parameter at a time and then we combine variations of two or more parameters (Table A.2.1, Appendix).

The starting point of our experiments here was the comparison of the LQ and HQ scenarios described in Figures 2.6 and 2.7. These results show, that (i) the rate of employment growth (REG) is systematically higher in the LQ scenario, and that (ii) the rate of income growth (RIG) is initially higher for the LQ scenario but becomes higher for the HQ scenario at later times. In the following experiments, we investigate the impact of the three above parameters on (i) the time required for HQ income to catch up and overtake LQ income, which we called ICUT, (ii) the relative REG for the two scenarios, and (iii) the variance of income determined by the change from conservative (CP) to progressive (PP) preferences. ICUT was measured as the time at which the HQ income crossed the LQ income curve (see Figure 2.6). ICUT is plotted as a function of the weight of human capital in the production function (Figure 2.8) and of the wage parameter k_w (Figure 2.9).

The most general trend observed is a fall in ICUT when both k_{Hi} or k_w increase. This means that the (LQ$\rightarrow$HQ) transition would have occurred earlier if a higher intensity of human capital and a higher wage rate had been used in the economic system. However, the behavior of ICUT becomes more complex when the increases in the above two parameters are combined with increasing values of B_{hi}. In this case, ICUT alternately rises or falls for different ranges of

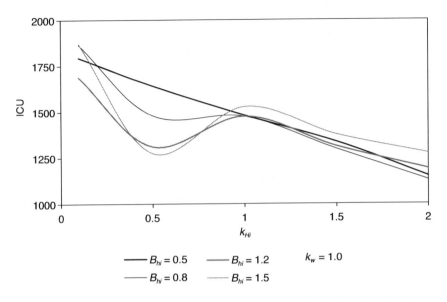

Figure 2.8 Effect of changing the weight k_{Hi} of Hi in the production function for different values of barrier in human capital B_{hi} (source: own elaboration).

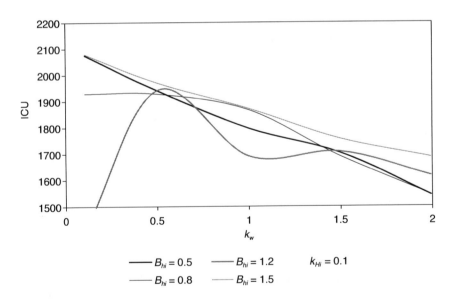

Figure 2.9 Effect of changing the wage parameter k_w for different values of barrier in human capital (source: own elaboration).

values of either k_{hi} or k_w. These more complex types of behavior could be understood by bearing in mind that the introduction of a human capital barrier excludes some workers from the labor force. The resulting outcome would be due to the balance between the higher wages of the employed workers and the absent wages of the unemployed ones. The general point to be made here is that wages are a source both of costs and of revenues. The effect of rising wage rates and of rising levels and intensity of human capital depends on the balance of their effects on revenues and on costs. Also, we have to bear in mind that the introduction of an h_i barrier in the present state of TEVECON is equivalent to an internal differentiation of the labor force. Thus, introduction of a low h_i barrier into an economic system which has low wages and low human capital can have a very different effect than the introduction of a higher h_i barrier into an economic system which has high wages and high levels and intensity of human capital. The effect of the human capital barrier on the ICUT falls for higher values of both k_{Hi} and k_w. Thus, a system which already has high wages and high levels and intensity of human capital is less affected by the introduction of a human capital barrier than a system which has low wages and low levels and intensity of human capital.

Finally, we can observe that the LQ income curve is virtually unaffected by the changes in the three above parameters. This is the result of the fact that human capital and output quality are almost constant in the LQ case.

The same set of experiments described in Table A.2.1 was carried out for the relative REG of the LQ and HQ scenarios. The result described in Figure 2.7 showed that REG(LQ) was systematically higher than REG(HQ). In fact, the two curves diverged continuously. Furthermore, both curves were approximately linear in time. In the vast majority of the experiments we carried out, REG(LQ) was greater than REG(HQ). However, for particular values of the parameters used, REG(HQ) increased considerably, showing an inflection point in the employment curve (see, for example, Figure 2.10).

After the inflection point, the HQ employment curve can sometimes overtake the LQ one. The inflection point occurs at very long development times, which correspond to high levels of economic development. In other words, similarly to

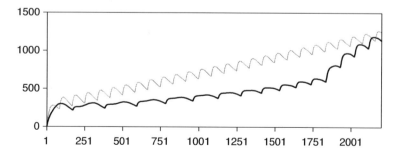

Figure 2.10 Employment for the LQ (light line) and HQ (heavy line) scenarios for $B_{hi}=0.5$ and $k_{Hi}=2.0$ (source: own elaboration).

what happened for income, the evolution of employment shows a self-accelerating character in the HQ case which is absent in the LQ case. In the HQ employment case, this self-accelerating character seems to arise fairly suddenly, while in the HQ income case it was continuous. However, even in the HQ employment case, we can see premonitory signs of the inflection in the shortening of the ILCs, which starts occurring from the beginning, a phenomenon which does not occur at all for the LQ scenario. Such shortening of the ILCs can be explained by (i) the increasing quality and internal differentiation of goods and services which lengthens the life cycles of the sectors producing them, as can be seen by comparing the LQ and HQ cases (see also Saviotti *et al.*, 2007); (ii) the increasing quality and internal differentiation of output can become faster the more knowledge-creating resources are present in the economic system. As in the income case, the employment curve of the LQ scenario is almost unaffected by the changes in parameters used in our experiments. As for the income case, this different sensitivity of the LQ and HQ cases to changes in parameters affecting human capital or wages can be explained by the much weaker feedback loop between demand and search activities existing in the LQ case.

The relative dynamics of income in the LQ and HQ scenarios is affected also by a change in preferences. Figures 2.11 and 2.12 compare the impact of preferences on the income curves for the LQ and HQ scenario with different parameter settings. Figure 2.11 corresponds to our standard scenario (experiment 1 in Table A.2.1), while Figure 2.12 corresponds to experiment 27. The results can be summarized as follows:

i   The variance in income induced by a change of preferences from conservative (CP) to random (RP) and then to progressive (PP) for both the LQ and LQ cases increases in the course of time – that is, the more highly developed an economic system is. In what follows we call this variance

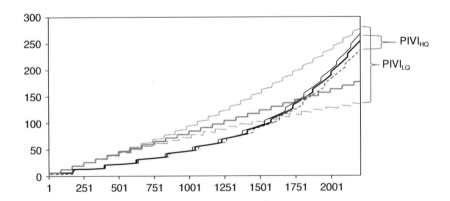

Figure 2.11 Income curves for the LQ (grey curves) and HQ (black curves) cases showing the impact of different preferences on income generation. The parameter settings correspond to the standard scenario (source: own elaboration).

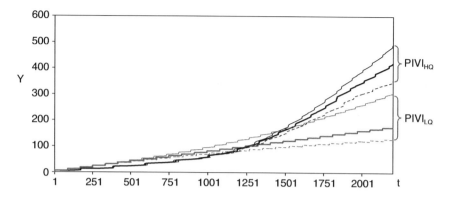

Figure 2.12 Income curves for the LQ (grey curves) and HQ (black curves) cases
showing the impact of different preferences on income generation. The parameter settings correspond to higher values of the B_{hi} barrier in human capital
and in the weight of human capital in the production function (experiment
27 in Table A.2.1) (source: own elaboration).

PIVI and we measure it as the difference between the income levels corresponding to PP and CP, respectively, at the maximum time at which we ran
our model (the intercepts of the income curves with the vertical axis on the
right of the diagram).

ii At equivalent times in our standard scenario (experiment 1, Table A.2.1)
PIVI is larger for the LQ than for the HQ case.

iii When the barrier to human capital, the weight of human capital in the production function and the wage parameter are increased, either individually
or in combination (experiments 2–44, Table A.2.1) PIVI grows also for the
HQ case and it can become comparable to that of the LQ case.

iv For very high values of k_{Hi} the income curve for the HQ case starts growing
very rapidly at fairly long times and then abruptly stops. In these conditions,
the process of economic development becomes so unbalanced that it cannot
proceed any further.

The previous results can be interpreted as implying that the impact of
changing preferences is likely to increase as economic development proceeds.
In other words, differences in consumer preferences are likely to have a
greater effect on the growth of income on those which are already rich than on
relatively poor ones. In an economic system in which most people can afford
just basic necessities, the disposable income required to buy new goods and
services would be absent or very scarce. In these conditions, preferences could
hardly exert any impact on income generation. Preferences can be expected to
start exerting an impact when there is a disposable income with which consumers could choose to purchase different goods and services in addition to
necessities.

While the previous conclusion makes sense in general, it is not immediately clear why different preferences should have a greater impact on income formation in the LQ than on the HQ case. If we remember that in the LQ case the only choice consumers could have is that amongst different types of goods and services, but that within each type quality remains constant. As a consequence, ILCs would be shorter and the rate of growth of disposable income would initially be faster. Yet the effect of preferences on PIVI would still be lower even after HQ income had overtaken LQ income. PIVI for the HQ case can start growing and become comparable to that of the LQ case only after barriers to human capital, a higher weight of human capital in the production function and a higher wage rate had been introduced. Thus, although for both the LQ and the HQ cases different preferences start exerting an effect on the rate of growth of income, the time at which preferences start affecting income varies depending on the case and on the parameter setting used in the experiments. In particular, barriers to human capital, a higher weight of human capital in the production function and a higher wage rate seem to have a much higher impact on the HQ than on the LQ case. This in understandable because both levels of human capital and wages remain relatively flat in the LQ case, while they increase in the HQ case.

Let us conclude this section by pointing out that that the term policy needs to be interpreted carefully in this context. Usually policies have a relatively short-term orientation with respect to the time horizon we are envisaging in this paper. The parameters we explored are related to human capital and to wages, two variables the importance of which in modern economic systems is still, and is likely to remain, very high. We have seen that rising wages and rising levels and intensity of human capital played a fundamental role in capitalist economic development by allowing to create both the competencies required to produce goods and services of higher quality and internal differentiation and the disposable income required to purchase them. These results cannot be interpreted as implying that economic development will always be positively affected by raising wages and levels and intensity of human capital. There are many examples in which a reduction in wages can positively contribute to economic performance. What matters is not wages per se but the combination of wages, human capital and other variables. Thus, even if rising wages and levels and intensity of human capital are required to sustain the long-term development of the economic system, short-term adjustments in their *combination* can be required to compensate for temporary slowdowns or bottlenecks. What matters is not wages or human capital per se but the way in which their co-evolution can create, in a coordinated way, new demand and the required purchasing power and preferences.

As for preferences, it is quite clear from our results that their impact on growth and development becomes increasingly important as the economic system becomes richer. As a consequence, the scope for activities which help consumers to form preferences for emerging goods and services increases with the level of economic development. This is particularly true for high levels and intensities of human capital and for high wage rates. However, we must remember that, if facilitating the formation of preferences for emerging goods and services can positively affect economic development, a balance must be maintained in the economic system between speeding up the introduction of new goods and services and reducing the weight of pre-existing ones.

4 Summary and conclusions

In this paper, we have studied the co-evolution of innovation and demand and tried to understand how it could have contributed to the long-run development of the capitalist economic system by means of our TEVECON model. We have shown that the economic system can create the disposable income required for consumers to be able to purchase the new, higher quality and more differentiated goods and services created by innovation. The creation of such disposable income is due to the combination of growing productive efficiency (trajectory 1), growing variety (trajectory 2) and growing output quality and internal differentiation (trajectory 3). Furthermore, we have shown that consumer preferences can affect observed macroeconomic development paths. In particular, we showed that consumers with progressive preferences led to higher rates of growth of output and of income than consumers with conservative preferences, where progressive preferences imply a strong relative propensity to purchase new goods and services at the expense of older ones. Thus, our results confirm that demand matters and that observed patterns of economic development can be explained by the co-evolution of innovation and demand.

After having established this point, we explored the economic development paths that could be generated by different combinations of growing variety (trajectory 2) and growing output quality and internal differentiation (trajectory 3). This was done by choosing two rather extreme scenarios, one including only growing variety, which we called low quality (LQ), and one including both growing variety and growing output quality and internal differentiation, which we called high quality (HQ). The HQ scenario gives rise to a slower but richer growth path. The LQ scenario has a higher rate of creation of new sectors and consequently a higher rate of growth of employment but at the expense of having lower wages, lower sectoral demand and lower levels of human capital.

An important result of our comparison was that the HQ income was initially lower than the LQ one, but that at later times the situation was reversed with HQ income becoming dominant. We called this phenomenon the (LQ→HQ) transition. This is important because it seems to map some observed paths of economic development, in particular what we call the transition from necessities to imaginary worlds. Admittedly, the two transitions are not identical but they both include the emergence of higher quality and more internally differentiated goods and services at a later stage of economic development. We then explored further the (LQ→HQ) transition to better understand long-run mechanisms of economic development. To do this, we varied some TEVECON parameters affecting human capital and wages. We found that growing wages and growing levels and intensity of human capital favor long-run economic development. We then hypothesized that the (LQ→HQ) transition could have been the outcome of a virtuous circle in which growing human capital and growing wages provided both the competencies needed to produce higher quality and more internally differentiated goods and services as well as the disposable income required to purchase them. Our TEVECON model proves that this virtuous circle is possible but that it is not necessary. As in all co-evolutionary processes, the necessary ingredients are required with the appropriate coordination.

Furthermore, we show that the LQ and HQ cases are both affected, although differently, by changing consumer preferences. In both cases, the variance in income produced by progressive (PP) and conservative (CP) consumer preferences tend to grow as economic systems become progressively richer. This points towards an important scope for policy, especially for those activities which help consumers to learn about new goods and services, a necessary condition for them to have clear preferences.

We conclude this paper by pointing out that the policy implications we can derive here are long term. Thus, we have seen that growing wages and growing levels and intensity of human capital favor long-run economic development. This conclusion cannot be translated into the short-term prescription to keep raising wages and levels and intensity of human capital under any circumstances. What matters are not the individual values or trends of wages and of human capital but their combinations. Many adaptations can be required to overcome short-term bottlenecks and to restore long-run trends.

Appendix

Table A.2.1 Parameter sets on the rate of growth of income and on the rate of growth of employment

	h_i entry barrier (B_{hi}) a	Weight of H_i in production function(k_{Hi}) b	Wage function parameter (k_w) c	
1	0.0	0.1	1	Standard
2	0.5	0.1	1	Entry barrier experiments
3	0.8	0.1	1	
4	1.2	0.1	1	
5	1.5	0.1	1	
6	0.0	0.5	1	Production function
7	0.0	1.0	1	experiments
8	0.0	1.5	1	
9	0.0	0.1	0.5	Wage function
10	0.0	0.1	1.5	experiments
11	0.0	0.1	2.0	
12	0.5	0.5	1	a&b
13	0.5	1.0	1	
14	0.5	1.5	1	
15	0.5	2.0	1	

	h_i entry barrier (B_{hi}) a	Weight of H_i in production function (k_{Hi}) b	Wage function parameter (k_w) c	
16	0.8	0.5	1	a&b
17	0.8	1.0	1	
18	0.8	1.5	1	
19	0.8	2.0	1	
20	1.2	0.5	1	
21	1.2	1.0	1	
22	1.2	1.5	1	
23	1.2	2.0	1	
24	1.5	0.5	1	
25	1.5	1.0	1	
26	1.5	1.5	1	
27	1.5	2.0	1	
28	0.5	0.1	0.1	a&c
29	0.5	0.1	0.5	
30	0.5	0.1	1.5	
31	0.5	0.1	2.0	
32	0.8	0.1	0.1	
33	0.8	0.1	0.5	
34	0.8	0.1	1.5	
35	0.8	0.1	2.0	
36	1.2	0.1	0.1	
37	1.2	0.1	0.5	
38	1.2	0.1	1.5	
39	1.2	0.1	2.0	
40	1.5	0.2	0.1	
41	1.5	0.1	0.1	
42	1.5	0.1	0.5	
43	1.5	0.1	1.5	
44	1.5	0.1	2.0	
45	0.5	0.5	0.1	a,b&c
46	0.8	1.0	0.5	
47	1.2	1.5	1.5	
48	1.5	2.0	2.0	
49				

Source: own elaboration.

References

Acemoglu, D. and Zilibotti, F. (1997) Was Prometheus unbound by chance? Risk, diversification and growth, *Journal of Political Economy*, 105(4): 709–751.

Aghion, P. and Howitt, P. (1992) A model of growth through creative destruction, *Econometrica*, 60: 323–335.

Amendola, M. and Gaffard, J.L. (1998) *Out of Equilibrium*, Oxford: Oxford University Press.

Andersen, E.S. (2001) Satiation in an evolutionary model of structural economic dynamics, in Witt, U. (ed.) *Escaping Satiation, the Demand Side of Economic Growth*, Berlin: Springer.

Andersen, E.S. (2007) Innovation and demand, in Hanusch, H. and Pyka, A. (eds) *Elgar Companion to Neo-Schumpeterian Economics*, Cheltenham: Edward Elgar.

Aoki, M. and Yoshikawa, H. (2002) Demand saturation-creation and growth, *Journal of Economic Behavior and Organization*, 48: 127–154.

Aversi, R., Dosi, G., Fagiolo, G., Meacci, M. and Olivetti, C. (1999) Demand dynamics with socially evolving preferences, *Industrial and Corporate Change*, 8: 353–399.

Bianchi, M. (ed.) (1998) *The Active Consumer*, London: Routledge.

Ciarli, T., Lorentz, A., Savona, M. and Valente M. (2010) The effect of consumption and production structure on growth and distribution. A micro to macro model, *Metroeconomica*, 61(1): 180–218.

De Benedictis, L., Gallegati, M. and Tamberi, M. (2009) Overall trade specialization and economic development: countries diversify, *Review of World Economics*, 145: 37–55.

Diamond, J. (1997) *Guns, Germs and Steel: the Fates of Human Societies*, New York: Norton.

Dosi, G. (1982) Technological paradigms and technological trajectories: a suggested interpretation of the determinants and directions of technical change, *Research Policy*, 11: 147–162.

Foellmi, R. and Zweimuller, J. (2006) Income distribution and demand induced innovations, *Review of Economic Studies*, 82: 95–112.

Grossman, Gene M. and Helpman, Elhanan (2001) *Special Interest Politics*, Cambridge; London: MIT Press.

Hobsbawm, E. (1968) *Industry and Empire*, Harmondsworth: Penguin Books.

Imbs, J. and Wacziarg, R. (2003) Stages of diversification, *The American Economic Review*, 93(1): 63–86.

Kaldor, N. (1957) A model of economic growth, *Economic Journal*, 67: 591–624.

Kirman, A. (1998) Self-organization and evolution, in Schweitzer, F. and Silverberg, G. (Eds) *Evolution und Selbstorganisation in der Ökonomie, Jahrbuch für complexität in den Natur, Sozial und Geissteswissenschaften*, Vol. 9, Berlin: Duncker & Humboldt.

Lazonick, William (1990) *Competitive Advantage on the Shop Floor*, Cambridge, Mass: Harvard University Press.

Maddison, A. (2007) *Contours of the World Economy, 1–2030AD*, Oxford: Oxford University Press.

Matsuyama, K. (2002) The rise of mass consumption societies, *Journal of Political Economy*, 110: 1035–1070.

Metcalfe, J.S. (2001) Consumption, preferences and the evolutionary agenda, *Journal of Evolutionary Economics*, 11: 37–58.

Murmann, J.P. (2003) *Knowledge and Competitive Advantage: the Co-evolution of Firms, Technology and National Institutions*, Cambridge: Cambridge University Press.

Murphy, K, Schleifer, A. and Vishny, R. (1989) Industrialization and the big push, *Journal of Political Economy*, 97: 1003–1026.

Nelson, R.R. (1994) The co-evolution of technology, industrial structure, and supporting institutions, *Industrial and Corporate Change*, 3(1): 47–63.

Nelson, R.R. (2008) What enables rapid economic progress: What are the needed institutions?, *Research Policy*, 37: 1–11.

Nelson, R.R. and Consoli, D. (2010) An evolutionary theory of household consumption behaviour, *Journal of Evolutionary Economics*, 20: 665–687.

Nelson, R. and Winter, S. (1982) *An Evolutionary Theory of Economic Change*, Cambridge, Mass: Harvard University Press.

Nicolis, G. and Prigogine, I. (1989) *Exploring Complexity: An Introduction*, New York: Freeman.

Pasinetti, L.L. (1981) *Structural Change and Economic Growth*, Cambridge: Cambridge University Press.

Perez, C. (1983) Structural change and the assimilation of new technologies in the economic system, *Futures*, 15: 357–375.

Polanyi, Karl (1944) *The Great Transformation* (11th edn, 1971), Boston MA; New York: Beacon Press; Rinehart & Company.

Pyka, A. and Fagiolo, G. (2007) Agent based modeling: a methodology for neo-Schumpeterian economics, in Hanusch, H. and Pyka, A. (eds) *Elgar Companion to Neo-Schumpeterian Economics*, Cheltenham: Edward Elgar.

Pyka, A. and Saviotti, P.P. (2011) Economic growth through the emergence of new sectors, in Mann, S. (ed.) *Sectors Matter – Exploring Mesoeconomics*, Heidelberg, Dordrecht, London, New York: Springer.

Pyka, A. and Saviotti, P.P. (2012) Economic development – more creation than destruction, in Krämer, H., Kurz, H. and Trautwein, H.-M. (eds) *Macroeconomics and the History of Economic Thought – Festschrift in Honour of Harald Hagemann*, London and New York: Routledge.

Romer, P. (1990) Endogenous technical progress, *Journal of Political Economy*, 98: 71–102.

Rosenstein-Rodan, P.N. (1943) Problems of industrialisation of eastern and south-eastern Europe, *The Economic Journal*, 53 (June–September): 202–211.

Saviotti, P.P. (1996) *Technological Evolution, Variety and the Economy*, Aldershot: Edward Elgar.

Saviotti, P.P. (2001) Variety, growth and demand, *Journal of Evolutionary Economics*, 11: 119–142.

Saviotti, P.P. and Frenken, K. (2008) Export variety and the economic performance of countries, *Journal of Evolutionary Economics*, 18: 201–218.

Saviotti, P.P. and Metcalfe, J.S. (1984) A theoretical approach to the construction of technological output indicators, *Research Policy*, 13: 141–151.

Saviotti, P.P. and Pyka, A. (2004a) Economic development by the creation of new sectors, *Journal of Evolutionary Economics*, 14(1): 1–35.

Saviotti, P.P. and Pyka, A. (2004b) Economic development, qualitative change and employment creation, *Structural Change and Economic Dynamics*, 15: 265–287.

Saviotti, P.P. and Pyka, A. (2008) Micro and macro dynamics: industry life cycles, inter-sector coordination and aggregate growth, *Journal of Evolutionary Economics*, 18: 167–182.

Saviotti, P.P. and Pyka, A. (2010) The co-evolution of innovation, demand and growth, paper presented at conference "Technical change, history, economics and policy," SPRU, Freeman Centre, University of Sussex, March 29–30, 2010.

Saviotti, P.P., Pyka, A. and Krafft, J. (2007) On the determinants and dynamics of the industry life cycle, presented at the EAEPE conference "Economic growth, development, and institutions – lessons for policy and the need for an evolutionary framework of analysis," Porto, November 1–3, 2007.

Schumpeter, J. (1934, original edition 1912) *The Theory of Economic Development*, Cambridge, Mass: Harvard University Press.

Veblen, T. (1915) *Imperial Germany and the Industrial Revolution*, New York: MacMillan.

Witt, U. (2001) Learning to consume: a theory of wants and the growth of demand, *Journal of Evolutionary Economics*, 11(1): 23–26.

3 The competent demand-pull hypothesis

Cristiano Antonelli and Agnieszka Gehringer

1 Introduction

Recent advances in the economics of knowledge crucially contribute to our understanding of the economic complexity of innovation. In particular, one of the main contributions of the economics of knowledge consists in providing the necessary micro-founded conceptual tools to an analysis of the innovation generation process. Consequently, more in-depth analysis of user–producer interactions – crucially based on the market-driven exchange of newly generated knowledge – can be conducted.

With these conceptual tools, we are equipped to offer a fresh view on the demand-pull hypothesis originating from the insight of Adam Smith (1776) and Allyn Young (1928) and subsequently elaborated in seminal contributions by Kaldor (1966, 1972) and Schmookler (1966).

The Kaldorian demand-pull hypothesis has a strong macroeconomic basis, focusing on increasing returns from public intervention to support aggregate demand. Complementary to the analysis of Kaldor, Schmookler's work was crucial in clarifying the chain of effects and causal relationships linking the increase in aggregate demand to the impact on investment and, finally, on technological advance. More specifically, Schmookler's demand-pulling mechanism does not involve a generic demand, but rather derived demand, originating from private investment in certain sectors of the economy. The conceptual framework elaborated by Schmookler, although intuitively pointing to a disaggregated effect, remained macroeconomic in nature, as did subsequent debate on the demand-pull hypothesis.

We add to the still ongoing debate by providing the foundations for the competent demand-pulling hypothesis. Our present effort is based on three contributions (Antonelli and Gehringer, 2012, 2013a, 2013b) in which we elaborate the conceptual basis for the competent demand-pull hypothesis and empirically test its relevance. This chapter aims to rigorously summarize the theoretical foundations of the competent demand hypothesis and the empirical evidence, as well as discuss and offer crucial policy implications.

The rest of the paper is organized as follows. In Section 2, we trace the evolution of the demand-pull hypothesis since its original formulation by Adam Smith and its macroeconomic applications that have determined the standard view over the demand pull. Section 3 is dedicated to highlighting novel opportunities for a microeconomic understanding of the demand-pull hypothesis. Section 4 spells out the competent demand-pull hypothesis articulating the grafting of recent advances in the economics of knowledge onto the received macroeconomic body of analysis. Section 5 closes the discussion with some concluding remarks and important reflections on innovation policy.

2 Origins of the demand-pull hypothesis

2.1 Adam Smith: the original insight

The origins of the demand-pull hypothesis can be traced back to Adam Smith's 'An Enquiry on the Nature and Causes of the Wealth of the Nations'. In Book 1, Adam Smith suggests that there is a causal link between the extent of the market and the productivity of labour. More precisely, the causal loop of effects contends that the extent of the market defines the scope and limits of the division of labour. The latter determines the degree of specialization of an economic system. The opportunities for learning and accumulating knowledge in turn depend on the levels of specialization and define the general efficiency of the production process. An increase in the levels of human capital and technological knowledge embedded in physical capital would favour the introduction of superior production techniques with the ultimate result of increasing revenue and demand (Figure 3.1). This dynamic chain of effects leads to the first formulation of an endogenous growth theory where technological progress and structural change

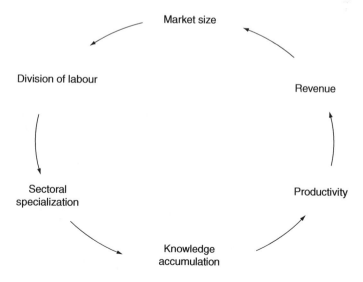

Figure 3.1 Smithian view on demand-pulling mechanism (source: own elaboration).

are intertwined and constitute the key components of a self-sustained dynamics. The increase in the extent of the market leads to increased levels of division of labour with the creation of new industries. Consequently, the structure of the system changes and at the same time higher levels of competence to be accumulated, making the introduction of technological innovations possible. The introduction of innovations enhances the general productivity of the system by increasing the generation of wealth and hence the extent of the market.

Careful reading of Book 1 of the founding book of economics as a specialized field of scientific activity leaves no doubts about Adam Smith's views on the endogenous dynamics of economic growth. Figure 3.1 synthesizes the founding pillars of the Smithian chain of causation.

Careful reading in Book 1 'of the causes of improvements in the productive powers of labour, and of the order according to which its produce is naturally distributed among the different ranks of the people', however, also makes it clear how much Adam Smith was aware of the central role played by the generation of technological knowledge as a key condition for the effective deployment of the endogenous dynamics of economic growth. Book 1 can be regarded as the first economic effort to implement a systematic analysis of the knowledge generation process.

According to Adam Smith, the introduction of innovations is a consequence of the division of labour:

> everybody must be sensible how much labour is facilitated and abridged by the application of proper machinery. It is unnecessary to give any example. I shall only observe, therefore, that the invention of all those machines by which labour is so much facilitated and abridged, seems to have been originally owing to the division of labour.
>
> (p. 15)

At the same time, the role of bottom-up learning processes in the accumulation of competence is well identified:

> Men are much more likely to discover easier and readier methods of attaining any object, when the whole attention of their minds is directed towards that single object, than when it is dissipated among a great variety of things. But, in consequence of the division of labour, the whole of every man's attention comes naturally to be directed towards some one very simple object. It is naturally to be expected, therefore, that some one or other of those who are employed in each particular branch of labour should soon find out easier and readier methods of performing their own particular work, whenever the nature of it admits of such improvement.
>
> (p. 10)

The bottom-up accumulation of competence is the primary input to the generation of the technological knowledge that makes innovations possible:

A great part of the machines made use of in those manufactures in which labour is most subdivided were originally the invention of common workmen, who, being each of them employed in some very simple operation, naturally turned their thoughts towards finding out easier and readier methods of performing it. Whoever has been much accustomed to visit such manufactures must frequently have been shown very pretty machines, which were the inventions of such workmen, in order to facilitate and quicken their own particular part of the work.

(p. 15)

Adam Smith identifies the variety of skills and competencies as a necessary condition for the actual generation of knowledge and raises the central issue of their effective coordination:

What a variety of labour, too, is necessary in order to produce the tools of the meanest of those workmen! To say nothing of such complicated machines as the ship of the sailor, the mill of the fuller, or even the loom of the weaver, let us consider only what a variety of labour is requisite in order to form that very simple machine, the shears with which the shepherd clips the wool. The miner, the builder of the furnace for smelting the ore, the feller of the timber, the burner of the charcoal to be made use of in the smelting-house, the brick-maker, the bricklayer, the workmen who attend the furnace, the millwright, the forger, the smith, must all of them join their different arts in order to produce them.

(p. 16)

In the discussion provided by Adam Smith, the role of top-down deductive efforts contributed by academics and vertical inter-industrial relations between users and producers of machinery is clearly acknowledged:

All the improvements in machinery, however, have by no means been the inventions of those who had occasion to use the machines. Many improvements have been made by the ingenuity of the makers of the machines, when to make them became the business of a peculiar trade; and some by that of those who are called philosophers, or men of speculation, whose trade it is not to do any thing, but to observe every thing, and who, upon that account, are often capable of combining together the powers of the most distant and dissimilar objects in the progress of society, philosophy or speculation becomes, like every other employment, the principal or sole trade and occupation of a particular class of citizens. Like every other employment, too, it is subdivided into a great number of different branches, each of which affords occupation to a peculiar tribe or class of philosophers; and this subdivision of employment in philosophy, as well as in every other business, improves dexterity, and saves time. Each individual becomes more expert in his own peculiar branch, more work is done upon the whole, and the quantity of science is considerably increased by it.

(p. 16)

Recent advances in the economics of knowledge give us a better understanding of the fact that Adam Smith was well aware of the contingent character of the knowledge generation process that is indeed stirred by a division of labour and by an increase in the extent of the market, but can take place only when an array of well-specified and highly localized circumstances concur to make the emergence of new technological knowledge possible. This leads us to suggest that the correct interpretation of the Smithian mechanisms of endogenous growth has a strong stochastic foundation that contrasts with the deterministic flavour retained in the literature. A correct understanding of the Smithian mechanism of endogenous growth would be that an increase in the extent of the market *may* favour: (i) an increase in the division of labour; (ii) which in turn *may* enable higher levels specialization; (iii) if, when and where the accumulation of competence is possible and if it *actually* enables (iv) its integration with codified and scientific knowledge that make the recombinant generation of new technological knowledge viable; (v) and hence are actually able to complete the set of complementary conditions that make the introduction of productivity-enhancing innovations *possible*. Appreciation of the stochastic character of the Smithian causation chain should have made it clear that, together with appreciation of the demand-pull effects, the focus of the enquiry should have been the identification of the conditional possibilities that make the working of the Smithian mechanism possible.

For quite a long time, the deterministic understanding of the legacy of Adam Smith, with the notable exception of Allyn Young (1928), had a much stronger following in the macroeconomics of growth than in the microeconomic analysis of the actual chain of conditions appearing in Figure 3.1, by means of which an increase in the extent of the market may actually favour the final introduction of innovations.

2.2   *The role of demand for growth in the macro framework*

While for Adam Smith the crucial demand-pulling mechanism was driven by division of labour and specialization, these factors were neglected in the subsequent foundation of the demand-pull hypothesis in the mid-1960s. In a macroeconomic and post-Keynesian framework of analysis, Nicholas Kaldor formulated the pioneering basis for the hypothesis (Kaldor, 1966, 1967, 1972). The main argument was based on recognition of the fact that increases in public expenditures would be able to support the expansion of aggregate demand with positive effects on output and productivity via interaction between the multiplier and the accelerator. Kaldor assumes that new technologies are available on the shelf at all times and that investments in tangible assets necessarily embody them. Technological change is necessarily biased and capital intensive.

Technological change is assumed to be necessarily associated with new machinery produced in the manufacturing industry with consequent emphasis on the central role of the secondary sector as the core of the accumulation process (Verdoon, 1949; Thirwall, 2003).

Building upon these somewhat naïve assumptions, Kaldor was able to articulate the view that an increase in public demand could foster aggregate demand via the multiplier and investments via the accelerator with final positive effects on productivity via capital accumulation. Additional flows of investments were expected to speed up the diffusion of technological innovations thanks to the new technological solutions embodied in the subsequent vintages of capital goods. In that way, the overall efficiency of the system would be improved and output would increase, allowing the economy to generate the necessary flows of fiscal receipts to repay the original public spending. This circular relationship is illustrated in Figure 3.2.

The Kaldorian approach to demand pull concentrated on the positive effects of the diffusion of innovations embodied in new waves of investment in capital goods, rather than on the actual creation of technological innovations. The process of diffusion is seen as an important ingredient for improvement in dynamic efficiency. Indeed, the increase in final demand that gives rise to accumulation of capital may foster an increase in total factor productivity through the diffusion of existing, most efficient, technological solutions. At the same time, however, the technologies being diffused would have already been developed and introduced. Consequently, demand-pulling effects would stem only from their diffusion, without any analysis of the mechanisms that had led to their original introduction. Most importantly, thus, the Kaldorian demand-pull hypothesis is successful in explaining the positive

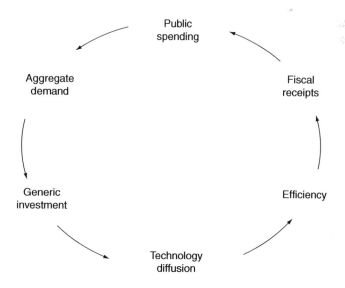

Figure 3.2 Kaldorian demand-pulling mechanism (source: own elaboration).

growth effects following the adoption and diffusion of the existing technologies, yet it is tacit on the reasons why and how additional investment should lead to the introduction of new technologies.

The motivations of the Kaldorian demand-pull hypothesis are clear, strong and sufficiently reasonable to adopt over the entire business cycle. On the contrary, the Keynesian recipes including deficit spending risked being considered only a special remedy for special economic crises that had little relevance. At a time of persisting full employment, deficit spending would lead to an excessive accumulation of debt. In this vein, the Kaldorian demand-pull hypothesis aimed to construct the building blocks for elaboration of an intertemporal equilibrium budget. Indeed, provided that the general efficiency of the system increases as a consequence of increases in output following an increase in aggregate demand, it can be easily shown that an increase in the public deficit to fund additional public expenditures at time t would lead to increased levels of output, hence, to augmented levels of fiscal receipts able to restore equilibrium budgets at time $t + 1$. In so doing, Kaldor provided a framework for justifying and motivating the extension of Keynesian macroeconomic policies beyond contingent crises, turning them into a tool to support economic growth, valid at all times.

Kaldor elaborated the macroeconomic demand-pull hypothesis by impinging on a very rough understanding of the microdynamics of technological change. As a matter of fact, Kaldor's view can be synthetized in terms of a reduction of the notion of technological change to a sheer and automatic process of diffusion of new technologies embodied in capital-intensive processes.

The contribution of Jacob Schmookler's *Invention and Economic Growth* (1966) is an important complement of the Kaldorian view. At the same time, however, Schmookler's sophisticated analysis constitutes a crucial advance in providing a more in-depth articulation of the causal chain of demand-pulling effects. From his contribution, indeed, new insights can be gained that explain the link between the initial increase in demand and capital accumulation and, finally, the actual generation of new technological knowledge and the adoption – as distinct from absorption – of technological innovations.

This new perspective is possible mainly thanks to the switching of the focus from the final, generic demand to the derived, specific demand for qualified capital goods and services. More precisely, Schmookler focuses attention on the rise in demand for specific activities or goods that is able to activate innovative firms to creatively meet such demand with new routines and new technological solutions. Thus, technology is not only diffused, but it is most importantly created and introduced. Finally, the efficiency of the system is enhanced and the generated income ensures positive flows of financial receipts, crucial in closing the cycle. The circular sequence of effects illustrating Schmookler's view is summarized in Figure 3.3.

The anecdotic evidence that he shows regards the US experience of waves of specific investments, occurring in a sequence of strongly interrelated activities in the construction of infrastructures, such as canals and railways, and in the provision of crucial utilities, such as electric power. These specific investment

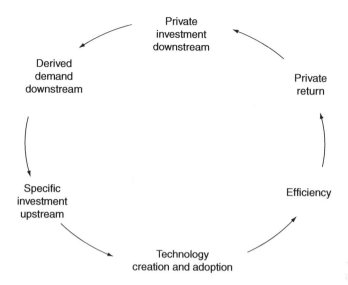

Figure 3.3 Schmookler's demand-pulling mechanism (source: own elaboration).

activities subsequently pulled the generation of technological innovations in the upstream sectors, being crucial suppliers of intermediate and capital goods in the construction of infrastructures. Moreover, thanks to the successful introduction of innovation, the profitability of innovators was enhanced, creating the necessary conditions for further investment. At the same time, a series of subsequent positive side effects occurred elsewhere in the system. Indeed, the creation of a new chain of canals connecting the Great Lakes with the ports of New York City and New Orleans was crucial in rendering agriculture viable in the Far West. Consequently, its inclusion in the American economy was assured. The construction of canals also induced the demand for transportation infrastructures, railways, as well as innovative transportation technologies in the machinery sector. In turn, investments in railways gave rise to a further demand-pulling effect of stimulus for the generation of innovative technologies in upstream industries supplying fixed capital and intermediary goods which were essential to the activity of the newly established industry (Antonelli and Gehringer, 2012).

Another crucial contribution of Schmookler consists in providing us with empirical evidence for his argument. He shows that the flows of technological innovations, as measured by patents, can be explained – with proper lags – by the flows of investments in the related industrial activities.

The contribution of Schmookler is important because, although it retains a macroeconomic nature, it provides consistent micro-foundations of the precise underlying mechanisms. Schmookler, indeed, is aware of the need to assure that the analysis has a microeconomic flavour. He observes that the additional derived demand through investment that is specific stirs not only the introduction of innovations and, finally, profitability of firms, but also the activity of 'inventors'. Schmookler, well aware of the crucial role of the generation of technological innovations, had pioneered one of the first empirical analyses of the economics of inventors by highlighting their motivations and incentives (Schmookler, 1957).

The empirical evidence regarding the role of derived demand and investment in stirring the generation of innovation could confirm the positive pulling of demand. This impact has been found to go through the enhancement of the rate of introduction of innovations. Also, the contribution of profitability in assuring the continuity of the demand pull has been found (Andersen, 2007).

This empirical evidence is rather broad, as it has been confirmed for different levels of aggregation. In particular, there are studies based on sector- and firm-level data (Brouwer and Kleinknecht, 1999; Piva and Vivarelli, 2007) as well as case study analyses (Walsh, 1984; Nemet, 2009; Guerzoni, 2010). Various measures of innovativeness have also been applied: patent counts measures (Scherer, 1982), R&D intensity (Jaffe, 1988; Kleinknecht and Verspagen, 1990), total factor productivity (Jaffe, 1988) and labour productivity (Crespi and Pianta, 2008).

2.3 Controversy over the demand-pull hypothesis

In subsequent economic discussion, consensus over the demand-pull hypothesis was substantially lacking. The main reason for this has been the controversy with those who sustained that it would be science and technology to shape and determine industrial development. The discussion intensified over the years and reached its high point in the 1970s when the scepticism regarding the role of demand became considerable and technology push dominated the stage (Di Stefano *et al.*, 2012).

From a methodological point of view, Mowery and Rosenberg (1979) advanced an important critique, stating that the early evidence based on the case study as well as on the first econometric investigations were unable to capture the pure demand-pulling effects. This methodological issue originates from the conceptual setting of the instantaneous interaction between the demand and supply side. The authors observe that an increase in demand could often derive from – and not be a determinant of – the introduction of an innovation. On the other hand, however, the role of demand could not be totally rejected since any kind of production activity is continuously confronted with demand-side conditions of marketability and profitability (Dosi, 1982).

However, probably the most serious drawback accompanying the discussion over the years was related to keeping the two sides completely distinct, as if moving on independent trajectories. As soon as one recognizes the possible complementarities between demand and supply forces, it becomes operational to analyse the simultaneous, although still distinct, contribution of both the demand and technological factors. Interestingly, the role of such complementarities was confirmed already in the analysed contribution of Adam Smith when describing the sources of improvements of machinery.

It was in this spirit of reconciliation that Klein and Rosenberg (1986) postulated for the construction of new models that were able to capture the two-sided impact on the generation of innovation. It seems that by now a reconciliation of the two approaches had been reached, with a crucial role confirmed for both, but a dominating nature assigned to technology push (Di Stefano *et al.*, 2012).

3 Competent demand and productivity growth

3.1 The need for micro-foundation

Much of the conceptual weaknesses in the original formulation of the demand-pull hypothesis derive from its macroeconomic focus. Indeed, the aggregated level of analysis prevents us from observing the precise within-system interactions that, conversely, stay at the heart of innovation dynamics. In such a disaggregated framework, both technology push in a top-down relationship and demand pull working in the opposite direction can simultaneously occur since nothing prevents each agent from being subject to positive influences from both its own suppliers and its qualified customers. Moreover, for the demand-side effects, users not only direct the derived demand towards producers, but such demand – being specific and qualified – delivers crucial impulses for the innovative activity upstream. In other words, derived demand is not generic, but competent and this explains why the positive impact on upstream productivity is achieved.

3.2 The ingredients of micro-foundation: knowledge generation and knowledge externalities

An analysis of the economic complexity of technological change based on recent advances in the economics of knowledge provides the necessary tools for reconsidering the demand-pull hypothesis in a microeconomic context. In such a framework, two crucial ingredients explain why derived demand is competent and how it contributes to positive productivity dynamics (Antonelli and Gehringer, 2013b).

The first ingredient refers to the very generation of technological knowledge. The process is a complex one since it requires the implementation and coordination of the existing pieces of knowledge available internally and externally to the knowledge generating units. With specific regard to external knowledge, it constitutes a crucial input in any innovative process (Antonelli, 2008). At the same time, however, no agent can instantaneously control all the pieces of external knowledge relevant for the internal generation of innovation. This implies that each agent who is willing to resist market competition will be involved in searching, screening, acquiring and adopting externally generated knowledge. The external source of knowledge can be very different, ranging from suppliers to competitors and customers. Among the latter, and depending on the precise characteristics of each industrial context, there will be qualified agents, often possessing technological capabilities that are crucial for the subsequent recombinant generation of knowledge at the upstream level. The demand for such qualified customers that reaches upstream agents is not generic but specific and competent. The access to existing knowledge incorporated in such competent demand is essential, as is the access to external knowledge from all the other sources (suppliers, competitors).

Sole access to the available stock of knowledge is a necessary though insufficient ingredient for efficiently coping with the market exigencies that accompany innovative activities (Weitzman, 1996, 1998). The second, complementary ingredient, indeed, reveals the relevance of user–producer transactions and interactions that have to support the acquisition and adoption of knowledge from external sources (Lundvall, 1985; Von Hippel, 1976, 1988, 1994, 1998, 2005). The main reason for the crucial role played by the market-driven interactions is the irreducible tacit content of technological knowledge that cannot be fully codified (Antonelli and Gehringer, 2013a). Consequently, the users of knowledge acquired from external sources need to interact with knowledge producers so that they are efficiently instructed on how to use it properly. Only by means of direct interactions between knowledge users and producers can the non-codified (tacit), but often crucial, pieces of knowledge be actually used. Since knowledge interactions are effected through market transactions, they are costly, requiring dedicated and by no means negligible financial resources.

Tacit knowledge provided by competent customers plays an important role in upstream production activities (Asheim and Gertler, 2005; Boschma, 2005). Their experience, based on exploitation of existing technological solutions, can be passed over to their own suppliers and used to develop new products or new, more efficient, ways of using existing technologies. Competent users therefore possess knowledge that can be acquired by producers by means of dedicated interactions, such as aftersale customer services.

It is important to stress that both codified and tacit knowledge as well as their interactive relationship are vital for the recombinant use of technological knowledge (Nonaka and Takeuchi, 1995). Moreover, both types of knowledge – codified or not – carry the characteristics of non-divisibility, non-excludability and limited appropriability. Due to such properties, the actual cost of acquiring knowledge is lower than the social value of the generated knowledge. As a result, knowledge externalities accompany market transactions and interactions based on external knowledge. This is illustrated in Figure 3.4 where the schedule of the private marginal benefit (PMB) represents, for each level of external knowledge, the average of the individual reservation price. The schedule of social marginal benefit (SMB) is obtained by vertically adding the PMB to the marginal external benefit (MEB). The latter is positive and upward sloping, since for higher levels of stock of external knowledge its pieces that cannot be fully appropriated become more numerous and thus the marginal benefit of the external stock of knowledge increases. For each positive level of external knowledge, there will be positive knowledge externality that will be the higher, the bigger the stock of knowledge available in an economy.[1]

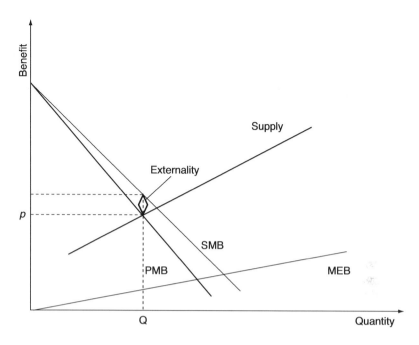

Figure 3.4 Market for external knowledge and equilibrium in the presence of knowledge externalities (source: own elaboration).

The availability of knowledge externalities originated when acquiring external knowledge as a complementary input in the underlying recombinant generation of knowledge has other essential consequences for the activity of each single agent and the economy as a whole. From the perspective of an individual innovative producer, knowledge externalities increase the relative attractiveness of external knowledge with respect to internal sources. The final consequence is that each single producer employs a higher absolute level (and a relative share) of external knowledge, experiences positive productivity dynamics and, finally, generates a higher level of output.

Such a positive sequence of effects regarding individuals can easily be extended to illustrate the general equilibrium consequences of the process. The production output of knowledge-intensive (horizontal) and non-knowledge-intensive (vertical) goods are represented graphically on the axes in Figure 3.5. It is plausible to expect that knowledge-intensive goods, say machines, are used in the production of non-knowledge intensive goods, for instance, textiles. The concave curves are the technological transformation frontiers. In particular, the one lying further away from the origins refers to a situation in which positive knowledge externalities, generated through the market interactions in the acquisition of knowledge from external sources, are at work.[2] These positive externalities exercise a positive influence on technology in the production of a

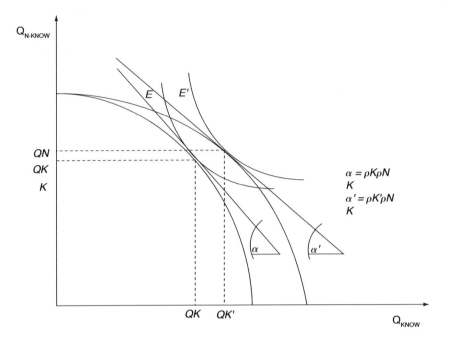

Figure 3.5 General equilibrium consequences of knowledge externalities (source: own elaboration).

knowledge-intensive good, in which higher cost efficiency is achieved (and thus the relative price ρ_K/ρ_{NK} decreases) and the output level increases. However, production of a non-knowledge-intensive good is also expanded. Indeed, its production process is positively influenced by enhanced efficiency in the production of a knowledge-intensive good. Overall, the total output of the economy and the welfare is increased since a higher indifference curve, E', can be achieved.

3.3 The Schumpeterian creative reaction

The analytical framework elaborated by Schumpeter (1947) provides the context in which the role of pecuniary knowledge externalities can be fully appreciated to assess the actual viability of the demand-pull hypothesis. According to Schumpeter (1947), firms, which are viewed as agents characterized by bounded and procedural rather than Olympian rationality, are exposed to continual discrepancies between the necessary plans and the actual conditions of product and factor markets. In order to cope with the ensuing out-of-equilibrium conditions, firms try to react. Their reaction will be adaptive if no or low pecuniary knowledge externalities are available. If no pecuniary knowledge externalities are available, the marginal product of knowledge matches its market price and no scope or opportunity for productivity-enhancing innovations is available. Firms can only move on the existing map of isoquants. When, on the other hand, pecuniary knowledge externalities are available, the reaction of firms may be creative as they have the opportunity to introduce productivity-enhancing innovations. The costs of the generation of new technological knowledge are, in fact, kept below equilibrium prices by pecuniary knowledge externalities (Antonelli, 2008, 2011).

The increase in demand is one of the typical factors of the mismatch between planned and actual market conditions. Figure 3.6 shows that the shift of the demand schedule from D1 to D2 may engender adaptive reactions when no knowledge externalities are available, or creative reactions when knowledge externalities are available.

In the former case, demand pull will only engender an increase in production costs and hence market prices. The supply schedule does not shift so that demand pull will only lead to inflation as the price level increases from p_1 to p_2. In the latter case, on the other hand, the supply schedule shifts from S1 to S2 because the introduction of innovations provokes the consequent reduction of production costs: demand pull can actually deliver the expected positive effects in terms of increased efficiency. If knowledge externalities are paramount, efficiency gains could lead – ceteris paribus – to a price level that is below the initial one.[3]

The availability of knowledge externalities becomes the discriminating factor that affects whether demand pull can yield just adaptive or creative reactions, and hence inflation or productivity growth. In this context, the role of user–producer

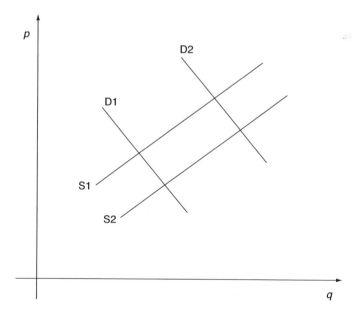

Figure 3.6 Demand pull and adaptive vs. creative reaction (source: own elaboration).

interactions as a crucial determinant of the general level of knowledge externalities can be fully appreciated. Demand pull as an unexpected change in product markets can actually lead to creative response and hence to the introduction of innovations only if pecuniary knowledge externalities are available. User–producer transactions rich of knowledge interactions are a crucial factor able to increase the amount of knowledge externalities available and hence increase the likelihood that demand expressed by competent users is actually able to pull the introduction of innovations.

The Schumpeterian framework of innovation as a creative reaction provides additional foundations for articulating and supporting the competent demand-pull hypothesis.

4 The competent demand-pull hypothesis

Depending on the precise source of external knowledge, the knowledge-based transactions and interactions for each agent will take place with different categories of agents located on the vertical chain of the *filiere productive*.[4] Thus, productivity dynamics can be enhanced thanks both to upstream linkages and through downstream linkages with qualified customers,[5] the latter equipped with specialized knowledge. It is crucial to recognize at this point that technological impulses are incorporated both in top-down relations with suppliers and in bottom-up relations with customers.

Most importantly in our framework, it becomes clear that customers become central carriers of technological knowledge and knowledge externalities that stay at the basis of the upstream innovative activities. The micro-founded framework is thus crucial to explaining the competent demand-pull hypothesis. Demand will actually pull the generation and adoption of new technological solutions only if and when the customers are sufficiently creative and their demand is consequently competent. But even if competent, demand alone is inactive, unless accompanied by insightful user–producer interactions. Thanks to such interactions, the access to external knowledge and to knowledge externalities is assured. Finally, the implementation of external knowledge and its combination with the internal stock readily available is the most important consequence of the interaction with the competent users.

The aforementioned conditions of competent – as opposed to generic – demand and of user–producer interactions are strictly complementary and as such necessary in order to observe positive productivity dynamics upstream. More precisely, if interactions take place in a context where the customers are not embodied with novel insights, the upstream firms cannot make their reaction creative. Consequently, even if demand increases, market adjustment of the firms will imply upward dynamics of prices since firms face a higher marginal cost in their production. Indeed, firms facing an excess in generic demand cannot take advantage of external knowledge and thus will be pushed to adjust their production techniques within the given maps of isoquants. More precisely, in the short run, an increase in the levels of production will be possible thanks to modification of the capital-to-labour ratio and a more intensive employment of labour, corresponding, however, to an increase in the marginal cost of production. However, even in the long run, when firms can adapt their fixed capital, they can achieve some reduction in their marginal costs. Nevertheless, this improvement in efficiency will not be enough to compensate for the initial efficiency losses and the cost levels remain above the initial levels prior to the demand increase. Thus, if demand is not competent, the reactions of the firms will be only adaptive with negative effects on efficiency.

On the contrary, if creative customers do not have the chance to be involved in effective market interactions with innovative upstream suppliers, the productivity potentials embodied in the competent demand will remain unused.

The appreciation of creative customers as actors with a crucial role in the marketplace and, specifically, in the generation of innovation has been till now left for discussion in the management literature (Mollick, 2005; Berthon *et al.*, 2007), although there, too, the tradition of research on the issue is still very young and incomplete. Indeed, the bulk of research efforts so far has concentrated on recognition of the potential role played by creative customers in business strategies and on their definition as 'underground innovators' (Mollick, 2005, p. 21) or as a 'gold mine of ideas and business opportunities' (Berthon *et al.*, 2007, p. 39).

Interestingly, there is a related concept of 'lead users' by von Hippel (1986) that suits our understanding of customers with innovative potentials.[6] According to von Hippel (1986, 2005), the role of lead users consists most importantly in expressing their specific, strong demand that, nevertheless, requires the medium-to-long run to be perceived by the market and be faced with the corresponding marketable and – more importantly – novel items. The precise time needed to satisfy this competent demand crucially depends on the ability of the lead users to clearly communicate their needs, but also on the effectiveness of market-based interactions with the firms responding to such needs.[7]

Conditioned by the presence of creative users and the framework where user–producer interactions effectively take place, knowledge interactions with knowledge externalities will result in positive productivity impulses upstream. It is, however, important to note that the effects of demand pull will differ across sectors and over time. In other words, competent demand pull works selectively, depending not only on the availability of knowledge possessed by creative customers, but also on its intensity and technological characteristics. In this sense, competent demand pull – like technology – remains localized. Moreover, the specific properties of user–producer interactions also matter in determining the effectiveness of demand-pull mechanisms. Such characteristics of knowledge and of knowledge-based interactions are strictly dependent on the internal and external conditions governing each industrial sector (Tödtling *et al.*, 2009). Internal conditions refer to the organization of knowledge generation as well as to the kinds of innovations being introduced (Breschi and Malerba, 2005). External conditions are determined by the knowledge management rules and mechanisms established by the relevant institutional system at the national (Lundvall,

1992; Nelson, 1993) and regional (Cooke *et al.*, 2000, 2004) level.[8] In particular, the working of knowledge management is influenced – among other things – by the design of the intellectual property rights protection, the adoption of technical standards, the organization of the exhibitions and the intentional actions aimed at collaborations between public research institutions and business agents. Again, both internal and external conditions differ from sector to sector and competent demand will therefore have a sector-specific impact.

The empirical evidence regarding the competent demand-pull hypothesis is still very young and limited. This notwithstanding, it clearly confirms the existence of qualified customers and their role played in enhancing upstream productivity dynamics. This evidence is based on our earlier empirical contributions studying the intersectoral system of knowledge-based interactions within the European manufacturing and service sectors in the time span 1995–2007 (Antonelli and Gehringer, 2012, 2013a, 2013b). In particular, in all three analyses, the competent demand-pull variable measures the sheer increase in the levels of intermediate input demanded by downstream customer sectors, weighted by their growth rates of total factor productivity. This multiplicative variable calculated for each single downstream sector is the main explanatory force determining the upstream productivity growth of each single supplying sector. As such, this variable is well distinct from the influences of the generic demand, generated by unqualified consumers. Moreover, by applying advanced econometric techniques permitting to account for endogeneity, we are able to separate the demand from supply forces.

The main results of all three investigations – based on the same European industrial systems, but looking at the intersectoral relations from different perspectives – point to the significant role played by some specific manufacturing sectors, namely: textiles and textile products; wood and products of wood; paper products, rubber and plastic; other non-metallic mineral products; machinery and equipment. This picture is a valuable confirmation of the anecdotic evidence regarding particularly textiles and textile products and machinery and equipment already discussed in Antonelli and Gehringer (2012). Interestingly, such evidence possesses a systemic flavour, as the demand impulses generated by the textile industry have an immediate implication on productivity growth in machinery and equipment. More precisely, rapid advances in the textile industry of the late 1990s led in the first place to innovations being generated within the sector. Subsequently, however, the wave of positive impulses, which were built upon innovative outcomes and upon the creative ideas of the textile producers, reached their suppliers of machinery and equipment who answered with novel technological solutions in textile production.

With respect to the geographic dimension, we find evidence of general, EU-wide effects through which demand positively pulls innovative performance across industries, countries and over time (Antonelli and Gehringer, 2012). At the same time, a more detailed investigation shows that the direction and strength of the impact differs between country groups within the EU. In particular, whereas in the EU, the dominating role in transmission of the demand-pulling effects was played by the manufacturing sectors, with only limited influence coming from services, the latter were actively contributing to demand-driven productivity growth, both in the eastern and southern EU members. In turn, appreciation of the great heterogeneity in the economic performance of single service sectors suggests that the difference between east and south exists as well and is remarkable. Indeed, for southern EU countries, it was financial intermediation, transportation and communication services that significantly and positively influenced upstream productivity growth. In eastern EU countries, on the other hand, hotels and restaurants played the most important role (Antonelli and Gehringer, 2013a).

5 Conclusions

The grafting of recent advances in the economics of knowledge onto the macroeconomic tradition of analysis of the demand-pull hypothesis makes articulation of a competent demand-pull hypothesis possible. We show that the hypothesis originates from the path-breaking intuition of Adam Smith. Adam Smith was well aware that an increase in the extent of the market would lead to enhanced levels of division of labour and specialization only if and when the knowledge generation process was effectively at work. With an analogous macroeconomic flavour, but crucially modifying the driving components of the mechanism, Kaldor (1966, 1967) and Schmookler (1966) laid an important basis for the demand-pull hypothesis.

The founding effort of the standard 'macroeconomic' demand-pull hypothesis is an important starting point for explaining how demand forces can be seen as effective drivers of overall economic performance. At the same time, especially during the last decades of the twentieth century, it became clear that aggregate demand pull can easily lead to inflation and to an actual decline in the general efficiency of an economic system. This is mainly because the generic, aggregate excess demand can easily push firms to produce in suboptimal conditions. Consequently, the conceptual decline of the demand-pull hypothesis followed this gloomy evidence.

A new, better understanding of the knowledge generation process and its complementarities with the innovation process enables us to grasp the crucial role of the context in which the demand pull actually takes place.

A reconstruction of the post-Keynesian approach in a new conceptual framework based on the recent advances in economics of innovation and knowledge enables us to qualify and reconsider the standard demand-pull hypothesis. As an important outcome of such a conceptual exercise, the competent demand-pull hypothesis emerges.

Whereas the standard demand-pull hypothesis by Kaldor (1966, 1967) and Schmookler (1966) was articulated in the post-Keynesian literature to deliver a justification for the active role of the public demand, the competent demand-pull hypothesis points to the role of creative customers by interacting with their innovative suppliers. As such, the competent demand-pull hypothesis does not neglect the role of the aggregate demand pulling the system in quantitative terms. The increase in output is a natural response to short-term excess demand. At the same time, the competent demand-pull approach is crucially motivated by qualitative improvements deriving from the more specific context of customers possessing specific knowledge and being able to effectively transfer such knowledge to the upstream producers. The latter not only receive valuable demand-side signals, but are subject to positive knowledge externalities that are a crucial engine in the subsequent productivity improvements and in higher production levels upstream. Thus, the aggregate output could and most probably will expand as well, in the same way as under the standard demand-pull hypothesis, but this expansion is a consequence of technological lead and not of a mere technical switch.

The policy implications of the competent demand-pull hypothesis are very important. Public support for the aggregate demand and public procurement may have the expected positive effects on productivity growth rather than the frequent experiences of just an increase in price levels. The condition for this positive influence is that public spending should be matched with research policy interventions that help to increase the amount of technological knowledge available within the system. Moreover, since competences, not only of producers but also of users, are essential, public intervention should aim to identify as well as train competent customers that are able to activate the key user–producer mechanisms of knowledge governance, making external knowledge available to producers.

Notes

1 It should be noted that the presence of positive knowledge externalities, although beneficial for whoever experiences it, implies an immediate welfare loss for the society as a whole. Indeed, if intellectual property rights were assigned in a way that entirely internalizes the externality, market equilibrium would be achieved at the intersection between the supply curve and the SMB curve, for a higher level of external knowledge and at a lower unit price. Nevertheless, it can be argued that such a deadweight loss is at least partly compensated for by the positive consequences of knowledge externalities as described below.

2 The precise position of the transformation frontier subject to knowledge externalities depends on the direction of technological advance taking place. We adopt a simple assumption that knowledge externalities have a positive impact on productivity only with the production of a knowledge-intensive good.

3 The precise effect depends additionally on elasticity of both the demand and the supply schedules and on the extent to which demand increases.

4 We focus on the vertical chain of relations. More generally, however, not only vertical but also horizontal knowledge linkages play a role. Consequently, in addition to suppliers and customers, competitors could also become an important source of relevant knowledge. Moreover, other sources of knowledge could come from agents belonging to a broader market environment, such as public and private research centres, universities and public institutions.

5 We refer interchangeably to qualified, creative, competent customers/users and define them as agents who direct specific demand to their suppliers and are able to generate impulses with technological content.

6 Berthon *et al.* (2007) stress the fact that the two concepts, namely creative customers and lead users, cannot be treated as synonyms. We recognize the operational differences between these concepts. Nevertheless, for the purposes of the economic foundation of the competent demand-pull hypothesis, these differences do not play a great role with both creative customers and lead users being able to direct the competent demand upstream.

7 Starting with the seminal contributions by von Hippel (1986), subsequent management literature concentrated on specific aspects linked to the market presence of qualified users, such as detailed characterization of lead users (Urban and von Hippel, 1988), and of innovators/innovations dependent on the involvement of lead users in innovation generation (Herstatt and von Hippel, 1992; Morrison *et al.*, 2000).

8 In the innovation systems approach by Edquist (2005), innovative firms interact with the non-business sector, namely, the science sector and policymakers.

References

Andersen, E.S. (2007). Innovation and demand. In: Hanusch, H. and Pyka, A. (eds), *The Elgar Companion to Neo-Schumpeterian Economics*, Cheltenham: Edward Elgar, 754–765.

Antonelli, C. (2008). *Localized Technological Change: Towards the Economics of Complexity.* London: Routledge.

Antonelli, C. (ed.) (2011). *Handbook on the Economic Complexity of Technological Change*. Cheltenham: Edward Elgar.

Antonelli, C. and Gehringer, A. (2012). Knowledge externalities and demand pull: the European evidence. LEI & BRICK – Laboratory of Economics of Innovation 'Franco Momigliano', Bureau of Research in Innovation, Complexity and Knowledge, Collegio Carlo Alberto, Working Paper, no. 201214.

Antonelli, C. and Gehringer, A. (2013a). Demand pull and technological flows within innovation systems: the intra-European evidence. Department of Economics 'S. Cognetti de Martiis', University of Turin, Working Paper, no. 03/2013.

Antonelli, C. and Gehringer, A. (2013b). The competent demand pull hypothesis: do services play a role? University of Turin and University of Göttingen, mimeo.

Asheim, B. and Gertler, M. (2005). The geography of innovation. In: Fagerberg, J., Mowery, D. and Nelson, R. (eds), *The Oxford Handbook of Innovation*, Oxford: Oxford University Press, 291–317.

Berthon, P.R, Pitt, L.F., McCarthy, I. and Kates, S.M. (2007). When customers get clever: managerial approaches to dealing with creative customers. *Business Horizons*, vol. 50, 39–47.

Boschma, R. (2005). Proximity and innovation: a critical assessment. *Regional Studies*, vol. 39, 61–74.

Breschi, S. and Malerba, F. (eds) (2005). *Clusters, Networks and Innovation*. Oxford: Oxford University Press.

Brouwer, E. and Kleinknecht, A. (1999). Keynes-plus? Effective demand and changes in firm-level R&D: an empirical note. *Cambridge Journal of Economics*, vol. 23, no. 3, 385–91.

Cooke, P., Boekholt, P. and Tödtling, F. (2000). *The Governance of Innovation in Europe: Regional Perspectives on Global Competitiveness*. London: Pinter.

Cooke, P., Heidenreich, M. and Braczyk, H.J. (eds) (2004). *Regional Innovation Systems*, 2nd edition. London: UCL Press.

Crespi, F. and Pianta, M. (2008). Demand and innovation in productivity growth. *International Review of Applied Economics*, vol. 22, no. 6, 655–672.

Di Stefano, G., Gambardella, A. and Verona, G. (2012). Technology push and demand pull perspectives in innovation studies: current findings and future research directions. *Research Policy*, vol. 41, no. 8, 1283–1295.

Dosi, G. (1982). Technological paradigms and technological trajectories. A suggested interpretation of the determinants and directions of technical change. *Research Policy*, vol. 11, no. 3, 147–162.

Edquist, C. (2005). Systems of innovation – perspectives and challenges. In: Fagerberg, J., Mowery, D. and Nelson, R. (eds), *The Oxford Handbook of Innovation*, Oxford: Oxford University Press, 181–208.

Guerzoni, M. (2010). The impact of market size and users' sophistication on innovation: the patterns of demand. *Economics of Innovation and New Technology*, vol. 19, no. 1, 113–126.

Herstatt, C. and von Hippel, E. (1992). From experience: developing new product concepts via the lead user method: a case study in a 'low tech' field. *The Journal of Product Innovation Management*, vol. 9, no. 3, 213–221.

Jaffe, A.B. (1988). Demand and supply influences in R&D intensity and productivity growth. *Review of Economics and Statistics*, vol. 70, no. 3, 431–437.

Kaldor, N. (1966). *Causes of the Slow Rate of Growth in the United Kingdom*. Cambridge: Cambridge University Press.

Kaldor, N. (1967). *Strategic Factors in Economic Development*. Ithaca, NY: New York State School of Industrial and Labor Relations, Cornell University.

Kaldor, N. (1972). *The Irrelevance of Equilibrium Economics*. Cambridge: Cambridge University Press.

Kleinknecht, A. and Verspagen, B. (1990). Demand and innovation: Schmookler re-examined. *Research Policy*, vol. 19, no. 4, 387–394.

Kline, S.J. and Rosenberg, N. (1986). An overview of innovation. In: Landau, R. and Rosenberg, N. (eds), *The Positive Sum Strategy: Harnessing Technology for Economic Growth*, Washington, DC: National Academy Press, 275–305.

Lundvall, B.A. (1985). *Product Innovation and User-Producer Interaction*. Aalborg: Aalborg University Press.

Lundvall, B.A. (ed.) (1992). *National Systems of Innovation: Towards a Theory of Innovation and Interactive Learning*. London: Pinter.

Mollick, E. (2005). Tapping into the underground. *Sloan Management Review*, vol. 46, no. 4, 21–24.

Morrison, P.D., Roberts, J.H. and von Hippel, E. (2000). Determinants of user innovation and innovation sharing in a local market. *Management Science*, vol. 46, no. 12, 1513–1527.

Mowery, D. and Rosenberg, N. (1979). The influence of market demand upon innovation: a critical review of some recent empirical studies. *Research Policy*, vol. 8, 102–153.

Nelson, R.R. (ed.) (1993). *National Innovation Systems: A Comparative Analysis*. Oxford: Oxford University Press.

Nemet, G.F. (2009). Demand-pull, technology-push, and government-led incentives for non-incremental technical change. *Research Policy*, vol. 38, no. 5, 700–709.

Nonaka, I. and Takeuchi, H. (1995). *The Knowledge-Creating Company*. Oxford: Oxford University Press.

Piva, M. and Vivarelli, M. (2007). Is demand-pulled innovation equally important in different groups of firms? *Cambridge Journal of Economics*, vol. 31, no. 5, 691–710.

Scherer, F.M. (1982). Demand-pull and technological invention: Schmookler revisited. *Journal of Industrial Economics*, vol. 30, no. 3, 225–237.

Schmookler, J. (1957). Inventors past and present. *Review of Economics and Statistics*, vol. 39, no. 3, 321–333.

Schmookler, J. (1966). *Invention and Economic Growth*. Cambridge, MA: Harvard University Press.

Schumpeter, J.A. (1947). The creative response in economic history. *Journal of Economic History*, vol. 7, 149–159.

Smith, A. (1776). *An Inquiry into the Nature and Causes of the Wealth of Nations*. London: W. Strahan and T. Cadell.

Thirlwall, A (2003). *Growth and Development with Special Reference to Developing Economies*, 7th Edition. London: Palgrave.

Tödtling, F., Lehner, P. and Kaufmann, A. (2009). Do different types of innovation rely on specific kinds of knowledge interactions? *Technovation*, vol. 29, no. 1, 59–71.

Urban, G.L. and von Hippel, E. (1988). Lead user analyses for the development of new industrial products. *Management Science*, vol. 34, no. 5, 569–582.

Verdoorn, P.J. (1949). Fattori che regolano lo sviluppo della produttività del lavoro, *L'Industria*, vol. 1, pp. 45–53.

Von Hippel, E. (1976). The dominant role of users in the scientific instrument innovation process. *Research Policy*, vol. 5, 212–239.

Von Hippel, E. (1986). Lead users: a source of novel product concepts. *Management Science*, vol. 32, no. 7, 791–805.

Von Hippel, E. (1988). *The Sources of Innovation*. Oxford: Oxford University Press.

Von Hippel, E. (1994). Sticky information and the locus of problem-solving: implications for innovation. *Management Science*, vol. 40, 429–439.

Von Hippel, E. (1998). Economics of product development by users: the impact of sticky local information. *Management Science*, vol. 44, 629–644.

Von Hippel, E. (2005). *Democratizing Innovation*. Cambridge, MA: The MIT Press.

Walsh, V. (1984). Invention and innovation in the chemical industry: demand-pull or discovery-push? *Research Policy*, vol. 13, no. 4, 211–234.

Weitzman, M.L. (1996). Hybridizing growth theory. *American Economic Review*, vol. 86, 207–212.

Weitzman, M.L. (1998). Recombinant growth. *Quarterly Journal of Economics*, vol. 113, 331–360.

Young, A.A. (1928). Increasing returns and economic progress. *Economic Journal*, vol. 38, no. 152, 527–542.

4 Market-based demand-driven innovation

Seven key principles and illustrative case studies

Amnon Frenkel and Shlomo Maital

1 Introduction: the simple logic of demand-driven innovation

To achieve excellence, organizations must excel in three generic 'value disciplines' (see Figure 4.1): operations (delivery of innovations), innovation (product leadership) and empathy (intimacy with customers) (adapted from Treacy and Wiersema, 1997). In other words: excel in innovation, excel in implementing innovative ideas and excel in building innovations on real customer needs. These are necessary conditions for market leadership and are perhaps even jointly sufficient.

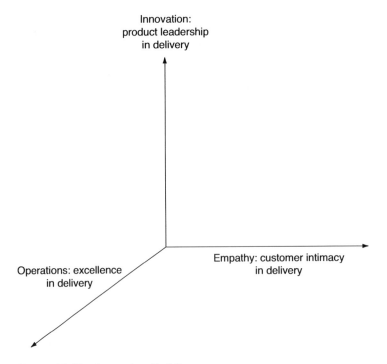

Figure 4.1 The three value disciplines.

Treacy and Wiersema argued back in 1997 that market leadership occurs at the intersection of these three disciplines, thus excellence is needed in only one of the three. However, today, most management educators believe that excellence in all three is vital because the intensity of global competition has greatly increased. And, of course, the three disciplines are closely linked. Customer intimacy should drive innovation. The reason for this is that successful innovation satisfies unmet wants; generally speaking, customers cannot and do not articulate those wants, but simply 'muddle through'. Only high-level customer intimacy can identify true needs that are unmet (see Treacy and Wiersema, 1993). Customer intimacy is also the basis (in part) of operational excellence – operations should always be tailored with the preferences of the end users in mind. All customer touchpoints in operations must be smooth, efficient and at the leading edge of best practice. Innovation is of little value unless the innovative service or good itself is delivered with excellence to the customer.

From this simple framework, we can see that customer intimacy is the core discipline that underlies both innovation (product leadership) and operational excellence. It is the discipline that drives the other two.

This essay comprises a series of stories or narratives about market-based demand-driven innovation. All relate, in one way or another, to customer intimacy. Our objective is to attempt to reveal the key success factors in demand-driven innovation through the stories of those who have implemented it in a variety of ways.

In management education, these stories are called 'case studies', whereas we prefer to adopt the term 'narratives'. Indeed, we believe the essence of a strong case study is a good story. It is in these stories of innovators who implement demand-driven innovation that we may find the complex truth of precisely how to leverage markets and demand to generate commercially successful innovations. We caution the reader: these are not conventional case studies, but rather unconventional narratives about real people that try to capture the human elements of demand-driven innovation rather than dry management facts. In many cases, our case studies are based on first-hand experiences, conversations and interviews. Many of the subjects of our narratives are unconventional (such as the pop-rock star Lady Gaga). But none, we hope, are boring, and all, we trust, are vivid and memorable. All our narratives reflect the fact that demand-driven innovation is an art, not a science.

We present seven key principles of demand-driven innovation and several stories that illustrate each principle, comprising 18 case-study narratives in all, covering many more specific innovations and businesses (see Table 4.1). In the next section, we discuss those principles and in the following section, we provide narratives that illustrate each. Our goal is to provide narratives that illustrate the essence of demand-driven innovation in the hope that 'practitioners' (entrepreneurs and those who seek to foster and encourage them) will embrace and implement innovation that is at least in part pulled by markets, demand and customers rather than pushed solely by governments and technology.

Table 4.1 List of case studies

1	A thousand true fans
2	Innovation management at Nokia
3	Intuit – quicken your sales, 'follow me home'
4	Crowd-sourced businesses
5	Get on the Lady Gaga bus
6	'Connect and develop' (Procter & Gamble)
7	Lego Mindstorms
8	SodaStream's bubbly business
9	Sara Blakely, Spanx
10	A man. A van. A plan
11	How strong minds raced so weak legs could walk
12	How ebooks were invented
13	Find yourself a 'squeeze box' – and think in it
14	Quingjie Shui – Tishlovet Water
15	Innovation where it counts
16	IKEA: can you feel small when you are really big?
17	Mellanox – warp speed for networks
18	From eggheads, golden eggs

Source: own elaboration.

2 Seven key principles of market-based demand-driven innovation

2.1 Bottom-up market-based innovation is superior to top-down innovation

One of the principles taught to generations of managers and management students is this: the larger the potential market for an innovation, the more attractive it is for investors and corporate backers. This has led to a familiar refrain in many business plans for innovative products and services, claiming that if only 1 per cent of a potential market is achieved, the result will still yield commercial success; 1 per cent of a $1 billion market is still $10 million.

This 'top-down' approach is now widely understood to be insufficient. If 99 per cent of customers prefer other products, why should 1 per cent prefer our innovation? A far more persuasive approach is known as 'bottom-up' innovation – identify and describe real, specific customers, one by one, who have expressed interest in the innovation and indicated willingness, in principle, to purchase it when available. Often, to launch an innovation, only one customer is needed. That customer provides invaluable feedback that generates other customers. And in the age of web-based businesses, no more than 1,000 'true fans' (see Figure 4.2 in the first case study) are often needed to sustain a business.

Even when the 'top-down' approach is used to estimate potential market size for an innovation, it is still vital to include a 'bottom-up' estimate, describing real potential customers and their initial responses to the innovation.

2.2 Open (crowd-sourced and lead-user) innovation surpasses closed innovation

Open innovation, in contrast to closed innovation, assumes that firms can and should use ideas acquired outside the firm as well as internally generated ones and employ both external and internal paths to market-based innovation. Accordingly, open innovation business models utilize wide 'sweeps' for innovative ideas that embrace customers, competitors and the firm's own R&D resources to create value. The open innovation paradigm also assumes that internally generated ideas can be taken to market through external channels outside the current core businesses of the firm in order to generate additional value (Chesbrough, 2006) – for example, IBM's establishment of an independent PC division in Boca Raton, Florida, far beyond its home base in New York State, to develop an innovation far outside IBM's core business, in the late 1970s.

Scientific research and development and in particular applied research is the foundation for innovation. Yet more and more evidence shows that a significant part of innovation arises not from institutionalized R&D funded by companies, but rather from tinkerers and users who identify a real, often very personal, need and solve it inventively with their own two hands.

Under this principle, organizations' innovation process includes, as a key element, the ideas, creativity and suggestions of those who use, like and buy the product or service. This includes: 'lead users', or key customers, as well as the general market of consumers (von Hippel, 1986).

The question then arises: how to innovate without invention? Lessons from Darwin may provide an appropriate answer. The first chapter of Darwin's *On the Origin of Species* (1859) sets the stage for showing how Nature 'evolves' its species through natural selection, by showing how human beings improve upon Nature by 'domesticating' species. This is done, for both plants and animals, as follows:

- Nature produces small (random) variations.
- Humans notice them and choose the ones they find useful and helpful for their own purposes.
- Humans select those variations for reproduction (through seeds, or cuttings, or by mating animals), rejecting the rest.

Many such random variations, Darwin notes, are almost imperceptible. But the keen eye of the gardener, farmer or breeder spots them and patiently strengthens and magnifies them over the years. It is not Nature, then, that selects, but human beings, in this case. Darwin's 'natural selection' suggests a demand-driven method for innovation which does not require the innovator himself to come up with the invention:

- Observe variations in how people use products and services, often in ways the producer did not intend.

- Replicate and standardize those variations by 'selecting' them and adapting them. It is 'natural selection', only you, not Nature, are the selector.

Car companies locate design shops in California and designers scout neighbourhoods to see how individuals 'customize' their cars, in paint, trim and in other ways. Fashion designers watch trendy neighbourhoods. Intuit (makers of Quicken accounting software) followed users home to observe how they use their product (they discovered it was used not to balance cheque books but to run businesses – a crucial discovery).

This is another reason why innovators should quickly get their products to market. Only when they are being used can users help you innovate, just as Darwin proposed. Watch for user-driven innovations. Adapt them. Then, observe again. You may end up with a winning product, utterly different from the one you began with. All through 'natural selection'.

User-driven and crowd-sourced innovation is thus market-driven innovation, which scans the world to find solutions already in use and in place in the market, to meet R&D challenges that otherwise might take years and millions of dollars to resolve. And it addresses one of the key stumbling blocks of innovation – the NIH (Not Invented Here) syndrome that has R&D departments defending only innovations that emerge from their own 'shop'. At the extreme, when companies receive innovative ideas from outside sources and forward them for evaluation to their R&D experts, the NIH syndrome has been known to kill a great many potentially revolutionary innovations. The logic underlying NIH is simple. Why should a company insist that all innovations come from its own R&D department if outsiders can come up with innovations that are sometimes superior? Lefley implemented a major change in Procter & Gamble's culture in order to replace NIH with PFE (Proudly Found Elsewhere). (See below, 'connect and develop'.)

Modern ICT technologies have enabled a phenomenon known as 'crowd sourcing' – using the knowledge, creativity and at times funding of a vast number of individuals, linked and networked by the internet. Organizations are now leveraging this key capability to radically alter innovation processes and transform them from closed (held within the boundaries of the organization) to open (to all who can provide creative feasible solutions).

2.3 Even supremely demand-driven innovation may require market education

The essence of innovation is identifying and meeting an unmet need or want. This places the understanding of markets and market demand at the core of innovation. But very often, consumers are so accustomed to overcoming challenges, difficulties or needs with what is available that they do not perceive the enormous advantages that pathbreaking innovations convey. In this situation, the innovator must not only meet an unsatisfied need, he or she must educate consumers and explain, communicate and teach how and why the innovation is superior to what is currently available, overcoming the inertia of habit that leads consumers to buy what they are accustomed to rather than what is new and unique. More than one innovation has the potential to create immense value, yet fails when introduced to the market, whereas the innovators were unable to help consumers perceive the added value created by the innovation. For this reason, market-based innovation often must include not only a differentiated product that satisfies unmet needs; it must also contain clever strategies to communicate the value-creating differentiators in order to alter customer perceptions.

2.4 The individual entrepreneurs themselves are often the most powerful market-demand researchers

Innovators often face a bitter dilemma. They require extensive market research to validate the commercial viability of their innovation, but lack the resources to acquire such research. The vicious circle is: market success generates resources that can fund market research, yet that market research itself is often a precondition for market success. One solution is to create 'minimum viable product' prototypes and introduce them to the market to get customer feedback even though the product is far from perfected. For this reason, 'time to market' is a crucial element of successful innovation.

Another solution is that of 'markets of one'. The innovator himself or herself becomes the market research. The reasoning is that the innovator is like many other persons with similar age, income, background, culture and needs. If the innovator believes he or she wants and needs the innovation, objectively, chances are good that many others will feel the same way. Thus, introspection and self-empathy are key tools for market-driven innovation. A great many successful innovations have been created when a single creative innovator brought into the world a product or service simply because he or she himself wanted and needed it – and many, many others, it emerged, had the same want and need.

2.5 'Reverse' (emerging-market-based) innovation can supply winning products for rich-country markets

In today's global economy, multinational corporations frequently produce their innovative products in Asia or in emerging Europe. But in general, they create and design those products in the West. Apple, for instance, has designers of its iPad in Silicon Valley, but factories in China. The result is that often products are designed for rich persons, in rich countries, and are then manufactured by the poor.

Suppose, however, that this logic were reversed. Suppose innovative products were created by those in poor countries, for the poor, and then adapted for rich persons. This is known as reverse innovation.

Why would one choose this approach? In increasingly price-sensitive markets in the West, value for money is becoming increasingly important. Cost-effective low-price innovative products developed for those with low incomes, in poor countries, can achieve major success in Western countries, at a time when marketing efforts increasingly stress value for money and cost saving.

A new book by Govindarajan and Trimble (2013), *Reverse Innovation: Create Far From Home, Win Everywhere*, makes this point. Despite the MBA/ Harvard-type title, the authors are right.

> Innovation in the rich world is based on the approach 'Spend money and innovate'. In the US, you can see this clearly in health care. We push the frontiers of medical science and technology with very little attention paid to cost. Our health-care system is prohibitively expensive, yet does not guarantee the highest quality; nor does it provide universal coverage. There is an alternative model of innovation: 'Spend less and innovate'. This is the only feasible model in poor countries that are resource-constrained. As some companies have discovered, constraints can be liberating. This notion is at the heart of reverse innovation.[1]

Remember former Curitiba (Brazil) Mayor Jaime Lerner's dictum? If you want to truly innovate, slash two zeros off your budget!

In his excellent YouTube talk, Prof. Govindarajan amplifies on his 'reverse innovation' idea:[2]

> What is reverse innovation? Why is it so important? What is it that multinationals must do to master reverse innovation? Think about the innovation paradigms inside GE, P&G, Pepsi, IBM, Cisco, Nestlé and others. Historically, MNCs design products in rich countries and sell them in poor ones. Reverse innovation involves the opposite, innovating in poor countries and bringing the products to rich ones. Clearly poor people want what rich people have. But why would a rich man want a poor man's product? That is the essence of reverse innovation.
>
> Nestlé: it is remaking itself as a health and wellness company. The place they are looking to innovate is emerging markets, because of the size of the consumer base. They innovated low fat healthy noodles in India under the brand name Maggy (noodles). It created a huge market in India, but is now sold successfully in rich countries.
>
> Tata Nano: $2,000 car. The cost of a DVD player in a BMW is much more! They target the two-wheeler population in India. Two-wheelers cost $1,500. A $2,000 car will win the two-wheeler population. You are converting non-consumers into consumers. This is fundamental innovation. Tata Motors plans to bring the Nano into Europe and the US.
>
> GE: five years ago GE pioneered an ultra-low cost portable ultrasound machine in China. It costs $15,000. Contrast that with the premium ultrasound machines sold for $350,000. Why do you need a portable machine in China? 90 per cent of China is rural. You have no hospitals. The hospital has to come to the patient. So the machine must be portable. The low-cost

portable machine, innovated for China, is now creating markets for GE all over the world, including the US. It is a $300 million global business for GE. In the US, you can put the portable ultrasound machine in an ambulance when there is an accident.

Why has reverse innovation become so important? It is because of the 2008–9 Great Recession, which has fundamentally reset the world. Growth has shifted from developed to developing countries, from rich to poor. Fifteen years ago, GE used to prepare its global strategy so there was a strategy for the US, Europe, Japan and the rest of the world. Today, GE has a BRIC strategy for the Mid-East and the rest of the world. This is a fundamental change. MNEs have taken the seven billion people on earth and divided them into two billion rich people and five billion poor. The latter were left to government and charity. This is outmoded. We need to bring the five billion poor into the consumer base. They cannot consume the same products consumed by the ywo billion rich base. There is no product created for middle America ($50k pcap) that can be adapted to capture middle India ($800 pcap).

What should the MNEs do to master reverse innovation? (1) Have a big dream for emerging markets. Unless you think big, you won't become big. (2) Make 'amplifying weak signals' a core competence. The future is unknowable. There are many 'weak signals' in emerging markets, MNEs are unused to hearing them. They must become expert at it. You cannot wait for the weak signal to become clear before you act because, by the time the signal is clear, the game is over. The golden rule is, spend a little, learn a lot and keep the cost of failure cheap. Then you can fail more often. Failure is converting assumptions into knowledge. Fail early, fail fast, fail cheap. (3) Fundamentally change the centre of gravity of your organization. You have to massively redeploy resources from rich lands to poor ones. Delegate power. Localize power and resources in emerging markets. This is hard for MNEs.

2.6 Demand-driven process innovation often surpasses product innovation

Traditionally it is customary to distinguish product innovation from process innovation. According to the Oslo Manual (OECD/Eurostat, 2005, pp. 149, 151), *product innovation* is 'the introduction of a good or service that is new or significantly improved with respect to its characteristics or intended uses. This includes significant improvements in technical specifications, components and materials, incorporated software, user friendliness or other functional characteristics.' A *process innovation* is 'the implementation of a new or significantly improved production or delivery method. This includes significant changes in techniques, equipment and/or software.'

This distinction led us to accept the premise that process innovation contributes more and yields a higher rate of return than product innovation, thus to a fundamental fallacy in many innovators' efforts. It assumes that innovation is solely about new products or services. In fact, research shows that process innovation generally yields a higher rate of return than product innovation and, indeed, excellence in process innovation may be a necessary condition for successful product innovation (Segerstrom, 2000).[3] For this reason, innovating in processes – for instance, in the processes with which products are manufactured, distributed, packaged, serviced, maintained, advertised and financed – can yield high returns even when the products themselves remain conventional. In addition, innovation in business designs – the way businesses are run – can create massive competitive advantage. Organizational innovation is generally regarded as separate and distinct from process innovation. But in fact, if we perceive business design as the complete system of business processes with which a business is operated, then it becomes a subcategory of process innovation. The leading proponent of this view is Hamel (2006).

The basis of process innovation, in general, is the intimate knowledge of customer needs, so that innovation in processes can create value and satisfy unmet needs stemming not solely from the product but also from the way the product is made and delivered. Often, the manner in which orders are fulfilled and products and services are delivered (both are processes) can be critical in determining the success or failure of a product innovation.

Milkshake marketing: how a 'jobs-to-be-done' perspective spurs innovation[4]

In *Innovation Management*, D.V.R. Seshadri and Shlomo Maital suggest that innovators should listen to four 'voices' – those of the product, the organization, the customer/client and your internal intuitive voice. All these voices 'speak' – except the product. How can products make their voice heard?

Now comes Harvard Business School Professor Clay Christensen's 'milkshake marketing' perspective to reinforce this point. Readers will know Christensen from his famous 'disruptive technology' work. Here is our 'take' on Christensen's approach, which says products are simply things that do a job. Find what that job is and you can innovate successfully. He suggests writing as if we were a milkshake.

> Hi! I'm a milkshake. My mom is a fast-food chain. She wants to sell more of me. So she did everything the MBA marketing texts say to do. And nothing worked. Then, she did the obvious – she asked me, the milkshake itself. *So I asked my buyers.* Turns out I'm bought mainly in the morning by commuters, who want something they can hold in one hand and relieve the boredom of the long commute to work. So we made the 'morning milkshake' thicker, so it lasts the whole trip, and more interesting, with chunks of fruit. Also kids like milkshakes. But it takes them forever to finish them, because they are so thick, so parents balk. So I told mom to make thinner milkshakes for kids. It worked! Sales doubled!

Christensen says:

> Looking at the market from the function of a product really originates from your competitors or your own employees deciding what you need, whereas the jobs-to-be-done point of view causes you to *crawl into the skin of your customer* and go with her as she goes about her day, always asking the question as she does something, 'why did she do it that way?'.

2.7 Startups require a strategic partner with a strong market presence

In general, large organizations struggle to sustain innovativeness and creativity, as they leverage the advantages of scale but suffer the stultifying tangle of bureaucracy and operational discipline. This is in part why many large companies seek to acquire innovative ideas through acquisition of small startups. At the same time, startups often acquiesce to acquisition offers (exits), partly because small (startup) enterprises face bottlenecks when seeking financial resources for sustaining their innovative processes and scaling up globally.

3 Seven principles in search of implementation: case studies

3.1 Bottom-up market-based innovation is superior to top-down

Case study 1: a thousand true fans[5]

There are two places where innovators look for ideas. One is the 'long tail' – esoteric niche markets, on the long largely unoccupied tail of the normal curve. The density of users and buyers here is too low to support activity, generally. The second is the fat middle, where ordinary people reside. Here, competition is fierce, advantages lie with incumbents and habit dominates (ever tried to get people who love vanilla ice cream to try chocolate?).

The alternative is to find 1,000 'true fans' (defined as people who will buy anything and everything you produce). Here is the calculation: if each of the 1,000 true fans spends one day's wages of $100 per year supporting what you do, that comes to: $1,000 \times \$100 = \$100,000$. Presto – you have a business!

If you are patient, if you add one true fan a day, it will only take you three years to build a real business. But, you have to maintain contact with your true fans. Web 2.0 and 3.0 (the advanced versions of the world wide web used as the basis of new web-based products) enable that. And the circle of true fans is surrounded by lesser fans, who will sometimes buy what you sell.

You don't need a hit to survive according to the '1,000 true fan' approach. There is a place in the middle, not the fat middle, and not the long tail. An 'artist' can aim for this spot, but only on one condition. Be sure you are passionate about the offering you are making to your true fans. If you are not, then you are

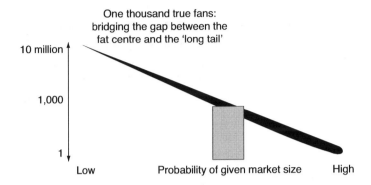

Figure 4.2 Markets of 1,000 (source: own elaboration).

doing it only for money and that means *you* yourself are not a true fan, so you can't expect 1,000 others to be one.

For example, using the logic of a street performer, the author of a book goes directly to the readers before the book is published; perhaps even before the book is written. The author bypasses the publisher and makes a public statement on the order of: 'When I get $100,000 in donations, I will release the next novel in this series.' Readers can go to the author's website, see how much money has already been donated and donate money to the cause of getting his novel out. Note that the author doesn't care who pays to get the next chapter out; nor does he care how many people who didn't pay read the book. He just cares that his $100,000 pot gets filled. When it does, he publishes the next book. In this case, 'publish' simply means 'make available', not 'bind and distribute through bookstores'. The book is made available, free of charge, to everyone: those who paid for it and those who did not. In 2004, the author Lawrence Watt-Evans used this model to publish his newest novel. He asked his true fans to collectively pay $100 per month. When he got $100, he posted the next chapter of the novel. The entire book was published online for his true fans and then later on paper for all his fans. He is now writing a second novel this way. He gets by on an estimated 200 true fans because he also publishes in the traditional manner – with advances from a publisher supported by thousands of lesser fans.

Case study 2: innovation management at Nokia – if you don't execute, you will be executed

In 2007, the second author of the current paper visited the Nokia headquarters on a benchmarking visit with a group of Israeli managers. We heard from top Nokia leaders, including Jorma Olilla, and were deeply and profoundly impressed by what they told us. We were shown what appeared to be the leading-edge top system for linking massive market research with new product development.

A Nokia VP, Jonas Gøst, told us about his 'four-screen' analysis – the first screen was movies (individual enjoyment); the second screen, TV (individual enjoyment); the third screen, computer (individual enjoyment), but the fourth screen was MMD (multi-media device) and the experience was communal/networked. MMD of course is a 'smart phone'. Nokia truly 'got it' early. They did their homework thoroughly. They surveyed 300,000 cell phone users, understood their needs, segmented the market into 12 segments and designed and marketed a phone specially tailored for each (see Figure 4.3). Nokia mapped its customers in two dimensions: Involvement (degree to which they are connected with, and involved with, other people); and Aspiration (degree to which they aspire to be 'cool', i.e. to use cutting-edge technology). It identified specific, coherent market segments according to their location on the 2x2 map. Then Nokia 'E' and 'N' cell phones were designed to meet the specific needs of each market segment.

By all odds, Nokia should today *rule* the smart phone market worldwide. The actual result: as of Q3 2010, Nokia's global cell phone market share fell in just 12 months, from 36.7 per cent down to 28.2 per cent, a huge drop of 8.5 per cent in just a year (Ben-Aaron, 2010). Nokia's mobile operating system, Symbian, once ruled the world and is now plummeting, overtaken by Android. Nokia has lost the American smart phone market to Apple and has nearly disappeared from that key market. It has now sold its cell phone operations to Microsoft for what seems to be a rather low price.

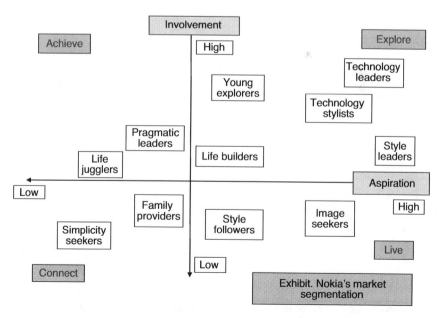

Figure 4.3 Nokia's 2×2 market map (source: own elaboration, based on a presentation by senior Nokia marketing managers).

The mobile operating system Symbian was complex, hard to use and failed to enlist masses of developers. Nokia's decision to make it 'open source' Symbian, spun off into a non-profit foundation, was a huge error. The Nokia smart phones were well designed, well conceived, but failed to excite – they had no 'wow'! Nokia focused on the 'what' of product development, not on the 'for whom?' (for those who love cool stuff, for example). Nokia dropped Symbian, in favour of Microsoft software, but perhaps too late.

An innovator can have the greatest strategic innovation plan in the world. If it is not executed flawlessly, your products will be executed – and so will you. Olli-Pekka Kallasvua, the Nokia CEO, has been fired and replaced by former Microsoft executive Stephen Elop. Elop's first decision has been to radically revamp Symbian, re-integrate it into Nokia and improve it radically. By rights, Nokia should have dominated the smart phone market, at least at its origins. Instead, it has been almost erased, by Apple, from it. And this, despite having perhaps the best market research-linked-to-R&D system in the business.

3.2 Open (crowd-sourced and lead-user) innovation surpasses closed innovation

Lead users

Eric von Hippel is an MIT scholar who pioneered research showing 'lead users' can be enormously valuable to companies who want to improve their products. This is because lead users are users of a product or service that currently experience needs still unknown to the public and who also benefit greatly if they obtain a solution to these needs (von Hippel, 1986).

With a British study funded by the British government, he conducted the first large-scale survey of consumer innovation.[6]

The result was astonishing: the amount of money individual consumers spent on making and improving products was more than twice the amount spent on product research and development by all British companies combined, over a three-year period. It makes sense – there are probably 20 million British consumers and perhaps 1/100 that number of R&D engineers. Von Hippel will replicate his study in Finland and in Portugal (see von Hippel and von Krogh, 2003).

Harvard Business School professor Carliss Baldwin says, 'we've had on a set of mental blinders', because we have missed, or underplayed, this key source of inventive progress.

'We've been missing the dark matter of innovation', von Hippel said, meaning, just as dark (i.e. not visible or detectable) matter exists because otherwise the universe would not be expanding, even though we can't really see it, so does consumer-driven innovation exist, though we don't really see it (until now). Von Hippel says: '77 per cent of scientific instrument innovation comes from users in the field. One of the implications? Change patent law, to enable people to build on others' ideas without fear of law suits.'[7]

Does von Hippel practise what he preaches? He does indeed. His book *Democratizing Innovation* is available for free by download from his personal website, even though the standard print version is published by MIT Press. I wonder how he managed to persuade MIT Press that free downloads actually boost print book sales.

This type of small-scale, one-off innovation is crucial. Think of all the times you have taken a product and in small ways changed it to improve it. Now, imagine if you had shared these ideas with the world, using the internet, the way Daniel Reetz did.

Reetz built a commercial book scanner, which normally costs $10,000, out of two old Canon A590 Powershot cameras, using parts rescued from junk piles. Total cost: $300. He can scan a 400-page book with it in 20 minutes! Reetz uploaded his do-it-yourself product to DIYbookscanner.org and 1,000 people joined his forum on that site, with 50 people actually building the scanner.

There is a strong positive correlation between the degree to which innovations are 'attractive' and the extent to which the users who initiate them are identifiable as 'lead users' (customers who receive great perceived value from the product) (see Figure 4.4).

Case study 3: Intuit – quicken your sales, 'follow me home'

This case study explains the three-step approach of Intuit[8] and its founder Scott Cook for market-driven innovation: (a) observe, (b) capture data, (c) reflect and analyse.

OBSERVE

Intuit is the leading producer of book-keeping software. In 1984, in Palo Alto, California, near Intuit's hometown of Menlo Park, Intuit founder and president Scott Cook observes several well-dressed women, members of Palo Alto Junior League, sitting at keyboards trying to use computers to write cheques. Cook watches, empathizes and learns.

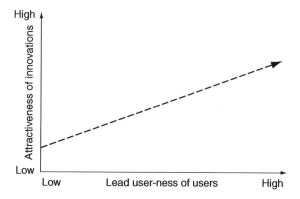

Figure 4.4 Lead users as a source of quality (source: adapted from von Hippel, 1994).

CAPTURE DATA

Intuit developed a version of empathic design known as 'Follow Me Home', in which Intuit managers closely observe customers as they buy Quicken, open the cellophane wrap, load it on their computers and begin to use it. They never intervene, even when tempted, but observe, take notes and sometimes videotape.

REFLECT AND ANALYSE

A year earlier, in 1983 Cook had an epiphany. Realizing that more and more consumers and small businesses were buying PCs, he saw that software that would write cheques and keep financial statements should be a hit product because software could automate dull, humdrum book-keeping tasks. The problem was that there were already dozens of such products on the market. Cook had to find a way to compete. He asked a group of women from the Palo Alto Junior League to sit in front of computers and operate Quicken. Some had never touched a computer in their life. 'People couldn't be bothered learning a complex program', he found. There was a big market but the product had to be cheap, fast, hassle-free and easy to use. Cook benchmarked Quicken not against other software but against the leading competitor, the pencil. The first conclusion: Quicken had to be very cheap, priced at between $20 and $50, because pencils sell for a dollar a dozen. By matching the pencil's ease-of-use (making Quicken exceedingly simple to load and run) and adding other features that pencils lack (speed, accuracy), Quicken's product profile dominated that of the pencil. It lacked a large number of optional features that competing software had – but people did not find those options important. As a result of another empathetic insight, Intuit observed that buyers of Quicken were not using it to manage their cheque books – they were managing their small businesses with it! This insight was vital in Intuit's continued success. Quicken was quickly adapted to the way customers were using it. Success might not have been attained had it not been for the 'Follow Me Home' approach.

Case study 4: crowd-sourced businesses: innovating how, *not what!*

How do you create great innovative new products? With a dynamic (and hugely expensive and inevitably expansive) R&D department?

Not according to made.com, an online-only furniture retailer. It has no inventory and no warehouse. Products are crowd-sourced. Visitors to its website submit designs. The best become prototypes and are posted. Registered made. com members then vote. The most popular furniture pieces are then made in China, shipped in containers and delivered to buyers directly from the port.

Threadless.com founders Jake Nikell and Jacob DeHart launched a 'thread' asking people to post t-shirt designs. The designer gets cash and some free t-shirts, the best of which can be made. Ten years later, threadless.com has nearly $30 million (2009) in revenue, 1,200 designs a week are submitted and winners get $2,000 plus $500 in vouchers.

Fluevog, a Canadian shoe company, launched OpenSource footwear in 2002. Customers (known as Fluevogers) upload designs. Winners have shoes named after them.

Is this cheap exploitation? Is it destroying the jobs of R&D engineers and designers? Or is it a new wave of management innovation, one that focuses on the 'how' things are done rather than on the 'what' is done?

Case study 5: get on the Lady Gaga bus – what can we learn from Stefani Germanotta?

If you believe the phenomenon known as Lady Gaga is not serious – think again! We can all learn a great deal from her.[9] Most albums are recorded in soundproof high-tech studios where electronic wizardry shapes songs to perfection. This is how it is done. This is the rule. Rent time in a studio and make your album.

But not Lady Gaga. In May 2011, she released the album 'Born This Way'; it reached No. 1. She made it while on tour in her Studio Bus. This is an extra bus filled with equipment and comprising a recording studio on wheels. Her engineer and two producers travelled with her on tour for a whole year. 'Basically, after the shows [back-breaking energy-draining two-hour shows], I would go on the Studio Bus and I would work all night. Then we would pull the buses over and I would get back on my bus and go to sleep.'

Of course, all the experts argued with her. 'We can't do your vocals now!' because of the sound of the bus and the reverberations. Said Lady Gaga:

> Turn on the mike and let's do this! I get so inspired and ready to go and I'm not the kind of person that can hold in my creativity.... Because of the thrill of the show and the crowd's energy ... I get so many ideas looking out into the crowd, like: I know what you want to hear. I know what you need.

Lady Gaga is a powerful innovator. Have you noticed that music videos are choreographed to move on the second and fourth beats of 4/4 time? Like – da DAH, da DAH ... Not Lady Gaga. She moves on the first and third beats, DAH da, DAH da. Partly for that reason, radio stations refused for six months to play her first single, *Just Dance*. But she won.

Make no mistake. Stefani Germanotta is a 24/7 performer. She says her very life is 'performance art'. But at the bottom she is an innovative musician. She never lip-syncs. And she writes her songs to meet what she understands her fans want and need – and she knows what they want, because she interacts with them almost every single night.

For innovators, a major lesson from Lady Gaga is to create the equivalent of her Studio Bus. Get your R&D people out of their sterile labs and into the real world. Get them to interact with the people who might or will use the stuff they create. Get them on the Lady Gaga bus. And, for a start, play one of her albums for your innovators. Despite what you think when you look at her fantastic costumes, beneath them there is the heart of a truly passionate musician.

Case study 6: 'connect and develop'[10]

Procter & Gamble (P&G) runs one of the most productive, widely imitated research and development operations in corporate history. But as the company grew to a $70 billion enterprise, the global innovation model it devised in the 1980s faced a major challenge. In order to grow revenues by a modest 5 per cent yearly, P&G had to create yearly a new business worth $3.5 billion! Then-CEO A.G. Lafley decided to search for external sources for innovation. Why? Suppose P&G has 7,000 talented R&D scientists. For each of them, there are perhaps 1,000 equally capable scientists outside P&G. Why not leverage 7,000,000 brains rather than just 7,000, asked Lafley? P&G's new strategy, connect and develop, used technology and networks to seek out new ideas for future products. 'Connect and develop will become the dominant innovation model in the twenty-first century', according to Larry Huston and Nabil Sakkab, both P&G executives. 'For most companies, the alternative invent-it-ourselves model is a sure path to diminishing returns.' P&G rapidly changed its innovation culture, from NIH ('Not Invented Here', rejecting any idea outside P&G's own R&D lab, a common syndrome in many organizations) to PFE ('Proudly Found Elsewhere', seeking ideas wherever they can be found, outside P&G).

Did this new approach work? Huston and Sakkab summarize:

> Today, more than 35 per cent of our new products in market have elements that originated from outside P&G, up from about 15 per cent in 2000. And 45 per cent of the initiatives in our product development portfolio have key elements that were discovered externally. Through connect and develop – along with improvements in other aspects of innovation related to product cost, design and marketing – our R&D productivity has increased by nearly 60 per cent. Our innovation success rate has more than doubled, while the cost of innovation has fallen. R&D investment as a percentage of sales is down from 4.8 per cent in 2000 to 3.4 per cent today. And, in the last two years, we've launched more than 100 new products for which some aspect of execution came from outside the company. Five years after the company's stock collapse in 2000, we have doubled our share price and have a portfolio of twenty-two billion-dollar brands.

Case study 7: Lego Mindstorms – when users innovate

Lego is a great serial innovator and is the world's fourth largest toymaker by sales. After the initial Lego brick invention, Lego innovated Lego Technic (advanced Lego bricks), Minifigures, Lego Technic computer control (with MIT Media Lab), Legoland theme parks, Lego Mindstorms (the intelligent Lego brick, integrated with robot technology), Lego retail stores, Clikits (a new design for girls) and Bionicle (combines construction toys and action themes).

Despite these successful innovations, for Lego it is an uphill battle. Increasingly children prefer computer video games. Lego is squeezed at the high end of the market by these games and by low-price, Asia-made imitations at the low end. As a result, Lego lost money in three of the past five years despite its innovations, cost-cutting and restructuring. Yet, had it not been for innovations like Mindstorms, Lego would have disappeared long ago. In competitive industries like Lego's, sometimes survival is an even bigger achievement than achieving growth and profit in less competitive industries.

'In Billund, Denmark, (Lego's manufacturing centre), not only is the customer right, he's also a candidate for the R&D team', notes a journalist, writing in *Wired* magazine. How is this done?

Lego's innovative Mindstorms product, which combines Lego bricks with programmable robots, debuted in 1998 and, with no advertising, became Lego's all-time bestseller. It sold 80,000 units in its first three months and 1 million units in all. But six years later, it needed an update. Lego lost $238 million in fiscal 2003.

In September 2004, Lego executives felt the Mindstorms innovation team needed a fresh perspective. Lego decided 'to outsource its innovation to a panel of citizen developers' known as a Mindstorms User Panel (MUP). Such panels often serve as 'beta' sites (testers of prototypes and working models). But Lego's MUP was different. It would actually design and invent. Four members were chosen from a shortlist of 20. They received no pay and even paid their own airfare! They met with Soren Lund, head of Mindstorms, in Washington DC, to hammer out the final details of the upgrade, known as NXT. Why are you doing this?, Lund asked them. Because, they said, they were playing a vital role in shaping a product they loved. According to *Wired* magazine, 'opening the (innovation) process engenders goodwill and creates a buzz among the zealots, a critical asset for products (like Mindstorms) that rely on word-of-mouth evangelism'. If NXT is a hit, the 'democratized' innovation process may be extended to the full range of Lego products.

3.3 Even supremely demand-driven innovation may require market education

Case study 8: SodaStream's bubbly business – making money from air[11]

Daniel Birnbaum had a great job, heading Nike Israel, from 2003–2006. In early 2007, he was offered the job of CEO of a failing Israeli company, Soda Club, selling an old-fashioned product (devices to carbonate water using CO_2 cartridges). He took the job – and the rest is history. Today, SodaStream, the reincarnation of Soda Club, is a $300 million annual business, with $35 million net income, operating in some 50 countries, selling cool, colourful carbonating devices with a powerful 'razorblade' model (most revenues come from selling the flavours so the one-time sale of the machine is no longer a key part of the money model). One family in every five in Sweden has a SodaStream device.

How did he do it? A key innovation was not in the product, but in how it is advertised. Birnbaum does not hire expensive ad agencies who spend millions on ads, half of which are worthless (but, the old cliché goes, 'you never know which half'). Instead, SodaStream uses public relations firms whose job is not to buy media time but to get SodaStream into the public consciousness and create 'buzz'. For instance, Daniel Birnbaum has been photographed with Susan Sarandon, Hollywood movie star and environmental crusader. They were shown at a Chicago homeware exhibition alongside a 'cage' containing 10,657 empty bottles and cans, collected by high school kids from a Malvern, PA school. In the photo, Birnbaum holds one SodaStream bottle – sufficient to replace all those cans and bottles. If a picture was ever worth a thousand words, that is it. Sarandon was quoted as saying: 'The recycling rate in America is less than 35 per cent. Troubling news, to say the least, particularly considering that this means that 141 billion beverage cans and bottles go to landfill each year.' PR firms cost money, true – but far less than ad agencies and they are perhaps far more effective.

The latest SodaStream product is the bright red AquaBar, an on-demand tabletop device that provides hot, cold, ambient and carbonated water, designed by a leading Italian designer. The launch was at a design show.

SodaStream did an IPO on NASDAQ in August 2010, reached a market value of $1.5 billion a year later and is still worth nearly $700 million.

3.4 Individual entrepreneurs themselves are often the most powerful market-demand research

Case study 9: Sara Blakely hated how her butt looks – and made a billion!

On 27 February, Sara Blakely celebrated her 44th birthday. Who is Sara Blakely? Back in 2012, she became the youngest woman (an American) to reach Forbes' 'billionaire' list (416th), self-made, on her own, without husband or family wealth.

How did she do it? Here is her story.

She was working as a sales trainer by day and stand-up comedian by night. She knew zero about tights (except that she hated them) and had never taken a business class. 'I had only one source to operate from ... my gut', she says.

She hated the way her bottom looked, wearing regular pants. She decided to do something about it because she was sure many other women felt the same way. She developed a bottom-scrunching panty using Spandex, wrote the patent herself and it was approved. Then she trademarked the name Spanx. For months, she drove around North Carolina begging mill owners to manufacture her product. Finally, after many rejections, she found a mill owner who agreed. Why? He said, he had two daughters. It took a year to perfect the prototype because Sara was obsessed that her Spanx should be comfortable. (After all – she would wear them herself.) She chose the Spanx name carefully and it proved to be a winner. 'It's edgy, fun, catchy, and makes your mind wander', she says, 'and it's all about making women's butts better, so why not?'.

She took a bold new approach to packaging – if your product is innovative, its package has to look it – and chose a bold red package with three women on the front. She called the buyer at Neiman Marcus, a top-of-the-line department store chain. She agreed to give Sara ten minutes. Together, they went to the ladies' room and Sara showed the buyer her butt, in her cream pants, before Spanx ... and after! Three weeks later, Spanx was on the shelves of Neiman Marcus. She did the same with Saks, Nordstrom, Bloomingdales and others. She asked her friends to go to the stores and make a huge fuss over her product.

She had no money to advertise, so she hit the road. She did in-store rallies about Spanx with the sales associates, then stayed all day introducing customers to Spanx. And she got help from media women; her product was on the Oprah Winfrey show, for instance, and the Tyra Banks show. To get free publicity for Spanx, she even joined Richard Branson's reality show *The Rebel Billionaire*, leaving her business for three months to do daring tasks all over the world.

Sara has now launched a foundation to empower women all over the world. She summarizes: 'My energy and inspiration comes from inventing and enhancing products that promote comfort and confidence for women. Customer feedback is one of the key drivers of our business.'

How many millions of women looked in the mirror, turned around and did not like what they saw below the waist? One bold woman did something about it. And she's a billionaire. Annual revenues are $250 million and her net margin is estimated at 20 per cent. And she started with the huge sum of $5,000 in personal savings.

Case study 10: A man. A van. A plan[12]

A Planet Money blog discusses the key difference between those who complain bitterly and those who take action. Adam Humphreys, who lives in New York City, wanted to travel to China. He filled out a long form, downloaded from a website, and showed up at the Chinese consulate only to learn he had filled out the wrong form. At the nearby internet café, where he went to get the right form, he found many others in the same predicament.

Reaction? Anger. Grumbling. And ... resignation.

Not this time. Adam called his friend Steven Nelson. They rented a large Penske cargo van, parked it in front of the Chinese consulate and mounted a sign: Lucky Dragon Mobile Visa Consultants. Inside the van: two Mac laptops and a printer, and an old couch, 'cosy as a dorm room'. Confused visa applicants line up outside. Adam and Steve first charged $10. They were over-run. They then charged $40. Too high. So they settled on $20, with a $5 discount for Buddhist monks. Sweet spot! Just right. Just like Goldilocks and the Three Bears' porridge.

Adam says he can make $500 a day, but he's cagey about disclosing real numbers. After all, someone else can park a van next to theirs. It's called capitalism.

How many times have we complained about bureaucracy, red tape, delays, incompetency, rudeness ... and stopped there rather than finding an initiative, taking action and offering a solution or work-around?

That, clearly, is the difference between an innovator and a complainer. Not IQ, brains, creativity, or anything else. Simply – willingness to act, to do something. Recall that da Vinci, that great creative brain, never actually built most of his amazing inventions, but simply drew them. Five centuries later, we venerate him and recently a daring Swiss engineer built the parachute da Vinci sketched and leaped out of a helicopter with it – but most of us would like to change the world a little faster.

Case study 11: how strong minds raced so weak legs could walk[13]

A US National Football League charity campaign once used the slogan, 'Strong legs run so weak ones can walk'. The second author of this paper recalled this during a visit to an Israeli startup named Argo, launched by Dr Amit Goffer. Argo's product is called ReWalk and it is an exo-skeleton (outside-the-body skeleton) which, with electronics, enables those who cannot walk to stand on their own two feet and walk at 2 km per hour, a good clip. ReWalk can also enable people to climb stairs. You might call it, 'Strong minds race so that weak legs may walk'.

Dr Goffer told us that, following a terrible accident, which left him paralyzed and confined to a wheel chair, he asked an audacious question: how can I create a device that enables people who cannot walk to walk by themselves? Dr Goffer has three degrees in electrical engineering and worked for years at Odin Medical Technologies, which he started (real-time MRI images for brain surgery), and at Elscint (medical imaging). In 1998/9, he conceived ReWalk and built a prototype himself. He described his approach to entrepreneurship: 'not succeeding is not in my vocabulary. You create a corridor ... you see a light at the end of it, and there are no exits, once you start you have to go all the way to the end, until you succeed.'

Goffer estimates there are two million people in the US alone who are in wheelchairs and, of them, some 500,000 could use ReWalk. He is marketing the device to US rehabilitation hospitals, including the Veterans' Administration. There are two models: one for institutions, such as hospitals, and the other for purchase by individuals. Argo has venture funding and employs 15 people in Israel, one in Europe and four in the US. It has several patents. The essence of Goffer's innovation is his deep insight, stemming from his own disability, that paraplegics would greatly value the ability to stand upright and look others in the eye rather than perpetually facing upward and looking at people a metre taller than their eye level.

We saw a demonstration of ReWalk. Attached to a disabled person's legs, it uses an electronic sensor device on the person's wrist to move each leg forward, when the person (on crutches) leans forward. The battery power is carried in a small backpack. The device makes a whirring noise that is not unpleasant or loud. The price is currently $90,000 per device in the US and 90,000 euros in Europe. This price will decline as large-scale manufacturing occurs. It finds use both as a 'walker' and as a rehabilitation device to help those who have been injured. By putting those confined to wheelchairs on their feet, erect, it essentially moves them from 'disabled' to 'enabled'. Goffer himself cannot use his device as he is quadriplegic. But he nonetheless wants to get his device to market quickly. I told him I thought a great many people would be waiting for it. 'I know', he said. This is why he and his team are working very hard. Production currently takes place at the company's offices in Yokneam, a northern suburb of Haifa.

Case study 12: how ebooks were invented and how Michael Hart changed the world

The person who invented ebooks died recently, at the age of 64. His name was Michael Hart and his little-known story shows how one person with one idea can truly change the world.[14] Hart was a student at the University of Illinois. (Recall that this university was a major pioneer in computer science, thanks to Marc Andreessen, who thought up Mosaic while at the university; Mosaic later became Netscape, the internet browser.) He was given a user's account on a Xerox Sigma V mainframe computer in the school's Materials Research lab in 1971, an account worth, according to him, $100 million at the time. He tried to think up a project that would justify the cost, even though it was free for him. On 4 July 1971, he attended an Independence Day fireworks celebration and later stopped at a grocery store. With his purchases, he received a copy of the Declaration of Independence. Hart typed the document and intended to send it as an email to all the users of ARPANET (the precursor of the world wide web). But a colleague said this would crash the system! (The whole Declaration is only 1,357 words!) So instead, he posted a notice saying the text could be downloaded. Hart said he wanted to 'encourage the creation and distribution of ebooks' in order 'to help break down the bars of ignorance and illiteracy'.

Hart's initiative and modest idea gave birth to Project Gutenberg, which today lists more than 30,000 downloadable ebooks in 60 languages. The project got off to a slow start. Hart created only 313 ebooks by 1997. But by 2021, Project Gutenberg's 50th anniversary, it is predicted there will be a billion ebooks available – and, as Hart said in an email, 'you will be able to carry them all in one hand!'.

Hart once told a magazine called *Searcher*: 'I was just waiting for the world to realize I'd knocked it over. You've heard of cow-tipping? The cow had been tipped over, but it took 17 years for it to wake up and say, "Moo".'

3.5 'Reverse' (emerging-market-based) innovation can supply winning products for rich-country markets

Case study 13: find yourself a 'squeeze box' – and think in it; spend less – and innovate better!

Thinking 'outside the box' is vastly over-rated. The best creative thinking is done *inside* the box – but the right box. By 'box', we mean the things about reality you *cannot* ignore because they just won't go away. Like time, money and feasibility.

So, think different about thinking differently. In wealthy countries, VCs and MBA professors caution, 'You always need more money than you ask for – ask for more, and then raise money when you can, not when you need it.' Problem is, as all of us know, when you have money in the bank, you tend to spend it; you tend not to respect it. And then high burn rates kill the innovative companies. They run out of money because having money means you have time (to dawdle) – but you don't! Because time to market is crucial and urgent, and having money kills it.

So, find a 'squeeze box'. Find a tight constraint, a challenging one. Make sure it is credible. Use it to create urgency, the first step in transformative change. And then work hard inside that box. When John F. Kennedy made his famous 'we will go to the moon by the end of the decade' speech before a joint session of Congress, on 25 May 1961, he did precisely that. And just eight years later, in 1969, American put a man on the moon. The 'squeeze box' definitely helped. If he had said, 'well, we'll go to the moon, sometime before the year 2050', would it have happened?

RETHINKING INNOVATION: START AT THE BOTTOM, NOT THE TOP!

The *Global New York Times*' 'Dawn of the New Decade' ad insert seeking investment in Asia (as if Asia needs money and investment rather than the overspending America) has an interesting interview with Anil Gupta, INSEAD Professor and expert on globalization.[15]

Here is Gupta's 'take' on the changing world of innovation:

> Enterprises that hope to emerge as the global leaders in 2020 will also need to think differently about innovation. Traditionally, innovation has originated in the developed countries ... within industries, at the top of a product range, for example, a Lexus, and then worked its way down to, say, a Toyota Corolla. In order to capture the very large market opportunities in the low-to-middle segments [in emerging markets], the leading global enterprise of 2020 will need to be good at not just top-down innovation but also at frugal innovation, whose roots would lie in the low- and middle-income markets of emerging economies.

Prof. Gupta cites as an example Tata Group's Nano car, the world's cheapest, and its strategic plan to bring out an electric Nana in the EU and US, matching the performance of domestic equivalents at a third less cost. 'We'll see this phenomenon in many industries, from tractors to banking', he notes.

The innovator must ask: can I shift my focus from premium-priced 'toys' bought by those with scads of money, to low-priced products that even low-income groups in low-income countries can buy? The late C.K. Prahalad identified 'fortunes at the bottom of the pyramid' ... but apparently, according to Gupta, there are also superior innovation opportunities down there.

Case study 14: Quingjie Shui – Tishlovet Water[16]

BACKGROUND

Tishlovet Group is an Israel-based global food company focused on dairy, coffee and chocolate. Tishlovet Water is a kind of startup operating within H2Q Water Industries, owned 87 per cent by Tishlovet Group for making and selling water devices worldwide. Quingjie Shui Group is a large Chinese global consumer electronics and home appliances company, headquartered in Quingdao, China; the Quingjie Shui brand led the world market share in 'white goods' (kitchen appliances) with 6.1 per cent. Its annual revenue is an estimated 33 billion RMB (about $4.6 billion).

In October 2009, Tishlovet acquired Tana Industries, purchased by Tishlovet subsidiary H2Q for NIS 291 million. Tana Industries was owned by Kibbutz HaLamed Hai and made the Tami 4 water purifying device.

On 18 May 2011, Tishlovet Water and Quingjie Shui Group launched their joint venture in Shanghai to produce a home water filtration device, with a $4 million marketing campaign featuring the mantra 'Smart Water – Safe Home'. The device is based on ten pending patents. The heart of the device is a high-tech filter known as MAZE, developed by Israeli entrepreneurs and produced in Israel. The high-tech purifier not only filters water but also heats it to exactly the right temperature for making tea. Tishlovet and Quingjie Shui each invested $20 million in the joint venture. The device will be sold initially in Beijing, Shanghai and Quingdao (headquarters of Quingjie Shui), and later in Shenzhen and Guangzhou.

Israeli entrepreneur Haim Wilder invented MAZE, together with Hebrew university professor Avi Domb. MAZE is a unique water purification technology and a filter that works with zero water pressure and its technology is the core of the Quingjie Shui Tishlovet device. A key point is this: the Tami 4 appliance itself will be made in China. But the crucial high-tech MAZE filter is produced in Israel, at Kibbutz Netiv Halamed Hey, thus keeping both high-value-added jobs and sensitive technology at home.

On 12 July 2009, the Tishlovet Group Chair outlined Tishlovet's strategy for its water ventures:

> Several years ago the Tishlovet Group identified water as a strategic category presenting significant business opportunity, in line with the Group's long term business strategy and vision. We view the development of a technology that enables high quality drinking water for both home and offices as a means to improve the quality of life of millions of people worldwide. About three years ago we teamed up with a group of Israeli entrepreneurs and scientists, and invested in the H2Q venture which develops a water purifier using a breakthrough technology. Tishlovet's water activities, which highlight both its social responsibility and commitment to the environment, meet a genuine need of people around the world today.

INTERVIEW WITH R.R., CEO, TISHLOVET WATER

R.R. has a strong background in high-tech industry. He has a BSc degree in Electrical Engineering and an MBA degree. He is 48 years old and is married, with three children. R.R. joined Tishlovet Group to head Tishlovet Water as CEO about two and a half years before the Quingjie Shui Tishlovet joint venture. Though he had no experience with the food or water industries, with all of his managerial experience focused on high-tech, he was fiercely recruited by Tishlovet Group Chair Ofra Tishlovet and other Board members. They spotted in him qualities they felt would enable him to build a new venture within Tishlovet. Tishlovet's vision is to bring 'magic' to basic products and few things are more basic than water. In R.R.'s own words:

> Tishlovet Water is a company launched within Tishlovet Group. I became CEO of Tishlovet Water in January 2007. The Quingjie Shui Tishlovet joint venture was the result of an orderly disciplined process. We chose Quingjie Shui as our Chinese partner after a careful selection process. We engaged in a dialog with Chinese consumers and focused on a compelling reason to buy our joint-venture product, built on effective communication with consumers.

1   The starting point is this: Chinese consumers do not drink tap water. It is Chinese custom and culture that water is boiled. This is why the Chinese drink tea and serve tea to guests. Plain boiled water is not tasty. And in China it is considered impolite to offer cold water to guests.

2   There is high awareness in China of all the contaminants that enter into tap water. Moreover, water that 'stands' for one night is thrown out. This is a very clear code in Chinese culture. For this reason, bottled water is widely sold and there is strong penetration of bottled water, in terms of per capita consumption.

At the same time, there are already a variety of home water devices, many of the local varieties are very cheap, some of the imported ones are quite expensive.

We felt that the size of the potential market for a home water device was very large and attractive. But a strong compelling value proposition had to be built.

I was hired by the Chair of Tishlovet Group and grand-daughter of the original founders of Tishlovet to build Tishlovet Water. Tishlovet Water is a world leader in water purification and filtration technology. And the Chinese market is very attractive. We treated the issue of how to do business in China, and how to penetrate the Chinese market, as an issue in business development. We first decided to map the market and the players in the market in great detail. We entered into the joint venture with Quingjie Shui only after we achieved a very deep understanding of the market.

There are a number of key points vital for doing business in China:

1   We understood that business in China is driven by interests. It is some-
    times claimed that the Chinese do not keep agreements, even signed
    legal ones. This is, in my view, not the case. The Chinese do keep
    agreements, *provided it is in their strong interest to do so*. And the
    agreement has to be win-win. In the West, a deal is a deal. In China this
    is not the case when the deal turns against China's interest.

2   In China, the process of building a deal and reaching agreement is
    crucial. It is very important that in this process, Chinese leaders main-
    tain 'face' and honour. We have learned this from experience. To head
    our China operations with Quingjie Shui, we opened an office in Shang-
    hai and hired a very sophisticated CEO, local Chinese. This is very
    important.

3   Mutual trust is very important. We were very patient and invested time
    in getting to know our Chinese partners and letting them get to know us
    as well as building the trust needed as the foundation of our joint
    venture. Our joint venture is built as much on trust and mutual respect
    as it is on capital or on technology.

4   To make a joint venture with Quingjie Shui, we engaged in a very long
    screening process, beginning with a long list that was sorted down to a
    short list. We chose Quingjie Shui as the best of two candidates. In this
    process, we used a local consultant. The key role played by this local
    person was crucial. It is also very important to establish trust with key
    local officials. Local government officials in China have strong powers
    in regulating business in their area. Their approval and goodwill are
    crucial.[17]

5   There is a widespread view, especially among Israelis, that proprietary
    technology should not be brought to China, even as part of a joint
    venture, because the Chinese will quickly copy and appropriate it. At
    Tishlovet Water, we disagree. The only real protection for unique tech-
    nology is to continue to develop it, one step ahead of competition. If
    you cannot do this, you will lose out, no matter how heavily you patent.
    The Chinese bring their own unique 'technology' – the ability to
    'design for manufacturability', to take complex technologies and make
    them suitable for efficient production. This is as important as the pat-
    ented core technology.

There were three separate signing ceremonies, over a two-year period. The
Board Chair and CEO of Tishlovet Group took part in one of them. In the
second signing ceremony, it was held in Israel. The Chairman of the Board
of Quingjie Shui himself came to Israel, along with Quingjie Shui's CEO,
and stood behind the CEO during the signing ceremony. However, the Chair
did not sign. I asked him, why? 'It is sufficient that I am standing here', he
said. The fact that the Chair of Quingjie Shui literally stood behind this

agreement, and made this known to all his managers, was vital. Without this, deals are not stable.

The third signing ceremony involved the full detailed agreement, including 'route to market'. Quingjie Shui has 7,000 retail outlets all over China. We (Tishlovet Water) are responsible for the product itself; we are in full control of making the product.

China has a detailed Five Year Plan. It includes supplying improved infrastructure throughout China, including high-quality water. The plan also includes raising the value-added of goods made in China. We studied the Chinese government's interest and goals and also Quingjie Shui's key interests, related to its Quingdao region and city. Quingjie Shui itself insisted that we had to have an engineering setup in China. For China, simply making a product in China is not sufficient. There has to be a component which involves some element of learning for China, in terms of technology.

Israeli engineers are very good at innovating new products. However, they are not good at 'engineering to cost' and 'designing to cost' or 'designing for manufacturability'. A Chinese engineer will take a product and reduce the number of parts in it from 100 to, say, 30, to make it faster cheaper and easier to make. But Israeli engineers do not have this mindset. However, Israeli engineers are very good at creativity and inventing new things. *Israeli engineers will make things work. Chinese engineers will make them commercially viable. This is a strong and positive collaboration.*

The MAZE high-tech filter that is at the heart of our devices is currently produced in Israel, on Kibbutz HaLamed Hai. Eventually, it may be produced elsewhere, perhaps in China. However, Israeli engineers will continue to develop advanced versions of the filter. As the filter becomes more and more commoditized, more sophisticated versions will be developed and we will work on this process continually.

Quingjie Shui has set up an organization as part of our joint venture. The CEO used to run the small appliances branch of Quingjie Shui. We have an Israeli marketing manager and an Israeli finance manager in our China operation. It is our intention to be in China over the long term. Our Tishlovet Water CEO in China is Joanna Chao Gu.

Our pricing plan will unfold over time. At the launch, our device is high priced at $692. Next year, we will introduce a medium-priced device. Over time, we will also introduce affordable devices. This is the opposite of the market penetration plan used by Japanese car and motorcycle firms in America, which began at the low end, to attract young customers, and moved up to the very high end (Lexus, for instance). In future, we plan to introduce this device in other countries, perhaps the UK.

We considered other large Asian nations, such as India. We chose not to go to India; there are water purifying devices there, they are very inexpensive and only involve purification. The Indian market is complex.

What should Israeli companies know in order to go to do business in China?

First, you must structure the joint venture so that it is relevant over time and the Israeli partner brings significant value added to the agreement, in the eyes of the Chinese partner. When you become irrelevant to the deal, which often happens, you will likely be sidelined. Second, you must structure sustainable win-win benefits for both the Israeli partner and the Chinese partner. This is crucial. The win-win must be sustainable over time.

When you consider engaging in a joint venture in another country, you must decide not only in which country to operate, but you should decide carefully in which countries *not* to operate. And above all, analyse very carefully, what are the other side's interests in the agreement?

At the heart of Tishlovet Group's strategy is the view that the most basic of human needs, food and water, are growth industries.

The Green Revolution pioneered by American agronomist Norman Borlaug caused grain prices to fall by 75 per cent between 1950 and 1990. Then, the price of rice, corn, soybeans and wheat has effectively doubled since 2007, causing the number of hungry people in the world to rise to one billion, or one person in every seven. Grain prices are poised to rise again, because of climate change, drought, rising population, local wars and biofuels. A joint report by the UN Food and Agriculture Organization and the Organization for Economic Cooperation and Development warns that wheat and grain prices will be 15–40 per cent higher over the coming ten years. That means even more hungry people and major social unrest.

The problem is not lack of land. There is enough land in the world, over six acres per person. But there is not enough good, fertile land – only one arable acre per person. So the world needs to find ways to grow more food on poor land. And it needs to find ways to deliver pure drinking water as increased use of fertilizers degrades ground water and endangers the health of millions of people. Food and water are about to reclaim their place as a central concern of policy and business.

Tishlovet Water is not confining its strategic expansion plans to China alone. Tishlovet recently announced that it has teamed with another innovative company, Virgin (specifically, Virgin Green Fund, a private equity fund affiliated with Virgin and focusing on green technologies), to form a new joint venture. The JV will bring Tishlovet Water purification products and services to Britain and to Ireland, later expanding to France, Australia and South Africa. Under a 30-year agreement, Virgin Tishlovet Water will use the Virgin brand to market Tishlovet Water products.

In a press release, Tishlovet Water CEO R.R. said:

I am proud of the fact that Virgin Group chose to establish a partnership with us in view of our expertise and excellent ability to provide consumers with pure, tasty water at point of use – highest quality, affordable and easy to use hot and cold water. Tishlovet Water is currently operating a successful partnership with Quingjie Shui Group in China to market its products there, and I am confident that our expertise and technology, combined with Virgin's leadership in understanding and meeting consumers' needs, will result in the creation of a company that specializes in the supply of pure, safe and tasty drinking water to consumers in countries around the world.

The joint venture described here is a strong example of reverse innovation – initially designing and launching products in emerging markets, then migrating them to developed countries. It is likely we will see a great many more examples of this process; emerging markets offer growth and a growing middle class, as well as production expertise. Demand-driven innovation will increasingly seek to satisfy needs and wants in emerging markets, first and foremost.

3.6 Demand-driven process innovation often surpasses product innovation

Case study 15: innovation where it counts – save lives, don't invent gadgets

A simple idea in economics is this: put your money where it brings the highest marginal return. In medical care, America is disastrously failing to do this. The result costs thousands of lives! According to a study by AARP (American Association of Retired Persons), published in their March 2012 Bulletin, 'hospital errors cause 100,000 deaths yearly in the US'. These are all preventable deaths, notes the author Katharine Greider. These deaths are equivalent to a hurricane that would wipe out the entire population of South Bend, Indiana!

A Medicare study found that one in seven patients died or were harmed by their hospital care! How about those odds: 14.2 per cent, you'll be harmed or die. 'The number of patients who die each year from hospital errors is equal to four jumbo jets crashing each week', notes the author. US surgeons operate on the *wrong body part* as often as 40 times a week!

A small investment in operations innovation could remedy this and substantially cut the death toll. For example: supply each nurse and doctor with an MDA (medical digital assistant) that provides instant comprehensive information on each patient and connects to a central databank. Some 1,500 lives were saved in 18 months in Michigan intensive care units when a checklist was introduced for handling catheters! Just a checklist!

Yet America continues to spend $8,000 a year on medical care, double that of France or Canada, investing in extremely expensive procedures instead of investing in innovations that improve operations, prevent errors and save lives. For example: open heart surgery costs $324,000, a heart transplant, $287,000, a liver transplant, $235,000, and a heart valve procedure, $133,000. These operations are done all the time.

It is true in general that there is massive underinvestment in strategic operations innovation, in companies. But in hospitals, this costly mistake kills huge numbers of people – and it is simply ignored. Process innovation is desperately needed – and could be hugely profitable.

Case study 16: IKEA – can you feel small when you are really big?
Anders Dahlvig thinks you can't!

Consider IKEA. This Swedish company, founded by Inqvar Kamprad at his Uncle Ernst's table in 1943, has revolutionized the global furniture business. It is the world's largest furniture retailer and its innovation is its business model, not its products. There is now a book, *The IKEA Edge*, by Anders Dahlvig, who rose from store manager to become Kamprad's right-hand man. Here is what *Fortune* magazine said about this book:

> Dahlvig does give a brief history of Ikea's evolution into the privately held retail giant that generated $31 billion in 2009, with 125,000 employees (ran 300 stores, operated in 38 countries and was the third largest buyer of wood in the world). But more often than not, the book is about management – motivating and inspiring employees, keeping an entrepreneurial streak as a company grows, creating loyalty and diversity, the role of a CEO. The book is rich in ideas about how to take a brand that has a strong regional culture and make it global. While some of these lessons are helpful and refreshing (Dahlvig suggests having numerous people report to you so you don't have time to micromanage or hover), I wanted more of a personal story about his time at the company. Instead the book is written in the style of Ikea itself: practical and no-frills.

What is IKEA's secret of success? Fierce supply-chain management, bulk buying and the creation of a unique customer experience. Consider IKEA's restaurants. Their real purpose?

> Take, for example, the fact that its restaurants generate $1.5 billion in sales. But the main reason behind those 15 Swedish meatballs for $3.99 is not to make a profit – it's to highlight the store's low prices and get the customer to shop longer.

Dahlvig knows clearly why IKEA and any company exists: 'A company's reason for existence should be to contribute to a better society.'

It is hard to imagine these words coming out of the mouths of most US CEOs, says *Fortune* magazine. But it might serve them well if they at least read the book.

IKEA's founder is now 88 and only recently retired. Prior to his retirement, Dahlvig was worried. He told the BBC's *Business Daily*:

> What will happen when the founder of IKEA is not around? What will happen to IKEA? The founder is 85, this transition is about to happen. He is less visible in the business. Transition is on the way. My biggest worry for the company is, the loss of the values, he is the guardian of that. This is the soul of the company. The consequence of losing the values is, the loyalty of

employees declines, and we become like every other company. This is our first generational change. That's a worry. The fact that IKEA is becoming bigger, a bureaucracy, the small company feel is declining, maybe inevitable, but I'm worried about that, and worried about the loss of the culture and the values. And I don't have a solution, how you can act like a small company when you are the size of IKEA.

Case study 17: Mellanox – warp speed for networks

On 19 July 2012, shares of an Israeli semiconductor company, Mellanox, rose by almost 50 per cent in a single day on both the Tel Aviv stock exchange and the NASDAQ. Lucky shareholders saw their stocks double in value in one year. The market value of Mellanox shares is now $3.7 billion and exceeds that of Bank Leumi, Israel's second largest bank. Mellanox and its entrepreneur, Eyal Waldman, identified a key process – data transfer between companies and clients – and the need to greatly speed up that process, and found a way to do so. Even though the innovation itself is a high-tech product, the objective is the *process* that the technology enables. And Mellanox's success is largely due to its ability to improve the data transfer speed not by a small amount but by entire orders of magnitude.

Despite the global recession, Mellanox shares rose from $7.70 in 2008 to around $100 in 2012, before falling back to $43.50 in February 2015. The reason is Mellanox's phenomenal profitability (71 per cent gross margin) and revenue growth (from $48.5 million in 2007 to a possible $600 million in 2012). Investors love rapid growth. And what has driven Mellanox's speedy growth is speed, loads of it.

In the TV series *Star Trek*, 'warp speed' was a faster-than-light propulsion system. The secret of Mellanox's success is 'warp speed' technology connecting companies and their clients with enterprise data processors – but it is not science fiction. Mellanox hardware can transfer 100 gigabits per second, or a hundred 2,600-page *Encyclopaedia Britannicas* every second. Mellanox's remarkable attainment of market-leading 'warp speed' for networks is the result of a decade-long quest, led by a talented entrepreneur and engineer, who identified a burgeoning embryonic market need well before other competing companies did. The need is, simply, to move data, in networks, faster.

Mellanox was founded in 1999. Founder Eyal Waldman is a serial entrepreneur and, many believe, a genius, though in a recent interview with him he denied both labels. After graduating from Technion-Israel Institute of Technology, he worked for Intel from 1989–93 as part of a highly successful team that developed the Pentium microprocessor, led by Dadi Perlmutter, now a senior Intel VP. Waldman left in 1993 along with several others in his Intel team to co-found Galileo with Avigdor Vilentz. When Galileo, which made high-speed communications hardware, was acquired by an American firm, Marvell, in 1999, Waldman left to found Mellanox. It is based in Yokneam, a Haifa suburb, and in Sunnyvale, CA.

Waldman had a key insight earlier than most other entrepreneurs. He saw that computing would shift to the 'cloud', a system where businesses keep their data and software at distant sites and access them through a network, named for the cloud-like shape of the diagram that describes the system. This will mean that the bottleneck in computing, Waldman reasoned, will not be computing power, memory or data storage, but speed – how fast you can transfer data over the network. Mellanox hardware delivers speed, more of it than its competitors, including giant Intel. Calling Mellanox a semiconductor company is like calling Ferrari a car firm. As a small 'David', Mellanox has slain much bigger Goliath competitors.

In a recent speech at a Technion conference, Waldman explained one unusual reason why data transfer speed is so important – electricity. Facebook, he notes, spends a third of its operating budget on electricity because its thousands of servers burn huge amounts of kilowatts. 'Warp speed' data transfer simply means using fewer watts of power.

'At Mellanox, we have almost daily challenges', Waldman said, when I interviewed him recently.

> We have many obstacles. We did a round of capital-raising in the third quarter of 2001, just around the time of 9/11! The conditions were nearly impossible. We had only $4 million in the bank at the time. This was enough to survive for only three more months. We once did a life-saving project for the company in only three months! This was impossible, unheard of. The team did and saved the company. I don't know of another team that would even have attempted it.

Why has Mellanox not been acquired, like most other startups, swallowed by a giant US firm? For one, Waldman truly wants to build a global giant, not do an 'exit' and bank a huge cheque, and he seems capable of doing it. For another, thank Oracle founder Larry Ellison. Oracle sells database software, about $11 billion worth every quarter. Oracle sells speed in accessing and using huge databases ('10x more speed!') and Mellanox helps provide it. Ellison bought 10 per cent of Mellanox stock. This investment acts as both a good housekeeping seal of approval for Mellanox and a kind of 'poison pill', deterring other companies who know that Oracle wouldn't agree to sell its shares.

Mellanox is one of a handful of Israeli high-tech firms that have outsourced some of its engineering to the West Bank. It has hired Palestinian engineers from Ramallah through a Palestinian outsourcing firm. Waldman believes business partnerships between Israelis and Palestinians can contribute to peace in the region, and I strongly agree.

3.7 *Startups require a strategic partner with a strong market presence*

Case study 18: from eggheads, golden eggs

'Egghead' is an epithet describing intellectuals (such as professors) who are out of touch with reality and lack common sense. Senior high-tech executive and entrepreneur Dan Vilenski believes he knows how to help eggheads lay 'golden eggs' (startups that generate wealth, jobs and exports). It's not just a theory.

Vilenski has 'proof of concept', with successful startups emerging from the highly productive lab of Technion optical physics Professor Steve Lipson. Lipson and Vilenski, in interviews, explained the winning formula for transferring technology from university labs to the marketplace.

Vilenski brought three major American high-tech companies to Israel – Kulicke & Soffa, KLA and Applied Materials. As head of BIRD-F (the US–Israel Binational Industrial R&D Foundation), he found many strategic US partners for struggling Israeli startups. Lipson served as his scientific mentor for over 20 years.

The term 'technology transfer' doesn't begin to convey how hard it is to convert basic research into market success. Many experts prefer the term 'Valley of Death' – the huge gap between the lab and the market, where startups trying to turn science into products lack funds, management skill, expertise and sales channels, and often stumble and die as a result.

A student project in Lipson's lab led to an idea – use a known technology (known as surface plasmon resonance) in a new way to identify proteins on a 'biological chip', or microprocessor, able to classify 36 different proteins at one time. With Lipson's knowhow, a startup, ProteOptics, was launched in 2000, with Lipson's student, Ariel Notcovich, as CEO. Lipson says most of his graduate students work in industry rather than in academia.

Vilenski brokered a 'marriage'. He found a US company called Bio-Rad that for over 50 years had produced and sold innovative lab equipment. Bio-Rad is led by its founder, Norman Schwartz, and his son David. Lipson, too, is part of an extended father–son team. His textbook *Optical Physics* was co-authored with his late father, Henry and his son, Ariel.

Bio-Rad invested in ProteOptics, starting in 2001, and eventually acquired the firm outright in 2006. Bio-Rad thought Lipson's technology could generate a new device for analysing proteins, just what scientists needed at a time when genomics (study of genes) was evolving into 'proteomics' (study of proteins triggered by genes). Bio-Rad was an ideal strategic investor. It brought intimate knowledge of the marketplace (in this case, scientific laboratories doing research on proteins), along with brand-name credibility that helped sell innovative products to cautious customers. The role of Bio-Rad as a strategic partner for ProteOptics was absolutely crucial, in two key ways. First, Bio-Rad provided ongoing financing, not as a one-time sum but as an annual cash flow, according to ProteOptics' needs. Second, and more importantly, Bio-Rad brought crucial intimate knowledge of the market and the potential customers, guiding ProteOptics away from one technological direction and towards a different alternative one, which turned out to be a crucial turning point. Without this wisdom, ProteOptics' development of its device may well have failed. Few startups have such intimate knowledge of the market, without the help of a veteran strategic partner like Bio-Rad.

'A strategic partner understands the market, can finance the development, has a business approach and has a world sales and service infrastructure', Vilenski argues. 'In my opinion all these elements are served better by a proper strategic partner than a financial partner.'

'A Bio-Rad director asked us, at an early stage, will this work?' Lipson said. 'We did some lab experiments, reflected, and changed direction from "interferometry" to "absorption". This switch was crucial. Bio-Rad was patient and supportive all along.'

Today, ProteOptics is Bio-Rad Haifa, sited on the Technion campus. Its technology is the heart of a $250,000 machine with a consumable bio chip widely used by pharmaceutical firms and other scientists and sold globally by Bio-Rad.

Lipson's ideas have created at least two other successful startups, both located in a development town, Migdal HaEmek – CI Systems, which also makes test equipment for labs, and Applied Spectral Imaging (ASI), whose spectral technology colours images with multiple colours, beyond the basic red, green and blue previously offered by digital cameras.

Lipson himself is firmly and irrevocably a bench scientist. But he has a rare knack of seeing how his discoveries can potentially become commercial products. He patents them before publishing. And his students love to do the implementation, aided by strategic partners.

'For instance is not a proof', goes a Yiddish saying. Scientists like Steve Lipson and dynamic matchmakers like Dan Vilenski are quite rare. As a result, golden eggs from eggheads remain the exception rather than the rule.

4 Conclusion

Readers may justifiably feel rather baffled after reading our narratives on demand-driven innovation. These are often (though not always) stories of rather eccentric individuals who often have weird ideas and take personal risks to implement them. The core of demand-driven innovation is always an idea born in a single brain, to an individual who has intuitive and/or evidence-based understanding of needs and wants that are currently unmet.

There is a fundamental paradox, and often a major misunderstanding, related to market-based demand-driven innovation. Market research, based on marketing 'science', is often not the friend of innovation, but rather the sworn enemy of innovation. The reason, as John Kearon notes in his challenging article 'The death of innovation' (2010), is that marketing science is based on what exists, not on what does not yet exist. Kearon claims:

> When originating a new category, everything has to be invented, everything is new and by definition contrary to the way things are. Trying to research new category ideas is pretty near impossible since people are notoriously bad at predicting whether they will adopt new behaviors in the future and generally reject such changes as alien and odd. Examples of hugely successful brands that originated their category but which failed disastrously in market research include Sony Walkman, Bailey's Irish Cream, Post-Its, Perrier (in the UK), Red Bull and cashpoint machines.

Market research often reveals what consumers are buying now rather than what they might wish to buy in future. Radical innovation, of the 'blue oceans' variety, can create market leadership. Market-based demand-driven innovation is not necessarily innovation driven by massive conventional market research (as our Nokia narrative above suggests). Most breakthrough innovations appear to occur because individual entrepreneurs achieve deep insights into market needs that others seem to lack. Innovation systems that give such individuals both the freedom to innovate and the infrastructure and resources to do so will ultimately triumph. However, a caveat is in order: it is certainly true that incremental innovations can sometimes *generate* radical innovations, simply by showing innovative companies what consumers regard as helpful and value-creating. An incremental innovation can become a blue ocean radical innovation when it is pushed to an extreme.

Notes

1 Source: http://mobile.businessweek.com/articles/2012-04-17/the-case-for-frugal-thinking, excerpted from Govindarajan and Trimble (2013).
2 Source: YouTube, www.youtube.com/watch?v=1KUFkQBDo74.
3 Not so long ago, innovative products could be made using processes that were developed in earlier generations. But this is no longer true for many manufacturing sectors, especially in a global economy in which demand is driven by product performance and value. For companies in these sectors, it is imperative that product innovation excellence be backed up by process innovation excellence. However, Segerstrom (2000) argues that government support for process improvement (by improving product quality) is a vertical growth engine that creates slower growth than government support for product R&D.
4 Clay Christensen's 'Milkshake marketing', Carmen Nobel, *HBS Working Knowledge*, 14 February 2011.
5 Source: http://kk.org/thetechnium/archives/2008/03/1000_true_fans.php.
6 See: Patricia Cohen, 'Turning innovation on its head', *Global New York Times*, 11 February 2011, p. 18.
7 S. Maital, 'Where does innovation come from? R&D? Or "dark matter"?', *Innovation Blog*, 2011, https://timnovate.wordpress.com/2011/02/11/.
8 Intuit is an American software company that develops financial and tax preparation software and related services for small businesses, accountants and individuals.
9 See Jon Parels, 'Lady Gaga's roaring retort', *New York Times*, 21–22 May 2011, p. 17.
10 Source: Larry Huston and Nabil Sakkab, 'Connect and develop: inside Procter & Gamble's new model for innovation', *Harvard Business Review*, Vol. 84, No. 3, March 2006.
11 Based on a case study by Yaara Ben-Nahum, Knowledge & Innovation Center, Technion; and on S. Maital, 'Marketplace', *Jerusalem Report*, May 2012.
12 Source: www.npr.org/blogs/money/2012/01/04/144636898/a-man-a-van-a-surprising-business-plan.
13 Additional source: www.argomedtec.com.
14 See William Grimes, 'Michael Hart, 64, pioneer in e-book distribution', *Global New York Times*, 10–11 September 2011.
15 'Emerging economies change the game for global corporations', *Global New York Times*, 27 August 2010, Dawn of the New Decade.
16 'Qjingjie Shui', or 'clean water' in Chinese, is a pseudonym for a large global Chinese consumer electronics company. 'Tishlovet', or conglomerate in Hebrew, is a

pseudonym for a large global Israeli company. Neither company has yet formally approved the release of this case study to the general public although senior executives have read and commented on it.

17 An extreme example is the Souzhou Science Park, about 30 minutes outside Shanghai. The Singapore government invested an enormous sum to build it – but few companies signed up to occupy the space. The logjam was broken only when a major portion of the equity in the park was transferred to the Souzhou City administration.

References

Ben-Aaron, D. (2010). 'Nokia's share slips as unbranded phonemakers, Apple gain ground', www.bloomberg.com/news/2010-11-10/nokia-s-market-share-slips-below-30-as-smaller-vendors-grow-gartner-says.html.

Chesbrough, H. (2006). 'Open innovation: a new paradigm for understanding industrial innovation'. In: Chesbrough, H., Vanhaverbeke, W. and West, J. (eds), *Open Innovation: Researching a New Paradigm* (pp. 1–12). Oxford: Oxford University Press.

Govindarajan, V. and Trimble, C. (2013). *Reverse Innovation: Create Far From Home, Win Everywhere*. Cambridge, MA: Harvard Business Press.

Hamel, G. (2006). 'The why, what, and how of management innovation', *Harvard Business Review*, 84(2), 72.

Kearon, J. (2010). 'The death of innovation', *Market Leader*, Quarter 4, pp. 20–24.

Nobel, C. (2011). 'Clay Christensen's Milkshake Marketing', *Harvard Business School Working Knowledge*, February 14.

OECD (Organization for Economic Cooperation and Development)/Eurostat. (2005). *Guidelines for Collecting and Interpreting Innovation Data – The Oslo Manual*, 3rd edn. Paris: OECD.

Segerstrom, P. (2000) 'The long-run growth effects of R&D subsidies', *Journal of Economic Growth*, 5, 277–305.

Treacy, M. and Wiersema, F. (1993). 'Customer intimacy and other value disciplines', *Harvard Business Review*, 71(1), 84–93.

Treacy, M. and Wiersema, F. (1997). *The Discipline of Market Leaders: Choose Your Customers, Narrow Your Focus, Dominate Your Market*. New York: New York.

von Hippel, E. (1986). 'Lead users: a source of novel product concepts', *Management Science*, 32(7), 791–805.

von Hippel, E. (1994). *The Sources of Innovation*. New York: Oxford University Press.

von Hippel, E. (2005). *Democratizing Innovation*. Cambridge, MA: MIT Press.

von Hippel, E. and von Krogh, G. (2003). 'Open source software and the "private-collective" innovation model: issues for organization science', *Organization Science*, 14(2), 209–223.

Zwillig, M. (2013). '5 rules of relevance every startup needs to adopt', http://blog.startup-professionals.com/2013/06/5-rules-of-relevance-every-startup.html.

Part II
The supply-side dimensions

5 Characterizing the evolution of the EU R&D intensity gap using data from top R&D performers

Jurai Stančík and Federico Biagi

1 Introduction

R&D activity, defined by the Frascati manual as 'creative work undertaken on a systematic basis in order to increase the stock of knowledge and the use of this stock of knowledge to devise new applications', has long been recognized as a source of productivity at the micro, meso and aggregate level. This is as true for business R&D as it is for government R&D.

Business R&D activity impacts on firms' productivity through the development of new and improved goods, services and production processes.[1] Studies that look at the direct relationship between productivity and business R&D using firm-level data typically find values for the R&D output elasticity of between 1 per cent and 25 per cent, centred on around 8 per cent (see Hall *et al.*, 2010). However, the effect of R&D on own labour productivity (or TFP) is not the only relevant one. In fact, the whole endogenous growth theory is based on the intuition that R&D activity generates relevant knowledge spillovers[2] which permit long-run growth as a result of market-driven accumulation (as opposed to external forces driving technological change, as in a typical Solow-type model). The existence and economic relevance of such spillovers is empirically confirmed.[3]

While providing an exhaustive review of the relationship between R&D and productivity (at the micro, meso or macro level) is outside the scope of this work, we believe that there is sufficient evidence supporting the hypothesis that R&D activities matter for productivity and growth.

This conclusion is important in the context of the US–EU productivity gap: if R&D is important for growth and given the existence of both a productivity and a R&D gap, closing the R&D gap is a precondition for closing the productivity gap[4] (for a different perspective, see Havik *et al.*, 2008).

In order to account for differences in country size, the R&D gap is often presented in terms of R&D intensity gap (R&D over GDP). When comparing countries, focusing on the measured R&D intensity gap is especially interesting if one of the countries is at the technological frontier because it shows how far any other country is from the 'optimal' level of R&D, given its size (as measured by GDP). Hence, a positive US–EU gap means that, relative to its size, the EU is not spending enough in R&D, and this, given the positive relationship between

R&D and productivity, implies that the EU is not improving its productivity at a satisfying rate.

In fact, this is exactly the perspective that the EU Commission and the EU Council have taken, first in the Lisbon Agenda and later in the Europe 2020 strategy,[5] when setting the 3 per cent target for (public and private) R&D spending as a percentage of GDP. Apart from the fact that setting a target based on the R&D/GDP ratio is debatable and risky[6] (see Mathieu and van Pottelsberghe, 2008), the 3 per cent target for R&D intensity indicates that knowledge-led growth is among the main objectives of the EU.

In this study, we present the evolution of the R&D intensity gap – and of its structural and intrinsic components – between the EU and its major competitors (US, Japan, BRIC, Asian Tigers), looking at four basic macro sectors defined in terms of their R&D intensity (as proposed by the OECD; see Hatzichronoglou, 1997). By decomposing the overall gap into a structural component (which reflects the role of differences in sectoral composition for a given average sectoral intensity) and an intrinsic component (which reflects the within-sector R&D intensity gap, for a given average sectoral composition), we can better understand the sources of the overall gap, at a given point in time or over a certain time horizon.[7]

Evidence on the role of the structural vs. the intrinsic component is not uncontroversial and this has important consequences in terms of policy implications (see O'Sullivan, 2007). In fact, if the intrinsic component dominates it means that, on average, the EU has a lower R&D intensity across the board, which also implies that there is a list of candidate policies to increase R&D spending (and hence intensity) that might be effective, even in the short run. These include tax credits to R&D activity, improving intellectual property rights and favouring foreign direct investment. If, on the contrary, the structural effect prevails, the ability to reduce the gap in the short run is greatly reduced by the fact that the latter arises from the structural composition of the economy, which is not likely to be altered simply by horizontal policies. In this case, sectoral policies might also be necessary.[8]

Erken and van Es (2007), using the OECD ANBERD and STAN database over the period 1987–2003 for 15 countries (including the US) and 36 industries, find that the intrinsic component dominates the structural one, and this is mostly driven by differences in R&D intensity within the service industry (in the manufacturing sector, the role of the intrinsic component is greatly reduced). These results might appear at variance with those obtained by Mathieu and van Pottelsberghe (2008), who – studying the evolution of the R&D intensity gap in the manufacturing sector using sectoral data from OECD ANBERD and STAN – find that a large share of cross-sector, country and time variation in business R&D intensity can be explained by variation across sectors,[9] hence pointing to the role of industrial specialization as one of the major determinants of aggregate R&D intensity (casting doubts on the usefulness of an across-the-board target). It should be stressed that Mathieu and van Pottelsberghe look at industries within the manufacturing sector, hence excluding services: this is crucial to delivering their results since one of the drivers of the US–EU R&D intensity gap is the different R&D intensity in the service industry[10] (especially in trade service industries).

Moncada-Paternò-Castello *et al.* (2010), using firm-level data obtained from the 2008 *Industrial Scoreboard*,[11] look at the structural vs. intrinsic component of the EU–US (and Japan) R&D intensity gap. From their analysis, it is clear that the structural component is absolutely dominant since it accounts for 4/5 of the overall gap[12] (in fact, the intrinsic effect works in reducing the EU gap relative to the US). The role of the structural component is also stressed by the 'Knowledge for Growth Expert Group'.

A slightly different story is found in Uppenberg (2009) where the focus is on the three industries that show the highest R&D intensity (chemicals and pharmaceuticals, transport equipment, ICT and other non-transport equipment). The author finds evidence pointing to within-sector lower R&D intensity in the EU relative to US and Japan; at the same time, he documents that the EU is more specialized in technology-intensive manufacturing.[13]

In the context of the R&D intensity gap, there have been some attempts to look more in depth at the sources of the structural gap, by considering firm demographics. This is related to the literature pointing to large EU–US differences in post-entry performance, and hence to the role of factors hindering firms' growth[14] (see Bartelsman *et al.*, 2003, 2004). If EU firms are not able to grow as fast as their US counterparts, and this is true even in high-growth, high-tech sectors, the effect in the context of the R&D intensity decomposition[15] is that the structural component dominates, simply because the economies of the EU are not able to expand in the high R&D intensive sectors.[16] The empirical counterpart of this literature in the context of the R&D intensity gap is the analysis of the gap across different age groups. Veugelers and Cincera (2010), using data from the 2008 *Industrial Scoreboard* dataset, find that: (1) a large fraction of leading innovators (34 per cent) are young (i.e. born after 1975); (2) young leading innovators (*yollies*) are especially R&D intensive; (3) *yollies* tend to be especially present in high-tech sectors (especially internet, biotechnology and software); (4) about 55 per cent of the EU–US R&D intensity differential can be accounted for by the lower R&D intensity of EU *yollies* as compared to US *yollies*; and (5) 92 per cent of this intensity differential can be explained by the different sectoral composition (i.e. EU *yollies* are not in high R&D intensive sectors), and in particular by the size of the biotechnology, pharmaceutical, semiconductors and internet sectors.

The policy implications arising from these results are immediate: in order to close the gap, policies must be directed towards stimulating the growth of young firms in highly R&D intensive sectors (see also Veugelers, 2009; Schneider and Veugelers, 2008).

Our work extends the work by Moncada-Paternò-Castello *et al.* (2010) by looking at a longer period (2002–2010). This is very important because a time dimension is needed if one wants to look at the evolution of the gap and of its components.[17] Besides, drawing conclusions from a single snapshot, while tempting, may be risky, if anything because of the simple reason that the EU and the US may not be perfectly aligned in terms of cycles (which affect both R&D investment and sales, but not necessarily in the same way).

Our study proceeds as follows. In Section 2, we discuss our approach and present the data. In Section 3, we look at the aggregate picture emerging from our exercise. Section 4 concludes our work.

2 Data

In this paper, we use data from the *EU Industrial R&D Scoreboard* database[18] (henceforth the *Scoreboard*) in which R&D investment data and economic and financial data from the last four financial years are presented for the 1,000 largest EU and 1,000 largest non-EU R&D investors.[19] This database covers about 80 per cent of all company R&D investments worldwide. All data within the *Scoreboard* are presented in EUR, applying the latest available exchange rate for the whole period (i.e. all data in year *T Scoreboard* use the exchange rate measured in year *T-1*, even if the observations refer to *T-2*, *T-3*, *T-4*). As a result, data from different *Scoreboards* are not directly comparable (in fact, data for the same company in the same reference year often differ across *Scoreboards*).[20] Therefore, to make them comparable, we first transform all data into nominal values applying the exchange rate from the reference year and then we apply the correct exchange rate to each observation in the reference year.[21] We then create a panel by joining all available *Scoreboards*.[22]

The *Scoreboard* database only collects information on top R&D investors and hence omits small companies, which tends to bias the sample in favour of large firms. By applying our approach, which fills in missing firm-year observations for companies below the R&D investment threshold with information from subsequent *Scoreboards*, we actually decrease this bias.

Another concern with the *Scoreboard* is that it applies different thresholds to EU and non-EU companies. For instance, the 1,000th EU company invested €4.5 million in R&D in 2010, while the 1,000th non-EU company invested €32.7 million in the same year.[23] In order to make the EU and non-EU samples more comparable, we choose to keep firms with at least 50 employees (so that the conditioning variable is not the same as R&D, the subject of our analysis).

The resulting panel consists of 3,034 unique companies from 32 countries, covering the period 2002–2010. In total, it comprises 19,207 firm-year observations. This panel is thus unbalanced (on average, each company stays in our sample for about six years). In a typical year, there are over 2,000 companies in the data and this amount varies between 1,651 (in 2002) and 2,466 (in 2006). Time distribution of our data is provided in Table 5.1.

Summary statistics of all firm-level observations used in the analysis are provided in Table 5.2.

As for sectors, we adopt an aggregation that is in line with the OECD methodology,[24] hence grouping the original ICB sectors[25] according to their average R&D intensity (across regions and time). We generate the following macro-sectors:

Table 5.1 Number of companies by year

	N	%
2002	1,651	8.60
2003	1,854	9.65
2004	2,139	11.14
2005	2,444	12.72
2006	2,466	12.84
2007	2,450	12.76
2008	2,257	11.75
2009	2,077	10.81
2010	1,869	9.73
Total	19,207	

Source: own elaboration.

- *high R&D intensity* aggregation (in which the average R&D intensity is above 5 per cent): biotechnology, electronic office equipment, health care equipment and services, internet, leisure goods, pharmaceuticals, semiconductors, software, telecommunications equipment;
- *medium to high R&D intensity* aggregation (in which the R&D intensity is between 2 and 5 per cent): aerospace and defence, alternative energy, automobiles and parts, chemicals, commercial vehicles and trucks, computer hardware, computer services, electrical components and equipment, electronic equipment, general industrials, household goods, household goods and home construction, industrial machinery, support services;
- *medium to low R&D intensity* aggregation (where R&D intensity is between 1 and 2 per cent): fixed line telecommunications, food producers, media, oil equipment, services and distribution, other financials, personal goods, tobacco
- *low R&D intensity* aggregation (where R&D intensity is below 1 per cent): banks, beverages, construction and materials, electricity, food and drug retailers, forestry and paper, gas, water and multi-utilities, general retailers, industrial metals, industrial metals and mining, industrial transportation, life insurance, mining, mobile telecommunications, nonlife insurance, oil and gas producers, travel and leisure.

Table 5.2 Summary statistics

	N	mean	sd	min.	max.
R&D (mil. EUR)	19,207	177	565	0	7,610
Sales (mil. EUR)	19,207	5,573	15,936	0	329,760
R&D intensity (R&D/sales)	19,207	3	187	0	18,478
Profit (mil. EUR)	19,207	499	2,257	−91,960	59,356
Employment	18,067	20,558	50,131	50	1,600,000
Age	14,041	49	47	0	440

Source: own elaboration.

This sectoral aggregation, together with broad ICB categories, is described in Table 5.3.

In terms of regional aggregation, in Section 3 we focus on five world regions: EU, US, Japan, BRIC and Asian Tigers. A complete description is provided in Table 5.4.

It should be noted that the *Scoreboard* attributes each company's total R&D investment to the country in which the company has its registered headquarters and to one single sector, regardless of the actual location in which R&D are performed and of the fact that some of the performed R&D might refer to sectors that are different from the main one. We acknowledge that these limitations may affect our analysis since they may impact both the geographical and the sectorial allocation of R&D activities. At the same time, we point out that this issue is inborn to the *Scoreboard* data and that all the studies based on this dataset are affected by it.

3 R&D intensity gap decomposition on macroeconomic data: EU versus US, Japan, Asian Tigers and BRIC

In order to analyse the sources of the R&D intensity gap between main world regions, we decompose the aggregate gap between region A and region B into an intrinsic and a structural component:

$$RDI_t^A - RDI_t^B = \sum_i (RDI_{it}^A - RDI_{it}^B) w_{it}^{AB} + \sum_i (w_{it}^A - w_{it}^B) RDI_{it}^{AB} \qquad (1)$$

with

$$w_{it}^{AB} = \frac{w_{it}^A + w_{it}^B}{2}; RDI_{it}^{AB} = \frac{RDI_{it}^A + RDI_{it}^B}{2} \qquad (2)$$

Table 5.3 Sector division by ICB1 categories and R&D intensity

	N	%
Oil and gas	445	2.32
Basic materials	1,577	8.21
Industrials	4,929	25.66
Consumer goods	2,609	13.58
Health care	2,888	15.04
Consumer services	777	4.05
Telecommunications	249	1.30
Utilities	410	2.13
Financials	580	3.02
Technology	4,743	24.69
Low R&D intensive	2,531	13.18
Medium to low R&D intensive	2,312	12.04
Medium to high R&D intensive	6,960	36.24
High R&D intensive	7,404	38.55

Source: own elaboration.

Table 5.4 Regional division

Country region	N	%
Austria	302	3.01
Belgium	366	3.65
Czech Republic	33	0.33
Denmark	408	4.07
Finland	595	5.94
France	1,131	11.29
Germany	1,955	19.51
Greece	61	0.61
Hungary	24	0.24
Ireland	143	1.43
Italy	481	4.80
Latvia	4	0.04
Luxembourg	73	0.73
Malta	10	0.10
Netherlands	510	5.09
Poland	44	0.44
Portugal	52	0.52
Slovakia	4	0.04
Slovenia	22	0.22
Spain	241	2.41
Sweden	744	7.43
UK	2,815	28.10
EU	**10,018**	**52.16**
USA	5,621	29.27
US	**5,621**	**29.27**
Japan	2,410	12.55
Japan	**2,410**	**12.55**
Brazil	64	17.49
China	135	36.89
India	142	38.80
Russia	25	6.83
BRIC	**366**	**1.91**
Hong Kong	57	7.20
Singapore	44	5.56
South Korea	229	28.91
Taiwan	462	58.33
Asian Tigers	**792**	**4.12**

Source: own elaboration.

where RDI_{it}^A is the R&D intensity (defined as R&D expenditures over sales) of sector i in year t in region A and w_{it}^A denotes the share of sector i sales within region A total sales in year t. The first term in equation (1) represents the intrinsic effect, while the second term is the structural one.

In practice, region A is always the EU[26] (which is our reference region), while region B is – one at a time – the US, Japan, BRIC countries and Asian Tigers, respectively.

The structural component measures the difference in R&D intensity due to industrial composition. In other words, it basically tells us whether EU firms are more or less specialized (compared with any of the other regions) in R&D intensive sectors. On the other hand, the intrinsic component captures the cross-regional differences in within-sector R&D intensity.

The results of these decompositions are shown in Figure 5.1. Since the EU is always the reference region, a negative value means that a given region is more R&D intensive than the EU, whereas a positive value would indicate a relatively higher R&D intensity for the EU.

Considering the EU–US comparison (see the upper left corner of Figure 5.1), our analysis shows that EU firms[27] are, on average, less R&D intensive than US firms[28] (by about 2 percentage points) and that this gap has increased over time (dotted line). The structural component (dashed line) shows a very similar pattern and matches almost perfectly the total gap also in terms of its nominal value. It follows that the intrinsic component is almost negligible: EU firms – within sectors – are on average as intensive as US firms. In fact, between 2002 and 2005, the contribution from the intrinsic component tended to lower the overall gap. However, since 2006, the positive contribution from the intrinsic component has decreased (with some evidence of a recent catching up). The broad picture that emerges from this simple decomposition is that there is an R&D intensity gap relative to the US, that such gap has not decreased and that it is fundamentally a structural gap: within sectors, EU companies do not exhibit

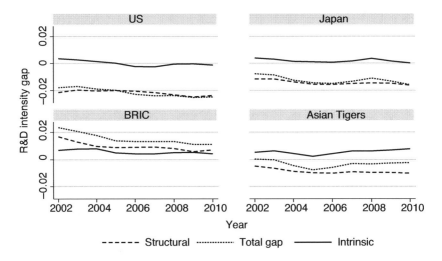

Figure 5.1 Decomposition of the R&D intensity gap into structural and intrinsic components (source: own elaboration).

Note
This figure presents the decomposition of the R&D intensity gap into structural and intrinsic components for four major world competitors of the EU. R&D intensity is defined as a ratio of sector R&D over sales. The reference region is always the EU. A negative value means that a region is more R&D intensive than the EU, while a positive value indicates a higher R&D intensity than the EU.

lower R&D intensity than their US competitors; however, the EU economy is more specialized in sectors characterized by a relatively low R&D intensity. Overall, the two effects result in a negative R&D intensity gap.

The comparison between the EU and Japan exhibits a similar pattern (see upper right corner of Figure 5.1). As a consequence of the different sectoral composition of the two regions, Japanese firms are more R&D intensive than EU firms.[29] While EU firms, on average, tend to be more R&D intensive within sectors, this effect is completely offset by the structural component, which is even larger than the total R&D intensity gap. A similar pattern can be found also when comparing EU firms with companies located in the Asian Tigers (lower right corner of Figure 5.1).

The comparison with the BRIC countries (lower left corner of Figure 5.1) is the only one that shows different results: overall, EU companies are more R&D intensive than BRIC companies and this gap is caused both by its within-sector higher R&D intensity and its sectoral composition.

Figure 5.2 describes the relationship between the R&D intensity gap and its structural/intrinsic components from a slightly different angle:[30] it depicts four graphs where the comparison between the EU and its four major world

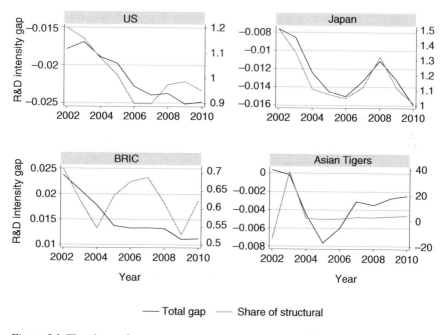

Figure 5.2 The share of structural component in the total R&D intensity gap (source: own elaboration).

Note

This figure presents the evolution of the total R&D intensity gap and the share of structural component in it for the four major world competitors of the EU. The reference region is always the EU. The right-hand-side axis represents the ratio of the structural component in the total gap (continuous line).

competitors concerns the evolution of the total R&D intensity gap and the share of the structural component in it. The two upper graphs – where we compare the EU to the US and Japan – exhibit almost identical patterns in which the structural component closely follows the evolution of the total gap. When the total gap becomes more negative (i.e. it increases in absolute value), the importance of the structural component decreases while, symmetrically, the one of the intrinsic component grows. This is likely to be due to cyclical phenomena that either increase R&D intensity by non-EU (i.e. US or Japanese) firms or reduce R&D intensity by EU firms in a way that is, on average, similar across sectors.[31] Once such short-run phenomena disappear, the structural effect becomes once again dominant.

For the BRIC region (lower left corner of Figure 5.2), the share of the structural component oscillates between 0.55 and 0.7, leaving 'room' for the intrinsic component (which is likely to respond, once again, to short-term variation in R&D intensity within sectors).[32]

Finally, the graph for the Asian Tigers (lower right corner of Figure 5.2) shows an overall rather negligible total R&D intensity gap. Nevertheless, values for the share of the structural component above 1 (with the exception of year 2002) suggest a strong and opposite role of the intrinsic component, which is also confirmed by our previous results.

Overall, our analysis shows that the total R&D intensity gap relative to any of the other four regions exhibits a decreasing trend up to the years 2005–2006. This means that, in the period 2002–2005, the gap between EU firms and firms based in the regions that, on average, exhibit a higher R&D intensity (US, Japan and Asian Tigers) has increased, while it has narrowed when considering firms located in regions that have a lower R&D intensity (i.e. BRICs). In both cases, these effects work to the detriment of the EU. After 2005–2006, there is some evidence that the position of the EU is improving relative to Japan and, especially, to the Asian Tigers, but it is worsening relative to the US and to the BRICs (especially after 2008).

Now we will look more closely at both the intrinsic and the structural components.

We start with the intrinsic component. In Figure 5.3, we plot the R&D intensity gap separately for each of the four macro-sectors described at the end of Section 2 (all countries are compared to the EU within each macro-sector). From the upper left graph, it is evident that there are almost no differences in R&D intensities among our five world regions within low R&D intensive sectors (those with R&D intensity below 1 per cent), as all four lines are very flat and close to the zero line (all of them are in negative values, which means that EU firms, on average, exhibit lower R&D intensity). The graph for the medium-to-low R&D intensive sectors (those with R&D intensity between 1 and 2 per cent), however, shows some diversity: firms in the BRIC region tend to be less R&D intensive than EU firms, while the opposite holds for Japanese firms; firms in Asian Tigers and in the US do not perform very differently from EU firms (the gap is close to zero but there is

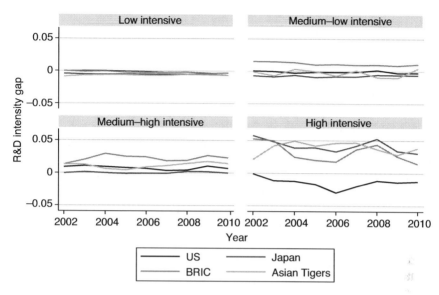

Figure 5.3 R&D intensity gap across regions and sectors (source: own elaboration).

Note
This figure presents the R&D intensity gap for four major world competitors of the EU and for four sectoral categories defined in the Data section. The reference region is always the EU. A negative value means that a region is more R&D intensive than the EU, while a positive value indicates a higher R&D intensity than the EU.

some variation for Asian Tigers). An interesting result comes from the bottom left graph about medium-to-high R&D intensive sectors (those with R&D intensity between 2 and 5 per cent): except when compared with Japanese firms (relative to which the difference is close to zero), EU firms tend to be more R&D intensive than firms belonging to the remaining three regions. Finally, the biggest differences are shown in the bottom right graph, which focuses on high R&D intensive sectors (those with R&D intensity above 5 per cent) and documents a very contrasting result for the EU: on the one hand, EU firms tend to be more R&D intensive than firms in Japan, Asian Tigers or the BRIC (by about 3–5 per cent), but on the other hand, EU firms show an average R&D intensity that is about 2 percentage points lower than that observed for US firms.

These results suggest that, although they may not be visible from the global economy perspective (Figure 5.1), there are some relevant cross-country, within-sector differences, implying that the intrinsic component has some relevance. This seems to be particularly evident when comparing the EU with the US and Japan: US companies are more R&D intensive than EU firms especially in high intensive sectors, whereas Japanese (and Asian Tigers) companies are more R&D intensive mainly in low and medium-to-low intensive sectors.

In the last part of this sub-section, we document the evolution of the differences in sectoral weights (across the five regions) for each macro-sector (Figure 5.4). This exercise is meant to clarify the evolution of the sectoral composition and, hence, the sources of the structural component. This simple analysis tells us that EU firms are more specialized in low and medium-to-low R&D intensive sectors, when compared with firms belonging to the three regions with higher overall R&D intensity (US, Japan and Asian Tigers). At the same time, EU firms are clearly at a disadvantage in the medium-to-high and high R&D intensive sectors when compared with US and Japanese firms (and also with Asian Tigers companies in the medium-to-high R&D intensive sectors). In other words, firms based in regions such as the US, Japan or Asian Tigers are more specialized in sectors that require higher R&D intensity which, in sum, tends to raise the R&D intensity gap with the EU. On the other hand, companies located in the BRIC countries – when compared with EU firms – tend to be more specialized in low R&D intensive sectors and less in medium-to-high and high R&D intensive sectors, which makes BRIC countries less R&D intensive than the EU.

When we put the pictures emerging from Figures 5.3 and 5.4 together, we notice that the position of the EU relative to the US is of special interest. On the one hand, the EU is not able to shift from low to high R&D intensive sectors at a satisfying rate (relative to the US, the positive gap in the low and the negative

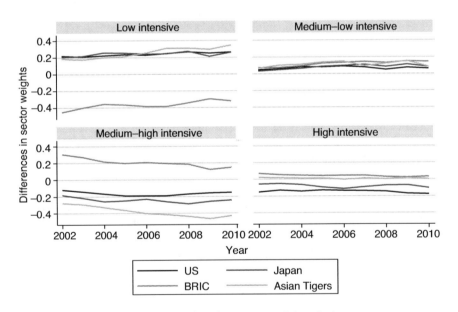

Figure 5.4 Sector weights across regions (source: own elaboration).

Note
This figure presents the difference in macro-sector weights for the four sectoral categories defined in the Data section and for four major world competitors of the EU. The reference region is always the EU. A negative value means that a sector in a region has greater weight in its economy than the same sector within the EU economy.

gap in high intensive sectors are both increasing). On the other hand, when we look within R&D intensive sectors, EU firms are less R&D intensive than their American counterparts. Overall, the first effect greatly dominates over the second (the structural component dominates over the intrinsic component), but the problem is that they both work to the detriment of the EU relative to the US.

4 Conclusions

In this study, using data from the *Industrial Scoreboard* from 2002 to 2010, we have looked at the R&D intensity gap between companies based in the EU and companies based in its major competitors. Our analysis reveals that EU firms are less R&D intensive than US, Japanese or Asian Tiger firms. This gap is, however, not caused by a within-sector lower intensity but rather by different sectoral compositions. In the comparisons with these three regions, the structural component plays a dominant role, leaving little room for the intrinsic components. This shows that, on average, EU companies are relatively more specialized in sectors with low or medium-to-low R&D intensity, whereas US, Japanese and Asian Tigers firms are more oriented towards high R&D intensive sectors. In fact, when we look within sectors, we find that sometimes EU firms are even more R&D intensive than firms belonging to these three regions.

When compared with the BRIC region, EU firms tend to be more R&D intensive. However, in this case, it is a consequence of higher R&D intensive activities within sectors as well as of a sectoral composition in favour of highly R&D intensive industries.

The fact that the lower R&D intensity of EU firms relative to that of firms based in the US, Japan and Asian Tigers is mostly attributable to the specialization patterns has important implications for the design of appropriate policies.

Policies directed at stimulating R&D intensity – such as an R&D tax credit – are not likely to be able to induce the reallocation patterns that are necessary to close the R&D intensity gap with the US, Japan and the Asian Tigers, unless they are accompanied by other horizontal and, possibly, vertical policies.

First, the EU should eliminate barriers to entry, exit and firm growth, especially in highly innovative sectors. In particular, the EU should try to reduce fragmentation of the single market – particularly for digital products – and improve access to external finance for innovative European firms. There is ample evidence that, in the EU, the venture capital market is not fully developed and that firms, especially SMEs, are facing credit constraints that have become tighter with the crisis. Designing correct measures to ensure that firms can invest in R&D and innovative activities is among the top policy priorities and we are reassured by the fact that the EU Commission – with the Horizon 2020 programme – is moving in the right direction.

Many researchers have also pointed to the role of labour market rigidities: inefficient regulation (especially with respect to employment protection legislation) may reduce the willingness of firms to invest and hire workers, especially if such investment is in new and risky technologies, which is often the case for firms operating in high-tech sectors. This effect ultimately reduces the number, size and growth potential of EU firms in the most innovative sectors.

These two interpretations, which stress the need for policies directed at correcting market or institutional failures, are often contrasted to another view according to which innovation is really a systemic process, which implies that more attention should be given to all the factors that stimulate and support the creation and growth of innovative companies (and hence to their share in production and value added), such as knowledge transfer (between research centres, universities and firms), public–private partnership directed at stimulating innovation and public procurement (the experience of the US Federal Government is often mentioned). Others claim that Europe needs a more (and better) targeted industrial policy, addressing the innovation potential of those sectors that, in non-EU countries (mainly the US), have proven to be driving growth, such as the ICT and the biotech sectors.

Our opinion is that these approaches should be seen as complementary and not as alternative, and that the European Commission, together with Member States and sub-national authorities, should implement the correct mix of policies, which will largely depend upon existing endowments and specialization patterns. In particular, we think that future research should try to understand and compare the efficiency and effectiveness of the various policies, and policy mixes, that are available at the European Union, Member State and sub-national government level.

Disclaimer

The views expressed in this paper are purely those of the authors and may not in any circumstances be regarded as stating an official position of the European Commission.

Notes

1 R&D activity not only directly affects the ability of a given organization (or country) to innovate and henceforth improve its productivity. It also increases its 'absorptive capacity' (see Cohen and Levinthal, 1989), creating an environment that is more receptive to innovation stimuli coming from outside. Disentangling the direct effect from the latter is far from easy, but there is empirical evidence that the indirect effect is sizeable (see Griffith *et al.*, 2003; additional evidence in favour of the absorptive capacity role of R&D emerges from studies that document the positive correlation between foreign R&D and productivity; see Coe and Helpman, 1995).

2 As argued by Hall *et al.* (2010), from a firm's perspective, spillovers can come from R&D activity performed (1) by other firms in the same sector; (2) by firms in other sectors; (3) by public research laboratories and universities in the same country; and (4) by firms' laboratories and government policies of other countries. From the domestic country perspective, the first three sources are components of the social or aggregate return to R&D, while only the fourth is a spillover. So 'whether we label something a spillover depends on whether it is being created by the unit under the investigation or by an entity external to that unit'. This also means that estimates of spillover effects tend to be larger when evaluated at the firm level, relative to the sector or country level.

3 Guellec and van Pottelsberghe (2001), using country-level data, estimate a long-run elasticity of TFP to business R&D of about 0.13, which is interpreted as a potential estimate of the social return to R&D. They also notice that the social return to R&D has been increasing with time, confirming the hypothesis that R&D is becoming an increasingly important activity in the knowledge-based economy. Additional results show that higher values for R&D intensity positively affect the elasticity of TFP to R&D, pointing to some form of increasing return to R&D investment, while the share of government spending in defence-related R&D activities has a negative impact on the elasticity of TFP to R&D stock.

4 For a study on the productivity gap using micro data, see Ortega-Argilés *et al.* (2011), where the effectiveness of R&D in the EU relative to the US is evaluated. For a survey on the EU–US R&D gap, see Ortega-Argilés (2012). For studies that look at the productivity gap at a macro level, using a sectoral decomposition, see O'Mahony and van Ark (2003) and Denis *et al.* (2004). See also Bassanini *et al.* (2000).

5 The Lisbon Agenda sets a target of about 3 per cent for the R&D intensity ratio for the year 2010, two-thirds of which are to be funded by the business sector and the rest by governments. This target is confirmed (for the whole EU) in the Europe 2020 strategy.

6 Using R&D intensity as a target, as opposed to selecting a given nominal value, has two main advantages: it does not depend on inflation (as long as the same price index can be used for GDP and R&D) and it makes cross-country-sector comparability possible. To take into account the large cross-country (i.e. Member States) variation in observed R&D intensities, the overall 3 per cent target is complemented with country-specific targets (compatible with the 3 per cent value for the whole EU; see European Commission (2011). Still, the possibility of reaching these (country-specific and overall) targets depends on the ability to transfer employment and value added from low R&D intensive sectors to high R&D intensive sectors in each Member State (see van Pottelsberghe, 2008).

7 In general, the relevance of the structural effects tends to rise as the number of sectors used for the decomposition increases. This is to be expected given that within-sector differences in R&D intensity are likely to be reduced when we move to a more disaggregated sectoral composition. Moreover, the result of the decomposition is very sensitive to the measurement of R&D in the service industry, which, in itself, is a very complex task due to lack of homogeneity across countries.

8 However, even horizontal policies may have a differential impact across sectors since they affect marginal costs and benefits from R&D activity differently.

9 For public sector R&D intensity, the bulk of the variation can be explained by country-specific factors.

10 This is also due to a different approach to sectoral classification of R&D activities across the Atlantic. In the EU, most countries use a product-based classification, so that most R&D expenditures are attributed to the manufacturing sector producing the good for which the R&D activity was performed, whereas in the US the 'principal activity of the firm' approach is typically used. In fact, the National Science Foundation (NSF) has estimated that roughly 93 per cent of the R&D expenditures recorded under the US trade services industry should be allocated to the manufacturing industry. Following this advice and using the NSF estimates, Duchene *et al.* (2010) re-evaluate the EU–US gap and get a more balanced view: the gap is both in manufacturing and services, and the gap in services is lower while the one in manufacturing is higher.

11 Here are the main differences between *Scoreboard* and BERD data: *Scoreboard* data record R&D investment by a given company, irrespective of the location where the R&D is performed, hence capturing global corporate funding. BERD data refer to R&D activities within a given territory. BERD includes non-company sources of R&D while *Scoreboard* does not (so that the portion of R&D financed by public

funding is excluded). *Scoreboard* collects data from audited financial accounts and reports, while BERD uses a stratified sample methodology. Moreover, *Scoreboard* provides information on sales, while BERD provides information on value added, so that R&D intensity can be defined in terms of R&D/sales for the former and R&D/value added for the latter. Finally, BERD uses NACE classification, while *Scoreboard* uses ICB classification.

12 This result applies to the case in which the authors consider the full set of EU companies. The relevance of the structural gap is even higher when a reduced set of EU companies is used.

13 The picture changes when, instead of nominal value added, the computations are made in real value added. Within the ICT and other non-transport equipment industry, US and Japan are particularly specialized in ICT equipment production where (compared with other sectors) prices tend to decline much faster, increasing the contribution of the ICT-producing sector to the economy.

14 Such factors are identified in the cost of funds, administrative costs, lack of fully integrated market, lack of appropriate skills and presence of labour and product market regulation, all of which are believed to generate a comparative disadvantage for the EU relative to the US.

15 On the role of the R&D gap in the ICT sector, see Lindmark *et al.* (2010).

16 If firms within these sectors grew, the sectors would grow as well and this would likely result in higher value added shares for such R&D intensive sectors.

17 For a regression-based approach to a question similar to ours, see Ortega-Argilés and Brandsma (2010), where they use the four waves of the 2006 *Industrial Scoreboard* to test whether there is evidence of cross-sector and cross-country variation in R&D intensity.

18 http://iri.jrc.ec.europa.eu/research/scoreboard_2010.htm.

19 The first issue, the 2004 *Scoreboard* (covering the period 2000–2003), comprises only the top 500 EU and 500 non-EU R&D investors, while *Scoreboards* between 2005 and 2007 include the top 700+700 R&D investors. Since 2008, *Scoreboards* include the top 1,000 EU and 1,000 non-EU R&D investors.

20 The *T Scoreboard* covers a period of four years, from *T-4* to *T-1*. Year *T-1* is called the base year, while *T-2*, *T-3* and *T-4* are reference years. The *Scoreboard* applies the *T-1* exchange rate to transform data from other currencies to EUR for both the base year and the three reference years.

21 Note that no further data transformation (deflation or PPP measures) was applied. The reason for this is twofold. First, by construction, the *Scoreboard* allocates all the R&D activities performed by a given firm to the place (and hence the country) in which the firm is based (irrespective of the actual place in which these R&D activities are performed). This implies that R&D activities of firms that have R&D centres around the world are allocated to the place in which these companies are based. By applying deflations or PPP measures, we would create a measurement error that would distort our results. Second, we want our results to be directly comparable with other European Commission studies, which are typically based only on nominal values.

22 If, for a given year, a base-year observation is available, we drop the reference-year observations. If the base-year observation is missing and if more than one reference-year observation is available, we employ the one from the more recent *Scoreboard*. To illustrate this, consider the following example: a company from the 2007 *Scoreboard* is included with a base year 2006 and three additional reference years, 2003–2004–2005, thus covering the last four financial years. Given that this company also belongs to the top 1,000 R&D investors in 2007, this company can also be found in the 2008 *Scoreboard*; it is there with a base year 2007 and reference years 2004–2005–2006. Let's assume that the same company can also be found in the 2009 and 2010 *Scoreboards*. We then have four firm-year observations (one base and three references) pointing to the same year, 2006. In this case, for the year 2006, we drop

all three reference-year observations and we only keep the base-year observation. At the same time, this company is not among the top R&D investors in any of the 2004, 2005 or 2006 *Scoreboards*. Therefore, we use its reference years coming from the 2007 *Scoreboard* to fill in missing firm-year observations for the years 2003–2004–2005. A general rule is that first we use all base-year observations and only if they are missing, we employ reference-year observations.

23 This is the result of both the data-gathering process and the actual distribution of firms performing R&D across countries. In particular, since the *Scoreboard* selects only the top 1,000 EU R&D performers and the top 1,000 non-EU R&D performers, and since both the number and size of non-EU R&D performers tend to be larger, the R&D expenditure for the 1,000th non-EU R&D performer turns out to be higher than the one of the 1,000th EU R&D performer.

24 See Hatzichronoglou (1997).

25 The Industry Classification Benchmark (ICB) is a system categorizing over 70,000 companies and 75,000 securities worldwide, enabling companies to be compared across four levels of classification and national boundaries. The ICB system is supported by the ICB Database, an extensive data source for global sector analysis, which is maintained by FTSE International Limited.

26 We also looked at the within-EU decomposition and found that firms from the newly added countries tend to have R&D intensity that is smaller than that observed for companies belonging to the EU15 countries. However, given the small relative size of such companies, the R&D intensity time profiles for the EU15 and the EU27 are basically identical. Hence, in the study we concentrate on the whole EU.

27 By this, we mean firms that are based in the EU.

28 By this, we mean firms that are based in the US.

29 The EU R&D intensity gap relative to Japan is lower than the one relative to the US.

30 The share of the intrinsic component is omitted here since it would just be a mirror image of the share of the structural component.

31 Perhaps reflecting the impact of some public policy directed at stimulating R&D in the US or Japan or simply the fact that economic cycles are not aligned across countries.

32 It is also possible that this variation depends upon the sample composition (i.e. the small number of firms belonging to the BRIC countries).

References

Bartelsman, E.J., Haltiwanger, J. and Scarpetta, S. (2004), 'Microeconomic evidence of creative destruction in industrial and developing countries', *IZA Discussion Paper*, n. 1374.

Bartelsman, E.J., Scarpetta, S. and Schivardi, F. (2003), 'Comparative analysis of firm demographics and survival: micro-level evidence for the OECD countries', *OECD Economics Department Working Papers*, n. 348, OECD Publishing.

Bassanini, A., Scarpetta, S. and Visco, I. (2000), 'Knowledge, technology and economic growth: recent evidence from OECD countries', *NBB Working Papers*, n. 6, May.

Coe, D. and Helpman, E. (1995), 'International R&D spillovers', *European Economic Review*, 39:5, pp. 859–887.

Cohen, W.M. and Levinthal, S. (1989), 'Innovation and learning: the two faces of R&D', *The Economic Journal*, 99, pp. 569–596.

Denis, C., McMorrow, K. and Rogers, W. (2004), 'An analysis of the EU and US productivity developments a total economy and industry perspective', *European Economy Economic Papers*, n. 208.

Duchene, V., Lykogianni, E. and Verbeek, A. (2010), 'R&D in service industries and the EU-US R&D investment gap', *Science and Public Policy*, 37:6, July.

Erken, H. and van Es, F. (2007), 'Disentangling the R&D shortfall of the EU vis-à-vis the US', *Jena Economic Research Papers*, n. 2007, 107.

European Commission (2011), *Innovation Union Competitiveness Report*, 2011 edition, Luxembourg.

Griffith, R., Redding, S. and Van Reenen, J. (2003), 'R&D and absorptive capacity: theory and empirical evidence', *Scandinavian Journal of Economics*, 105:1, pp. 99–118.

Guellec, D. and van Pottelsberghe, B. (2001), 'R&D and productivity growth: panel data analysis of 16 OECD countries', *OECD Economic Studies*, n. 33, 2001/II.

Hall, B.H., Mairesse, J. and Mohen, P. (2010), 'Measuring the returns to R&D', in Hall, B.H. and Rosenberg, N. eds. *Handbook of the Economics of Innovation*, vol. 2, pp. 1033–1082, Elsevier.

Hatzichronoglou, T. (1997), 'Revision of the high-technology sector and product classification', *OECD Science, Technology and Industry Working Papers*, 1997/1992, OECD Publishing.

Havik, K., McMorrow, K., Roger, W. and Turrini, A. (2008), 'The EU-US total factor productivity gap: an industry perspective', *European Economy Economic Papers* n. 339.

Lindmark, S., Turlea, G. and Ulbrich, M. (2010), 'Business R&D in the ICT sector: examining the European ICT R&D deficit', *Science and Public Policy*, 37:6, pp. 413–428.

Mathieu, A. and van Pottelsberghe, B. (2008), 'A note on the drivers of R&D intensity', *CEB Working Paper* n. 008/002.

Moncada-Paternò-Castello, P., Ciupagea, C., Smith, K., Tubke, A. and Tubbs, M. (2010), 'Does Europe perform too little corporate R&D? A comparison of EU and non-EU corporate R&D performance', *Research Policy*, 39, pp. 523–536.

O'Mahony, M. and van Ark, B. (2003), 'EU productivity and competitiveness: an industry perspective. Can Europe resume the catching-up process?', Luxembourg: Office for Official Publications of the European Communities.

Ortega-Argilés, R. (2012), 'The Transatlantic productivity gap: a survey of the main causes,' *Journal of Economic Surveys*, 26:3, pp. 395–419.

Ortega-Argilés, R. and Brandsma, A. (2010), 'EU-US differences in the size of R&D intensive firms: do they explain the overall R&R intensity gap?' *Science and Public Policy*, 37:6, pp. 429–441.

Ortega-Argilés, R., Piva, M. and Vivarelli, M. (2011), 'The Transatlantic productivity gap: is R&D the main culprit?', *IZA Discussion Paper* n. 5586, 2011.

O' Sullivan, M. (2007), 'The EU's R&D deficit and innovation policy', Expert Group on Knowledge for Growth.

Schneider, C. and Veugelers, R. (2008), 'On young innovative companies: why they matter and how (not) to policy support them', OR 0807, Department of Managerial Economics, Strategy and Innovation, Katholieke Universiteit Luven.

Uppenberg, K. (2009), 'Innovation and economic growth', *EIB Paper*, 14:1.

van Pottelsberghe, B. (2008), 'Europe's R&D: missing the wrong targets?', Bruegel Policy Brief, n. 03/2008.

Veugelers, R. (2009), 'A lifeline for Europe's young radical innovators', *Bruegel Policy Brief*, Issue 2009/01.

Veugelers, R. and Cincera, M. (2010), 'Young leading innovators and the EU's R&D intensity gap', *Bruegel Policy Contribution*, Issue 2010/09.

6 Good governance, firm performance and policy recommendations

Is the shareholder value counter-revolution obsolete?

Jackie Krafft and Jacques-Laurent Ravix

1 Introduction

Since the 1980s, the literature on corporate governance has developed in three directions: promotion at a theoretical level of a normative model of 'good governance' based on shareholder value principles; progressive elaboration of metrics and scores of this model of corporate governance at the empirical level; development of policy recommendations in line with the dominant theoretical and empirical results in the academic world. For a long time, these directions were closely related since dominant models (based on Principal-Agent reasoning) served as a reference to the elaboration of metrics and to the principles of good governance (shareholder value oriented) to be implemented at the policy level as well.

In a series of critical works on the US economy, Lazonick and Mazzucato (2013), Lazonick (2007), Lazonick and O'Sullivan (2002) and O'Sullivan (2000) explain the process of corporation financialization that has taken place over the last decades and the emergence of the shareholder value model of corporate governance that legitimizes such financialization. They show how the role of stock markets has been perverted towards the increasing use of stock buybacks, generating an explosion in executive pay. The current chapter is in line with these previous works. We mostly document here the academic work at the origins of the common belief that the model of corporate governance aimed at defending shareholders' interests and primacy and defined as 'good governance' should apply to all firms, independently of their age, size, activity and home country, and leading to policy recommendations promoting this model for efficiency reasons. This 'shareholder value counter-revolution', as we could label it in opposition to the concept of 'managerial revolution' previously coined by Alfred Chandler (1977), was grounded on several key academic contributions over the last 30 years, including Jensen and Meckling (1976), Fama (1980), Fama and Jensen (1983), Jensen (1986) and, more recently, Hart (1995), Shleifer and Vishny (1997), Holmstrom and Kaplan (2001), Hermalin and Weisbach (2003), Gompers *et al.* (2003), Klapper and Love (2004), Durnev and Kim (2005), Black *et al.* (2006) and Core *et al.* (2006).[1] We also stress that evolution in global consensual thinking has occurred recently, coinciding with the emergence of the financial crashes in the 2000s. New bodies of theoretical research have emerged and empirical evidence on the beneficial effects of the shareholder value model tends to be contested as soon as the institutional context, cross-country comparisons and the expected impact on long-term outcomes in terms of innovation are taken into consideration. As far as policy recommendations are concerned, the emergence of the crisis reveals a gap between how corporate governance in advanced economies is understood before this event and after. Before, corporate scandals multiplied because good governance was inappropriately adopted by firms, either because critical mass of adopting firms was not reached or because the attributes of good governance were not all covered. Afterwards, debates at the academic and societal levels started to develop more fundamental criticisms of the rationale of the adoption and implementation of corporate governance oriented towards maximization of shareholder value. Instead of adopting good governance for more efficiency in firms, the emphasis is now more on reframing corporate governance for viability reasons at the firm level.

The chapter is structured as follows.[2] In Section 2, we document the theoretical and empirical results, and political recommendations that led to identifying the shareholder value model as being in the best position to promote better efficiency at the firm level. In Section 3, we describe how, all over the financial crashes, theory, empirics and policy start considering a reframing of principles of good governance directed towards less efficiency and more viability, maybe making the shareholder value model obsolete. Section 4 concludes and discusses its obsolescence.

2   Promoting good governance for efficiency reasons

In this section, we document at a theoretical, empirical and policy level how good governance characterized by the adoption of the shareholder value model of corporate governance has been considered as the norm in (i) realigning the incentives of the manager in the interests of the shareholder, (ii) guaranteeing better security, high cash flow and low cost of capital, and (iii) using resources more efficiently and stimulating growth.

2.1   At the theoretical level

There is a major shift here from a 'normative' view of the separation ownership-control and its supposedly bad consequences on the system as a whole to a more 'predictive' approach trying to elaborate on the causal relations between agency problems, governance practices and corporate performance. At the origins, the issue of corporate governance is first related to firms' internal efficiency. The separation between property and control is considered as a normative mismatch, an inadequacy of the US capitalist system. The control over the firm is no longer based on property rights (Berle and Means, 1932) and this results in a new power given to the directors. The directors represent a new social class emerging from this 'managerial revolution' (Chandler, 1977). This situation is expected to generate major coordination failures and negative impact on performance of firms and the structure of industry and the only remedy to this anomaly is to go back to the genuine system in which the owners are restored in their legitimate rights. This reasoning is at the basis of the initial agency-based literature applied to corporate governance. Berle and Means (1932) advocate that the separation property-control in US corporations results in a conflict of interest between managers and shareholders that creates inefficiencies in large corporations. In the 1980s, most of the early contributions to agency theory (Jensen and Meckling, 1976; Fama, 1980; Fama and Jensen, 1983) consider that managers' private information creates managerial discretion and self-serving leading to agency problems and costs. These difficulties, they argue, can be reduced by the definition of an optimal contract between managers and shareholders which is able to restore efficiency in decision-making by facilitating the monitoring from shareholders, securing their right to a better reward and the full benefit of their investment, and thus improving corporate performance. Besides internal efficiencies considerations, the impact of corporate governance tends to be more and more related to market performance, while monitoring is also provided by the market for corporate control based on hostile takeovers. This corresponds to the emergence of the theory of shareholder value which codifies the relationship between shareholders and managers (Jensen, 1986).

The mid-1990s brought new theoretical explanations onto the scene, resulting in an explosion of empirical work (Shleifer and Vishny, 1997). New developments tended to exhibit a direct relation between agency problems, corporate performance and the implementation of good governance practices. Agency models demonstrated that corporate governance affects firm value and performance through two basic channels: the expected cash flow for investors and the cost of capital. First, agency problems make investors pessimistic since they believe that future cash flow will be diverted. Alternatively, good governance increases investors' trust and willingness to pay more while it also renders managers' diversion costly and expropriation unlikely. With good governance, 'more of the firm's profit would come back to (the investors) as interest or dividends as opposed to being expropriated by the entrepreneur who controls the firm' (La Porta *et al.*, 2002, p. 1147). If normally risk and expected return are negatively related since riskier stocks have to be compensated by a higher expected rate of return and involve higher costs in terms of monitoring, investors perceive well-governed firms as less risky and better monitored. Consequently, they tend to apply a lower expected rate of return, which leads to a higher firm valuation. As already shown by the first predictive model of positive agency theory (Jensen and Meckling, 1976), better governed firms may have more efficient operations, resulting in a higher expected future cash-flow stream.

Second, the cost of capital is negatively related with measures of protection of shareholder rights and positively related with general measures of the quality of legal institutions (La Porta *et al.*, 2002; Gompers *et al.*, 2003). In that perspective, good governance thus decreases the cost of capital since it reduces shareholders' monitoring and auditing costs (Drobetz *et al.*, 2004; Lombardo and Pagano, 2002; Errunza and Miller, 2000). Therefore, better corporate governance structure and practice leads to better corporate performance, lower agency cost and higher stock performance.

2.2 At the empirical level

In the early 1990s, a number of consulting firms attempted to translate the positive principles of agency theory in terms of operational indicators. Measures of the impact of good governance on the value of company shares started to flourish, including Shareholder Value from McKinsey, Total Return Share/Total Business Return from the Boston Consulting Group and Economic Value Added/ Market Value Added from Stern Stewart. Rankings for investors were then developed according to the way in which companies met these criteria and how the companies themselves introduced this information in their annual reports of business activity. These rankings, based originally on observations of the impact of the mode of corporate governance (using one attribute of corporate governance as a proxy) on the performance of markets for US companies (especially the evolution of stock values), tend to emerge as a standard that is widely spread internationally.

By the mid-1990s, the new theoretical assessments based on different quantifiable determinants marked the advent of multiple attributes corporate governance. Meanwhile, empirical work at that time continued to measure the impact of one single attribute of governance on company performance. The gap between theoretical and empirical work can be explained by a lack of access to comprehensive data on all aspects or attributes of corporate governance. It follows nevertheless that the results obtained in the different contributions often remained inconsistent, even contradictory. For example, Hermalin and Weisbach (2003) showed in a seminal paper that the predominance of outside members on boards of directors increases the stock market performance, whereas Bhagat *et al.* (2004) argued instead that firms using long-term relationships with investors (relational investors) are the ones with the best results.

The early 2000s were characterized by the emergence of more robust empirical work on the multi-attributes of governance that coincided with the development of databases exclusively dedicated to this issue (Gompers *et al.*, 2003; Core *et al.*, 2006). Several databases were developed: RiskMetrics/International Shareholder Services (RM/ISS), The Corporate Library (TCL) and Governance Metrics International (GMI). The predictive quality of the theory was then in a situation to be tested by the data produced. Analysing in more detail what went wrong with the governance of firms, especially at the time of the burst of the high-tech bubble at the end of the 1990s, became possible. For instance, in the case of Parmalat and Ahold, corporate governance deficiencies appeared not to have been causal in a strict sense. Rather, they tended to facilitate (or at least did not prevent) practices that resulted in poor performance. Enron and Worldcom failures point to issues regarding auditor and audit committee independence and deficiencies in accounting standards. The reassessment of companies that have turned out to be corporate scandals – as an illustration, in 2001, Enron was evaluated as doing better in terms of corporate governance than 42.1 per cent of other companies listed in the S&P financial index (source: issproxy.com) – becomes possible on the basis of the exploitation of large, international databases using multi-attributes measures of corporate governance.

2.3 At the policy level

Over the last three decades, the notion of corporate governance at the policy level has referred almost exclusively to 'shareholder value' – that is, the idea that the governance of a corporate firm must be organized under the control and in the interest of shareholders or investors. This shareholder value corporate governance is considered to be the 'best practice' to obtain good business results and performance and it must therefore be diffused and adopted as largely as possible in modern economies. The traditional 'best practice' definition of corporate governance as the way to organize relationships among members of the firm in order to satisfy shareholders and investors as residual claimants is a normative definition based on the assumption of market efficiency.

New policy principles were adopted first in Anglo-Saxon countries where they were intended to give back to shareholders the capacity of control over managers, for two main reasons: the need to be better rewarded for their investments and to get safer conditions if discretionary and sometimes adventurous managerial behaviour was displayed. In the 1990s, corporate governance became a much-debated topic in the European Union. Reports were published in the UK, France and elsewhere. These reports were mainly intended to solve purely pragmatic problems (public image of firms and top managers, European single market, privatizations). Interestingly, these reports were soon followed by more formal principles designed and diffused by the OECD.

As Mairi Maclean explains, the capitalist systems and beliefs which UK and France adhere to were quite different: 'Yet, the origins of the corporate governance debate which has been sparked in the 1990s on both sides of the Channel are remarkably similar' (Maclean, 1999, p. 88). Reference reports were issued by private sector initiatives (Cadbury Report in the UK and Viénot Report in France) and the main recommendation was that necessary reforms needed to 'be achieved through the initiatives of directors and shareholders alone rather than by legislative change' (Maclean, 1999, p. 90). The Cadbury Report structured the debate in the UK, concentrating corporate attention on matters of regulation, responsibility and reporting to shareholders, board effectiveness, auditing and accountability. The Report outlined a 'code of best practice' for all listed companies registered in the UK, which covered directors' service contracts, interim reporting, audit objectivity and the role of institutional investors. The implementation was left to the Hampel Committee, established in November 1995. The Cadbury Report was soon followed by the Greenbury Report on the sensitive problem of directors' pay. All decisions and initiatives remained largely at the private level in the UK.

This was also the case in France as a working group organized by the French employers' associations (CNPF, AFEP)[3] was set up under the chairmanship of Marc Viénot (head of Société Générale), regarding the mission, composition and functioning of the board of directors. The Viénot Report advocated the removal of the cross-shareholdings and cross-directorships which were a distinctive feature of French corporations, together with nomination and remuneration committees, and the appointment of at least two independent non-executive directors.

As explained again by Maclean (1999, pp. 90–94), the underlying causes of these reporting activities and the need for a debate on corporate governance were the following. The first cause was the takeover mania stimulated in Europe by the need to prepare the 1992 Single Market. In France and the UK, firms overstretching themselves in order to acquire the critical mass soon suffered the burden of debt and external growth cost, at a time of rising interest rates. The second cause came from many business scandals arising in the 1980s and early 1990s in both countries. In the UK, Guinness insider trading, Maxwell's self trading, and the fraudulent collapse of the BCCI and Barings (Britain's oldest merchant bank covering up trader Nick Leeson's fraudulent dealings) were among the much publicized names involved. In France, big companies such as Carrefour, Société Générale and Pechiney were also involved in business scandals. By 1996, a quarter of the CEOs of France's top 40 listed companies were under investigation for fraud or corruption (Saint-Gobain, Bidermann, Bouygues, SNCF, Paribas, EDF, Auchan, GMF and Renault).

Privatization was the third cause underscoring the need for better corporate governance. Privatization programmes implemented in the 1980s and 1990s led to public outrage because of inflated pay awards, stock options and bonuses to senior executives. In the UK, the sale of public utilities in the Thatcher era – telecommunications, gas, water authorities, electricity, railways – with their monopoly markets gave a 'millionaire status' and a public image of 'fat cats' to the executives concerned (Maclean, 1999, p. 89). In France, after Mitterrand's long-lasting resistance, massive privatization was undertaken in the late 1990s to meet 'convergence criteria' for the monetary union of 1999. Still, the French habit of bundling public–private together remains a difficulty for corporate governance matters.

The pragmatic solutions proposed by the Cadbury and Viénot Reports to develop private rules of corporate governance and restore the image of top managers and big companies were later transformed into more formal principles in two documents issued by the OECD in 1999 and 2004. The universal aspect of corporate governance, inspired by agency theory, clearly marks the preamble of these documents, which specifies:

- 'The Principles focus on publicly traded companies. However,... they might also be a useful tool to improve corporate governance in non-traded companies, for example, privately held and state-owned enterprises' (OECD, 2004, p. 11).

- 'The Principles represent a common basis that OECD member countries consider essential for the development of good governance practices' (ibid.).
- 'Good corporate governance should provide proper incentives for the board and management to pursue objectives that are in the interests of the company and its shareholders and should facilitate effective monitoring' (ibid.).
- '(T)he Principles focus on governance problems that result from the separation of ownership and control' (ibid., p. 12).

The lesson to be learnt at the policy level is twofold. First, if a company has low performance, very often the reason lies with the fact that governance of this company is not in close conformity with the principles of good governance and that efforts still need to be made at the company level to attract investors. Second, the list of principles of good governance is incomplete due to the imperfect integration of the latest findings at the theoretical and empirical level and the regular introduction of a new series of provisions is part of the learning process derived from the reassessment of critical cases. In sum, companies have to do much better in terms of corporate governance, and policy recommendations in that matter have to adapt to this important challenge.

3 Reframing governance for viability reasons

The general crisis has led to some important changes in the issue of corporate governance and a more cautious definition and implementation of the principles of good governance. Here we document such changes at the theoretical, empirical and policy level, in view of going beyond the obsolescence of the shareholder value model.

3.1 At the theoretical level

At the theoretical level, the change can be illustrated first by a renewal of interest in an early literature that advanced the theory that a model of corporate governance – being shareholder value oriented or stakeholder value oriented – cannot be considered apart from the institutional context where it is implemented. One of the arguments structuring this literature is that different national systems of corporate enterprise co-exist. In many countries (Japan, Germany, France), a tradition of insider corporate governance is in place which cannot be reduced to the dilemma shareholders versus managers. Aoki (1984) developed the cooperative theory of the Japanese firm in which the different parties (or stakeholders) are all engaged in a bargaining game of corporate governance. The accumulation of specific financial and human resources that produce a quasi-rent is only possible if (i) shareholders and investors gain a sufficient return for their investments; (ii) employees evolve in revenues and careers; and (iii) managers coordinate the bargaining game. In the meantime, limits to this model are well known: bilateral relations between a bank and a company that supports the Japanese banking system appears to outperform significantly in a financial market where the evaluation is public and diffused to a large community of competing investors; this system is also less suitable in a situation of unpredictable demand and irregular technical progress.

At a more general level, other arguments started to emerge in the field of corporate governance. The stakeholder perspective is the main alternative to maximization of the shareholder value promoted by agency theory. The stakeholder perspective argues that there are numerous parties that contribute to a firm's economic performance and value. Consequently, all these stakeholders (not just the suppliers of capital) must be considered residual claimants (Blair, 1995; Donaldson and Preston, 1995; Kelly *et al.*, 1997; Zingales, 2000; Hansmann, 1996; Driver and Thompson, 2002).

Commentators also argued that there are some assumptions behind the normative, best practice-oriented, uniform model of shareholder primacy that may render the model inapplicable in most modern economies. Allen (2005) noted that, in the absence of complete markets, the beneficial properties of shareholder dominance did not necessarily apply and firms that pursue broader interests may outperform them. In a similar perspective, Aglietta and Rébérioux (2005) characterized the incongruence of shareholder dominance with economies where markets are liquid, investors short-termists and financial markets highly instable. Coffee (2005) complemented the argument by stressing that the structure of ownership, highly dispersed in the Anglo-American system and more concentrated in the continental European one, is important in explaining the performance implications of corporate governance. Finally, Hansmann (1996) showed that stock value maximization may not be in the best interests of shareholders themselves.

On the other hand, there are commentators that maintain that the institutional context has changed significantly over the last decade and that there is a convergence of corporate systems and regulation (Martynova and Renneboog, 2011; Bebchuk and Weisbach, 2010), possibly unravelling the existence of prominent differences. Up to the mid-1990s, most work on corporate governance was in the context of US firms. However the influential work of La Porta *et al.* (1997, 1998, 1999, 2000a, 2000b, 2002) has stimulated a large body of work on international comparisons (Levine, 2005; La Porta *et al.*, 2008). Much of this work focuses on differences between countries' legal systems and studies how these differences relate to differences in the way that economies and capital markets perform. It should be noted that convergence can mean different things – from incorporation of a system of corporate governance identified as 'superior' to a gradual diffusion of rules and practices that lead to a mix of co-existing systems. In this literature on convergence in corporate governance regimes, the first sense is basically the reference and the Anglo-American model of shareholder value model of corporate governance is the norm. The reason may lie in Hoelzl (2006)'s explanation that conventional models take no account of the institutional context because, in the long run, international competition will supposedly force firms to minimize costs. Cost minimization requires firms to adopt rules to raise external capital at the lowest cost. Competition is assumed to ensure that all corporate governance systems converge on the most efficient system. Countries that fail to adopt the 'right' system will inflict costs on their firms which will be less able to raise capital and may migrate from the country if inappropriate corporate rules are adopted. Because of this mechanical relationship between international competition and governance, supporters of agency theory and related models of corporate governance usually argue that the shareholder value model is based on best practice and is intrinsically superior to other models.

Finally, a series of arguments concern the inadequacy of the shareholder value model to adapt to the development of innovation and growth in a business history context. Influenced by agency theory, a large majority of economists have assumed that the market mechanism is the best way of allocating resources to achieve superior economic performance. This idea is however problematic in the case of corporate governance because 'powerful industrial corporations have remained central to the resource allocation process (Lazonick and O'Sullivan, 2002, p. 13). Indeed, US firms have used different ways of organizing internal resource allocation and these regimes of corporate governance have profoundly structured the recent history of US industry. The US national system of corporate governance displayed two radically different regimes of internal resource allocation during the twentieth century:

- a 'Retain & Reinvest' regime, based on retention of corporate earnings and reinvestment in corporate growth, mainly operated from the 1920s to the 1970s;
- a 'Downsize & Distribute' regime, i.e. downsizing of corporate labour forces and distribution of corporate earnings to shareholders, underlying the rise of shareholder value over the 1980s and the 1990s; top corporate managers were encouraged by institutional investors to align their own interests with financial interests rather than with the productive activities of the firm. This alignment with shareholder interests resulted in the explosion of top management pay and wage inequality. Large downsizing programmes and distribution of dividends were considered a panacea for the US industry, particularly in traditional sectors, even if the 'Retain & Reinvest' strategy remained temporarily at work in the new economy to keep highly educated professionals and finance innovation during company take-offs (e.g. Microsoft, Intel).

But the market also imposed a change in the financial rationale of the new economy which became involved in shareholder value. People in charge of resource allocation in large companies must 'cooperate' with stock markets in order to acquire new technologies and new competences through M&A by means of stock-for-stock exchanges that need to maintain a high level of stock value. After having benefited from the positive image of the new economy, the shareholder value model suffered from the explosion of the internet market, which called into question the capacity of the model to provide a stable development of a science-based economy.

These contributions originally drawn from the economics of innovation show that the model of shareholder value corresponding to the 'Downsize & Distribute' regime may have increased the ups and downs that innovative firms and innovative industries faced during and after the financial crash, leading to the conclusion that adopting this model is not neutral and even detrimental in some cases to the evolution of innovative firms and industries (Lazonick, 2007; Fransman, 2004; Krafft and Ravix, 2005, 2008a, 2008b). Alternatively, the 'Retain & Reinvest' model would spur innovation since it allows the accumulation of capital and capabilities and the generation of huge revenues. In turn, 'corporations tended to retain both the money that they earned and the people whom they employed, and they reinvested in physical capital and complementary human resources, providing the financial foundations and capabilities for corporate growth' (Lazonick and O'Sullivan, 2002). Indeed, this model corresponds to what companies such as Google and Apple are implementing today, suggesting they have adopted a different model of corporate governance leading to poor performances in the company scores referring to the shareholder value model as the norm.

3.2 At the empirical level

For a long time, the belief was 'better governance will result in higher firm value and more profitable firm performances' with the underlying idea that, if it was true there, it would be true everywhere and for any kind of investments, including innovative ones. In the last five years, however, the main question addressed at the empirical level has been: do we really have robust evidence for this? Contributions have concentrated on two major issues: the issue of international comparisons and the issue of innovation.

International comparisons

Until the mid-1990s, most of the work on corporate governance was in the context of US firms. A substantial body of research into US firms showed that cross-firm differences in governance have a substantial effect on firm value and performance (Gompers *et al.*, 2003; Bebchuk *et al.*, 2008; Core *et al.*, 2006), using the Investor Responsibility Research Center (IRRC), which publishes detailed listings of corporate governance criteria for individual US firms. However, how non-US firms perform when they adopt the US best practice is much less documented.

Klapper and Love (2004) used Credit Lyonnais Securities Asia (CLSA) firm-level data of 374 firms from 14 emerging countries. CLSA provided rankings in corporate governance, drawn from a questionnaire circulated among 495 companies. The sample was selected based on two criteria: firm size and investor interest. The CLSA corporate governance questionnaire covered seven broad categories in 25 countries (US and non-US). The questionnaire was then completed by Credit Lyonnais analysts, who added one point to each answer in favour of the best practice, and the percentage of positive responses to questions in each category was then reported. The authors reported that better corporate governance is highly correlated with better operating performance and higher market valuation. This gives some support to the fact that non-US firms increasingly adopt US firm practices in terms of corporate governance.

Black *et al.* (2006) constructed a Korean Corporate Governance Index (KCGI) for 515 Korean companies, based on a survey of corporate governance practices by the Korea Stock Exchange in 2001, sent out to all listed firms on the Korea Stock Market. The authors extracted 38 variables from the survey questions, which were classified into four sub-indices, and then combined sub-indices into the overall index-KCGI. They reported an increase in KCGI and predicted a 0.47 increase in Tobin's Q.

Drobetz *et al.* (2004) documented a positive relationship between governance practices and firm valuation for German public firms by constructing broad corporate governance rating related to the German Corporate Governance code. They sent out questionnaires to 253 German firms in different market segments and received answers from about 36 per cent of these firms. Results exhibit again a positive, significant relation.

Beiner *et al.* (2006) sent out a questionnaire based on the suggestions and recommendations of the Swiss Code of Best Practice to all Swiss firms quoted on the Swiss Stock Exchange in 2003. The index consisted of 38 governance attributes divided into five categories. They reported that an increase in the corporate governance index by 1 per cent causes an increase in market capitalization of roughly 8.52 per cent.

These contributions are all in line with an increasing convergence in systems of corporate governance. However, there are several limitations with these studies: most of the studies are based on one single year, or work under the assumption of constant historical ratings; a longer period of study is required to draw general results; a country case study raises the question of generalization with other countries; empirical studies should be based on data that explicitly considers several countries.

Krafft *et al.* (2014) aimed to provide an empirical contribution to the adoption of the US best practice by non-US firms (24 countries, more than 2500 firms), over the period 2003–2008, using the ISS Risk Metrics data – that is, the largest corporate governance data provider. The corporate governance variable was the CGQ, score metrics developed by the data provider based on 55 governance factors spanning eight attributes of corporate governance. They found a positive and significant impact of an increase in CGQ on stock market performance (positive relationship between CGQ and Stock Return, significant at 1 per cent [2SLS], positive relationship between CGQ and Dividend Yield, significant at 1 per cent [OLS]), on firm value (positive relationship between CGQ and Tobin's Q, significant at 1 per cent [OLS], significant at 5 per cent [FE]) and on operating performance (positive relationship between CGQ and ROA, significant at 1 per cent [2SLS], positive relationship between CGQ and NPM, significant at 10 per cent [OLS], significant at 5 per cent [FE]).

Table 6.1 synthesizes the recent results using international comparisons. Convergence seems at work then. However, immediate efforts should be made to refine the results obtained so far, which are necessarily highly contingent on the US-centric nature of the datasets used and do not account fully for non-US specificities. So up to this stage, the conclusion is yes, we have robust evidence that convergence operates, but sound international comparisons require data that is less US-centric in terms of the model of corporate governance to be applied.

The issue of innovation

Here the debate is as follows. On the one hand, because good governance involves better monitoring, greater transparency and public disclosure, an increase in investor trust, a decrease in manager discretion and rent expropriation, less risk, more efficient operations, etc., it should be beneficial to all investments, especially innovative ones. On the other hand, because good governance puts a large emphasis on the interests of the shareholders as a primary goal, it may be detrimental to innovative investments since (i) shareholders and investors are mostly interested in dividends and returns on investments and not R&D strategy, and (ii) it introduces a short-term perspective while innovation is long term.

Driver and Guedes (2012) contributed to the debate by testing the possibility of a perverse effect of 'good governance' on uncertain, long-term investments. The data came from the Manifest global proxy governance and voting service database, UK investor data. They considered 91 UK manufacturing and service (excluding financial) firms, with the highest averaged R&D expenditure in the period 2000–2005. They ended up with the following results. The governance variable in levels was significantly negative in all specifications (FE and GMM), suggesting that there is a long-run negative effect of governance on R&D, which is consistent with views that argue that the adoption of the best practice may have contradictory or perverse effects when innovation is taken into account.

Table 6.1 Evidence on the impact of good governance on company performance

	Multiple attributes	*Country*	*Firms*	*CG results performance*
Gompers *et al.* (2003)	Yes	US	1500	Positive
Bebchuk *et al.* (2008)	Yes	US	1500	Positive
Core *et al.* (2006)	Yes	US	1500	Positive
Klapper and Love (2004)	Yes	Emerging countries	374	Positive
Black *et al.* (2006)	Yes	Korea	515	Positive
Drobetz *et al.* (2004)	Yes	Germany	162	Positive
Beiner *et al.* (2006)	Yes	Switzerland	~100	Positive
Krafft *et al.* (2014)	Yes	Non-US	2500	Positive

Source: own elaboration.

Lhuillery (2011) used Vigéo Data regrouping 5,528 firms belonging to 110 large French listed business groups. He noted that there was no significant influence of good governance on R&D decisions (GMM and FE), resulting in possible doubts regarding the 'Anglo-Americanization' of some European firms.

Finally, there is also a focus on the impact of anti-takeover provisions on firm innovation. Here, the issue is knowing whether the *managerial myopia hypothesis* (Stein, 1988) or the *quiet life hypothesis* (Bertrand and Mullainathan, 2003) prevails. According to the first hypothesis, the threat of hostile acquisition can lead managers to avoid undertaking long-term, risky investments because these projects can lead to a wide divergence between market and intrinsic values. Takeover provisions may shield managers from concerns related to short-term performance and permit more long-term, value-maximizing investment strategy that encourages greater innovation. Alternatively, according to the second assumption, if the presence of takeover protection reduces the effectiveness of the external disciplinary market, then the manager may exploit the opportunity to avoid difficult and risky investments, especially if these reveal that managers are of lower quality.

Becker-Blease (2011) used the IRRC and merged the data with financial accounting standards and NBER patent database. The study covered the period 1984–1997 and the sample comprised 600 US firms. The results showed that higher levels of 23 takeover provisions were associated with innovation efforts (R&D expenditures, awarded patents, quality of patents, number of patents awarded per $ of R&D), suggesting that innovation is positively correlated with anti-takeover provisions. Indeed, some provisions appear more important than others in this positive correlation and firm-level provisions are significant in this positive correlation, whereas state-level provisions are not.

O'Connor and Rafferty (2012) also used IRRC together with Compustat and constructed a sample of 1,719 firms (1990–2005). With static models (OLS), they obtained a negative but non-robust relationship between corporate governance index and R&D activity. With dynamic models (GMM), there was no relation any more, or only a slightly positive one.

Krafft *et al.* (2008) used Risk Metrics/International Shareholder Services, with 2500 firms from 25 industries in 24 countries (non-US), over the period October 2003 to December 2008. They showed that good governance principles have a stronger impact on stock market performance in innovative industries compared with more traditional ones. Also, variations of CGQ are much more important in innovative industries than in more traditional ones, suggesting that adoption of the best practice amplifies the ups and downs of industrial development and innovative industries in particular. (See Table 6.2 for a summary of the findings in this section.)

What emerges from the empirical work is that corporate governance is not neutral to innovation, suggesting that short-term oriented models of corporate governance such as the shareholder value model are probably interacting with the long-term perspective of innovation, leading to potential mismatch.

Table 6.2 Evidence on the impact of good governance on innovation

	Multiple attributes	Takeover defences	Country	Firms	CG results on innovation
Driver and Guedes (2012)	X		UK	91	Negative
Lhuillery (2011)	X		F	110	Not significant
Becker-Blease (2011)		X	US	600	Positive
O'Connor and Rafferty (2012)		X	US	1719	No relation: slightly positive with GMM, negative but not robust with OLS
Krafft et al. (2008)	X		Non-US	2500	Positive, potentially amplifying ups and downs

Source: own elaboration.

3.3 At the policy level

Today, most commentators consider that the recent crisis that began in 2008 with the subprimes is the most serious crisis since the Great Depression. At the macroeconomic level, monetary policy in most advanced countries is far too expansive, with the result that interest rates fall together with risk premia. This generates a boom in asset prices, especially in the housing sector where lending expands rapidly. With lower interest rates, investors privilege the search for higher yields and tend to neglect the risk in their decision to invest since they think that the new financial instruments available intrinsically play the role of risk spreading throughout the whole financial system. This is now a well-known story, with highly detrimental consequences all around the globe.

In a recent series of publications (OECD, 2009; Kirkpatrick, 2009; OECD Steering Group on Corporate Governance, 2010), the OECD draws some key lessons from the financial crisis on the issue of corporate governance. These are important contributions, first, because much of the attention in both the academic and the business world has been centred so far on macroeconomic drivers of the economic downturn, whereas more microeconomic determinants have often been neglected, and, second, because corporate governance is considered a major cause that has led to the most important crisis since the Great Depression.

The OECD publications assess three different channels through which corporate governance had a negative effect: (i) the failures and weaknesses in corporate governance arrangements which did not serve their purpose of safeguarding against excessive risk-taking in a number of companies; (ii) the accounting and regulatory requirements that have also proved insufficient in some areas; and (iii) the remuneration systems that have not been closely related to the strategy and risk appetite of a company and its longer term interests. Based on disclosure of information and financial primacy, the shareholder model that inspired the OECD Principles of Corporate Governance[4] required, at a practical level, companies to change the composition of their boards of directors and audit committees to achieve a super majority of external members in order to favour internal controls related to financial reporting. In the meantime, risk management remained largely neglected. Companies also systematically tracked charter and bylaw provisions as well as anti-takeover provisions and increasingly linked executive and director pay to stock market performance. According to Kirkpatrick (2009, p. 12), this generated a 'general concern about incentive systems that are in operation in non-financial firms and whether they lead to excessive short term management actions and to "rewards for failure"'.

What emerges as a novel element is that commentators also tend to find microeconomic causes for the general crisis, essentially related to corporate governance. On the issue of risk, the OECD principles in 2004 state that 'the board should fulfil certain key functions including reviewing and guiding corporate strategy, major plans of action, risk policy' (VI.D.7); while on the issue of remuneration, the recommendation is to align 'key executive and board remuneration with the longer term interests of the company and its shareholders' (VI.D.4).

However, in practice, principles of good governance reward high levels of risk-taking and the incentive systems promoted by good governance increases the failures of risk management. Kirkpatrick (2009) argues that this occurs basically for two reasons: first, because most of the time information is not necessarily available to the board and, second, because the board's lack of banking and financial experience often prevents appropriate treatment of the information when available. Paradoxically, the deficiency of a low experience in banking and finance at board level is especially predominant in the banking system where:

> Bear Sterns had been taken over by JPMorgan with the support of the Federal Reserve Bank of New York and financial institutions in both the US (e.g. Citibank, Merrill Lynch) and in Europe (UBS, Credit Suisse, RBS, HBOS, Barclays, Fortis, Société Générale) were continuing to raise a significant volume of additional capital to finance, *inter alia*, major realized losses on assets, diluting in a number of cases existing shareholders.
>
> (Ibid., p. 4)

4 Conclusion

This chapter intended to review the major analytical and empirical reasons for the dominance of the shareholder value model and the implications in terms of policy of what good governance should be. It also discussed the potential demise of this model due to new results in theory and empirics developed in a context of financial crashes. The managerial revolution à la Chandler has indeed been replaced by the shareholder value counter-revolution, but should the shareholder value counter-revolution be considered obsolete? We can summarize our views as follows.

In the early 2000s, with the explosion of the high-tech bubble, the first trend was clearly oriented towards the adoption of good governance for efficiency reasons. The crisis only affected some sectors and required the introduction of new provisions to the incomplete list of principles of good governance. On the contrary, at the height of the subprime crisis in the late 2000s, good governance finally appeared as one cause of the emergence of the economic and financial downturn, leading to discussions on its implementation.

Throughout the 2000s, these criticisms did not, however, have a decisive impact on the model of corporate governance to be implemented or on the way this model was adopted. The belief was rather that principles of good governance were not sufficiently detailed and complete, and that the sectoral crisis was more predominantly related to the explosion of a speculative bubble. The subprime crisis seems to suggest that this belief needs to be changed significantly, first, because in the concrete world information is never complete and perfect, and agents have intrinsic difficulties in using efficiently the information, and second, because shareholder primacy involves short-termism in decision-making.

In this post-crisis context, the primary lesson to be learnt is thus that firms, investors and policymakers should be aware that scores and measures of corporate governance tend very often to be short-term oriented and will never be complete, with the risk of leading to over- or under-estimates of the actual situation of companies in governance. In terms of policy recommendations, this suggests that corporate governance principles should be more oriented towards preserving a higher stability of firm performance than towards higher performance in itself. In that perspective, the development of metrics of corporate governance is useful, but should be perceived as volatile indicators on what firms really do in terms of corporate governance, also potentially involving cumulative performance volatility concerns at the stock market level.

Notes

1 The counter-revolutionary grounding of shareholder value as a good governance practice can be illustrated by the following quotations: 'The problem is how to motivate managers to disgorge the cash rather than investing it at below cost or wasting it on organization inefficiencies' (Jensen, 1986, p. 323). 'We want to know how investors get the managers to give them back their money' (Shleifer and Vishny, 1997, p. 738).
2 This is based on previous work: Krafft *et al.* (2014, 2011, 2008), Dietrich *et al.* (2008), Krafft and Ravix (2005, 2008a, 2008b).
3 CNPF: Conseil National du Patronat Français; AFEP: Association Française des Entreprises Privées.
4 Shareholder value is clearly promoted in both OECD Principles of Governance (1999, 2004). The 2004 version is only more explicit in the need to maintain an equitable treatment of shareholders and also introduces the role of stakeholders in corporate governance.

References

Aglietta, M. and Rebérioux, A. (2005). *Corporate Governance Adrift: a Critique of Shareholder Value*. Cheltenham: Edward Elgar.

Allen, F. (2005). Corporate governance in emerging economies. *Oxford Review of Economic Policy*, 21, 164–177.

Aoki, M. (1984). *The Cooperative Game Theory of the Firm*. Oxford: Oxford University Press.

Bebchuk, L., Cohen, A. and Ferrell, A. (2008). What matters in corporate governance? *Review of Financial Studies*, 22, 783–827.

Bebchuk, L. and Weisbach, M. (2010). The state of corporate governance research. *Review of Financial Studies*, 23(3), 939–961.

Becker-Blease, J. R. (2011). Governance and innovation. *Journal of Corporate Finance*, 17(4), 947–958.

Beiner, S., Drobetz, W., Schmid, F. and Zimmermann, H. (2006). An integrated framework of corporate governance and firm valuation-evidence from Switzerland. *European Financial Management*, 12, 249–283.

Berle, A. and Means, G. (1932). *The Modern Corporation and Private Property*. London: MacMillan.

Bertrand, M. and Mullainathan, S. (2003). Enjoying the quiet life? Corporate governance and managerial preferences. *Journal of Political Economy*, 111(5), 1043–1075.

Bhagat, S., Black, B. and Blair, M. (2004). Relational investing and firm performance. *Journal of Financial Research*, 27(1), 1–30.

Black, B., Jang, H. and Kim, W. (2006). Does corporate governance predict firms' market values? Evidence from Korea. *Journal of Law and Economics*, 22, 366–413.

Blair, M. (1995), *Ownership and Control: Rethinking Corporate Governance for the Twenty First Century*. Washington: Brookings Institution Press.

Chandler, A.D. (1977). *The Visible Hand: The Managerial Revolution in American Business*. Cambridge, MA: Harvard University Press.

Coffee, J. (2005). A theory of corporate scandals: why the USA and Europe differ. *Oxford Review of Economic Policy*, 21, 198–211.

Core, J., Guay, W. and Rusticus, T. (2006). Does weak governance cause weak stock returns? An examination of firm operating performance and investors' expectations. *Journal of Finance*, 61, 655–687.

Dietrich, M., Krafft, J. and Ravix, J.L. (2008). Regulation and governance of the firm. *International Review of Applied Economics*, 22(4), 397–406.

Donaldson, T. and Preston, L. (1995). The stakeholder theory of corporation: concepts, evidence and implications. *Academy of Management Review*, 20(1), 65–91.

Driver, C. and Guedes, M. (2012). Research and development, cash flow, agency and governance in UK large companies. *Research Policy*, 41(9), 1565–1577.

Driver, C. and Thompson, G. (2002). Corporate Governance And Democracy: The Stakeholder Debate Revisited. *Journal of Management and Governance*, 6(2), 111–130.

Drobetz, W., Schillhofer, A. and Zimmermann, H. (2004). Corporate governance and expected stock returns: evidence from Germany. *European Financial Management*, 10, 267–293.

Durnev, A. and Kim, E. (2005). To steal or not to steal: firm attributes, legal environment, and valuation. *The Journal of Finance*, 60, 1461–1493.

Errunza, V. and Miller, D. (2000). Market segmentation and the cost of capital in international equity markets. *The Journal of Financial and Quantities Analysis*, 35, 577–600.

Fama, E. (1980). Agency problem and the theory of the firm. *Journal of Political Economy*, 88, 288–307.

Fama, E. and Jensen, M. (1983). Separation of ownership and control. *Journal of Law and Economics*, 26, 301–325.

Fransman, M. (2004). The telecoms boom and bust 1996–2003 and the role of financial markets. *Journal of Evolutionary Economics*, 14(4), 396–406.

Gompers, P., Ishii, J. and Metrick, A. (2003). Corporate governance and equity prices. *The Quarterly Journal of Economics*, 118, 107–155.

Hansmann, H. (1996). *The Ownership of Enterprise*. Cambridge, MA: Harvard University Press.

Hart, O. (1995). Corporate governance: some theory and implications. *Economic Journal*, 105(430), 678–689.

Hermalin, B. and Weisbach, M. (1998). Endogenously chosen boards of directors and their monitoring of the CEO. *American Economic Review*, 88, 96–118.

Hermalin, B. and Weisbach, M. (2003). Boards of directors as an endogenously determined institution: a survey of the economic literature. *Economic Policy Review*, Federal Reserve Bank of New York, April, 7–26.

Hoelzl, W. (2006), Convergence of financial systems: toward an evolutionary perspective. *Journal of Institutional Economics*, 2(1), 67–90.

Holmstrom, B. and Kaplan, S. (2001). Corporate governance and merger activity in the United States: making sense of the 1980s and 1990s. *Journal of Economic Perspective*, 15, 121–144.

Jensen, M. (1986). Agency cost of free cash flow, corporate finance and takeovers. *American Economic Review*, 76, 323–329.

Jensen, M. and Meckling, W. (1976). Theory of the firm: managerial behaviour, agency costs and ownership structure. *Journal of Financial Economics*, 3, 305–360.

Kelly, G., Kelly, D. and Gamble, A. (eds) (1997) *Stakeholder Capitalism*. Basingstoke: MacMillan.

Kirkpatrick, G. (2009). The corporate governance lessons from the financial crisis. *Financial Market Trends, OECD*, 1, 1–30.

Klapper, L. and Love, I. (2004). Corporate governance, investor protection, and performance in emerging markets. *Journal of Corporate Finance*, 10, 703–728.

Krafft, J. and Ravix, J. (2005). The governance of innovative firms: an evolutionary perspective. *Economics of Innovation and New Technology*, 14, 125–148.

Krafft, J. and Ravix, J. (2008a). Corporate governance and the governance of knowledge: rethinking the relationship in terms of corporate coherence. *Economics of Innovation and New Technology*, 17, 79–95.

Krafft, J. and Ravix, J. (2008b). Corporate governance in advanced economies: lessons in a post financial crash era. *Recherches Economiques de Louvain*, 74(4–5), 419–424.

Krafft, J., Qu, Y., Quatraro, F. and Ravix, J.L. (2014). Corporate governance, value and performance of firms: new empirical results on convergence from a large international database. *Industrial and Corporate Change*, 23(2), 361–397.

Krafft, J., Qu, Y. and Ravix, J.L. (2008). Corporate governance, industry dynamics and firms performance on the stock market: an empirical analysis of a best practice model. *Recherches Economiques de Louvain*, 74(4–5), 455–478.

Krafft, J., Qu, Y. and Ravix, J.L. (2011). Gouvernance d'entreprise et performances sectorielles: une réévaluation de la fiabilité des scores et des mesures de bonne gouvernance. *Economie et Prévision*, 1–2(197–198), 145–158.

La Porta, R., Lopez-de-Silanes, F. and Shleifer, A. (1999). Corporate ownership around the world. *Journal of Finance*, 54, 471–517.

La Porta, R., Lopez-de-Silanes, F. and Shleifer, A. (2008) The economic consequences of legal origin. *Journal of Economic Literature*, 46, 285–332,

La Porta, R., Lopez-de-Silanes, F., Shleifer, A. and Vishny, R. (1997). Legal determinants of external finance. *Journal of Finance*, 52, 1131–1150.

La Porta, R., Lopez-de-Silanes, F., Shleifer, A. and Vishny, R. (1998). Law and finance. *Journal of Political Economy*, 107, 1113–1155.

La Porta, R., Lopez-de-Silanes, F., Shleifer, A. and Vishny, R. (2000a). Agency problem and dividend policies around the world. *Journal of Finance*, 55, 1–33.

La Porta, R., Lopez-de-Silanes, F., Shleifer, A. and Vishny, R. (2000b). Investor protection and corporate governance. *Journal of Financial Economics*, 58, 3–27.

La Porta, R., Lopez-de-Silanes, F., Shleifer, A. and Vishny, R. (2002). Investor protection and corporate valuation. *The Journal of Finance*, 57, 1147–1170.

Lazonick, W. (2007). The US stock market and the governance of innovative enterprise. *Industrial and Corporate Change*, 6, 983–1035.

Lazonick, W. and Mazzucato, M. (2013). The risk-reward nexus in the innovation-inequality relationship: who takes the risks? Who gets the rewards? *Industrial and Corporate Change*, 22(4), 1093–1128.

Lazonick, W. and O'Sullivan, M. (eds) (2002). *Corporate Governance and Sustainable Prosperity*. New York: Palgrave.

Levine, R. (2005). Law, endowments, and property rights. *Journal of Economic Perspective*, 19, 61–88.

Lhuillery, S. (2011). The impact of corporate governance practices on R&D efforts: a look at shareholders' rights, cross listing, and control pyramid. *Industrial and Corporate Change*, 20(5), 1475–1513.

Lombardo, D. and Pagano, M. (2000). Legal determinants of the return on equity. Working Paper No. 193 (Stanford Law School).

Maclean, M. (1999). Corporate governance in France and the UK: Long term perspectives on contemporary institutional arrangements. *Business History*, 41(1), 88–116.

Martynova, M., and Renneboog, L. (2011). Evidence on the international evolution and convergence of corporate governance regulations. *Journal of Corporate Finance*, 17, 1531–1557.

O'Connor, M. and Rafferty, M. (2012). Corporate governance and innovation. *Journal of Financial and Quantitative Analysis*, 47(02), 397–413.

OECD (1999). *Principles of Corporate Governance*. Paris: OECD, www.oecd.org.

OECD (2004). *Principles of Corporate Governance*. Paris: OECD, www.oecd.org.

OECD (2009). *Corporate Governance and the Financial Crisis: Key Findings and Main Messages*. Paris: OECD, 1–59.

OECD Steering Group on Corporate Governance (2010). *Corporate Governance and the Financial Crisis*. OECD, 24 February 2010, 1–34.

O'Sullivan, M. (2000). *Contests for Corporate Control: Corporate Governance and Economic Performance in the United States and Germany*. Oxford: Oxford University Press.

Shleifer, A. and Vishny, R. (1997). A survey of corporate governance. *Journal of Finance*, 52, 737–783.

Stein, J.C. (1988). Takeover threats and managerial myopia. *The Journal of Political Economy*, 96(1), 61–80.

Zingales, L. (2000). In search for new foundations. *Journal of Finance*, 55(4), 1623–1653.

7 The geography of inter-firm knowledge spillovers in bio-tech

Ron Boschma, Pierre-Alexandre Balland and Dieter Kogler

1 Introduction

Evolutionary Economic Geography has recently drawn a lot of attention from scholars in economic geography (Boschma and Frenken, 2006; Martin and Sunley, 2006; Boschma and Martin, 2007; Boschma and Frenken, 2011). An evolutionary approach to economic geography centres on historical processes that have led to certain spatial patterns, such as the clustering of economic activity. The spatial distribution of economic activity is thus understood as an outcome of largely contingent, yet path-dependent, historical processes. Much of the explanatory framework is based on firm-level theorizing. That is, rather than taking the region, or any other spatial entity, as the unit of analysis, the firm is considered the locus of development and change. Economic evolution can therefore be understood as stemming from innovation leading to new organizational routines and their selective transmission across firms (Nelson and Winter 1982).

This book chapter aims to illustrate how basic concepts of evolutionary economic geography such as firm heterogeneity, proximity and path dependence can be fruitfully applied to the study of the geography of inter-firm knowledge spillovers. We will argue that firms develop firm-specific routines, which makes it hard for firms to connect to and learn from other firms. Having said that, knowledge spills over across firms now and then, and the proximity of a firm to other firms on various dimensions (such as geographical, social and cognitive proximity) may be a conditioning factor in this respect. In addition, we account for self-producing, path-dependent processes in which knowledge dynamics are grounded in and build on pre-existing knowledge and previously formed network ties. In doing so, we make the case that an evolutionary perspective on the spatial dynamics of inter-firm knowledge spillovers is very different from a knowledge production framework that is commonly applied in the knowledge spillover literature.

Since the 1990s, economic geographers have embarked on the study of the geography of knowledge spillovers. Not only did they show that geographical distance forms a real barrier to knowledge spillovers (Jaffe *et al.*, 1993; Feldman, 1994; Acs *et al.*, 2002), they also observed a high degree of spatial concentration of research and development (R&D) spending and patenting in a small number of regions (Storper, 1992; Acs *et al.*, 1994; Audretsch and Feldman, 1996;

Caniels, 2000; Cantwell and Santangelo, 2002). These studies often relied on patent citations as a proxy for knowledge flows and used information on the geography of citing patents and cited patents to determine the geography of knowledge spillovers. What they demonstrated is that knowledge spillovers are often geographically localized and that place matters for knowledge production and knowledge exchange.

Network studies have demonstrated that knowledge networks are not randomly structured but highly skewed – that is, some nodes are highly connected while other nodes are not (Ozman, 2009). This might be attributed to geographical proximity as a potential driver of network formation, but not necessarily, as there may be other network drivers involved (Breschi and Lissoni, 2003). Only recently, economic geographers have started to conduct network studies on knowledge spillovers by investigating the geography of inventor networks and collaborative research projects (Breschi and Lissoni, 2003; Balconi *et al.*, 2004; Ejermo and Karlsson, 2006; Gluckler, 2007; Ponds *et al.*, 2007; Maggioni *et al.*, 2007; Hoekman *et al.*, 2009; Boschma and Frenken, 2010). In this respect, networks are conceptualized as 'space of flows' (Castells, 1996) and perceived as important vehicles of knowledge transfer and diffusion (Ter Wal and Boschma, 2009).

In this chapter, we analyse the geography of knowledge spillovers in an evolutionary economic geography framework by investigating the way in which knowledge ties are organized. Following a relational account of knowledge spillovers, we depict knowledge networks as complex evolving structures that build on preexisting knowledge and ties. In doing so, we describe knowledge spillovers as complex and dynamic relational structures that contain important features of knowledge production and diffusion. In economic geography, there is still little understanding of how the structure of knowledge networks are formed over time and how the current network structure impacts on future network states. The objective of this chapter is to explain the dynamics of inter-organizational knowledge spillovers – that is, we aim to explain the driving forces behind the decision of actors to cite patents produced by other actors. In particular, we directly address the endogenous forces of knowledge dynamics because we claim that the special structure of knowledge ties provides unequal positions in terms of opportunities, cost and risks. Our study investigates the knowledge spillover networks of biotech firms by means of inter-organizational citation patterns based on USPTO biotech patents in the years 2008–2010.

The structure of the chapter is as follows. Section 2 briefly discusses the theoretical background, Section 3 explains the biotech patent database, Section 4 will introduce the statistical modelling of the knowledge network, Section 5 presents the main variables and Section 6 sets out the main findings. Section 7 concludes.

2 Spatial networks of knowledge spillovers

In economic geography, the study of the geography of knowledge spillovers took off in the 1990s. There were very good reasons to expect that geographical distance acts as a barrier to knowledge spillovers, due to the tacit and complex nature of knowledge that requires face-to-face interaction (Storper, 1992). This expectation has been confirmed in many empirical studies that used patent citations as a proxy for knowledge flows (e.g. Jaffe *et al.*, 1993; Feldman, 1994; Audretsch and Feldman, 1996; Caniels, 2000; Acs *et al.*, 2002). In addition, studies often found high correlations between inputs to knowledge (such as R&D) and output to technical knowledge (such as patent intensity) to explain the geography of innovation. These studies demonstrated that knowledge spillovers are often geographically bounded and what mattered for knowledge exchange and innovation is the space of place (Castells, 1996).

However, these studies did not analyse knowledge spillovers from a network perspective. Networks studies observe again and again that knowledge networks are not randomly structured but very biased (Newman, 2003; Ozman, 2009), just as knowledge spillovers are geographically biased. With structure, we mean that the set of links between nodes in a network is very different from the properties of a random network – that is, the properties one obtains by randomly connecting nodes to create a network structure. In reality, the degree distribution of nodes in networks is skewed almost by rule: few nodes have a high degree while many nodes have a low degree, meaning that some nodes are more popular to link with than other nodes. In addition, clustering is a very significant feature of networks, meaning that friends of friends are often friends with one another, and some nodes are so much more than other nodes. This implies that networks are not random but structured or organized and therefore require a full explanation (Boschma and Frenken, 2010).

Preferential attachment can provide an explanation for differences in the degree of nodes. The process of preferential attachment describes the growth of a network in which the probability that a new node will link to a certain other node is proportional to the number of links this nodes (that is, its degree) already has (Barabási and Albert, 1999). As a result, central nodes tend to become more central, whereas peripherally positioned nodes stay peripheral (Orsenigo *et al.*, 1998; Powell *et al.*, 2005). This mechanism reflects the benefits of linking to nodes with high degree since such 'hubs' provide new nodes with short pathways to many other nodes in the network. Closure can explain clustering of nodes in networks. In this case, new network relations follow on from existing relations as two actors are introduced to one another by a third actor with whom both already have a relationship. The reason for the establishment of such triangle relationships is that each actor can be informed by the common third party about the other in terms of its trustworthiness and the knowledge it possesses, and once the relationship is established, the two partners have less incentive to behave opportunistically since they may jeopardize their relation with the third actor. Ter Wal (2014) found in a study on the evolution of co-inventor networks that closure is particularly relevant as a mechanism of network formation in exploitation rather than exploration contexts.

However, there might be limits to the number of network relations a node can meaningfully maintain, as is the case of inter-firm networks (Holme *et al.*, 2004). This implies that well-connected nodes will often not be responsive to proposals for networking and will select only the most beneficial partners (cf. Giuliani, 2007). In addition, there is a tendency of new nodes to connect to nodes with lower degree when these are more proximate or similar to them in a number of dimensions (Boschma and Frenken, 2010). Geographical proximity might be a crucial driver here since a node may opt to collaborate locally to save on travel time and transportation costs, and to circumvent linguistic and cultural barriers. In that case, firms will connect not necessarily with the most central firms that are located in other regions, but will connect to those that are close by in a geographical sense (Guimera and Amaral, 2004). But there may be other forms of proximity that bias the partnering choice to similar firms. Breschi and Lissoni (2003) argued that it is not geographical proximity itself that causes knowledge spillovers to be geographically bounded. Instead, it is the underlying social networks of inventors and the mobility of inventors across firms that tend to be geographically localized and in turn cause knowledge spillovers to have a limited geographical reach. Firms also tend to select partners that are cognitively similar. Cognitive proximity favours collaboration between agents because absorptive capacity is needed to communicate and to interpret and exploit the knowledge that is exchanged (Cohen and Levinthal, 1990). That is, their own cognitive bases should be close enough in order to understand and absorb each other's knowledge (Breschi and Lissoni, 2006; Nooteboom, 2000).

Nevertheless, it is not necessarily true that all forms of proximity may matter equally in partnering decisions. Proximity dimensions in knowledge networks may actually be substitutes rather than complements (Boschma, 2005). Singh (2005) found evidence that geographical proximity is especially important in the establishment of interdisciplinary research collaboration (when cognitive proximity is low), while inventors working in the same field (high cognitive proximity) collaborate on average over longer geographical distances. Agrawal *et al.* (2006) found that knowledge is transferred between firms in different locations (so geographical proximity is low) by employees that are socially linked due to a shared past, such as a common working experience. Breschi *et al.* (2003) found similar results when analysing the social networks of US inventors who are mobile in space.

A drawback of the knowledge spillovers literature in economic geography is that it did not analyse knowledge spillovers from such a network perspective until very recently. Breschi and Lissoni (2003) were among the first to use patent data as true relational data. Economic geographers have started to conduct spatial network studies on knowledge spillovers by investigating inventor networks and collaborative research projects (Ejermo and Karlsson, 2006; Ponds *et al.*, 2007; Maggioni *et al.*, 2007; Hoekman *et al.*, 2009). Only a few of these network studies have applied the proximity framework and there is still little understanding of what role cognitive capabilities of agents, geographical proximity and social connectedness play in the spatial formation of knowledge networks. Moreover, as far as we know, no study has accounted for structural network forces (such as preferential attachment and closure) that shape the formation of knowledge networks, with two exceptions (Balland *et al.*, 2013; Ter Wal, 2014).

These structural forces account for the self-reproducing, path-dependent process behind knowledge dynamics, i.e. that knowledge production builds on pre-existing knowledge and previously formed ties. These structural patterns of knowledge spillovers are often left unconsidered in statistical models of know-ledge spillovers. In this chapter, we incorporate these structural forces and the various proximity dimensions to explain the structure of the knowledge spillover network of biotech firms.

3 The biotech patent database

The biotechnology sector makes extensive use of patent protection (Kortum and Lerner, 1999). Essentially, if a firm or individual believes that a biotech inven-tion has potential economic value, there is a high probability that they will seek intellectual property protection in form of a patent. Most attractive in this context is to file for a patent in the largest economic markets, such as the United States (Niosi and Bas, 2001). Thus, one could argue that an analysis based on United States Patent and Trademark Office (USPTO) patent data, which is utilized in the present study, is potentially representative of the worldwide stock of know-ledge in a particular technology sector in which it is customary to patent. Fur-thermore, patent data provide a wealth of information regarding the individual inventors and assignees, as well as references to prior art, i.e. citations to previous patents, that were instrumental in the development of a new invention. Thus patent data provide an excellent opportunity to investigate the networks of knowledge spillovers of biotech firms, based on inter-organizational citation pat-terns (Gittelman and Kogut, 2003).

All patent data utilized in this study are originally from the United States Patent and Trademark Office (USPTO). Several publicly available patent data-sets as well as supplementary data were used to derive the various measures that are employed in our model. These include the 'Patent Network Dataverse' at the Institute for Quantitative Social Science at Harvard University (Lai *et al.*, 2011), the NBER Patent and Citations Data (Hall *et al.*, 2001) and the USPTO harmon-ization of names of organizations data file (USPTO, 2010).

The initial sample of USPTO biotech patents granted in the years 2008, 2009 and 2010 was selected according to the USPTO's definition of biotechnology based on US patent classes, i.e. primary and sub-class (USPTO, 2002).[1] We identified 1,081 organizations that were awarded at least three patents over the three-year time period, i.e. one patent per year on average, in order to formalize our network dimensions. Patents assigned to individuals rather than organiza-tions, which represent a very small fraction of total biotech patents granted, were excluded from the analysis. This selection procedure resulted in the inclusion of about 13,000 patents which represent over 75 per cent of all USPTO biotech patents awarded in the three-year time period analysed.

Subsequently, we identified all citation linkages between these organizations based on the generated sample of network patents and their respective assignees, i.e. the organizations listed as assignee on the actual patent document. This allowed for the construction of annual citation matrices between the 1,081 organizations in the sample which essentially indicate the occurrence of knowledge spillovers between each pair of firms. Over 90,000 individual citations are accounted for in the three matrices that indicate knowledge spillovers between the organizations of interest.

4 Statistical modelling of knowledge structures

Our objective is to explain the dynamics of inter-organizational knowledge spillovers – that is, we want to explain the driving forces behind the decision of actors to cite patents produced by other actors. Moreover, we want to address directly the endogenous forces of knowledge dynamics because the particular organization of knowledge ties provides unequal positions in terms of opportunities, cost and risks. Therefore, we are interested in modelling explicitly the complex interdependencies between organizations, which raises a set of econometrical issues.

A fundamental characteristic of structures of relationships is the existence of conditional dependencies between observations, i.e. the interdependencies between the set of pairs of actors that can be potentially linked. A first kind of interdependency is that dyads (pairs of actors) that have one actor in common cannot be assumed to be statistically independent. Such structural dependencies violate standard statistical procedures in generalized linear modelling that assume independence among observations. In this case, however, one can correct for this problem by introducing actor-level or dyadic-level fixed effects (Mizruchi and Marquis, 2005). However, in more complex interdependencies (such as indirect relationships), the resulting correlation between observations can lead to unreliable estimations of parameter coefficients and standard errors (Steglich *et al.*, 2010). A crucial point is that the structure of knowledge spillovers contains a lot of information in terms of hierarchy, cohesive sub-groups of actors and relational positioning of organizations that should not be left out in a study that investigates patent citations.

To model knowledge dynamics, we employ a class of statistical network models based on Markov chain Monte Carlo simulation procedures. This class of model is known as the class of Stochastic Actor-Oriented Models (SAOM), which are the most promising class of models allowing for statistical inference of network dynamics. An introduction to the SAOM can be found in Snijders *et al.* (2010), while the mathematical foundation of these models are detailed in Snijders (2001). In economic geography, there are some very recent applications (Balland, 2012; Ter Wal, 2014; Balland *et al.*, 2013, 2014; Giuliani, 2013; Giuliani and Matta, 2013). We use SAOM implemented in the RSiena[2] statistical software (Ripley *et al.*, 2011). In the literature, this class of models is also referred to as SIENA models. The acronym 'SIENA' stands for 'Simulation Investigation for Empirical Network Analysis'.

The basic principle of SAOM is to estimate parameters by simulating the evolution of a particular network structure from a given starting configuration (the observation of the network structure in t_0) to another given configuration (the observation of the network structure in t_1). Therefore, the dependent variable in SAOM is slightly different than the one employed in conventional econometrics since the variable to be explained is the structure resulting from knowledge spillovers between a set of actors, i.e. the particular way patent citations between actors are organized. In our study, the dependent variable is more precisely a set of consecutive (yearly) observations of the architecture of citations that firms decide to make between each other. More formally, these observations take the form of three successive square ($n*n$) matrices and we explain why knowledge ties are created or maintained between organizations.

Table 7.1 presents a simple description of the dynamics of knowledge spillovers we model, indicating the number of ties created, maintained and dissolved from one observation to another.[3] The ties between the n actors are represented by dichotomous[4] (0/1) and directed linkages, which means that we are analysing asymmetric adjacency matrices. To give an example, if organization i cites in the year 2008 one or more patents granted by organization j, then xij (2008) = 1. But if organization j does not cite any patent from organization i in the year 2008, then xij (2008) = 1 # xji (2008) = 0. The link is deleted in the next year if ego does not decide in a new patent to cite again organization j. Obviously, patenting is a necessary condition for the actors to have out-going ties, but they can receive ties (citations) without patenting during the observed year.

The dynamics of the structure of knowledge spillovers is modelled on the basis of several principles and assumptions. These assumptions are related to the modelling procedure since the evolution of the structure of patent citations is modelled as a Markov chain. This implies that change probability only depends on the current state of the network (t) and not on its past configurations ($t-1$). The second principle is related to the idea of non-simultaneity of events. Time runs continuously between observations and actors can only make one citation at a time. Three actors can only be connected as a result of a sequence of citations between the three pairs of actors. Finally, the observed network dynamics is supposed to be the result of the decisions of actors. Such relational choices are based on their preferences, constraints, costs or opportunities. It is assumed that organizations are actors that have the ability to elaborate on their own strategic decisions. It should be noted that these assumptions would be less realistic in the case of citations between patents directly since patents are not actors with their own strategy.

Table 7.1 Changes in citation ties between observations

Periods	$0 \rightarrow 0$	$0 \rightarrow 1$	$1 \rightarrow 0$	$1 \rightarrow 1$	Jaccard
2008–2009	1,158,167	3,723	3,598	1,992	0.214
2009–2010	1,157,845	3,920	3,676	2,039	0.212

Source: own elaboration.

A key principle of the model is that the dynamics of knowledge spillovers is driven by micro-level decision of actors to cite patents invented by others, which in turn will form an aggregated knowledge structure. Given that an actor i has the opportunity to make a relational change (determined stochastically), the choice for this actor is to change one of the tie variables x_{ij}, which will lead to a new state x, $x \in C(x^0)$. A traditional logistic regression is used to model choice probabilities (Snijders *et al.*, 2010):

$P\{X(t)$ changes to $x | i$ has a change opportunity at time t, $X(t) = x^0\}$

$$= p_i(x^0, x, v, w) = \frac{\exp\left(f_i(x^0, x, v, w)\right)}{\sum_{x' \in C(x^0)} \exp\left(f_i(x^0, x', v, w)\right)}$$

When actors have the opportunity to change their relations, the objective function describes preferences, opportunities or constraints of actors, for instance, to cite patents developed by organizations from the same technological class or from the same spatial area. Patent citations choices are determined by a linear combination of effects, depending on the current state (x^0), the potential new state (x), individual attributes[5] (v) and proximity (w):

$$f_i(x^0, x, v, w) = \sum_k \beta_k S_{ki}(x^0, x, v, w)$$

As detailed in Snijders (2001), the estimation of the different parameters β_k of the objective function is achieved by an iterative Markov chain Monte Carlo algorithm based on the method of moments. The stochastic approximation algorithm simulates the evolution of the network and estimates the parameters β_k that minimize the deviation between observed and simulated networks. The specification of the objective function used in the empirical section is described below.

5 Model specification: structural and non-structural variables

Figure 7.1 indicates the cumulative degree distribution of organizations over the period 2008–2010.[6] We can observe a typical statistical signature of knowledge structure, i.e. the fact that very few actors are active players, while most of the actors make or receive very few citations. This structural characteristic is known as the scale-free distribution in statistical physics (Barabási and Albert, 1999) and indicates the hierarchical nature of relational structures. Interestingly, we can observe that the shape of the citations received (in-degree) is even more hierarchical than the shape of the citations made (out-degree). It suggests that the production of successful patents (that will be highly cited) is more unequal than the production of patents.

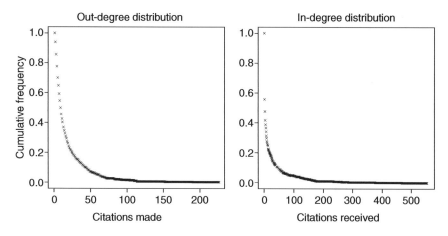

Figure 7.1 Degree distribution (2007–2010) (source: own elaboration).

To have a better idea of the centrality of the biggest players in the structure of knowledge spillovers in biotech, Table 7.2 indicates the top 20 companies in terms of in-degree and out-degree. This ranking confirms the influential role of universities in biotechnology (Zucker *et al.*, 1998, 2002). The relationships between the top 20 players[7] in terms of knowledge transfer are displayed in Figure 7.2. Since only the most important actors are considered, we observe a cohesive picture, with a central position in terms of knowledge accessibility occupied by the University of California.[8]

Table 7.3 shows further descriptive statistics for the structure of knowledge spillovers. The density is low (0.005), which indicates that only 0.5 per cent of the possible linkages are patent citations. In addition, 5 per cent of the citations are reciprocated within a year. It is more than what we can expect from a random network structure with the same characteristics, but lower than what we find in other networks, such as advice networks or friendship networks. Together with the highly unequal degree distribution, the relatively low level of reciprocity can be interpreted as another indicator of the hierarchical nature of knowledge spillovers. When we turn to the triadic level, we observe that knowledge spillovers are not only strongly localized in space, but also strongly localized in few parts of the global structure. Indeed, the clustering coefficient shows that inter-organizational citations occur between organizations that cite the same actor, creating triangles of relationships. The connectivity is also very high, which indicates that, even if actors are located in different parts of the world, they are still very close in terms of geodesic distance (average path length of approximately three steps).

These descriptive statistics confirm that the structure of knowledge spillovers contains a lot of information in terms of non-spatial positioning of actors.

Table 7.2 Key players in biotech: top 20 centrality scores (2007–2010)

Out-degree (top 20)		In-degree (top 20)	
Organizations	Citations made	Organizations	Citations received
University of California	224	University of California	554
US Health Human Services	208	Genentech	457
Cornell Research Foundation	181	US Health Human Services	423
University of Texas	161	Chiron	275
Genentech	159	Roche	268
Amgen	155	University of Texas	259
Sequenom	153	Abbott	243
Genprobe	138	Harvard University	231
Novartis	132	Stanford University	230
Monsanto	119	Johns Hopkins University	218
Merck	113	Amgen	212
University of Michigan	113	General Hospital Corporation, MA	209
California Institute of Technology	112	Du Pont	208
Ravgen	109	Genetics Institute	170
Human Genome Sciences	108	Merck	169
Life Technologies	108	Becton Dickinson	165
Columbia University	107	University of Wisconsin-Madison	162
Pioneer Hi-Bred	103	Eli Lilly	158
Wyeth	102	Human Genome Sciences	158
Stanford University	99	Massachusetts Institute of Technology	156

Source: own elaboration.

Therefore, this structure should be taken into account in models of knowledge spillovers. The main challenge is to operationalize this global structure into a set of structural variables at the micro-level and to model the decision of actors to cite other actors. Taking into account the observed structural patterns, we model explicitly the following structural variables using SAOM: density, transitivity, cyclicity and preferential attachment.

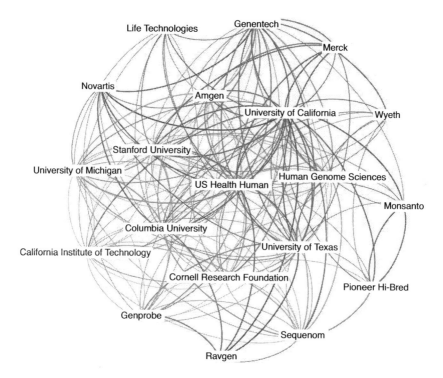

Figure 7.2 Knowledge exchanges between the top 20 actors (2007–2010) (source: own elaboration).

Table 7.3 Structural characteristics of knowledge spillovers

	2008	*2009*	*2010*
Number of nodes (organizations)	1,081	1,081	1,081
Number of edges (citation links)	5,590	5,715	5,959
Density	0.005	0.005	0.005
Average degree	5.171	5.287	5.512
Reciprocity	0.047	0.041	0.037
Average clustering coefficient	0.092	0.103	0.096
Diameter	10	8	8
Average path length	3.211	3.158	3.285

Source: own elaboration.

5.1 Structural variables

The structural variables accounting for the structural patterns of knowledge spill-overs are described below. All are visually represented in Table 7.4 to facilitate interpretation.

Density

This variable can be interpreted as the constant term in regression analysis. It is a structural determinant that indicates the general tendency of organizations to cite patents granted by others. As specified by Snijders *et al.* (2010), this variable should always be included in SAOM to control for the general likelihood of ties to appear. Density is measured by the out-degree of organizations: $D_i=\Sigma_j x_{ij}$ $D_i=\Sigma_j x_{ij}$.

Reciprocity

Reciprocity is a relevant variable for the dynamics of directed knowledge spill-overs. It indicates the general tendency of actors to cite patents of organizations that also cite their patents. Reciprocity is based on the counts of the number of reciprocal citations of actor *i*: $R_i=\Sigma_j x_{ij} x_{ji}$.

Table 7.4 Structural variables

Name	Visual representation
Reciprocity	
Transitivity	
Cyclicity	
Preferential attachment	

Source: own elaboration.

Note
The dashed arrows represent the expected link if the corresponding structural effect is positive.

Transitivity

We also control for the effect of transitivity, which leads to triadic network closure. A positive effect indicates that actor i and actor h are more likely to cite each other if they both already cite actor j. Although transitivity can be measured in several ways, the most common is based on the counts of number of transitive triplets, i.e. the number of times an actor i is tied with two actors that cite each other (Ripley *et al.*, 2011): $T_i = \Sigma_{j,h} x_{ij} x_{ih} x_{jh}$.

Cyclicity

Transitivity refers to local clustering of actors, but it does not account for the direction of linkages. Knowledge spillovers can be transferred as a cycle, from actor i citing actor j, then actor h citing actor i, and then actor j citing actor h. Such a cyclic process of knowledge spillovers would indicate a non-hierarchical structure and a collaborative way of producing knowledge. The cyclicity effect counts the number of three cycles in citations of actor i: $C_i = \Sigma_{j,h} x_{ij} x_{jh} \; x_{hi}$.

Preferential attachment

The preferential attachment variable models the in-degree distribution of actors, i.e. the fact that few actors are cited very often, while most of the actors receive very few citations. A positive effect would reflect the attractiveness of actors that already receive many citations, for instance, because they invented groundbreaking patents in the past that have been the basis for many further developments in the field. More precisely, we consider the square root version of the in-degree distribution, in order to avoid co-linearity issues with other structural effects and to smooth the in-degree distribution (Ripley *et al.*, 2011). Therefore, preferential attachment is measured as the sum of the square roots of the in-degrees (citations received) of the actors that actor i cites: $PA_i = \Sigma_j x_{ij} \sqrt{\Sigma_h x_{hj}}$.

5.2 Non-structural variables

Geographical proximity

The location of the 'inventive headquarter' of an organization was based on the primary location of knowledge production as indicated by the inventor residences.[9] Almost every firm in our sample has patents assigned to it that have been developed by inventors in various different places. However, organizations' inventor pools are not randomly distributed in space, but rather show distinct patterns of spatial clustering. This in turn enabled us to identify one primary place of knowledge production for each firm. In order to measure geographical proximity between organizations based on their primary locations of knowledge production, we computed the inverse of the natural logarithm of the physical distance (+1) between the locations of two organizations in kilometres. We subtract the results from the maximum distance obtained to convert the measure into a proximity measure.

Cognitive proximity

The cognitive proximity between two organizations is a result of their common-alities of patenting in similar biotech classes as defined previously. Specifically, we count the total number of technology classes that two firms have patents assigned to and then calculate the cognitive proximity measure based on the share of the total number of classes covered by each individual firm. The observation time frame to derive this asymmetric measure between all organizations in a network is the previous five-year window of the actual observation that is investigated. Essentially, cognitive proximity measures the similarity of two firms in terms of having patents granted in specific patent classes that comprise biotechnology and thus indicates the relatedness of the two organizations' technology expertise and focus.

Same country

We also control for belonging to the same country on the basis of the location of the organizations. The measure of the same country is binary: 1 if both organizations have their 'inventive headquarter' in the same country and 0 if they have not.

Absorptive capacity

In addition to the structural and the proximity variables, we also control for het-erogeneity in the patenting behaviour of organizations. Absorptive capacity is measured as the capacity of organizations to absorb knowledge produced by others. These organizations are also more likely to be leaders in the patent race and therefore they are more likely to diffuse knowledge (Alcacer and Chung, 2007), i.e. in our case, to receive citations. We measure absorptive capacity by computing the natural logarithm of the number of patents an organization developed in the biotech industry in the five years prior to our first observation, i.e. during the period 2003–2007. Indeed, by construction, organizations that patent a lot are more likely to cite patents from others (ego effect). Since we analyse the dynamics of knowledge spillovers as a directed process of know-ledge transfer, we also control for the fact that organizations that patent a lot are therefore more likely to be cited by others (alter effect).

Table 7.5 Descriptive statistics of the control variables

	Minimum	*Maximum*	*Mean*	*Standard deviation*
Geographical proximity	0	9	0.896	1.302
Cognitive proximity	0	10	3.967	3.693
Same country	0	1	0.338	0.473
Absorptive capacity	0	7	1.913	1.343

Source: own elaboration.

6 Estimation results

Table 7.6 presents the results of SAOM estimating the driving forces of the dynamics of inter-organizational knowledge spillovers for the period 2008 to 2010. Four different model specifications are reported. The first model is a 'baseline' model that only includes the tendency of actors to cite patents from other actors and the tendency to reciprocate citations. Then we explore more complex structural characteristics by including triadic-level effects (transitivity and cyclicity) and degree-related effects (preferential attachment) in the 'structural' model. A third model specification is employed to test the influence of variables that have been found to be important in the literature on knowledge spillovers (i.e. geographical proximity, cognitive proximity, belonging to the same country and absorptive capacity), but without taking the knowledge structure into account. The final model combines the variables of the structural and the non-structural model.

All parameter estimations are based on 1,000 simulation runs and convergence of the approximation algorithm is excellent for all the variables of the different models. This convergence is a way to evaluate the goodness of fit of the different models and it indicates if the deviation of the simulated structures compared to the observed structures is acceptable (t-values <0.1). The parameter estimates of SAOM can be interpreted as non-standardized coefficients obtained from logistic regression analysis (Steglich *et al.*, 2010). Therefore, the parameter estimates that are reported can be read as log-odds ratio, i.e. how the log-odds of tie formation (decision to cite a patent from another actor) change with one unit change in the corresponding independent variable. Because odds ratios are more easy to interpret, we will sometimes refer in the text to the odds ratios (OR) to discuss the results. Odds ratio can be computed as the exponentiated form of the coefficients of each predictor.

The different model specifications confirm the importance of endogenous, structural effects in the dynamics of knowledge spillovers. Although the coefficients of all predictors are very robust across the different specifications, we discuss the coefficients obtained in the final model in order to control simultaneously for the effect of other structural effects and control variables. The density coefficient is an indicator of the general tendency of actors to form linkages. The negative and significant density effect indicates that, on average, organizations cite very few other organizations (Est.=−3.529; OR=0.029). Organizations are more likely to cite patents from organizations that already cite them.[10] Other variables held constant, organizations are 38 per cent more likely (Est.=0.323; OR=1.381) to cite an actor that also cites them compared to an actor that does not. This result probably relates to the fact that there is a strong, cohesive group of actors (see Figure 7.2) that cite each other, but this should not be interpreted as an absence of hierarchy in knowledge spillovers dynamics.

Indeed, when we extend the analysis to the triadic level, we find that actors are more likely to create a sub-group of actors (positive effect of triadic closure), but they exchange knowledge in a non-cyclic, hierarchical manner (negative

Table 7.6 The determinants of inter-organizational knowledge spillovers, 2008–2010

	Baseline model	Structural model	Non-structural model	Final model
Structural variables				
Density	−2.848** [0.008]	−3.513** [0.009]	−3.441** [0.012]	−3.529** [0.012]
Reciprocity	1.270** [0.047]	0.439** [0.056]		0.323** [0.053]
Transitivity		0.175** [0.004]		0.146** [0.003]
Cyclicity		−0.067** [0.008]		−0.112** [0.008]
Preferential attachment		0.168** [0.002]		0.083** [0.004]
Control variables				
Geographical proximity			0.034** [0.006]	0.038** [0.005]
Cognitive proximity			0.020** [0.002]	0.019** [0.002]
Same country			0.415** [0.017]	0.242** [0.017]
Absorptive capacity [alter]			0.475** [0.005]	0.225** [0.008]
Absorptive capacity [ego]			0.183** [0.006]	0.122** [0.005]

Source: own elaboration.

Notes
Number of actors: $n = 1,081$. The asterisks indicate that the parameter estimates are significantly different from 0 at a 5 per cent level (*) and at a 1 per cent level (**).
Standard errors are reported in brackets.

cyclicity effect). The positive effect of transitivity means that actors are 15 per cent more likely (Est.=0.146; OR=1.157) to cite other organizations if they are already linked by one common intermediary.[11] This preference for closed local networks is an important determinant of knowledge spillovers and this structural configuration can capture other cognitive or social variables that are more difficult to observe in large-scale studies. These closed local networks, however, are hierarchical because the coefficient for cyclicity is negative (Est.=–0.112; OR=0.894). It indicates that the configuration where two actors, A and B, cite each other (regardless of the direction of the citation) and where these two actors cite the same actor C (that does not cite these two actors A and B in turn) is more likely to happen than a cyclic configuration where A cites B, B cites C and C cites A. In the non-cyclic configuration and if C is an active[12] actor, the position of C is an interesting position where C diffuses knowledge to A and B while C is absorbing knowledge elsewhere in the structure. The degree distribution (Figure 7.1) also provides important information on the individual capacity of actors to absorb and diffuse knowledge in the structure of the network. The preferential attachment coefficient is positive and significant, describing the behaviour of actors to cite actors that are already cited by many others (Est.=0.083; OR=1.086). This result reflects a certain status of organizations that is not necessarily achieved by producing many patents, but by producing successful/groundbreaking patents, such as Stanford's recombinant DNA method, which was one of the first biotech patents granted altogether.

Our results also confirm the effects of variables that do not operate at the structural level, but at the dyadic (geographical and cognitive proximity, same country) and organizational level (absorptive capacity). As expected, geographical proximity strongly influences the citation patterns of organizations (Est.=0.038; OR=1.038), even when we control for belonging to the same country. It means that organizations are 40 per cent more likely to cite an organization of the same spatial area compared to an organization located in the most remote location in the world.[13] Interestingly, this coefficient does not change from the non-structural to the final model, suggesting that the information contained in the structure of knowledge spillovers and in the geography of knowledge spillovers is different. The same conclusion can be drawn from the reading of the coefficient of cognitive proximity. Organizations that have patented in the same technological classes are more likely to cite each other in the future (Est.=0.019; OR=1.019). Obviously, the effect of cognitive proximity would be even stronger if different industries were included in the sample. In our case, since we only consider biotech organizations, cognitive proximity is a prerequisite to be part of the knowledge dynamics we model. In this case again, the inclusion of structural variables does seem to decrease the explanatory power of cognitive proximity. The belonging to the same country is an important determinant of knowledge spillovers (Est.=0.242; OR=1.273) but the coefficient is strongly reduced by the inclusion of structural variables. The absorptive capacity variable is positive and significant, and it simply controls for the fact that organizations that have substantially patented in the last years are more likely to cite other organizations in general (ego effect; Est.=0.122; OR=1.129), but also more likely to be cited (alter effect; Est.=0.225; OR=1.252). While our measure of absorptive capacity only counts the number of patents, the information contained in the actual distribution of citations (modelled via preferential attachment) seems to provide an additional explanation, probably about the technological value of the patents.

7 Conclusion

In this chapter, we have illustrated how basic concepts of evolutionary economic geography such as firm heterogeneity, proximity and path dependence can be applied to the study of the geography of inter-firm knowledge spillovers. Instead of using the common framework of a knowledge production function, we have explicitly adopted a 'relational' approach to knowledge spillovers, following the seminal claim by Breschi and Lissoni (2001). The different model specifications show that the structure of knowledge spillovers contains in itself important information that can explain patterns of knowledge dynamics and technological evolution. Therefore, we argue that not only should these complex interdependencies be included in traditional econometric approaches, but they should also be modelled explicitly through variables representing local clustering, hierarchical positioning and degree distributions, for instance. These variables provide additional explanatory power to the existing determinants of knowledge spillovers that have been discussed in the literature so far. In fact, evaluating the importance of structural effects in the dynamics of knowledge spillovers could allow the influence of geographical proximity per se to be evaluated more precisely. Moreover, such an approach also allows variables to be captured that are not easily observable, such as cognitive proximity or social proximity, because they strongly shape the structure of knowledge networks (Balland, 2012).

This chapter, however, should not be considered as an attempt to obtain the best model possible to describe the dynamics of knowledge spillovers, but more as a first step towards the analysis of endogenous effects of knowledge dynamics. This approach opens a set of research questions that should be investigated further. First, the model proposed is admittedly quite simple in terms of non-structural effects and further research should consider other variables that have been shown to be relevant in the literature on inter-organizational patent citations. Social networks constructed from teams of inventors play an important role in explaining knowledge spillovers (Singh, 2005; Breschi and Lissoni, 2009), but also R&D collaborations (Gomes-Casseres *et al.*, 2006; Frankort *et al.*, 2012) and labour mobility (Almeida and Kogut, 1999; Corredoira and Rosenkopf, 2010). Second, the model only considers a short period of time (2008–2010) in a specific industry (biotech). It should be noted, however, that the changing role of the drivers of network dynamics over time is an emerging research topic in economic geography and network theory (Rivera *et al.*, 2010; Hoekman *et al.*, 2010; Balland *et al.*, 2013; Ter Wal, 2014). Therefore, a next logical step would be to analyse how structural and non-structural effects influence differently the dynamics of knowledge spillovers at different stages of the technology life cycle. Moreover, an interesting research question concerns whether incremental and radical innovations are driven by the same forces and whether these forces are constant across industries. Third, we did not account for performance of organizations. It is often assumed that knowledge spillovers are important for economic performance of organizations, but it is rarely empirically assessed. Our approach provides an interesting opportunity to test whether the position of actors in knowledge structures influence their economic performance, and in turn, how the economic performance of actors influence their probability to diffuse (i.e. to be cited by other organizations) or to access (i.e. to cite other organizations) knowledge in the future. Such a research question could be an extension of our approach since the class of statistical models we use in this chapter allows for the analysis of the co-evolution between network dynamics and the performance of actors (Snijders *et al.*, 2010; Steglich *et al.*, 2010).

Notes

1 This specific definition of biotechnology has been previously used in other studies (Johnson, 2009; Lee, 2010) and includes the following US patent classes (primary and sub-classes): 47/1.1–47/1.4, 47/57.6–47758, 424/9.1–424/9.2, 424/9.34–424/9.81, 424/85.1–424/94.67, 424/130.1–424/283.1, 424/520–424/583, 424/800–424/832, 435/1.1–435/7.95, 435/40.5–43 5/261,435/317.1–435/975, 436/500–436/829, 514/2–514/22, 514/44, 514/783, 530/300–530/427, 530/800–530/868, 536/1.11–536/23.74, 536/25.1–536/25.2, 800, 930, 935.

2 The RSiena package is implemented in the R language and can be downloaded from the CRAN website: http://cran.r-project.org/web/packages/RSiena/. In this chapter, we use the RSiena version 1.0.12.167.

3 The Jaccard coefficient indicates the degree of stability of the network structure from one observation to another (Snijders *et al.*, 2010). Since we decide to set the duration of a tie to one year, the structure is quite dynamic and therefore the Jaccard coefficient is rather low, but does not affect the convergence of the algorithm.

4 The current implementation of RSiena does not allow easily weighted analysis, i.e. valued networks.

5 Individual and proximity variables are centred around the mean.

6 We aggregate the structure of knowledge spillovers in 2008, 2009 and 2010.

7 Top 20 players in terms of out-degree.

8 Patents that are assigned to 'The Regents of the University of California' as well as other sub-entities within the University of California university system on the official USPTO patent documents are generally referred to as 'University of California' in the present study.

9 Our attempt in this chapter is not to provide a detailed account of the diffusion of knowledge spillovers in space nor to find the best measure of geographical proximity. Such an approach would require more fine-grained measures of geographical proximity.

10 In a network where the nodes are patents, the coefficient of reciprocity would be negative since citations can only be made towards previous patents that, by their nature, cannot reciprocate the citation.

11 If two actors A and B are indirectly linked by more than one intermediary, the probability that a tie is created between A and B also increases because it would lead to the simultaneous closure of more than one triad.

12 If C is not an active node, this pattern may be artificially driven because if C does not patent, C cannot by definition contribute to close the knowledge spillover cycle.

13 The scale of geographical proximity is constructed in such a way that minimum geographical proximity = 0, and maximum geographical proximity = 9. Since the coefficients are not standardized, the odd ratio of choosing an organization from the same
spatial area versus an organization from the most remote spatial area should consider
the scale of the input variable: OR = exp (0.038*9) = 1.407.

References

Acs, Z.J., Anselin, L. and Varga, A. (2002) Patents and innovation counts as measures of
regional production of new knowledge, *Research Policy* 31(7): 1069–1085.
Acs, Z.J., Audretsch, D.B. and Feldman, M.P. (1994) R&D spillovers and innovation
activity, *Managerial and Decision Economics* 15: 131–138.
Agrawal, A., Cockburn, I. and McHale, J. (2006) Gone but not forgotten: knowledge
flows, labor mobility, and enduring social relationships, *Journal of Economic Geography* 6: 571–591.
Alcacer, J. and Chung, W. (2007) Location strategies and knowledge spillovers, *Management Science* 53(5): 760–776.
Almeida, P. and Kogut, B. (1999) Localization of knowledge and the mobility of engineers in regional networks, *Management Science* 45: 905–917.
Audretsch, D.B. and Feldman, M.P. (1996) R&D spillovers and the geography of innovation and production, *American Economic Review* 86(3): 630–640.
Balconi, M., Breschi, S. and Lissoni, F. (2004) Networks of inventors and the role of
academia: an exploration of Italian patent data, *Research Policy* 33: 127–145.
Balland, P.A. (2012) Proximity and the evolution of collaboration networks: evidence
from research and development projects within the Global Navigation Satellite System
(GNSS) industry, *Regional Studies* 46(6): 741–756.
Balland, P.A., Belso-Martinez, J.A. and Morrison, A. (2014) The dynamics of technolo-
gical and business networks in industrial clusters: embeddedness, status or proximity?,
Papers in Evolutionary Economic Geography 14(12), Section of Economic Geography,
Utrecht University.
Balland, P.A., de Vaan, M. and Boschma, R. (2013) The dynamics of interfirm networks
along the industry life cycle: the case of the global video game industry, 1987–2007,
Journal of Economic Geography 13(5): 741–765.
Barabási, A.L. and Albert, R. (1999) Emergence of scaling in random networks, *Science*
286: 509–512.
Boschma, R.A. (2005) Proximity and innovation. A critical assessment, *Regional Studies*
39(1): 61–74.
Boschma, R.A. and Frenken, K. (2006) Why is economic geography not an evolutionary
science? Towards an evolutionary economic geography, *Journal of Economic Geo-
graphy* 6(3): 273–302.
Boschma, R.A. and Frenken, K. (2010) The spatial evolution of innovation networks: a
proximity perspective. In R. Boschma and R. Martin (eds) *The Handbook on Evolutionary Economic Geography*. Cheltenham, UK: Edward Elgar, 120–135.
Boschma, R.A. and Frenken, K. (2011) The emerging empirics of evolutionary economic
geography, *Journal of Economic Geography* 11: 295–307.
Boschma, R.A. and Martin, R. (2007) Constructing an evolutionary economic geography,
Journal of Economic Geography 7(5): 537–548.
Breschi, S. and Lissoni, F. (2001) Knowledge spillovers and local innovation systems: a
critical survey, *Industrial and Corporate Change* 10: 975–1005.

Breschi, S. and Lissoni, F. (2003) Mobility and social networks: localised knowledge spillovers revisited. CESPRI Working Paper 142, Bocconi University, Milan.

Breschi, S. and Lissoni, F. (2006) Mobility of inventors and the geography of knowledge spillovers. New evidence on US data. CESPRI Working Paper 184, Bocconi University, Milan.

Breschi, S. and Lissoni, F. (2009) Mobility of skilled workers and co-invention networks: an anatomy of localized knowledge flows, *Journal of Economic Geography* 9(4): 439–468.

Breschi, S., Lissoni, F. and Malerba, F. (2003) Knowledge networks from patent citations? Methodological issues and preliminary results. DRUID summer conference.

Caniels, M. (2000) *Knowledge Spillovers and Economic Growth. Regional Growth Differentials across Europe*, Cheltenham: Edward Elgar.

Cantwell, J. and Santangelo, G.D. (2002) The new geography of corporate research in information and communications technology (ICT), *Journal of Evolutionary Economics* 12: 163–197.

Castells, M. (1996) *The Rise of the Network Society*, Oxford: Blackwell.

Cohen, W.M. and Levinthal, D.A. (1990) Absorptive capacity: a new perspective on learning and innovation, *Administrative Science Quarterly* 35, 128–152.

Corredoira, R.A. and Rosenkopf, L. (2010) Should auld acquaintance be forgot? The reverse transfer of knowledge through mobility ties, *Strategic Management Journal* 31(2): 159–181.

Ejermo, O. and Karlsson, C. (2006) Interregional inventor networks as studied by patent coinventorships, *Research Policy* 35(3): 412–430.

Feldman, M.P. (1994) *The Geography of Innovation*, Dordrecht: Kluwer Academic Publishers.

Frankort, H., Hagedoorn, J. and Letterie, W. (2012) R&D partnership portfolios and the inflow of technological knowledge, *Industrial and Corporate Change* 21(2): 507–537.

Gittelman, M. and Kogut, B. (2003) Does good science lead to valuable knowledge? Biotechnology firms and the evolutionary logic of citation patterns, *Management Science* 49(4): 366–382.

Giuliani, E. (2007) The selective nature of knowledge networks in clusters: evidence from the wine industry, *Journal of Economic Geography* 7(2): 139–168.

Giuliani, E. (2013) Network dynamics in regional clusters: evidence from Chile, *Research Policy* 42: 1406–1419.

Giuliani, E. and Matta, A. (2013) Impact evaluation with social network analysis methods, program for supply chain development in the province of Cordoba, Argentina, *Inter-American Development Bank* (ATN/ME-8112-AR).

Gluckler, J. (2007) Economic geography and the evolution of networks, *Journal of Economic Geography* 7(5): 619–634.

Gomes-Casseres, B., Hagedoorn, J. and Jaffe, A. (2006) Do alliances promote knowledge flows? *Journal of Financial Economics* 80: 5–33.

Guimera, R. and Amaral, L.A.N. (2004) Modelling the world-wide airport network, *European Physical Journal B* 38(2): 381–385.

Hall, B.H., Jaffe, A.B. and Trajtenberg, M. (2001) The NBER patent citations data file: lessons, insights and methodological tools, *NBER Working Paper* 8498.

Hoekman, J., Frenken, K. and Tijssen, R. (2010) Research collaboration at a distance: changing spatial patterns of scientific collaboration within Europe, *Research Policy*, 39: 662–673.

Hoekman, J., Frenken, K. and Van Oort, F. (2009) The geography of collaborative knowledge production in Europe, *Annals of Regional Science* 43(3): 721–738.

Holme, P., Edling, C.R. and Liljeros, F. (2004) Structure and time evolution of an internet dating community, *Social Networks* 26: 155–174.

Jaffe, A.B., Trajtenberg, M. and Henderson, R. (1993) Geographic localisation of knowledge spillovers as evidenced by patent citations, *Quarterly Journal of Economics* 108: 577–598.

Johnson, D.K.N. (2009) Not far from the madding crowd: the role of proximity in biotechnology innovation, *International Review of Business Research Papers* 5(2): 420–429.

Kortum, S. and Lerner, J. (1999) What is behind the recent surge in patenting, *Research Policy* 28: 1–22.

Lai, R., D'Amour, A., Yu, A., Sun, Y. and Fleming, L. (2011) Disambiguation and co-authorship networks of the US patent inventor database (1975–2010), https://thedata.harvard.edu/dvn/dv/patent.

Lee, J. (2010) Heterogeneity, brokerage, and innovative performance: endogenous formation of collaborative inventor networks, *Organization Science* 21(4): 804–822.

Maggioni, M.A., Nosvelli, M. and Uberti, T.E. (2007) Space vs. networks in the geography of innovation: a European analysis, *Papers in Regional Science* 86(3): 471–493.

Martin, R. and Sunley, P. (2006) Path dependence and regional economic evolution, *Journal of Economic Geography* 6(4): 395–437.

Mizruchi, M.S. and Marquis, C. (2005) Egocentric, sociocentric, or dyadic? Identifying the appropriate level of analysis in the study of organizational networks, *Social Networks* 28: 187–208.

Nelson, R.R. and Winter, S.G. (1982) *An Evolutionary Theory of Economic Change*, Cambridge MA and London: The Belknap Press.

Newman, M.E.J. (2003) The structure and function of complex networks, *SIAM Review* 45: 167–256.

Niosi, J. and Bas, T.G. (2001) The competencies of regions – Canada's clusters in biotechnology, *Small Business Economics* 17: 31–42.

Nooteboom, B. (2000) *Learning and Innovation in Organizations and Economies*, Oxford: Oxford University Press.

Orsenigo, L., Pammolli, F., Riccaboni, M., Bonaccorsi, A. and Turchetti, G. (1998) The evolution of knowledge and the dynamics of an industry network, *Journal of Management and Governance* 1: 147–175.

Ozman, M. (2009) Inter-firm networks and innovation: a survey of literature, *Economics of Innovation and New Technology* 18(1): 39–67.

Ponds, R., van Oort, F.G. and Frenken, K. (2007) The geographical and institutional proximity of research collaboration, *Papers in Regional Science* 86: 423–443.

Powell, W.W., White, D.R., Koput, K.W. and Owen-Smith, J. (2005) Network dynamics and field evolution: the growth of interorganizational collaboration in the life sciences, *American Journal of Sociology* 110(4): 1132–1205.

Ripley, R., Snijders, T. and Preciado Lopez, P. (2011) *Manual for RSiena*, University of Oxford, Department of Statistics, Nuffield College, 1 May.

Rivera, M., Soderstrom, S. and Uzzi, B. (2010) Dynamics of dyads in social networks: assortative, relational, and proximity mechanisms, *Annual Review of Sociology* 36: 91–115.

Singh, J. (2005) Collaborative networks as determinants of knowledge diffusion patterns, *Management Science* 51: 756–770.

Snijders, T. (2001) The statistical evaluation of social network dynamics. In M. Sobel and M. Becker (eds) *Sociological Methodology*. Boston and London: Basil Blackwell, 361–395.

Snijders, T., Van De Bunt, G. and Steglich, C. (2010) Introduction to actor-based models for network dynamics, *Social Networks* 32: 44–60.

Steglich, C., Snijders, T. and Pearson, M. (2010) Dynamic networks and behavior: separating selection from influence, *Sociological Methodology* 40: 329–393.

Storper, M. (1992) The limits to globalization: technology districts and international trade, *Economic Geography* 68(1): 60–93.

Ter Wal, A.L.J. (2014) The dynamics of the inventor network in German biotechnology: geographic proximity versus triadic closure, *Journal of Economic Geography* 14: 589–620.

Ter Wal, A.L.J. and Boschma, R.A. (2009) Applying social network analysis in economic geography: framing some key analytical issues, *Annals of Regional Science* 43(3): 739–756.

United States Patent and Trademark Office (2002) *Technology Profile Report: Patent Examining Technology Center Groups 1630–1650, Biotechnology*, Patent Technology Monitoring Division Report, United States Patent and Trademark Office, Alexandria, VA.

United States Patent and Trademark Office (2010) *USPTO Assignee Harmonization Data File*. Retrieved 8 October 2011, from www.uspto.gov/web/offices/ac/ido/oeip/taf/data/misc/data_cd.doc/assignee_harmonization/.

Zucker, L.G., Darby, M.R. and Armstrong, J. (2002) Commercializing knowledge: university science, knowledge capture, and firm performance in biotechnology, *Management Science* 48: 138–153.

Zucker, L.G., Darby, M.R. and Brewer, M.B. (1998) Intellectual human capital and the birth of US biotechnology enterprises, *American Economic Review* 88: 290–306.

8 Social capital and the innovative performance of Italian provinces*

Riccardo Crescenzi, Luisa Gagliardi and Marco Percoco

1 Introduction

The concept of social capital has been extensively applied by economists and other social scientists to the analysis of a wide range of phenomena: from economic growth (Knack and Keefer, 1997) and development traps (Woolcock, 1998) to political participation (Di Pasquale and Glaeser, 1999), institutional performance (La Porta *et al.*, 1997) and the spread of secondary education (Goldin and Katz, 1999). However, the analysis of the link between social capital and the genesis of innovation has remained relatively under-explored in 'mainstream' economics literature. Economists of innovation and economic geographers have recently tried to fill this gap but no clear consensus has emerged on the impact of social capital on innovative performance and on the underlying transmission mechanisms (Cohen and Fields, 2000; Hauser *et al.*, 2007; Kallio *et al.*, 2009; Laursen and Masciarelli, 2007; Patton and Kenney, 2003; Sabatini, 2009; Tura and Harmaakorpi, 2005).

Existing literature on the social capital–innovation nexus adopts a broad definition of social capital that simultaneously encompasses all its dimensions (associational activities, political participation, institutional thickness and trust). This broad definition has made it difficult not only to empirically operationalize the concept but also to account for the contradictory evidence on its impact on innovative performance: positive in some studies (e.g. Akcomak and Ter Weel, 2009) and negative in others (e.g. Florida, 2002).

This paper looks at the local endowment of social capital in terms of attitude towards civicness and pro-social behaviour. In this perspective, local trust, reciprocity and even altruism, by lowering transaction costs, are fundamental components of an environment congenial for (high-risk) innovation investments that benefit from ties based on trust and cooperation (Dettori *et al.*, 2012; Hauser *et al.*, 2007). Trust and cooperation shape the networks through which valuable knowledge is exchanged and re-combined (Audretsch and Feldman, 2004), stimulating relational proximity and preventing stagnation and lock-in (Boschma, 2005). In this framework, the impact of social capital on innovation depends simultaneously on the density of the network linking knowledgeable individuals and on the extension of their 'radius of trust' (Fukuyama, 1995). The wider the radius of trust in the network of knowledgeable individuals, the greater the likelihood that complementary knowledge will be exchanged (Knack, 2001) with a positive impact on innovative performance.

In order to study the impact of social capital on innovation, this paper builds upon existing literature in a number of innovative ways. First, the paper develops an operational definition of social capital and a clear conceptualization of its impact on innovation by cross-fertilising the literature on the socio-institutional determinants of innovation with the literature on social capital. Second, while the large majority of the existing analyses on the impact of social capital on regional innovation are based on qualitative methods, this paper adopts a quantitative approach. Third, the empirical analysis also explores the causal nature of the social capital–innovation nexus by explicitly addressing the potential endogeneity bias through a robust identification strategy based on a time lag instrumental variable approach.

The analysis looks at the Italian provinces, an exemplary case study in the literature on social capital (Guiso *et al.*, 2004; Ichino and Maggi, 2000; Putnam, 1993) although – to the best of our knowledge – the link between social capital and innovation has not been explored in depth. Recent studies on social capital in Italy are largely qualitative (Ramella and Trigilia, 2009); those based on a quantitative approach focused on selected geographical areas (e.g. industrial districts, as in Cainelli *et al.*, 2005) or adopted a firm-based perspective in order to address the impact of social capital on the firms' propensity to innovate and their willingness to invest financial resources in innovative activities (Arrighetti and Lasagni, 2010; Laursen and Masciarelli, 2007).

The paper is organized as follows: the second section provides an overview of the literature on the link between innovation and social capital, developing an operational definition of the concept and highlighting the transmission mechanisms at play. Section 3 discusses the estimation strategy and the data, while the fourth section presents some key results discussing their economic implications. Finally some conclusions are drawn underlining the fundamental role of social capital as a determinant of local innovative performance.

2 How social capital shapes local innovative performance

A growing body of literature suggests that innovation is a social process embedded in the local socio-institutional environment that, in its turn, is systematically affected by the strength and intensity of social ties. The emphasis on the social dimension of innovation led to the definition of innovation-prone and innovation-averse regions (Rodríguez-Pose, 1999), social filters (Rodríguez-Pose and Crescenzi, 2008), innovative milieux (Breschi and Lissoni, 2001; Camagni, 1995), learning regions (Florida, 1995; Morgan, 1997) and regional systems of innovation (Cooke *et al.*, 1997). In this context, social capital – together with other 'intangible' territorial assets – plays a very important role for the understanding of differential innovative performance at the territorial level (Dettori *et al.*, 2012). However, the analysis of the impact of social capital on innovation has suffered from the lack of consensus on its definition and from the complexity of its operationalization and measurement (Guiso *et al.*, 2010). While Coleman (1988) argued that it coincides with the social structure of a society that facilitated the actions of individuals, Putnam (1993) identified social capital in terms of trust-based relations and groups, and Fukuyama (1995) suggested that social capital has to be intended in terms of trust, civicness and network relations.

When looking at social capital from the perspective of the literature on the socio-institutional determinants of innovation, it is immediately apparent that both the 'network' and 'civic-engagement' dimensions of social capital are relevant to innovation dynamics. Innovation is simultaneously influenced by the extent, density and shape of the networks through which knowledge is channelled (Breschi and Lissoni, 2001) and by the 'rush and motivation' for the development (and maintenance) of these linkages used for the exchange of 'economically valuable' knowledge (Storper and Venables, 2004). Both dimensions play a crucial role in knowledge exchange, re-combination and generation (Dettori *et al.*, 2012).

The shape and density of networks matters for innovation given that 'bridging' networks – i.e. 'open' connections between heterogeneous groups – foster innovative capabilities by facilitating the diffusion of valuable and non-redundant knowledge and preventing stagnation and lock-in (Boschma, 2005; Dettori *et al.*, 2012). Relational networks connecting individuals, groups, firms, industries with different knowledge bases are a critical precondition for knowledge generation and transfer. In this context, innovation emerges from a cumulative process embedded in the social context and systematically affected by mechanisms of interactive learning stimulating the exchange and re-combination of knowledge (Asheim, 1999; Lundvall, 1992).

Social capital is then a pre-condition for innovation since it stimulates interpersonal interactions, the formation of networks and the circulation of valuable knowledge (Tura and Harmaakorpi, 2005; Capello and Faggian, 2005).[1] The so-called 'weak ties hypothesis' proposed by Granovetter (1973) is crucial in this context. Relationships between people can be characterized by either frequent contacts with deep emotional involvement or by sporadic interactions with low emotional commitment. The former category is generally identified as 'strong ties' – such as the relationships within families or close friends – while the latter is associated with the definition of 'weak ties' linking individuals characterized by loose acquaintances. When contextualizing Granovetter's argument into the analysis of innovation, 'weak ties' can be seen as a source of novel information and responsible for the diffusion of ideas (Granovetter, 1982; Rogers, 1995), while 'strong ties' increase the risk of exchanging redundant knowledge simply because they connect knowledge seekers with other individuals that are more likely to deal with 'known'/familiar information and knowledge (Levin and Cross, 2004).

In other words, weak ties are fundamental in spreading information because they operate as a bridge between otherwise disconnected social groups (Ruef, 2002). Weak ties serve as a bridging mechanism between communities within the same society, while strong ties function as a bonding device within homogeneous groups potentially hampering the degree of sociability outside restricted social circles (Beugelsdijk and Smulders, 2003).

> If knowledge stays too much inside ... bounded communities – when communities mistrust each other – then knowledge will have a limited and uneven spread. Bridging between communities in a context of generalized trust gives each communities confidence that their knowledge will be used by members of other communities to their mutual benefit.
>
> (Rodríguez-Pose and Storper, 2006: 8)

As a consequence, social capital – in terms of trust, reciprocity and even altruism – by lowering transaction costs (Diani, 2004), generates the incentives ('rush and motivation', as in Storper and Venables, 2004) for 'bridging' ties to be generated, maintained over time and actively used for valuable knowledge exchange, contributing to an environment congenial for (high-risk) innovation investment that benefits from 'open' ties based on trust and cooperation (Hauser *et al.*, 2007). In other words, social capital also influences innovation by means of reciprocity (motivation for knowledge exchange) in small groups or networks. This type of pro-social behaviour is often motivated by forms of expectations about the behaviour of other individuals and this, in its turn – as argued by Dodgson and Gann (2010) – results in a more efficient sharing of information and knowledge. Furthermore, it is worth noticing that pro-social behaviour, in its purest form, can also be motivated by altruism, i.e. a situation in which intrinsic motivation is overwhelmingly dominant with respect to extrinsic motivation (Benabou and Tirole, 2003). A wide range of human actions can be driven by altruism[2] or by the willingness to contribute to social welfare with no reward in exchange. In this regard, Dogson and Gann (2010) argue that collaborative efforts in developing freeware software is a 'special' case of pro-social behaviour largely driven by intrinsic motivation. However, in the case of formal product innovation, this situation is practically very rare: even in the particular case of 'purely' academic research, the extrinsic motivation of scientists in the form of career concerns remains crucial. When innovation is captured by means of patents (as in the standard quantitative literature based on the Knowledge Production Function), these forms of collaborative (altruistic) innovation are necessarily excluded from the analysis. Coherently with this framework – and under the significant constraints in term of data availability that a priori prevent the inclusion of direct proxies for the structure of local network relations – the empirical analysis will proxy social capital by means of data on blood donations and participation into voluntary associations. In light of the conceptualization and measure of innovation adopted in this paper, these proxies will be interpreted as signs of attitudes for pro-social behaviour, 'civicness' or civic values (as in Putnam, 1993) promoting simultaneously the production of public goods, the incentives for knowledge-sharing and acting as a pre-condition for its diffusion through 'bridging' networks.

The case of Italy is a particularly appropriate 'laboratory' to test these hypotheses. Putnam (1993) has suggested that one of the main reasons for the perpetuation of developmental differences between the north and the south of Italy is to be ascribed to the quality of the institutions and social capital. Arrighetti and Lasagni (2010) analysed the effect of these social conditions on the propensity to innovate of Italian firms and concluded that innovative firms tend to cluster in those provinces characterized by higher levels of 'positive social capital', defined as civicness and high social interactions, and lower levels of 'negative social capital', generally associated with opportunistic behaviour caused by the existence of groups lobbying for partisan interests. Following the same line of argument, but focusing on case studies such as the Emilia Romagna industrial districts, Cainelli *et al.* (2005) argued that extensive horizontal relationships among local economic actors generate positive network externalities favouring the exchange of valuable knowledge and fostering the innovative performance of local firms.

3 Model of empirical investigation

In order to assess the impact of social capital on the innovative performance of Italian provinces, the empirical analysis relies on a 'modified' Knowledge Production Function (KPF) approach. The analysis is based on the KPF (formalized by Griliches, 1979, 1986, and Jaffe, 1986) but adopts a place-based perspective, with Italian provinces (NUTS3 level) as units of observation. This specification of the KPF is customary in the literature on regional innovation (Audretsch, 2003; Audretsch and Feldman, 1996; Crescenzi and Rodríguez-Pose, 2011; Crescenzi *et al.*, 2007, 2012; Feldman, 1994; Fritsch, 2002; Moreno *et al.*, 2005a; O'hUallachain and Leslie, 2007; Ponds *et al.*, 2010; Varga, 1998) and it allows us to focus upon the territorial dynamics of innovation by taking account of our measure of social capital as determinant of regional innovative performance. The Regional Knowledge Production Function takes the following form:

$$Patents\_growth_{i,(t-T)\to t} = \beta_0 + \beta_1 Patent_{i,t-T} + \beta_2 SocCap_{i,t-T} +$$
$$\beta_3 Grad_{i,t-T} + \beta_4 privR\&D_{i,t-T} + \qquad \text{(Equation 1)}$$
$$\beta_5 X_{i,t-T} + \delta_i + \varepsilon_i$$

Where $Patents\_growth_{i,(t-T)\to t} = \dfrac{1}{T}\ln\left(\dfrac{Patents_{i,t}}{Patents_{i,t-T}}\right)$ is the logarithmic transfor-

mation of the ratio of patent applications in province i at the two extremes of the period of analysis $(t-T,t)$. Among the independent variables, $soccap_{i,t-T}$ is our variable of interest and represents the measure of social capital in each province i at time $(t-T)$; $patents_{i,t-T}$ is the log of the level of patent applications per million inhabitants at the beginning of the period of analysis $(t-T)$; $privrd_{i,t-T}$ is private expenditure in R&D as percentage of regional GDP at $(t-T)$; $grad_{i,t-T}$ is the number of graduates as a percentage of regional population at time $(t-T)$; $X_{i,t-T}$

is the matrix of additional controls (i.e. regional sectoral composition, population density and female unemployment) at $(t-T)$; finally, δ_i represents macro-regional dummies for southern, central and northern Italy and ε_i is the error term. A detailed description of the variables is included in Table A.8.1 in Appendix A.

Regional innovative performance – OECD patent data are used as a proxy for innovation. The generation of innovation is proxied by the logarithmic approximation of the growth rate of patents over the period 2001–2007.[3] Patent statistics are generally regarded as a reliable measure of innovative output providing comparable information on inventions across different regions and a broad range of technological sectors (OECD, 2001; Sedgley and Elmslie, 2004). Conversely, patent-based innovation indicators fail to account for either the differentiated degree of novelty of patented products (not all patented products are equally 'new' and/or valuable) or the non-patentability of many inventions (in particular as regards process innovation or 'open source' innovation as discussed above). In addition, different sectors appear to have intrinsically different propensities to patent inventions. In order to minimize any potential bias in our analysis: (a) there are controls for the initial patent intensity of each region; (b) there are also controls for the economic sectoral structure. The specification of the dependent variable in terms of growth rate is an attempt to overcome the lack of panel data and provide some evidence on the dynamic effect of social capital on innovation (Crescenzi *et al.*, 2007): after controlling for the effect of initial conditions in terms of innovative performance (initial level of patenting), social capital is tested as a predictor of a given region's capability to develop based upon existing technological infrastructure and hence improve its innovative performance (patent growth rate).

Initial patent intensity – the initial patent intensity in each province is used as a proxy for the existing technological capabilities and their distance from the technological cutting edge. It also controls for differences in the patenting propensity often related to pre-existent differences in sector specialization as discussed above.

Social capital – coherently with the conceptual framework outlined above, the analysis looks at the concept of social capital as propensity towards pro-social behaviour in terms of attitude for cooperation with anonymous others, participation in groups and associations and civicness. The rationale for the adoption of this definition is that 'positive' social behaviour tends to be generally associated with more successful economic outcomes (De Blasio and Nuzzo, 2010) and that a greater level of civic engagement and cooperation may, in its turn, facilitate the exchange of economically valuable (often non-codified or tacit) knowledge in 'open' networks. From this perspective, we refer to the idea proposed by Burt (1992: 32) that 'people who do better are somehow better connected' and that those people 'connected to certain others, trusting certain others, devoted to support certain others' can be identified as structural holes connecting different segments of the society. The concept of social capital interpreted in terms of civic virtues and propensity to cooperate has been operationalized through a composite indicator based on two key variables: 'blood donations per 100 residents' and 'voluntary associations per sq. km'.[4]

Both variables are interpreted as measures for altruism reflecting the attitude to develop horizontal relations fostering networks of civic engagement (Arrighetti and Lasagni, 2010; Beugelsdijk and van Schaik, 2005; De Blasio and Nuzzo, 2012) and are considered customary proxies for the participation of individuals in activities with positive social externalities (Cartocci, 2007) and pro-social behaviour (Putnam, 1993; Guiso *et al.*, 2004; Nannicini *et al.*, 2010).

The reliability of these variables as proxies for social capital is also reinforced by some specificities of the Italian case. First of all, it should be borne in mind that blood donations are completely free in Italy and national regulations do not allow for any form of monetary compensation for donors. In addition AVIS (Italian National Association of Blood Donors) data confirm that blood donations clinics are equally accessible and evenly distributed across provinces and regions in the entire country.[5]

Second, empirical evidence also makes it possible to rule out the possibility that the density of voluntary associations could be considered also as a proxy for urbanization economies: when the composite indicator for social capital is regressed on the 'number of firms per sq. km' there is no evidence of any significant correlation.[6]

Our composite indicator for social capital is computed in line with the indicators of technological capabilities (ArCo) by Archibugi and Coco (2005). The social capital indicator combines both variables with equal weights:

$$Socialcapital = \sum_{i=1}^{2} \lambda_i I_i$$

Where I_i represents each of the two variables adopted as proxy for social capital (blood donations and voluntary associations) and λ_i is the constant equal to ½. The index is then normalized to vary from 0 to 1 as follows:

$$I_i = \frac{Observed\_value - Minimum\_observed\_value}{Maximum\_observed\_value - Minimum\_observed\_value}$$

Social capital variables cover all Italian provinces (NUTS3 level)[7] and are available from ISTAT (Italian National Statistical Office).[8] The use of a composite indicator as proxy for social capital endowment is customary in the literature and reflects the multifaceted nature of this concept. In addition, the use of composite indicators is crucial for the identification strategy discussed below: given the significant constraints in terms of historical data availability at the sub-national level, it would be impossible to identify suitable instruments for each social capital variable separately.

Innovation input – 'private R&D as a share of GDP' and the 'number of graduates over the total population' are used as proxies for the key inputs of the 'standard' regional Knowledge Production Function (Crescenzi *et al.*, 2007; Moreno *et al.*, 2005b; O'hUallachain and Leslie, 2007; Ponds *et al.*, 2010;

Varga, 1998). On account of limited data availability, our R&D measure is available only at regional level (NUTS2), while the number of graduates is available for each province (NUTS3).

Controls – our specification of the knowledge production function includes controls for population density at the provincial level, labour market characteristics in terms of female unemployment rate and sector structure measured by the share of employment in agriculture and services.[9]

The sectoral composition is controlled for by using data on employment for three sectors: agriculture, industry and services and is interpreted as a measure of specialization. All controls are available at the provincial level (NUTS3) from ISTAT.

The analysis includes additional controls to minimize the impact of spatial autocorrelation in the error term. In particular, it includes the spatial lag of population density[10] as a measure of accessibility and macro-regional dummies (north, south and centre) in order to control for time-invariant area characteristics and other unobserved sources of spatial autocorrelation (Armstrong, 1995; Rodríguez-Pose, 1999).

Identification strategy – the next question is how to identify the link between innovation and social capital given the potential endogeneity of social capital on account of both reverse causality and omitted variable bias as well as the relevant risk of measurement errors implicitly associated with the adoption of proxies to measure the key variable of interest.

The main research hypothesis in this paper is that social capital can be treated as a determinant of innovation as it facilitates, through the promotion of cooperation and civic engagement, the development of networks between knowledgeable individuals and the circulation and diffusion of knowledge. Even if grounded in a large body of literature and supported by robust qualitative evidence, this argument may overlook the possibility that causality runs in the opposite direction: more innovative provinces might be able to generate – through economic incentives sufficiently high as to create valuable networks – a virtuous cycle based on cooperation and trust, stimulating civicness and a sense of community and providing greater incentives towards pro-social behaviours. In addition, an omitted-variable problem may also bias the estimation of the model. The measures of social capital are potentially correlated to local characteristics that cannot be fully controlled for. This is particularly problematic when considering neighbouring effects and spatial correlation: the omitted variable bias may depend on both local characteristics and neighbouring area features affecting local innovative performance.

Finally, the adoption of proxies and the construction of a composite indicator of social capital may potentially exacerbate the measurement errors in our variable of interest.

In order to minimize the impact of all these problems, the model controls for spatial correlation by including the spatial lag of social capital[11] and a set of macro-regional dummies. Furthermore, the potential endogeneity of social capital is dealt with by adopting an instrumental variable approach (2SLS). In particular, the level of social capital in each province is instrumented with the 'voter turnout in selected historical referenda'.[12] For the instrument, the analysis relies on regional-level[13] data due to the lack of historical quantitative information at the provincial level.

In order to understand the rationale behind our identification strategy, it is important to consider that, in the case of social capital, the selection of an appropriate instrument is constrained by two major factors. First, as discussed above, there is still no consensus on a single definition of social capital and its measure (Guiso *et al.*, 2010). This implies that the search for an appropriate instrument cannot build on the micro-foundations of the concept. Second, there are major problems in recovering reliable time series for the key social capital proxies, especially when the analysis is performed for sub-national geographical units. This also explains why it was impossible to use a panel structure for the empirical analysis and why it was also impossible to make use of the standard instrumental variables time lag approach based on the lagged values of the variables of interest (Putnam, 1993).

In order to overcome both shortfalls, the existent empirical literature on the economics of institutions and culture in general and on social capital in particular has made extensive use of alternative historical proxies as instruments.

The existing literature on the impact of social capital, by building on both the theoretical framework of the overlapping-generations model and the multidimensionality of social capital (Guiso *et al.*, 2008), has suggested that intergenerationally transmitted priors and social structures (measurable by means of different but correlated variables) affect individual decisions regarding whether to trust other members of the society or alternatively just the member of a restricted group (Tabellini, 2010). As a consequence, in line with the existing literature, the identification strategy is not based on the causal link between 'referenda turnout' and social capital indicators. On the contrary, the proposed instrumental variable – in the absence of reliable historical data on the social capital indicators at the beginning of the twentieth century – is considered as an alternative proxy for past stocks of social capital and adopted as a time lag instrument (Tabellini, 2010; Putnam, 1993; Tomassini, 1999).

The instrument – 'voter turnout in selected historical referenda' – is expected to be positively correlated with social capital as it is considered in the literature as an alternative proxy for civic participation and engagement and civic virtues (De Blasio and Nuzzo, 2012).

Furthermore, the historical turnout in referenda of 'general' relevance can be interpreted – in line with a large body of literature – as a proxy for the propensity of people to participate in social life showing positive social behaviour. This choice is also supported by Putnam's (1993) view of participation in 'general interest' referenda as radically different from turnout in political elections. While all parties involved in political elections are largely motivated by self-interest (being elected for candidates, having their instances represented in the relevant institutional bodies for their electors), participants (promoters, campaigners and voters) in referenda are directly interested in promoting change at the level of the entire society and their self-interest (if any) remains very limited (Putnam, 1993).

4 Empirical results

The cartographic representation of the key variables of interest (Figures 8.1 and 8.2) shows similarities between the spatial distribution of innovation and that of the composite measure of social capital. The geography of innovation is linked with social capital patterns and, although the fundamental north–south divide is apparent, the maps confirm the provincial level as the relevant spatial unit of analysis.

In order to further investigate this preliminary descriptive evidence, the Regional Knowledge Production Function specified in Equation 1 is estimated and results are presented in Table 8.1. The values of the R-squared and of the Moran's I test[14] for spatial autocorrelation in the regression residuals are reported for all specifications of the model, confirming the robustness of our results.

In the basic specification, only the 'traditional' inputs of the KPF (R&D expenditure and human capital) are included in the model together with the initial level of patenting in each province (Table 8.1, Col. 1). The initial number of patents per million inhabitants is statistically significant at the 1 per cent level and negatively associated with the dependent variable. This suggests a (weak) convergence in innovative performance in line with existing regional-level research on Europe and the United States (Crescenzi and Rodríguez-Pose, 2011; Crescenzi *et al.*, 2007; Moreno *et al.*, 2005b), and reflects a weak trend in (conditional)

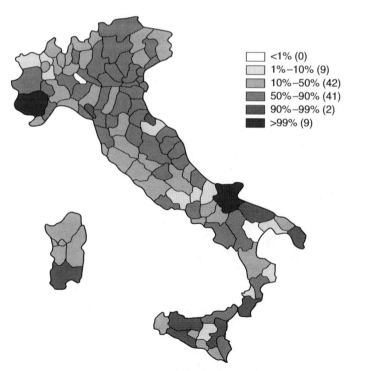

☐	<1% (0)
▨	1%–10% (9)
▨	10%–50% (42)
▨	50%–90% (41)
▨	90%–99% (2)
■	>99% (9)

Figure 8.1 Growth rate of patents (per million inhabitants), 2001–2007 (source: own elaboration).

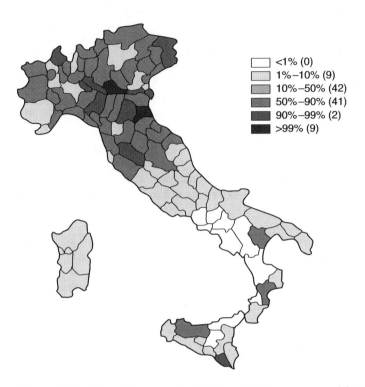

Figure 8.2 Social capital, composite indicator, 2001 (source: own elaboration).

technological convergence in advanced economies. In the Italian case, this trend also reflects the crisis of traditionally successful innovative areas (such as industrial districts) and the emergence of some new successful players. The 'core' long-established areas of 'Made in Italy' – such as the industrial districts specializing in the production of leather goods and shoes, mainly in Tuscany and Marches – experienced a negative dynamic in productivity, while other areas – in particular those specializing in chemistry and oil (spatially concentrated in Tuscany and Sicily) and metallurgy (Tuscany and Sardinia) or the industrial districts specializing in clothing (Veneto and Apulia) and eyewear (Veneto, Emilia-Romagna and Friuli-Venezia Giulia) – showed an economic performance significantly above the national average (ISTAT, 2007, 2008).

Regional investment in R&D is highly significant and positively associated with innovative performance. Investments in R&D are generally weak in Italy (1.2 per cent of GDP in 2010, the lowest rate in the EU-15), in sharp contrast with the above-EU-average intensity of the leading provinces in Lombardy and Emilia-Romagna, generating a highly localized geography of innovative efforts. However, in all specifications of the model, there is no evidence of any impact of human capital endowment on innovation. This result highlights one of the specificities of the Italian case: in contrast to the rest of Europe and the

Table 8.1 Estimation of the empirical model: regional knowledge production function with social capital – annual growth rate of regional patenting (2001–2007)

	(1)	(2)	(3)	(4)	(5)	(6)	(7)	(8)
Dep. var.: patent growth	OLS	OLS	OLS	OLS	OLS	OLS	OLS	2SLS
Patents (level in 2001)	−0.0407** (0.0104)	−0.0547*** (0.0101)	−0.0536*** (0.0099)	−0.0524*** (0.0100)	−0.0518*** (0.0100)	−0.0548*** (0.0088)	−0.0685*** (0.0115)	−0.0771*** (0.0113)
Private R&D	0.0373*** (0.0099)	0.0277** (0.0098)	0.0264** (0.0109)	0.0262** (0.0113)	0.0256** (0.0107)	0.0167 (0.0120)	0.0048 (0.0153)	0.0023 (0.0140)
Graduates	0.0766 (0.0488)	0.0386 (0.0515)	0.0376 (0.0507)	0.0460 (0.0562)	0.0889 (0.0700)	0.0759 (0.0660)	0.0545 (0.0649)	0.0239 (0.0649)
Social capital		0.182*** (0.0426)	0.185*** (0.0410)	0.180*** (0.0399)	0.191*** (0.0428)	0.207*** (0.0427)	0.169*** (0.0516)	0.458*** (0.0742)
Spatial lag of bridging social capital			−0.0126 (0.0117)	−0.0142 (0.0130)	−0.0149 (0.0119)	−0.0131 (0.0090)	−0.0191* (0.0103)	−0.0174 (0.0171)
Female unemployment				0.0090 (0.0145)	0.0145 (0.0218)	0.0093 (0.0204)	0.0133 (0.0194)	0.0107 (0.0189)
Employment in agriculture					0.0231 (0.0155)	0.0217 (0.0142)	0.0146 (0.0124)	0.0228 (0.0151)
Employment in industry					0.0526 (0.0426)	0.0338 (0.0374)	0.0247 (0.0404)	0.0573* (0.0340)
Population density						0.0294** (0.0120)	0.0301** (0.0111)	0.0372*** (0.0091)
Spatial lag of population density						−0.0018 (0.00318)	−0.0008 (0.00314)	−0.0008 (0.00300)
Macro-regional dummies							YES	YES
Constant	0.428** (0.165)	0.291 (0.172)	0.288 (0.170)	0.328 (0.196)	0.578* (0.294)	0.353 (0.293)	0.335 (0.282)	0.194 (0.278)
Observations	97	97	97	97	97	97	97	97
R-squared	0.181	0.276	0.281	0.285	0.303	0.355	0.399	0.209
Moran's I	0.0082	−0.0442	−0.0263	−0.0153	−0.0387	−0.0477	−0.0777	−0.0420
P-value	0.362	0.354	0.408	0.468	0.376	0.296	0.164	0.360

Source: own elaboration.

Notes

*** *p*<0.01.

** *p*<0.05.

* *p*<0.1.

Clustered – robust standard errors in parentheses.

US (Crescenzi *et al.*, 2007), the local endowment of human capital does not exert a direct impact on local innovation due to the fundamental mismatch between (southern) graduates' skill profile and their occupations (Iammarino and Marinelli, 2011).

Subsequently, our key variable of interest, namely social capital, is included in the regression (Table 8.1, Col. 2) showing a positive and highly significant correlation with the innovative performance of Italian provinces. The following specifications allow for the inclusions of additional regressors in order to check for the robustness of our preliminary findings. In Column 3, the spatial lag of social capital[15] is introduced into the model without any significant evidence of spatial correlation in the sample.[16] Subsequently, additional controls for labour market characteristics, sector structure, population density and its spatial lag (as a proxy for accessibility) are introduced into the model (Table 8.1, Cols 4, 5 and 6, respectively). Neither the level of female unemployment (proxy for the efficiency of the local labour market), nor the measures of sector specialization (the share of employment in agriculture and industry) are statistically significant. The highly regulated Italian labour market does not exert any influence on local-level innovative performance. The same is true for regional specialization patterns, which are heavily constrained by low factor mobility and lack of critical mass in average firm size. What matters for innovation – and this result remains robust in subsequent specifications of the model – are agglomeration economies: population density is positively associated with innovation with a 5 per cent significance level, while the spatial lag of population density is not statistically significant. The most innovative provinces seem to be those where density is higher: major urban areas with their functional hinterland. Finally, in order to minimize the persistence of additional omitted variables and residual neighbouring effects and spatial autocorrelation, macro-regional dummies were introduced. Given that the Moran's I test (computed for each specification of the model) does not detect spatial autocorrelation in the residuals, the combination of macro-regional variables and spatially lagged explanatory variables is able to capture a significant part of the total spatial variability of the data.

The measure of social capital remains positively associated with innovation with a significance level of 1 per cent in all the specifications. After fully controlling for the north–south divide and other spatial effects, social capital emerges as the most important predictor of innovative performance together with the proxy for agglomeration economies. Highly agglomerated provinces – where face-to-face contacts maximize the exchange of knowledge – with high levels of cooperation and associational activities show the best innovative performance. This result provides quantitative confirmation for the qualitative evidence of some existing studies on innovation and social capital (Biagiotti, 2008; Ramella and Trigilia, 2009, 2010), suggesting that the positive and significant effect of social capital on innovation is largely based on evidence of pro-social behaviour stimulating generalized trust and cooperation between otherwise disconnected communities. Such cooperative attitude allows for the access to non-redundant information, favouring the transfer and re-combination of valuable knowledge.

The robustness of these results is tested against a potential endogeneity bias by means of an instrumental variable (IV) approach: 2SLS results are shown in Table 8.1, Col. 8. The IV results strongly support the existence of a causal link between social capital and innovation (positive coefficient and statistically significant at the 1 per cent level). The first stage regression (Table 8.2a) confirms the validity of this instrumental strategy. The instrument, referendum turnout, is highly correlated to the instrumental variable, social capital, showing the expected sign and confirming the rational for its selection.

Table 8.2a First stage regression

Dep. var.	(1)
	Social capital
Patents	0.0084
(level in 2001)	(0.0224)
Private R&D	0.0004
	(0.0218)
Graduates	0.0743
	(0.0782)
Female unemployment	−0.0122
	(0.0342)
Population density	−0.0172
	(0.0142)
Spatial lag of population density	−0.0168
	(0.0225)
Employment in agriculture	−0.0159**
	(0.0064)
Employment in industry	−0.0502
	(0.0326)
Spatial lag of social capital	0.2355
	(0.1699)
Referendum	1.1679***
	(0.2923)
Macro-regional dummies	YES
Constant	−4.9766***
	(1.5394)
Observations	97
R-squared	0.628

Source: own elaboration.

Notes
*** $p<0.01$.
** $p<0.05$.
* $p<0.1$.
Clustered – robust standard errors in parentheses.

Being aware that the econometric literature on instrument validity suggests that it is possible to encounter the problem of weak instruments even with an unproblematic first stage regression (Staiger and Stock, 1997; Stock and Yogo, 2005) and in order to rule out any related risk the rule of thumb proposed by Staiger and Stock (1997) and Stock and Yogo's (2005) threshold values are applied. The F-statistic in the first stage is consistent with both criteria[17] (Table 8.2b), confirming that the instrumental variables strategy is robust and unaffected by any potential weak instrument bias.

To support the robustness of the statistical findings discussed above, a number of additional robustness checks were implemented. In Table 8.3, the OLS specification is reported, substituting the composite indicator of social capital with its two components, namely blood donations and voluntary associations. Both variables are positively correlated with innovation and statistically significant, confirming their reliability as proxy for social capital interpreted in terms of pro-social behaviour. Further robustness checks on the specification of the model are included in Appendix B.

Finally, in order to provide further support for the reliability of the instrument, it is necessary to check whether this variable is systematically correlated with alternative social capital proxies commonly adopted in the empirical literature. An extensive literature suggests that the multidimensionality of social capital has to be carefully taken into account when analysing its impact on any economic outcome. In particular, in the conceptual framework of this paper, substantially different effects may be produced by different extensions of the 'radius of trust' (Fukuyama, 1995). The extension of the cooperative networks in place and the typology of ties among the involved actors may affect the quality of information exchanged as well as its degree of novelty. Strong ties within closed groups are associated with the exchange of redundant knowledge and potential risk of lock in. This typology of networks and trust relations, commonly identified with the concept of bonding social capital, tends to be associated with intense relations among homogeneous individuals (Putnam, 2000; Beugelsdijk and Smulders, 2003) and often operationalized in terms of trust and relations with family and close friends (De Blasio and Nuzzo, 2012).

Checking for the existence of a systematic correlation between the selected instrument and the so-called 'bonding social capital' is particularly interesting in the case of Italy where the reliance on networks of family and friends has been traditionally associated with the potential emergence of negative social externalities. Since the seminal work by Banfield (1958), the low propensity to cooperate was associated with, among other things, the strength of family ties. In particular, Banfield (1958) pointed out the negative impact on economic development of the low propensity to cooperate, which, in turn, implies high transaction costs. This 'development trap' is the outcome of strong family ties (the so-called 'amoral familism'), high uncertainty and a highly unequal distribution of income and wealth. So far, there has been no conclusive empirical evidence confirming Banfield's hypothesis, but some recent research tends to support this view (Alesina and Giuliano, 2010; Giavazzi *et al.*, 2010; Duranton *et al.*, 2009).

Table 8.2b First stage statistics

Variable	Shea Partial R2	Partial R2	F(2, 19)	P-value
Social capital	0.1056	0.1056	15.97	0.008

Source: own elaboration.

Table 8.3 Robustness checks (1): estimation of the empirical model – regional knowledge production function with blood donations and voluntary associations; annual growth rate of regional patenting (2001–2007)

Dep. var.: patent growth	(1)
	OLS
Patents (level in 2001)	−0.0739***
	(0.0115)
Private R&D	0.0140
	(0.0133)
Graduates	0.0429
	(0.0687)
Voluntary associations	0.0514***
	(0.0115)
Blood donations	0.0855***
	(0.0257)
Female unemployment	0.0108
	(0.0179)
Employment in agriculture	0.0099
	(0.0128)
Employment in industry	0.0235
	(0.0353)
Population density	0.0220*
	(0.0112)
Spatial lag of population density	−0.0008
	(0.0032)
Macro-regional dummies	YES
Constant	0.243
	(0.342)
Observations	97
R-squared	0.430

Source: own elaboration.

Notes
*** $p<0.01$.
** $p<0.05$.
* $p<0.1$.
Clustered – robust standard errors in parentheses.

Table 8.4 Robustness checks (2): correlation between the instrument and alternative social capital proxies

Dep. var.:	(1)
	Referendum
	OLS
'Bonding' social capital	−0.0518 (0.0697)
Macro-regional dummies	YES
Constant	4.5060*** (0.0691)
Observations	97
R-squared	0.804

Source: own elaboration.

Notes
*** $p<0.01$.
** $p<0.05$.
* $p<0.1$.
Clustered – robust standard errors in parentheses.

Although recent studies pointed out the dangers of assuming a straight-forward correlation between the intensity of ties with family and close friends and the emergence of negative social behaviour (De Blasio and Nuzzo, 2010), the relevance of a pre-existent extensive literature building on this hypothesis deserves a deeper analysis. To rule out any doubt in this regard, a composite indicator for bonding social capital is computed by following the procedure adopted for the creation of our key regressor. In order to capture the strength of ties with family and friends, the analysis relies on two key indicators: 'the number of families having lunch at least once per week with relatives and close friends (per 100 households)' and 'the number of young adult individuals living with parents (per 100 young adults)'.[18]

The instrument – namely referendum turnout – is regressed on the composite measure of bonding social capital controlling for macro-regional dummies. Results reported in Table 8.4 confirm that the instrument is not significantly correlated with bonding social capital, supporting the reliability of our main findings and confirming that the empirical analysis is correctly identifying the impact of a very specific typology of social capital: pro-social behaviour and generalized trust between otherwise disconnected groups.

5 Conclusions

A large body of literature has looked at the very different ways in which social capital influences economic and social activities. The analysis of innovation has suffered from the lack of a suitable working definition for social capital and from the difficulties in operationalizing its links to innovation dynamics. This paper fills this gap by looking at social capital as a fundamental determinant of innovation that facilitates the generation and persistence of the networks favouring the diffusion and circulation of valuable non-redundant knowledge. In this perspective, the effect of social capital on innovation is shaped by the emergence of pro-social behaviour stimulating the attitude towards generalized trust and cooperation and facilitating the exchange of complementary knowledge between individuals belonging to different epistemic communities. This paper has empirically tested these hypotheses by means of the quantitative analysis of the innovative performance of Italian provinces. Notwithstanding the significant data limitations affecting all quantitative research on social capital and its effect, the results are clear-cut and robust.

Social capital – as propensity towards pro-social behaviour and generalized trust – is an important predictor of innovative performance after controlling for the 'traditional' knowledge inputs (R&D investments and human capital endowment) and for other characteristics of the local economy. The empirical analysis has devoted special attention to the potential endogeneity of social capital that might bias the estimation of its impact on innovation. The instrumental variable approach has made it possible to identify a clear causal link between social capital and innovation. The identification of these links suggests that – although changes in the local endowment of social capital are certainly hard to promote through public policies – carefully designed innovation policies can contribute towards creating incentives for cooperative behaviour. For example, policies based on the regional and inter-institutional mobility of 'knowledgeable individuals' and cooperative research projects can contribute to the generation of trust-based ties and reinforce the external projection of existing networks among innovative agents. Further exploration of these policy options remains in our agenda for future research but this paper is a step towards opening the way to a more systematic quantitative exploration of the link between innovation and social capital as an important pre-condition for policy analysis.

Acknowledgements

The authors are grateful to Sylvie Charlot, Guido De Blasio, Steve Gibbons, Ian Gordon, Andrés Rodríguez-Pose, Stefano Usai and participants in the ERSA Conference 2011 (Barcelona), the EU REAL-CRENos workshop (Cagliari), the Work-in-progress Seminars of the LSE Geography and Environment Department (London) and the Research Seminars of the Economics Department of Roma Tre University (Rome) for their comments on earlier drafts of this paper. The comments from the anonymous referees, which helped to improve the manuscript substantially, are also gratefully acknowledged. The research leading to these results has received funding from the European Union Seventh Framework Programme FP7/2007–2013 under grant agreement n SSH-CT-2010–266959. The research is also part of the UK Spatial Economics Research Centre. The usual disclaimer applies.

Appendix A

Variables included in the analysis

Table A.8.1 Variables list

Variables	Description	Source	Year
Patents growth	Logarithmic transformation of the ratio of patents per million inhabitants in region i at the two extremes of the period of analysis (t – T,t)	OECD RegPat database	2001–2007
Patents (level in 2001)	Logarithm of the level of patent applications per million inhabitants at the beginning of the period of analysis (t – T)	OECD RegPat database	2001
Private R&D	Logarithm of private expenditure in R&D as percentage of regional GDP at (t – T)	ISTAT Indicatori Ricerca e Innovazione	2001
Graduates	Logarithm of the number of graduates in population at time (t – T)	EUROSTAT Regional Database	2001
Female unemployment	Logarithm of the number of unemployed women in total female labour force	OECD Regional Database Regional Labour Market TL3 database	2001
Sectoral shares and Herfindal Index	Sector employment/total employment ratio defined for agriculture, industry and services. Herfindal calculated as the sum of the square of these ratios.	OECD – Regional Database Regional Labour Market TL3 dataset	2001
Population density	Logarithm of the population in respect to local surface	OECD Regional Database Demographic Statistics TL3 dataset	2001
Social capital *Civicness and pro-social behaviour*	Blood donations (number of blood donations per 100 residents)	Cartocci (2007)	2001
	Voluntary associations (number of voluntary associations per sq. km)	Cartocci (2007)	2001
Social capital 'Bonding' (robustness checks)	Weekly lunch (number of families having lunch at least once per week with relatives and close friends per 100 households)	ISTAT Rilevazione 'Parentela e Reti di solidarietà'	2001
	Adult children (number of young adult individuals living with parents per 100 young adults)	ISTAT Rilevazione 'Parentela e Reti di solidarietà'	2001
Instrumental variable Social capital *Instrument – referenda*	Logarithm of the voter turnout to the following historical referenda: 1946 (monarchy vs. republic), 1974 (divorce), 1978 and 1981 (abortion), 1985 ('scala mobile') and 1987 (nuclear power)	Nuzzo (2006)	1946–1974– 1978–1981– 1985–1987 (mean value)

Source: own elaboration.

Appendix B

Further robustness checks

Table A.8.2 reports the key instrumental variable regression re-estimated with the dependent variable in levels (rather than in growth rates). When compared to the initial specification, where patent growth rate was used as the dependent variable, while also controlling for the initial patent intensity in each province, this additional specification aims to capture the dynamic effect of social capital on innovation in a complementary manner. The measure of social capital is regressed against the innovative performance of Italian provinces in subsequent years in order to test for a path dependency associated with the social capital dimension.

Columns 1, 2 and 3 in Table A.8.2 report the estimation results using, respectively, the number of patents per million of inhabitants in 2002, 2005 and 2007 as dependent variables,[19] while controlling for the potential endogeneity of social capital by means of the instrumental variables approach. These additional results confirm the robustness of the relation between social capital and innovation and show that it is stronger over time, highlighting a path-dependency/cumulative effect of social capital on innovation.

The robustness of our result is further tested against changes in the specification of our estimation equation by re-estimating the instrumental variable regression and progressively eliminating all control variables (Table A.8.3). This showed that the effect of social capital remains consistent in all specifications of the model independently of the inclusion of additional regressors, suggesting that social capital has an independent effect on innovation above and beyond its potential second-order effect on physical and human capital.

Table A.8.2 Further robustness checks (1): estimation of the empirical model – regional knowledge production function with social capital; level of patents (2002, 2005, 2007)

Dep. var.	(1) Patents (level in 2002) 2SLS	(2) Patents (level in 2005) 2SLS	(3) Patents (level in 2007) 2SLS
Social capital	4.395*** (1.498)	4.024*** (1.419)	4.456*** (1.029)
Private R&D	-0.0297 (0.143)	-0.0228 (0.152)	0.0050 (0.155)
Graduates	0.485 (0.482)	-0.472 (0.343)	0.0558 (0.513)
Spatial lag of social capital	-0.809* (0.414)	0.180 (0.190)	-0.0523 (0.192)
Female unemployment	0.0962 (0.109)	-0.157 (0.106)	-0.0406 (0.158)
Employment in agriculture	0.159 (0.224)	0.241 (0.169)	0.226 (0.163)
Employment in industry	0.218 (0.393)	0.0030 (0.376)	0.311 (0.315)
Population density	0.274* (0.0998)	0.255*** (0.0980)	0.367*** (0.0775)
Spatial lag of population density	-0.0401 (0.0414)	-0.0289 (0.0469)	-0.0303 (0.0463)
Macro-regional dummies	YES	YES	YES
Constant	2.871* (1.744)	-0.101 (1.391)	1.398 (2.010)
Observations	97	103	103
R-squared	0.492	0.541	0.550

Source: own elaboration.

Notes
*** p<0.01.
** p<0.05.
* p<0.1.
Clustered – robust standard errors in parentheses.

Table A.8.3 Further robustness checks (2): estimation of the empirical model – regional knowledge production function with social capital; annual growth rate of regional patenting (2001–2007)

Dep. var.: patent growth	(1)	(2)	(3)	(4)	(5)	(6)	(7)
	2SLS	2SLS	2SLS	2SLS	2SLS	2SLS	2SLS
Social capital	0.458*** (0.0742)	0.424*** (0.0932)	0.425*** (0.0946)	0.431*** (0.0966)	0.446*** (0.101)	0.439*** (0.0988)	0.480*** (0.111)
Patents (level in 2001)	-0.0771*** (0.0113)	-0.0735*** (0.0110)	-0.0758*** (0.0122)	-0.0764*** (0.0119)	-0.0771*** (0.0121)	-0.0768*** (0.0123)	-0.0772*** (0.0132)
Private R&D	0.0023 (0.0140)	0.0116 (0.0141)	0.0120 (0.0147)	0.0122 (0.0145)	0.0152 (0.0138)	0.0161 (0.0131)	
Graduates	0.0239 (0.0649)	0.0419 (0.0693)	-0.0190 (0.0600)	-0.0238 (0.0559)	-0.0244 (0.0581)		
Spatial lag of social capital	-0.0174 (0.0171)	-0.0188 (0.0194)	-0.0184 (0.0211)	-0.0175 (0.0204)			
Female unemployment	0.0107 (0.0189)	0.0178 (0.0198)	0.0052 (0.0151)				
Employment in agriculture	0.0228 (0.0151)	0.0250 (0.0164)					
Employment in industry	0.0573* (0.0340)	0.0814** (0.0391)					
Population density	0.0372*** (0.0091)						
Spatial lag of population density	-0.0008 (0.0030)						
Macro-regional dummies	YES	YES	YES	YES	YES	YES	YES
Constant	0.194 (0.278)	0.489* (0.277)	0.143 (0.202)	0.117 (0.181)	0.109 (0.190)	0.178*** (0.0506)	0.147*** (0.0507)
Observations	97	97	97	97	97	97	97
R-squared	0.209	0.173	0.144	0.134	0.105	0.113	0.035

Source: own elaboration.

Notes
*** $p < 0.01$.
** $p < 0.05$.
* $p < 0.1$.
Clustered – robust standard errors in parentheses.

Appendix C

Spatial autocorrelation tests

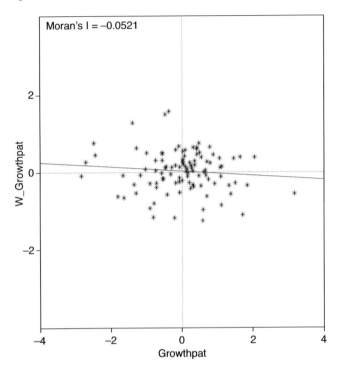

Figure A.8.1 Moran's I test on the dependent variable (patents' growth rate) (source: own elaboration).

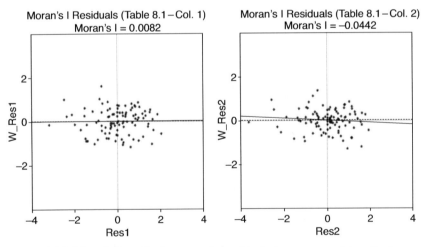

Figure A.8.2 Moran's I test for the regression residuals (source: own elaboration).

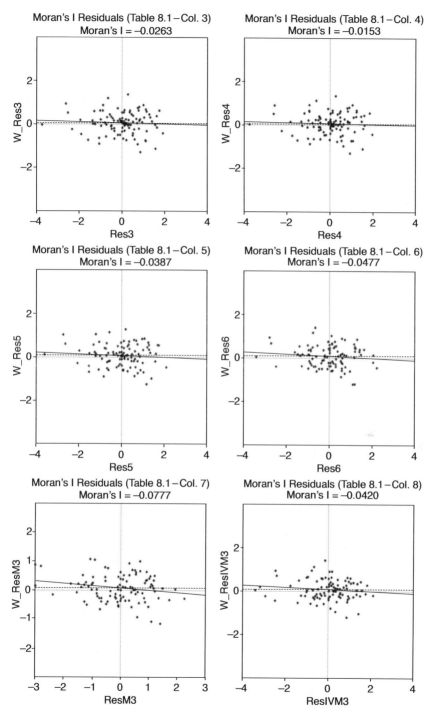

Figure A.8.2 Continued

Notes

* The material included in this chapter was previously published in Crescenzi, R., Gagliardi, L. and Percoco, M. (2013), 'Social capital and the innovative performance of Italian provinces', *Environment and Planning A*, 45(4): 908–929, London: Pion Ltd. www.pion.co.uk and www.envplan.com.

1 Kallio *et al.* (2009) suggested that the link between the social dimension and the emergence of an innovative outcome lies in local absorptive capacity that promoted the diffusion of knowledge within the regional system of innovation. Other authors argued that social capital has only a second-order effect and that it is mediated by increasing returns on investments in human (Bourdieu, 1986; Gradstein and Justman, 2000; Dakhli and De Clercq, 2004) or physical capital (Becker and Diez, 2004; Fritsch and Franke, 2004; Cainelli *et al.*, 2005).

2 We would like to thank one of the anonymous referees for raising this point.

3 Patent data at the NUTS3 level are in principle available for a longer time series; however, data on social capital and other control variables at the provincial level prior to 2001 are unavailable. The empirical analysis is forced to rely on 2001 Census data and some additional specialized data sources for social capital-related variables (Cartocci, 2007) for the computation of the independent variables. In order to capture the dynamic effect of social capital on innovation, the dependent variable is computed by covering the time interval between 2001 and the latest available year in the OECD PatStat database (i.e. 2007). Even though still relatively limited, the coverage of an eight-year period is a significant improvement on the existent quantitative literature on the link between social capital and innovation in the Italian provinces. All existing studies cover shorter time spans. For example, Cainelli *et al.* (2005) looking at the Emilia Romagna Industrial districts cover the 2002–2007 period; Laursen and Masciarelli (2007), whose analysis is focused on larger geographical units (NUTS2 regions), still cover a shorter time interval (2001–2003).

4 The two social capital indicators ('number of voluntary associations' and 'blood donations') are only made available with different standardization methods ('per sq. km' and 'per 1000 residents', respectively). However, the rationale for the focus on the spatial density of voluntary associations is that this proxy aims to capture the density of pro-social actions in terms of their spatial intensity, in line with the focus of the paper on the spatial/territorial dimension of social capital.

5 Blood donations clinics are generally present in each municipality with a standard deviation in the density of blood donations clinics per kmq of just 0.010. The table with descriptive statistics on the geography of blood donation clinics in Italy is not included in the paper but is available from the authors upon request.

6 This regression includes controls for additional covariates such as population density, spatial lag of population density, female unemployment, employment in agriculture and services and macro-regional dummies. All these regressors will also be included in the main specification of the KPF. The table with the results of this additional robustness check is available upon request.

7 103 observations.

8 See Table A.8.1 for further details.

9 Additional controls on sector structure (such as the Herfindal Index) were also included in the model with no statistically significant effect. In order to keep our specification as simple as possible (parsimony), these variables were excluded from the final specification of the model presented in the paper but additional regression tables are available on request.

10 Computed by means of a first-order 'queen contiguity' spatial matrix as customary in the literature.

11 Computed – as for other spatially lagged variables – by means of a first-order rook contiguity matrix.

12 The measure is constructed as the average political participation in the following referenda (voting is not mandatory): 1946 (monarchy vs. republic), 1974 (divorce), 1978 and 1981 (abortion), 1985 ('*scala mobile*') and 1987 (nuclear power). The average measure is used in order to limit the potential bias coming from peculiar ideological positions in different regions with respect to particular questions.

13 Available in Nuzzo (2006); see Table A.8.1 for further details.

14 Calculated by means of a customary first-order queen contiguity spatial matrix.

15 Measured by means of a customary first-order queen contiguity. Note that additional robustness tests using the rook version of the matrix were performed with no qualitative changes in the estimates.

16 This result is consistent with the Moran's I index of our dependent variable that shows a statistically non-significant spatial autocorrelation ($I = -0.0521$; P-value: 0.302) – Moran's I scatter plots available in Appendix C.

17 The F statistic is above all the Stock and Yogo (2005) threshold values for the instrument for bridging social capital and above the 15 per cent critical value for the instrument adopted for bonding social capital.

18 Strong family ties imply geographical proximity of adult children: young adults tend to stay longer with their parents and relationships within families are particularly strong and based on repeated interactions (Alesina and Giuliano, 2010). Reher (1998) distinguishes the 'weak family ties' tradition of Northern Europe, whereby children leave their parents' home relatively early in their life, from the 'strong family ties tradition' in Southern Europe, whereby children move away from their parents at a later stage. Manacorda and Moretti (2006) and Giuliano (2007) provide additional empirical evidence on the role of cultural factors in explaining co-residence of parents and children.

19 Note that the number of observations is different in 2002 because the dependent variable is available for only 97 of the 103 provinces.

References

Akcomak, S. and Ter Weel, B., (2009), 'Social capital, innovation and growth: evidence from Europe', *European Economic Review*, 53(5): 544–67.

Alesina, A. and Giuliano, P., (2010), 'The power of the family', *Journal of Economic Growth*, 15(2): 93–125.

Archibugi, D. and Coco, A., (2005), 'A new indicator of technological capabilities for developed and developing countries (ArCo)', *World Development*, 32(4): 629–54.

Armstrong, H.W., (1995), 'An appraisal of the evidence from cross-sectional analysis of the regional growth process within the European Union', in: R.W. Vickerman and H.W. Armstrong (eds), *Convergence and Divergence Among European Regions*, London: Pion Ltd.

Arrighetti, A. and Lasagni, A., (2010), 'Capitale sociale, contesto istituzionale e performance innovative delle imprese', *Scienze Regionali*, 10: 5–34.

Asheim, B., (1999), 'Interactive learning and localised knowledge in globalising learning economies', *GeoJournal*, 49: 345–52.

Audretsch, D.B., (2003), 'Innovation and spatial externalities', *International Regional Science Review*, 26: 167–74.

Audretsch, D.B. and Feldman, M.P., (1996), 'R&D spillovers and the geography of innovation and production', *American Economic Review*, 86: 253–73.

Audretsch, D.B. and Feldman M.P., (2004), 'Knowledge spillovers and the geography of innovation', in: J.V. Henderson and J.-F. Thisse (eds), *Handbook of Regional and Urban Economics*, vol. 4, Princeton, NJ: Elsevier.

Banfield, E. C., (1958), *The Moral Basis of a Backward Society*, Chicago: Free Press.

Becker, W. and Diez J., (2004), 'R&D cooperation and innovation activities of firms. Evidence for the German Manufacturing Industry', *Research Policy*, 33: 209–23.

Benabou, R. And Tirole, J., (2003), 'Intrinsic and extrinsic motivation', *Review of Economic Studies*, 70(3): 489–520.

Beugelsdijk, S., and Smulders, S., (2003), 'Bridging and bonding social capital: which type is good for economic growth?', Paper presented at the European Regional Science Association, Jyvaskila, Finland.

Beugelsdijk, S. and van Schaiik T., (2005), 'Social capital and growth in European regions: an empirical test', *European Journal of Political Economy*, 21: 301–24.

Biagiotti, A., (2008), 'I sistemi locali leader nei brevetti', in: C. Trigilia and F. Ramella (Eds), *Imprese e territori dell'alta tecnologia in Italia*, Prato: Iris.

Boschma, R.A., (2005), 'Proximity and innovation: a critical assessment', *Regional Studies*, 39(1): 61–74.

Bourdieu, D., (1986), 'The forms of capital', in: J. Richardson (ed.), *Handbook of Theory and Research for the Sociology of Education*, New York: Greenwood.

Breschi, S. and Lissoni, F., (2001), 'Localised knowledge spillovers vs. innovative milieux: knowledge "tacitness" reconsidered', *Papers in Regional Science*, 90: 255–73.

Burt, R., (1992), *Structural Holes*, Cambridge, MA: Harvard University Press.

Cainelli, G., Mancinelli, S. and Mazzanti, M., (2005), 'Social capital, R&D and industrial district', *Feem Working Papers* n. 744584.

Camagni, R.P., (1995), 'The concept of "innovative milieu" and its relevance for public policies in European lagging regions', *Papers in Regional Science*, 74: 317–40.

Capello, R. and Faggian, A., (2005), 'Collective learning and relational capital in local innovation processes', *Regional Studies*, 39: 75–87.

Cartocci, R., (2007), *Mappe del tesoro: atlante del capitale sociale in Italia*, Bologna: Il Mulino.

Cohen, S. and Fields, G., (2000), 'Social capital and capital gains: an examination of social capital in Silicon Valley', in: M. Kenney (ed.), *Understanding Silicon Valley*, Stanford: Stanford University Press.

Coleman, J.S., (1988), 'Social capital in the creation of human capital', *American Journal of Sociology*, 94: S95–S120.

Cooke, P., Uranga, M.G. and Etxebarria G., (1997), 'Regional innovation systems: institutional and organisational dimensions', *Research Policy*, 26: 475–91.

Crescenzi, R. and Rodríguez-Pose, A., (2011), *Innovation and Regional Growth in the European Union*, Berlin: Springer.

Crescenzi, R., Rodríguez-Pose, A. and Storper, M., (2007), 'The territorial dynamics of innovation: a Europe–United States comparative analysis', *Journal of Economic Geography*, 7: 673–709.

Crescenzi, R., Rodríguez-Pose, A. and Storper, M., (2012), 'The territorial dynamics of innovation in China and India', *Journal of Economic Geography*, 12: 1055–85.

Dakhli, M. and De Clercq, D., (2004), 'Human capital, social capital and innovation: a multi-country study', *Entrepreneurship and Regional Development*, 16(2): 107–28.

De Blasio, G. and Nuzzo, G., (2010), 'Individual determinants of social behaviour', *Journal of Socio-Economics*, 39: 466–73.

De Blasio, G. and Nuzzo, G., (2012), 'Capitale sociale e disuguaglianza in Italia' *Questioni di Economia e Finanza*, 116, Banca d'Italia, Italy.

Dettori, B., Marrocu, E. and Paci, R., (2012), 'Total factor productivity, intangible assets and spatial dependence in the European regions', *Regional Studies*, 46(10): 1401–16.

Diani, M., (2004). 'How associations matter. An empirical assessment of the social capital-trustvoluntary action link', in: S. Prakash and P. Selle (eds), *Investigating Social Capital. Comparative Perspectives on Civil Society, Participation, and Govern-ance*, New Delhi: Sage.

Di Pasquale, D. and Glaeser, E., (1999), 'Incentives and social capital: are homeowners better citizens?', *Journal of Urban Economics*, 45(2): 354–84.

Dodgson, M. and Gann, D.M., (2010), *Innovation: A Very Short Introduction*, Oxford: Oxford University Press.

Duranton, G., Rodríguez-Pose, A. and Sandall, R., (2009), 'Family types and the persist-ence of regional disparities in Europe', *Economic Geography*, 85(1): 23–47.

Feldman, M.P., (1994), *The Geography of Innovation*, Boston: Kluwer Academic Pub-lishers.

Florida, R., (1995), 'Towards the learning region', *Futures*, 27(5): 527–36.

Florida, R., (2002), *The Rise of the Creative Class: and How It's Transforming Work, Leisure, Community, and Everyday Life*, New York: Basic Books.

Fritsch, M., (2002), 'Measuring the quality of regional innovation systems: a knowledge production function approach', *International Regional Science Review*, 25: 86–101.

Fritsch, M. and Franke, G., (2004), 'Innovation, regional knowledge spillovers and R&D cooperation', *Research Policy*, 33: 245–55.

Fukuyama, F., (1995), *Trust: The Social Virtues and the Creation of Prosperity*, New York: Free Press.

Giavazzi F., Schiantarelli F. and Serafinelli, M., (2010), 'Attitudes, policies and work', Working Paper.

Giuliano, P., (2007), 'Living arrangements in Western Europe: does cultural origin matter?', *Journal of the European Economic Association*, (5): 927–52.

Goldin, C. and Katz, L., (1999), 'Human capital and social capital: the rise of secondary schooling in America, 1910–1940', *Journal of Interdisciplinary History*, 29: 683–723.

Gradstein, M. and Justman, M., (2000), 'Human capital, social capital and public school-ing', *European Economic Review*, 44: 879–91.

Granovetter, M.S., (1973), 'The strength of weak ties', *American Journal of Sociology*, 78: 1360–80.

Granovetter, M., (1982), 'The strength of weak ties: a network theory revisited', in: P. Marsden and N. Lin (eds), *Social Structure and Network Analysis*, Beverly Hills, CA: Sage.

Griliches, Z., (1979), 'Issues in assessing the contribution of research and development to productivity growth', *Bell Journal of Economics*, 10: 92–116.

Griliches, Z., (1986), 'Productivity, R&D, and the basic research at the firm level in the 1970s', *American Economic Review*, 76: 141–54.

Guiso, L., Sapienza, P. and Zingales, L., (2004), 'The role of social capital in financial development', *American Economic Review*, 94(3): 526–56.

Guiso, L, Sapienza, P. and Zingales, L., (2008), 'Long term persistence', *NBER Working Paper* 14278.

Guiso, L., Sapienza, P. and Zingales, L., (2010), 'Civil capital as the missing link', *NBER Working Paper* 15845.

Hauser, C., Tappeiner, G. and Walde, J., (2007), 'The leaning region: the impact of social capital and weak ties on innovation', *Regional Studies*, 41(1): 75–88.

Iammarino, S. and Marinelli, E., (2011), 'Is the grass greener on the other side of the fence? Graduate regional mobility and job satisfaction in Italy', *Environment and Plan-ning A*, 43(11): 2761–77.

Ichino, A. and Maggi, G., (2000), 'Work environment and individual background:

explaining regional shirking differentials in a large Italian firm', *Quarterly Journal of Economics*, 115: 1057–90.

ISTAT (2007), 'Rapporto annuale: la situazione del Paese', Rome: Istat.

ISTAT (2008), 'Rapporto annuale: la situazione del Paese', Rome: Istat.

Jaffe, A., (1986), 'Technological opportunity and spillovers of R&D: evidence from firms' patents, profits and market value', *American Economic Review*, LXXVI: 984–1001.

Kallio, A., Harmaakoorpi, V. and Pihkala, T. (2009), 'Absorptive capacity and social capital in regional innovation system: the case of the Lahti region in Finland', *Urban Studies*, 47: 303–19.

Knack, S., (2001), 'Trust, associational life and economic performance', in: J.F. Helliwell (ed.), *The Contribution of Human and Social Capital to Sustained Economic Growth and Well-being*, Ottawa: HDRC.

Knack, S. and Keefer, P., (1997), 'Does social capital have an economic payoff? A cross-country investigation', *Quarterly Journal of Economics*, 112(4): 1252–88.

La Porta, R., Lopez de Silanes, F., Shleifer, A. and Vishny, R.W., (1997), 'Trust in large organizations', *American Economic Review*, 87(2): 333–8.

Laursen, K. and Masciarelli, F., (2007), 'The effect of regional social capital and external knowledge acquisition on process and product innovation', DRUID Working Paper.

Levin, D. and Cross, R., (2004), 'The strength of weak ties you can trust: the mediating role of trust in effective knowledge transfer', *Management Science*, 50: 1477–90.

Lundvall, B., (1992), 'Introduction', in: B.-Å Lundvall (ed.), *National Systems of Innovation. Towards a Theory of Innovation and Interactive Learning*, London: Pinter Publishers.

Manacorda, M. and Moretti, E., (2006), 'Why do most Italian youths live with their parents? Intergenerational transfers and household structure', *Journal of the European Economic Association*, 4(4): 800–29.

Moreno, R., Paci, R. and Usai, S., (2005a), 'Spatial spillovers and innovation activity in European regions', *Environment and Planning A*, 37: 1973–812.

Moreno, R., Paci, R. and Usai, S., (2005b), 'Geographical and sectoral clusters of innovation in Europe', *Annals of Regional Science*, 39: 715–39.

Morgan, K., (1997), 'The learning region: institutions, innovation and regional renewal', *Regional Studies*, 31: 491–504.

Nannicini, T., Stella, A., Tabellini, G. and Troiano, U., (2010), 'Social capital and political accountability', Università Bocconi, mimeo.

Nuzzo, G., (2006), 'Un secolo di statistiche sociali: persistenza o convergenza tra le regioni italiane?', *Quaderni dell'Ufficio Ricerche Storiche*, 11, Bank of Italy.

O'hUallachain, B. and Leslie, T.F., (2007), 'Rethinking the regional knowledge production function', *Journal of Economic Geography*, 7(6): 737–52.

OECD (2001), 'Using patent counts for cross-country comparisons of technology output', *STI Review*, 27: 129–46.

Patton, D. and Kenney, M., (2003), 'Innovation and social capital in Silicon Valley', *BRIE Working Paper* 155, Berkeley, CA.

Ponds, R., van Oort, F. and Frenken, K., (2010), 'Innovation, spillovers and university–industry collaboration: an extended knowledge production function approach', *Journal of Economic Geography*, 10(2): 231–55.

Putnam, R.D., (1993), *Making Democracy Work: Civic Traditions in Modern Italy*, Princeton: Princeton University Press.

Putnam, R.D., (2000), *Bowling Alone: The Collapse and Revival of American Community*, New York: Simon & Schuster.

Ramella, F. and Trigilia, C., (2009), 'Le strategie dell'innovazione. Indagine sui brevetti europei delle imprese italiane', *Economia e Politica Industriale*, 36(2): 199–213.

Ramella, F. and Trigilia, C., (2010), 'Legami forti e deboli nella costruzione sociale delle invenzioni', *Stato e Mercato*, 88 (April): 78–102.

Reher, D.S., (1998), 'Family ties in Western Europe: persistent contrasts', *Population and Development Review*, 24(2): 203–34.

Rodríguez-Pose, A., (1999), 'Innovation prone and innovation averse societies: economic performance in Europe', *Growth and Change*, 30: 75–105.

Rodríguez-Pose, A. and Crescenzi, R., (2008), 'R&D, spillovers, innovation systems and the genesis of regional growth in Europe', *Regional Studies*, 42(1): 51–67.

Rodríguez-Pose, A. and Storper, M., (2006), 'Better rules or stronger communities? On the social foundations of institutional change and its economic effects', *Economic Geography*, 82(1): 1–25.

Rogers, E.M., (1995), *Diffusion of Innovations* (4th edn), New York: The Free Press.

Ruef, M., (2002), 'Strong ties, weak ties and islands: structural and cultural predictors of organizational innovation', *Industrial and Corporate Change*, 11: 427–49.

Sabatini, F., (2009), 'Il capitale sociale nelle regioni italiane: un'analisi comparata', *Rivista di Politica Economica*, 99: 167–220.

Sedgley, N. and Elmslie, B., (2004), 'The geographic concentration of knowledge: scale, agglomeration and congestion in innovation across US states', *International Regional Science Review*, 27: 111–37.

Staiger, D. and Stock, J.H., (1997), 'Instrumental variables regression with weak instruments', *Econometrica*, 65: 557–86.

Stock, J.H. and Yogo, M., (2005), 'Testing for weak instruments in linear IV regression', in: J.H. Stock and D.W.K. Andrews (eds), *Identification and Inference for Econometric Models: A Festschrift in Honour of Thomas Rothenberg*, Cambridge: Cambridge University Press.

Storper, M. and Venables, A.J., (2004), 'Buzz: face-to-face contact and the urban economy', *Journal of Economic Geography*, 4: 351–70.

Tabellini, G., (2010), 'Culture and institutions: economic development in the regions of Europe', *Journal of the European Economic Association*, 8(4): 677–716.

Tomassini, L., (1999), 'Il mutualismo nell'Italia liberale (1861–1922)', in: Ministero per i Beni e le Attività Culturali, *Le società di mutuo soccorso in Italia e i loro archivi*, Rome: Ministero per le Attività ed i Beni Culturali.

Tura, T. and Harmaakorpi, V., (2005), 'Social capital in building regional innovative capability', *Regional Studies*, 39: 1111–25.

Varga, A., (1998), *University Research and Regional Innovation*, Boston: Kluwer Academic Publishers.

Woolcock, M., (1998), 'Social capital and economic development: toward a theoretical synthesis and policy framework', *Theory and Society*, 27(2): 151–208.

Part III

Innovation and systemic technology policy

9 The ontology of complexity and the implications for innovation policy

Verónica Robert and Gabriel Yoguel[1]

1 Introduction

The corpus of evolutionary neo-Schumpeterian economics is neither unique nor completely integrated. Instead, it is made up of several heterogeneous contributions that have appeared over the last 30 years. Since its very beginnings, different sets of contributions to neo-Schumpeterian evolutionism have been close to the complexity approach (Silverberg *et al.*, 1988; Dosi and Kaniovski, 1994; Arthur *et al.*, 1997; Arthur, 1989, 1990, 2009; Cantner *et al.*, 2000; Metcalfe and Foster, 2007; Dopfer and Potts, 2004; Dopfer, 2005; Saviotti and Pyka, 2004; Foster, 2005; Durlauf, 2005; Boschma and Martin, 2010; Frenken, 2006; Antonelli, 2011). This approach allows the micro, meso, and macro levels of analysis to be integrated. Also, it can account for micro-heterogeneity, self-organization, path dependence, non-linear interactions, and divergent paths. In particular, the complexity approach represents a break with both reductionist and holistic explanations. Emergent properties are the result of micro–meso–macro interactions. This group of characteristics defines a set of ontological suppositions about complexity that are related to the ontological suppositions about current neo-Schumpeterian evolutionism.

Several elements of the ontology of complexity can also be found in different authors from the history of economic thought that are frequently quoted in evolutionary economics, including Smith, Marshall, Schumpeter, Hayek, Kaldor, Young, and Hirschman. In this regard, the precedents for complexity theory in economic thought may follow two possible paths: the first is mainly concerned with order and the transformation problem associated with it. This path, pointed out by Metcalfe (2010), starts with Smith and ends with Hayek. The second path is mainly concerned with development, cumulative causations, and divergence. This path starts also with Smith but ends with structuralism and the development school (Robert and Yoguel, 2011).

The two paths are also precedents for the evolutionary contributions that constitute the basis for very divergent interpretations as two forms of intervention in economy, a situation which is reflected by the diversity of policy recommendations deriving from them. These include, on the one hand, bottom-up policies, such as capacity building and the development of institutions that promote innovation and economic development as emergent properties. On the other hand, the recommendations also include top-down policies, such as the selection of specialization sectors and fostering structural change. These two forms of conceiving public intervention have often been put forward at the same time by evolutionist authors, despite their different conceptual roots.

In this chapter, we argue that the complexity approach could be a theoretical and conceptual starting point that would allow the integration of different contributions from neo-Schumpeterian evolutionism and the economic policy recommendations deriving from it.

This chapter has three interconnected aims that are relevant for the perspective of development. First, to compare different evolutionist streams of thought taking into account the various dimensions of the ontology of complexity that they support, be it explicitly or implicitly. Second, to evaluate how close each group is to the two historical traditions of economic thought mentioned above. Third, to discuss the political actions that derive from each of these two historical traditions and the way in which evolutionist contributions articulate them to different degrees. This articulation will depend on how far they adhere to the different dimensions of complexity: the more points they have in common, the easier it will be to derive policy recommendations that articulate both bottom-up and top-down processes.

This chapter is organized into three main sets of building blocks. In Section 2, on the basis of different trans-disciplinary definitions of complexity, we present the ontological assumptions of complexity. As such, the first set of building blocks is made up of the five dimensions of complexity that we identify. In Section 3, we identify two traditions in the history of economic thought into which a set of complexity-related ideas can be read. These ideas constitute the second set of building blocks. In Section 4, we propose a typology of the contributions that make up neo-Schumpeterian evolutionary economics. The typology, based on the main concerns addressed by each group, is the third set of building blocks. In Section 5, we mix the three sets of blocks up, showing the different starting points for each of the groups' contributions, how they are related to the abovementioned traditions in economic history, and how the various dimensions of complexity are emphasized differently. In Section 6, we present the policy implications and how they are related to the historical traditions and the complexity dimensions. Finally, in Section 7, we discuss the main conclusions.

2 Towards an ontology of complexity

It is difficult to say that complexity is a theory; but it is, in any case, an approach that includes a set of conceptual fundamentals and methodological tools. As an approach, it is also associated with theories such as dissipative systems and networks, with specific application areas. Prigogine and Stengers (2002) suggest that the complexity approach is essentially a new relationship between science and nature that comes in response to a new view of the world, characterized not only by its unpredictability but by the impossibility of addressing its structure and dynamics through general and immutable laws. Since then, complexity has been associated with self-organization, out-of-equilibrium dynamics, irreversibility, and indeterminacy, and the notions of irreversibility and uncertainty have come to predominate over stability and equilibrium in systems dynamics.

However, Prigogine's position has been strongly criticized by Bricmont (1995), arguing that complexity is not in contradiction with Newtonian thinking. This illustrates how far complexity has been a subject of debate even within the hard sciences.

The development of complexity as a concept has led to the description of a set of deep features relating to the functioning of complex systems. These features can account for many different situations. In this sense, a definition of complexity should aim to cover this diversity but should also describe the main features of the system itself (components, rules, etc.). Its application to social phenomena has given rise to a variety of contributions, showing how broad the reach of complexity can be.

According to Rosser (2007), a broad definition of complexity may be attained by discarding what is undoubtedly not complex, i.e. 'those systems that do not generate endogenously or deterministically well behaved dynamics'. Nevertheless, the vagueness of the definition goes against its practicality. Rosser also quotes Day's definition (1994), which indicates that a system is complex if it tends, endogenously and asymptotically, to something different than a fixed point, a limited cycle, or an explosion. In this case, the definition is more precise but it is circumscribed to an evaluation of the system in terms of its results, not of its composition and characteristics. Kwapieña and Drożdż (2012) provide a definition that aims to describe the system through its components and not its behaviour or outcome. According to these authors, a complex system is comprised of a large number of components which interact in a non-linear way, exhibiting collective behaviour and being easily able to modify their internal structure and/or activity patterns from data or energy exchanges with the environment. While these approaches are not stringent enough to enable one to decide whether a system is complex, they are useful for identifying when a system is clearly non-complex.

Beyond these few-word definitions of complexity and the epistemological explanations of Prigogine and Stengers, efforts to characterize complexity have tended to list the set of characteristics that a system must have in order to be called complex. For example, the definition proposed by Nekola and Brown (2007) identifies several characteristics that a complex system should present: (i) micro-heterogeneity; (ii) interactions between system components and with environment in many different ways and on multiple spatial and temporal scales; (iii) complex structures and non-linear dynamics; (iv) dynamics neither completely stochastic nor entirely deterministic, but instead a combination of randomness and order; (v) positive and negative feedback mechanisms, causing either amplification or damping of temporal and spatial variation; (vi) openness, which means that systems exchange matter and energy with the environment to reach an organized state far from equilibrium; (vii) historical contingent, system configurations reflect the influence of initial conditions and subsequent perturbations; and (viii) hierarchical organizations, which means that systems are nested within others.

These kinds of definition are also predominant in evolutionary economics. For example, Arthur *et al.* (1997) quote six key features of complexity applied to economic systems: (i) heterogeneous agents interact with each other within a specific local environment in a given space; (ii) the absence of a global controller that can exploit all the opportunities or interactions of the economy, although there may be weak global interactions; (iii) a hierarchical organization with many intersectoral interactions; (iv) continuous adaptation through learning and evolutionary agents; (v) continuous innovation, new markets, technologies, behaviours, and institutions that create new niches within the system; and (vi) non-equilibrium dynamics with either no equilibrium states or multiple ones which are unlikely to reach a global optimum.

Metcalfe and Foster (2007) and Dopfer and Potts (2004) consider that: (i) a complex system is a network structure made up of components and linkages; (ii) its linkages allow information and knowledge to circulate; (iii) its structure is modular; (iv) it is open to new components and new interactions between them, and (v) it has a hierarchy since each component is also a complex system. From the evolutionary geography perspective, Martin and Sunley (2007) stress the following features: (i) the distributed nature of the systems; (ii) the several scales of analysis; (iii) the systems are open to novelty that comes from environment; (iv) there are non-linear dynamics and feedbacks between components; (v) a complex system cannot be decomposable or its decomposability is limited; (vi) it may exhibit emergence and self-organization; (vii) the components are adaptive and they interact with the environment; and (viii) the system is not deterministic or traceable.

Kirman (2010) and Helbing and Kirman (2013) give a definition of complexity that emphasizes the relevance of interactions between system components. According to these authors: (i) The connections between heterogeneous components are incomplete and chosen by the components according to different criteria (cost, benefits, capabilities, history, etc.). Each component has a limited number of connections to others in the neighbourhood. (ii) The system's behaviour cannot be understood from the properties of its components, but rather from the interactions between them. In this sense, the interaction processes and coordination of the network structure are more important in explaining the aggregate results than individual behaviour. (iii) The system may exhibit emergent properties such as network structure, the heterogeneity of components and the rules that guide the components' behaviour. Therefore, system behaviour is often counter-intuitive. (iv) Feedback and unexpected side effects are common. The system may feature cascade effects and extreme events. The probability of extreme events is higher than expected according to a normal (Gaussian) distribution and their impact may take on almost any size (in particular, it may be global in scale). Since the interactions are constrained by the neighbourhood, extreme events do not affect all components simultaneously, but the scope and velocity of these events depend on the system's network structure. (v) System behaviour is hard to control in a centralized or top-down fashion. The components will often fail to behave the way they wish or as they should, because they cannot act independently. Therefore, the system cannot be strictly optimized in real time, even with the biggest supercomputers. (vi) The system may spend long periods of time far from equilibrium, even when an equilibrium exists in principle. The system may have multiple equilibria, but these equilibria may be unstable.

It is interesting to note that when the definitions of systems are based on a list of features, it is not clear in general whether a system is complex if it satisfies one, several, or all of the features listed; therefore, such definitions entail a strong underlying ambiguity. Moreover, many of these features are associated with one another or are mutually implied. At the same time, although there is some overlapping among the listed characteristics, the coincidence is not perfect.

Combining all the above definitions, we propose the following four dimensions to synthesize the 15 elements which are present in the different definitions of complexity: (i) micro-heterogeneity, (ii) network architecture, (iii) interactions, disequilibrium, and divergence, and (iv) emergent properties (see Table 9.1).

Micro-heterogeneity refers to different features of component, subsystems, and systems (micro-meso) in terms of capacities, behaviour, and performance. It is related to the ability of the system's components to generate variety, adapt, and evolve. This feature, in turn, is combined on the one hand with the possibility of generating novelty endogenously – creativity – and on the other by

Table 9.1 Four dimensions of the ontology of complexity

Ontological assumptions of complexity

I Micro-heterogeneity	1 Evolutionary heterogeneous agents, with creative capacity 2 Learning and adaptation 3 Heterogeneity of systems (meso)
II Network architecture	4 Linkages more relevant than components 5 Hierarchical organization 6 Decomposable modular structure 7 Partial and local information. No global controller. 8 Lack of global optima
III Interactions, disequilibrium, and divergence	9 Positive feedbacks 10 Far-from-equilibrium dynamics 11 Indeterminacy and uncertainty 12 Non-ergodic path dependence
IV Emergent properties	13 Multiscale analysis 14 Novelty 15 Micro variability consistent with macro stability

Source: own elaboration, based on the cited works.

selecting the relevant attributes on the basis of interaction with the environment, the learning process, and capability building. These features make complex systems adaptive. Heterogeneity manifests itself at different levels of analysis: firms, local or sectoral systems, and national economies.

The second dimension is associated with the network architecture of interactions that complex systems present. Linkages are more relevant then components. The presence of hierarchy, in the sense put forward by Simon (1969), can be described as a complex system that consists of other subsystems that are also complex. The presence of modular structures explains why interactions within subsystems are denser than interactions with each other. The modular system is resilient: it is able to absorb exogenous shocks and remain functional. The network architecture defines the characteristics of the information circulation within the system and between the system and environment. The information is local and therefore partial; however, the overall system can process information based on its distributed operation. While global interactions are possible (each component simultaneously exchanges information with the rest of the system's components), they will tend to be weaker than local interactions (each component exchanges information with neighbouring components in the multidimensional space with which it is linked). In this regard, the prevailing partial information prevents the existence of a global controller. Therefore, because of the absence of a global controller, there is no guarantee of reaching a global optimum.

In the third dimension, interactions, disequilibrium, and divergence are closely related to each other. The interactions between components of a complex social system are intentional and are located in the network architecture. This means that the components can change their location and their specific links from moving along this network. The complex systems are out of equilibrium: there is order, but this does not imply that they are in a state of equilibrium. Feedback processes manifest in interactions between the heterogeneous components of the system and between them and the environment. This explains why such systems show far-from-equilibrium dynamics. In this context, the system is indeterminate. The system dynamics are associated with its initial conditions and its own history (path dependency) which can result in the dynamics leading to divergent paths and lock-in situations.

Finally, emergent properties are the result of multiple interactions on different scales of analysis. The fact that complex systems present various scales of space and time means that the results of each scale cannot be derived linearly from lower scales, each of which show specific attributes in each case. The macroscopic regularities which support small-scale variability are themselves emergent properties of the system.

3 Two paths of complexity in economic history

Different conceptual elements of the complexity approach that have currently been adopted by several economists can also be read in the contributions of different authors throughout the history of economic thought. Actually, the adoption of the complexity approach by evolutionary economics is grounded in the fact that the contributions of its predecessors are consistent with many of the ontological assumptions of complexity discussed in Section 2. In this section, we will show two possible paths for the history of economic thought in which different aspects of the five dimensions of the ontology of complexity can be recognized. The first path, identified by Metcalfe (2010), is focused on coordination problems and the links between this and economic change (Smith–Marshall–Schumpeter–Hayek–Knight). Metcalfe, therefore, refers to this path as one that focuses on self-organization and self-transformation issues. However, there is a second, alternative path that can be identified behind the concepts of feedback and divergence. This second path is much more related to accumulation and transformation problems (Smith–Marshall–Young–Schumpeter–Kaldor–Myrdal–Hirschman).

Metcalfe (2010) traces a path of complexities ideas in economics from Smith to Hayek, including Marshall, Schumpeter, and Knight, in whose work a connection between interdependence and order can be found. Metcalfe proposes that these authors' ideas are of great importance, particularly those related to our understanding of the division of labour and the role of innovation in stimulating the processes of coordination and self-transformation. The authors belonging to this path share the idea that the economic system is in disequilibrium, which is generated by innovation – economic growth reflects the growth of human knowledge – and therefore order became a better concept than equilibrium for coping with the problem of coordination (Metcalfe, 2010).

Metcalfe suggests that the division of labour, which is closely linked to coordination problems, leads to the division of labour in the production of knowledge, and therefore to innovation and transformation. Consequently, the problem of organizing production is analogous to the problem of generating new knowledge. The first deals with complementarity in the production of goods and services, and the second with the complementarity between different types of knowledge – both internal and external to the firm. The interactions between diverse parts of the systems lead to a complexity approach that can account for subsystems that are loosely coupled with each other but its components are highly connected. Redundancy of linkages allows the system to have meta-stability properties like the distributed systems described by Simon (1969).

All these ideas are consistent with a Schumpeterian view of innovation, including new combinations of existing knowledge and Smith's idea of innovation driven by specialization, which leads to further learning and deeper and more detailed command of different spheres of knowledge. However, the generation of new knowledge is largely produced by combining complementary types of expertise that already exist in the system. Therefore, interactions, although always local (not only because of bounded rationality agents but because there is an incomplete net of interactions) are sufficient and therefore effective for giving order to the system (Hayek, 1945). In this context, the self-organization (coordination problem) and the self-transformation of the system (change issue) are closely linked. However, order is not general equilibrium since it does not require global interactions but local ones, which means perfect connections between all parts of the system.

According to Metcalfe, after 1945, the dominant stream in economics favoured the idea of equilibrium, a natural consequence of their main concern: 'the rational coherence of economic relations' (Metcalfe, 2010: 47). Hayek's idea of order (1948), as opposed to equilibrium, is the response to the need to recognize some level of predictability in the economy but also emergent novelty from within the system. Therefore, the system can never be in equilibrium because of the very nature of the process of economic competition that leads to innovation.[2] This issue is present in Hayek's work but can also be found in Schumpeter, although the latter differs strongly from the former in that the equilibrating forces he considered are continuously threatened by the creative destruction processes that tend to continuously introduce new sources of quasi-rents. Contrary to equilibrium, the idea of order does not eliminate endogenous heterogeneity or emerging novelty. Schumpeter conceived the economic system as one of disequilibrium, but within which there is a tendency towards order that derives from the process of market selection.

Similarly, Metcalfe (2010) states that Hayek differs from Marshall in their treatment of market equilibrium. Hayek believes that a competitive equilibrium is a contradiction in terms: 'racing is a verb, a verb is a word that expresses a doing, an action, a process. However, in the steady state of perfect competition it refers to no action, but a state of inaction.' Hayek's main question concerns how a society solves the problems of knowledge processing when information is distributed, and therefore knowledge is scarce and partial. The answer given by Hayek – which is claimed by evolutionary authors such as Metcalfe and Antonelli – is related to the very definition of competition. According to these authors, the process of competition is first, and above all, a process for discovering new knowledge based on the combination of specialized and scarce private knowledge. This has disturbing consequences, says Metcalfe: in a broad sense, competition is the answer to a problem that is never solved, because each solution process opens up new possibilities and new demands. At this point, Metcalfe breaks with the problem of scarcity and moves on from the question of self-organization to the question of self-transformation. Hayek argues that scarcity is a problem and problems invite solutions, so scarcity becomes the instigator for the search for new knowledge. In fact, this is the most dynamic of the concepts and is more incompatible with the idea of a steady state in knowledge dynamics. Within this line of thought, the origin of change relies on scarcity and on the problem of self-organization that derives from it.

As post-war neoclassical economics is guided by its concern for coherence and rationality, the path stressed by Metcalfe is guided by his concern for the emergence of novelty and structural change under disequilibrium conditions that are nonetheless ordered and coordinated. As we will argue, he is not interested in the causes that lie behind the divergent economic structures with unequal levels of development. His idea of transformation and structural change refers to the continuous changes that occur in the participation of firms competing in different populations. Therefore, the path that leads to Metcalfe links this set of authors from Smith to Hayek ontologically, but downplays issues such as feedback and divergence.

Conversely, if the main concern is the divergence of development patterns and their relations with the productive structures, then a different but complementary path can be traced. This second path coincides with the one proposed by Metcalfe, but it differs in others. It is a complementary path because it deals with the relationship between feedback and system divergence at meso and macro level.

This second path goes from Smith to Myrdal and Hirschman, via Marshall, Young, Schumpeter, and Kaldor, and it may extend to the present day if we include the new contributions of Latin American structuralism (Cimoli and Porcile, 2013). On this path, notions of interactions between heterogeneous agents, feedbacks, emergence, and far-from-equilibrium dynamics are considered. On the other hand, it is also connected with convergent or divergent dynamics of production systems, be they local, sectoral, or national innovation systems. This path is also characterized by its interest in the relationship between increasing returns and development that has had an important place in economic thinking. It was originally formulated in Smith's famous thesis about the connection between division of labour and market size. Smith's perspective refers to productivity gains associated with market expansion, which in turn lead to a greater division of labour and to the subsequent introduction of innovations. However, Walrasian economics led to a shift of interest from a dynamic and evolving economy to a static and equilibrium-focused one, where the mechanism of self-transformation of endogenous structures was absent. Smith's famous thesis was thus set aside from the neoclassical road, although there were, of course, noteworthy exceptions.

First, Marshall made a major contribution by analysing the micro-complexity arising from the interactions between organizations in a specific territory and the emergence of localized externalities. Marshall's distinction between increasing returns inside firms, on the one hand, and those external to the firm but internal to the industry, on the other, was important not only because it justified why increasing returns do not always lead to monopoly, but also because it gave an explanation of the relationship between market growth, division of labour, knowledge generation, and increasing returns in industrial activity. In this sense, Marshall has pointed out the existence of a feedback link between the micro dynamics of individual firms and the generation of external economies at industry level.

> Good work is rightly appreciated, inventions and improvements in machinery, in processes and the general organization of the business have their merits promptly discussed: if one man starts a new idea, it is taken up by others and combined with suggestions of their own; and thus it becomes the source of further new ideas.
>
> (Marshall, 1920: 271)

Therefore, his conception of economic dynamics is not associated with equilibrium but with evolution.

Second, Young (1928) has linked increasing returns with economic progress, including notions of micro-evolution, structural change, and disequilibrium. In that direction, he has pointed out that the dynamics of the economy are characterized by novelty and qualitative change:

> Out beyond, in that obscurer field from which it derives its external economies, changes of another order are occurring. New products are appearing, firms are assuming new tasks, and new industries are coming into being. In short, change in this external field is qualitative as well as quantitative. No analysis of the forces making for economic equilibrium, forces which we might say are tangential at any moment of time, will serve to illuminate this field, for movements away from equilibrium, departures from previous trends, are characteristic of it.
>
> (Young, 1928: 528)

At the same time, he has stressed the importance of both internal and external economies to firms arising from changes in direct and indirect methods of production and labour productivity associated with market expansion. According to Young, the production structure is not an exogenous characteristic of an economy but an endogenous result of capitalist dynamics which from today's complexity approach would be understood as an emergent property of the productive system. Young has shown that every change in each part of the system changes the composition and organization of the system structure and feeds new waves of technological change through new flows of externalities.

Furthermore, Schumpeter is also part of the second tradition, as he considered that those systems in which competition processes are based on new combinations tend to diverge, in development terms, from those in which it is based on pricing.[3]

So far it is clear that in this path the focus is on structural change and development as a disequilibrium process in which industry-level increasing returns and complementarities among sectors prevail, and in which new sectors appear and disappear within a framework of a strong volatility of entry and exit of firms in the competitive process. If the central question were about self-organization and, in particular, were focused on the understanding of how to make development, self-transformation, and structural change compatible with economic order, then Hayek would be the one to provide the answer. However, if the central question were about feedbacks and divergence, then the development school would be the one to collect this background on increasing returns, interaction, and structural change in order to explain the phenomenon of divergence between productive systems. That is, beyond the order exhibited by systems taken as interdependent units, divergence between systems is caused by increasing returns at the industry level that result from interactions. This is the starting point of development theory: how to account for the differences between economies. Many of these arguments, as is discussed below, are in line with the complexity approach.

Third, Kaldor has established a long-term relationship between the growth of output and the growth of productivity, popularized as the Kaldor–Verdoorn relationship. He has analysed the effect of this relationship on the existence of development paths under disequilibrium conditions. During the 1960s, Kaldor developed his theory of cumulative causation and its effects on dynamic increasing returns, growth, and productivity. In this context, the Kaldor–Verdoorn law summarizes some effects of non-linear dynamics and feedbacks arising from the relationship between output and productivity growth. Although his work was not undertaken from the complexity perspective, it is related to complex systems in which the presence of feedbacks leads to non-linear dynamics. Other Keynesian and structuralist authors (such as Thirlwall, 1979) followed a similar path and also considered the relevance of the economic structure and the pattern of trade specialization in terms of the income elasticity of different exports and imports. Thus, these authors, faithful to the Keynesian tradition, have been thought to demand a key role in explaining the differential rates of growth of output and have emphasized how demand side and supply side (production structure) interact.

Fourth, the school of economic development (Hirschman, 1958; Rosenstein-Rodan, 1943; Prebisch, 1959; Myrdal, 1957) framed many of these issues in a discussion of the specific problems of underdevelopment. From this perspective, the productive structure of developing countries was a key factor limiting their development. This is explained by a pattern of productive specialization where products that use abundant resources (agricultural and mining commodities as well as cheap unskilled labour) prevail. These activities show a low presence of positive feedbacks and increasing returns, short productive chains, and few horizontal and vertical linkages with the rest of the production system. Dual structures with one highly productive sector and others with low productivity levels tend to give rise to processes of exchange rate appreciation that further limit development of the low productivity sectors.

In this case, the feedbacks do not refer to interaction among firms but among productive sectors that lead to the emergence of externalities, and among macroeconomic aggregates causing diverging dynamics between developed and developing countries. For example, Myrdal (1957) showed that the divergent paths between countries are due to the existence of cumulative causation processes between immigration, wages, and employment. He claimed that the investment rate depends positively on income levels for the previous period, which was reinforced through various mechanisms such as the existence of increasing returns, increased productivity, and immigration flows.[4]

In sum, in a stylized description, these two paths could be organized in terms of two key dimensions: coordination – vis-à-vis transformation – in production systems and the prevalence of heterogeneity and divergence between production systems, as opposed to the consideration of a single economic system that does not distinguish between developed and developing economies. The first tradition would be located under the 'coordination and unique system' quadrant, while the second tradition would be under the 'transformation and divergence among systems' quadrant (see Table 9.2).

Table 9.2 Two alternative paths of complexity in economic thinking

	Coordination	*Transformation*
Monoeconomics (unique economic system)	First path: Smith–Marshall–Schumpeter–Hayek–Knight	
Divergence between multiples and heterogeneous economic systems		Second path: Smith–Marshall–Young–Schumpeter–Kaldor–Myrdal–Hirschman

Source: own elaboration.

These two paths are taken up by different authors of the current evolutionary economics discussed in the following sections. It is relevant to note that both traditions ultimately derive from a complexity perspective, although from a development perspective the second path seems more attractive. Nevertheless, it could be enriched from the perspective associated with self-organization and self-transformation, i.e. giving more prominence to competition in microeconomic processes. To do this, we need to understand to what extent the different streams within evolutionary thinking are coherent. That is the aim of the following sections.

4 A possible typology of evolutionary contributions

Current evolutionary trends in economics – and, in particular, neo-Schumpeterian evolutionism – are strongly heterogeneous. Although this heterogeneity is reflected in specific ontological assumptions from different contributions, there are some common starting points accepted by most authors.

Evolutionary economics has made a great effort to discuss its own ontological bases. Some examples of this are Dosi and Nelson (1994), Metcalfe (1998), Potts (2000), Nelson and Winter (2002), Dopfer (2004, 2005), Dopfer and Potts (2004), Hodgson (2004), Knudsen (2004), Andersen (2004), Witt (2004, 2008) and Vromen (2004). These works are not only the basis for the construction of evolutionary ontology, but have also established the specificity of current neo-Schumpeterian evolutionary economics from another group of evolutionary thinking in economics, i.e. the old American institutionalism. In this regard, Witt (2008) and Hodgson (2004) have suggested placing evolutionary thinking among other streams of thought, based on a discussion of the ontological and methodological assumptions that underlie it.

In this section, we present a conceptual typology for the contributions made by different evolutionary authors. We have identified five conceptual axes: (i) habits and routines, (ii) innovation systems, (iii) cumulative causation, (iv) self-organization/self-transformation, and (v) feedbacks and increasing returns.

We started by proposing a list of papers that we considered to be most relevant to evolutionary neo-Schumpeterian tradition. Therefore, this first selection was built from our own experience and has been tested with several scholars at different international seminars. We then built a database with the references of the selected papers. As a consequence, we identified 39 contributions to the canon from 43 authors[5] that allowed us to build a database of 2844 cited contributions and around 1090 authors – that is, an average 2.6 contributions per author, since several authors appeared more than once. Of the total 2846 works cited, 61 per cent (1727) are degree 1 – that is, they are cited by a sole author out of the 39 that make up the canon. Likewise, 24 per cent of the citations (692) are within the canon. Of these, the contributions of the authors that are most often cited represent around 80 per cent of the citations from the canon (Nelson, Dosi, Freeman, Metcalfe, David, Antonelli, Arthur, Cohen, Levinthal, Hodgson, Lundvall, Saviotti, Boschma, Foster, Teece, Pavitt, and Winter). At this first stage, the group that represents the first conceptual area (habits and routines) accounts for 25 per cent of the citations within the canon; the group we refer to as 'systems', 29 per cent; cumulative causation, 13 per cent; self-organization/self-transformation, 16 per cent; and feedbacks and increasing returns, 17 per cent.[6] When we take into account only those mentioned by at least two of the 38 contributions included in this exercise (degree 2), the proportion of citations within the canon out of the total citations is somewhat higher (26 per cent). There are also some changes in the share of each theoretical area: the habits and routines group represents a great proportion of citations within the canon, the systems group is unchanged, and the remaining groups have smaller proportions.

Using this database, we established a distance measure between papers according to similarities in the references for each article. We try to identify different branches in evolutionary neo-Schumpeterian literature that together constitute a loosely coupled network of contributions. We found some correlations between contribution and authors, namely that contributions from a given thematic group tend to cite members of the same group more than authors belonging to other groups.

Since the initial selection of articles was subjective, and we realize that it may be influenced by our own readings and interests, we decided to verify our guesses using a systematic procedure. Econlit, the American Economic Association electronic database, was used to identify papers for the second stage.[7] This database indexes over 1600 journals and also collects books, collective volume articles, dissertations, working papers in economics, and full-text book reviews from the *Journal of Economic Literature* (JEL). Each record has information on title, authors, source (type of document, publication name, editor, and ISBN), an abstract, and a publication date.

During this second stage, we selected a group of journals that had included articles on evolutionary neo-Schumpeterian economics. These included the main journals on evolutionary economic thinking: the *Journal of Evolutionary Economics* (JEE) and the *Journal of Economic Issues* (published by the Schumpeter Society and the Association of Evolutionary Economics, respectively). We also considered those journals on industrial dynamics, corporate change, and business where the most relevant papers from the evolutionary stream are published:

Research Policy (RP), *Industrial and Corporate Change* (ICC), *Industry and Innovation, Economics of Innovation and New Technology, Structural Change and Economic Dynamics, Journal of Economic Behavior and Organization, Technology Analysis and Strategic Management,* and the *Harvard Business Review.* A set of mainstream journals were also taken into account since some of the most cited papers on evolutionary thinking were published there, including American association papers: the *American Economic Review,* the *Journal of Economic Literature,* the *Journal of Economic Perspectives,* and the *Economic Journal* (published by the Royal Economic Society). Finally, we included the *Cambridge Journal of Economics* (CJE), one of the most relevant journals on heterodox economics.

We then performed several searches using different key words for each thematic group. These allow us to increase the number of contributions (68 papers) belonging to each group enormously, even though most were papers that were not frequently quoted or were written by authors without a long academic career. We therefore proceeded to discard those papers that were cited less than 100 times, and those written by authors with less than 20 articles in academic journals or less than 40 publications in journals, books, proceedings, etc. Using these criteria, we removed 29 papers and selected 45 papers by 59 authors in order to build the canon. Using this methodology, we included some articles and authors the relevance of which we had not initially appreciated (Cohendet and Llerena, 2003; Foss, 2003; Loasby, 1998; Mathews, 2003; Asheim and Coenen, 2005; Niosi, 2002; Carlson and Stankiewicz, 1991; Buenstorf and Klepper, 2009; Cooke, 2001; Setterfield, 1997; Cantner and Pyka, 2001). Of the final database of 45 papers, some 2807 cited works were identified, which corresponded to around 1100 authors. From those total citations, around 35 per cent were of the selected group of authors from the canon. Once again, when studies that were cited only once are eliminated, the proportion of works from within the canon increases to 37 per cent of degree 2 citations.

As a consequence of this procedure, we propose the following groups of articles:

i   Habits and routines (13 articles, mostly from ICC and mainstream journals: Cohen and Levinthal, 1989; Cohendet and Llerena, 2003; Cowan and Foray, 1997; Dosi, 1988; Foss, 2003; Hodgson, 1998; Loasby, 1998; Mathews, 2002; Nelson and Winter, 1973, 2002; Nelson, 1991; Pavitt, 2002; Teece and Pisano, 1994).

ii   Innovation systems (13 articles, mostly from RP: Antonelli, 1999; Ashein and Coenen, 2005; Boschma and Lambooy, 1999; Breschi and Lissoni, 2001; Buenstorf and Klepper, 2009; Carlson and Stankiewicz, 1991; Cook, 2001; Edquist and Hommen, 1999; Freeman, 1995; Lundvall *et al.*, 2002; Malerba, 2002; Niosi, 2002; Pavitt, 1984).

iii   Cumulative causation (six articles, mostly from the CJE: Dosi, 1982; Metcalfe *et al.*, 2006; Saviotti, 2001; Saviotti and Pyka, 2004; Cimoli *et al.*, 2010; Setterfield, 1997).

iv   Self-organization/self-transformation (six articles from the CJE and JEE: Cantner and Pyka, 2001; Dopfer *et al.*, 2004; Dosi and Nelson, 1994; Foster, 2005; Metcalfe, 1995; Witt, 1997).
v   Feedback and increasing returns (seven articles, mostly from mainstream journals: Arthur, 1989; Blume and Durlauf, 2005; David, 1985; Durlauf, 2005; Krugman, 1991; Lane and Maxfield, 2005; Audrestcht and Feldman, 1996).

The first group, habits and routines, is defined by their interest in learning processes at the firm level and in the behaviour of economic agents and institutions within a framework that is not always strictly evolutionary because it is also related to institutionalism (Hodgson) and management studies (Teece and Pisano). The contributions of this group have defined a set of ontological assumptions for evolutionary thinking in economics. They stress the presence of bounded rationality and environmental uncertainty which limit access to information, capacity building, and the organization's perception of preferences and representations of the world. Bounded rationality and non-modellable uncertainty explain why firms act through routines that are generated along their evolutionary path (Nelson and Winter). These routines constitute the organizational memory through which firms develop their productive and commercial activities. They include instructions that allow firms to replicate one another and imitate other firms. The routines are tested when conflicts appear and deliberative actions are needed. In that case, innovation emerges in the form of changing existing routines and creating new ones (Pavitt). This routinized behaviour is coherent with Hodgson's habit-driven behaviour, in which he stresses the importance of habits over rational choice in the behaviour of economic agents. He considers that agents act within socially pre-established parameters to cope with uncertain and changing environments. These habits are defined locally depending on the scope of the actors' connections.

This group's clearest backgrounds are to do with industrial organization, the theory of the firm, and management, on the one hand, and the American institutionalism on the other, as opposed to the Austrian school of thought.

The second group, innovation systems, includes contributions which have emphasized the systemic dimension of innovation and technological change on the basis of concepts such as clusters and local, regional, sectoral, and national innovation systems. This group is the largest because of the scope of its subject matter. On the one hand, it includes contributions from Freeman, Edquist, Nelson, and Lundvall, who are associated with the national innovation systems (NIS) approach. On the other hand, it includes different contributions related to innovation systems (local and sectoral) within an evolutionary framework (Malerba, Pavitt, Breschi, Lissoni, Cook) and others closer to the complexity approach (Boschma and Antonelli). Common to all these contributions is the consideration of the systemic nature of innovation. They place innovation and learning process in a central position, adopting a holistic, interdisciplinary approach and employing a historical perspective. They emphasize the differences between systems and recognize the existence of divergent paths among them. Their analysis highlights elements such as interdependence, non-linearity, and the centrality of institutions.

The third group is cumulative causation. It includes contributions that stress the demand side, such as Dosi, Saviotti, and Pyka, and those on international trade by evolutionary contributions, such as Cimoli, Porcile, and Rovira. Although they are mainly focused on economic aggregates, they recognize the relevance of micro- and meso-dynamics. They emphasize the complementarity of Keynesian, Schumpeterian, and Kaldorian sources of growth (Dosi, Setterfield). The centrality of absolute advantage in determining the specialization on international trade – based on exploiting opportunities of an expanding demand – can be recognized in Kaldorian ideas of feedbacks between demand and productivity. Therefore, in these contributions, the presence of persistent heterogeneity in preferences, endowments, routines, and performance and the immanent possibility of novelty are taken as two strong ontological assumptions (Metcalfe, Foster, and Ramlogan).

The fourth group, self-organization/self-transformation, is characterized by its strong evolutionary and Austrian roots. The former can be seen in contributors' interest in explaining the self-transformation of economic systems and population dynamics driven by variation, selection, and retention. The Austrian contributions emphasize economic order as an endogenous result of decentralized disequilibrium interactions among system components. The contributions included in this group come from Dopfer, Metcalfe, Potts, Witt, Foster, Cantner, and Pyka, among others. In particular, Dopfer has proposed an axiomatic construction that explains the workings and dynamics of a neo-Schumpeterian evolutionary system. The contribution of this group is the articulation of the micro and macro levels based on the meso level. The meso level is characterized by various features to implement a rule generated at the micro level: different sets of routines corresponding to the production of goods and services in a population of firms competing in the same market. The macro dimension, in contrast, includes a set of heterogeneous rules generated at the micro level, representing the state of the technological and organizational practices at a given moment in time (without discarding the heterogeneity present within each population) of all available goods and services traded on the market. Thus, the ontology present in this group is not reductionist from the macro to the micro.

Finally, the fifth group, which we call feedback and increasing returns, consists of a large stream of thought identified with complexity economics at the Santa Fe Institute (Arthur, Durlauf, and Lane). These contributions – motivated by a desire to explain substantive empirical phenomena – have been applying different ideas from the complexity approach to economics, focusing especially on (i) historical studies, (ii) the identification of data patterns which are consistent with some of the features of complex environment (power law), and (iii) social interactions. Specifically, they are focused on analysing decentralized interactions at the micro level and the feedback and non-equilibrium dynamics derived from it. These feedbacks lead to the presence of increasing returns and divergent paths among systems. They have applied non-linear dynamics not only to innovation processes but also to other economic fields, such as finance and stock markets. They have also emphasized that feedback mechanisms can even be perceived between behaviour and institutions. This direction includes the contributions on competitive technologies and standard diffusion (Arthur) and economics of 'qwerty' (David).

5 Evolutionism-cum-complexity: current trends in complexity and innovation, common elements, and conceptual differences

Having defined the evolutionary groups, in this section we will focus on the degree of agreement of each group with the five dimensions that account for the ontology of complexity: (i) heterogeneity, (ii) network architecture, (iii) interactions, disequilibrium, and divergence, and (iv) emergent properties. We have explored the relationships between them in order to find common traits and try to articulate them from a complexity perspective. In the five evolutionary groups identified, we have found similarities and differences in terms of the ontological dimensions of complex systems. In Table 9.3, we present the relationship between the typology outlined above and the four dimensions of the ontology of complexity discussed in Section 2.

The habits and routines group is characterized by the importance of heterogeneity of habits, routines, and capabilities derived from differentiation strategies of firms endowed with bounded rationality. In this scenario, firms interact in an uncertain environment.[8] Firms change their routines and therefore innovate when non-trivial problems appear or are discovered (Nelson and Winter, 1982). According to Hodgson (2009), habits, beliefs, and procedural rationality are the effective ways through which firms and institutions face uncertainty. Differentiation is the starting point for analysing the competition dynamic in which learning processes, developed through firms' evolutionary paths, are a key factor. Differentiation strategies are based on problem-solving heuristics leading to the emergence of innovation processes, which in turn will increase the initial heterogeneity between firms.

The firms interact in a hierarchical and modular network architecture. In terms of Nelson and Winter (1982), the hierarchy can be found when passing from individual learning (skills) to organizational learning (routines). This means that the economic systems are complex at different levels of analysis even though micro-level analysis is paramount. Besides, modularization can be seen in the way routines and sub-routines are articulated. As a consequence, from this perspective, firms can be defined as a set of routines organized into a modular structure that lets firms maintain functionality beyond exogenous shocks.

Departing from this network architecture, interactions with the environment and firms' access to local information let them complement their internal capabilities. In this sense, the firm's individual behaviour is partially determined by systemic conditions and idiosyncratic traits. Meanwhile, institutions shape the behaviour of the agents, although micro interactions based on local learning and

Table 9.3 Assumptions regarding the ontology of complexity by thematic group/author

	G1 Habits and routines	G2 National, local and sectoral innovation systems	G3 Cumulative causation	G4 Self-organization/self-transformation	G5 Feedback and increasing returns
I Micro-heterogeneity	Heterogeneity in routines, habits, and capacities derived from differential learning processes and adaptation to the environment.	Heterogeneity within and between innovation systems.	Heterogeneity of productive and technological trajectories.	Micro-heterogeneity is the fuel of the evolutionary process.	Heterogeneous agents interacting locally in a decentralized way.
II Network architecture	Structured hierarchy of routines and subroutines.	Incomplete linkages. Local connections in a multidimensional space. Connections have costs.	Network structure is not key in the analysis. Priority is given to the role of demand.	Partial local information is articulated from network interaction to give rise to collective knowledge.	Location determines connections and network structure. No global controller information can be local or global (externalities). Hierarchical organization and multiple scales of analysis.
III Interactions, disequilibrium, and divergence	Interaction with the environment for capability building Uncertainty about the nature of the innovation process. Disequilibrium and dynamic path dependence.	Interactions between firms lead to feedbacks processes and give rise to local learning, externalities, and divergence between systems.	Feedback processes with demand, and structural change derived from disequilibrium and path-dependent dynamics.	Distinction between order and equilibrium. Interactions in the adaptive process produce positive feedback, disequilibrium and generation of variety and selection.	There are multiple equilibria (or attractors) undetermined a priori. Positive feedback and increasing returns, network economies, and network externalities.
IV Emergence	Institutional structures, rules, and habits.	Innovation systems.	Structural change leading to the emergence of new sectors and complexity of the existing sectors.	Emergence of order and structure.	Order: arrives at an attractor of the system between different possible attractors. No guarantee of global optimality.

Source: own elaboration.

imitation can lead to changes in these rules and institutions. Interactions between firms and their surroundings show certain characteristics of their own: in the first place, the competition process as a whole conditions the dynamic of each individual firm. In terms of disequilibrium and divergence, the contributions of this group come from the idea that system dynamics are always path dependent and out of equilibrium. However, in this case, path dependence refers to the paths that firms and their context have travelled along. Disequilibrium is also reflected in the presence of positive feedbacks in the learning processes at the micro level and by the uncertainty present in the very nature of the innovation process (Nelson, 1991), which moves the system away from the equilibrium.

The way heterogeneity, network architecture, interactions, and disequilibrium interact explains the group's emergent properties. What emerge in this group are institutional structures, new routines, rules, and habits. Additionally, in their firm theory, organizations can be understood as complex systems because feedback mechanisms between variables and emergent properties are present. These feedback processes necessarily lead to divergent paths among firms competing in a market but not to divergence among systems.

The innovation systems group of contributions distinguish between micro and system heterogeneity. In particular, contributions linked to local and sectoral innovation systems stress the importance of heterogeneity within systems made up of different firms and institutions. There is a continuous generation of micro-diversity but also a process of resolution of this variety via local knowledge diffusion. As long as each system was idiosyncratically articulated, each of them performed differently, accounting for meso- and macro-heterogeneity. In this regard, they are closer to the second tradition, which emphasized system divergence.[9]

Interactions between system components are local, taking into account the specific characteristics of technology and knowledge (synchronic and diachronic complementarities) and information and rationality (incomplete and bounded). From the perspective of national systems of innovation, Freeman (1995) states the importance of inter-firm relationships as well as external linkages and linkages between economics sectors. According to him:

> The success of any specific technical innovation, depended on other related changes in systems of production. As three major new 'generic' technologies (information technology, bio-technology and new materials technology) diffused through the world economy in the 1970s and 1980s, systemic aspects of innovation assumed greater and greater importance.
>
> (Freeman, 1995: 11)

From the perspective of local innovation systems, the localization of interactions are also affected by the functioning of the institutions embedded in the territory (Maskell and Malmberg, 1999). The interactions take place in an incomplete architecture of connections. In the discussion held within evolutionary geography on the role of territory in a context of ICT diffusion, various contributions have stressed the need to expand the dimensionality of space beyond the geographical dimension. In particular, Boschma and Martin (2010) and Antonelli (2011) are interested in analysing the network architecture in multidimensional space in a framework of incomplete network of connections. For example, social distance is taken into account by using social network analysis (SNA). This tool also allows the network structure and the relative position of firms in the network to be considered. It is also relevant to understanding both the individual dynamics – central or peripheral or bridge positions are not equivalent – and the global dynamics; some network structures favour the differential creation and circulation of knowledge.

Interactions are relevant in local, sectoral, and national innovation systems; nevertheless, the idea that interactions have costs is stressed mainly by the local and sectoral contributions. Interactions between components can generate positive feedbacks that amplify individual responses, resulting in aggregate dynamics that cannot be deduced from the linear aggregation of its components. In this sense, the interactions between firms and its surroundings lead to aggregate dynamics that lead to persistent heterogeneity. The responses of each firm to changes in environmental conditions or to changes made by other co-located firms lead to answers that can be multiplied at the system level. As such, interactions that generate externalities multiply through feedbacks leading to increased returns and divergent dynamics.

The system and its global functioning is by itself an emergent property. In Edquist *et al.* (2001) and Edquist (1997), innovation systems are considered emergent because they are the result of a historical process within a framework of interdependences of its components. Therefore, they are a result of a co-evolution between knowledge, institutions, and organizations. Meanwhile, in the contributions related to the new evolutionary geography (Boschma, 2005; Boschma and Martin, 2010; Martin and Sunley, 2007), which has strong links with the complexity approach, emergence precisely refers to local and sectoral innovation systems on the basis of local interactions. Antonelli (2011) additionally postulates that innovation is an emergent property which is considered as the result of both the intentional and the creative actions of firms and meso–macro conditions. The introduction of novelty is the combined result of the conditions of the system as a whole and the characteristics derived from firms' idiosyncratic capabilities.

The contributions of the cumulative causation group are focused on understanding long-term growth processes based on an expansion of demand. The Smithian idea that market expansion is an engine of economic diversification, creating opportunities for innovation, appears as the key link between Schumpeterian, Kaldorian, and Keynesian dynamics of growth. In this context, the possibility of emerging externalities that trigger growth and diversify the productive structure relies on the characteristics of the productive structure itself which would lead to feedback growth in the framework of the Kaldor–Verdoorn relation. Global interactions predominate over local ones, at least within the system, regardless of the scale of analysis. These issues bring them close to structuralism and lead them to understand divergence between economic systems beyond feedback related to knowledge and technology. In this context, they stress the importance of cumulative causation process and explain why the dynamic processes lead to temporal, structural irreversibility, and path dependence. In this group, micro-heterogeneity is partially present in agent-based modelling to account for the emerging macro or sectoral dynamic,[10] but a macro or industry analysis prevails in most contributions. Interactions become evident especially between different sectors and economics aggregates. In this regard, they are mostly global since the structural conditions act as a signal to all agents within a system. In turn, micro interactions would be absent or would arise from externalities (global interactions).[11] Dosi (2014) states that micro-heterogeneity and far-from-equilibrium interactions induce the co-evolution of aggregate variables (employment, production, etc.) and institutional set-ups. Therefore, the macro structure can be considered an emergent property.

Regarding disequilibrium, Saviotti and Pyka (2004) consider that the dynamics of the system are explained by a continuous passage from Schumpeterian circular economy (equilibrium) to disequilibrium. In contrast, Dosi (2014) holds that there is a dynamic that is continuously out of equilibrium. As in all cases where feedback processes may play an important role, these contributions stress the possibility of lock-in situations caused by non-linear interactions. They refer to learning and adaptation processes that lead to co-evolution between demand and technological and production conditions.

The contributions of this group stress different emergent properties. On one hand, structural change, new sectors, and new products emerge as a result of a larger disposable income that arises from the technological change itself (Saviotti and Pyka, 2004). On the other hand, as the unintended result of the collective interactions of the agents in a learning situation, new organizational forms and institutions emerge (Dosi, 2014). Moreover, Dosi stresses that stable relationships observed between aggregate variables might arise from interactions and turbulent microeconomic disequilibrium. He argues that this emergence may appear as both an aggregated and a collective phenomenon (e.g. macro regularities) but also at the industrial and firm levels.

In the self-organization/self-transformation group, contributions can easily find an underlying evolutionary ontology that is strongly linked to the ontology of complexity. In this group, which is faithful to the Hayekian tradition, the notion of order is preferred to the equilibrium one. The authors' opposition to equilibrium relies on their understanding of the architecture of connections as incomplete, which leads to the idea of partial information (Foster, 2005; Saviotti, 2001). Potts (2000) states that the economic structure is a complex system in which connections are incomplete and local. Local information is articulated into a larger network of interactions, giving rise to collective knowledge. In turn, links and information are more important than system components (Kirman, 2010) when explaining system dynamics.

In this group, network architecture is hierarchical because multiple scales of analysis (micro–meso–macro) are considered. In Dopfer, micro-heterogeneity is preserved at the meso level and meso-structure heterogeneity is kept at the macro level. The significance of hierarchy and modularization can be seen in Dopfer and Potts's (2004) definition of a complex system: a complex system is modular, open, and with hierarchies. It is modular because it consists of a set of specific parts which are functional and connected. It is open because the parts interact with some degrees of freedom and can therefore continually change their connections. Finally, it is hierarchical because each module is a complex system in itself.

The emergent properties here are order and structure, which do not invalidate micro-heterogeneity. These authors are well aware of the assumption of variability at the micro level and constancy at the macro level. As Dopfer posits, what emerges depends on the dimension from which we analyse the system, either at the micro, meso, or macro level. Thus, at the micro level, a rule (routine) emerges; at meso level, multiple updates of this rule made by the agents of a population emerge; and at macro level, populations of rules and updates to them emerge. Metcalfe stresses that the evolutionary process explains how populations change over time and how structure is an emergent property, resulting from the interaction and interdependence among agents. This idea of a path-dependent resilient structure sets Metcalfe apart from Hayek, for whom only self-organization emerges. More specifically, Metcalfe considers that structural change emerges as a consequence of the competition process. Like Kirman, Metcalfe thinks it is possible that the organizational structure of the market emerges. Besides, depending on the level of market organization, the structure may or may not reach the point where it is able to promote specialization, coordination, and economic change.

From this evolutionary perspective, innovation produces changes in the selective features of product and processes within a population. As a consequence, this is not just a random Darwinian perspective because Darwinian selection is not cumulative and it is inefficient since there are too many alternatives to be selected.

Coordination is the main problem tackled by this group of contribution. Transformation is a problem that arises from the coordination issue. It regards how different agents combine different pieces of knowledge, and how different pieces of knowledge are accumulated along their path dependence combined with the old ones is the main concern of this group. Therefore, there is space for local interactions and divergence of agents or systems, but they are mainly focused on the fact that the selection process is continuously discarding heterogeneity (which is the fuel of evolutionary process), leading little space for assuming divergence as a main trend of economic development. The restless capitalism of Metcalfe refers more to the continuous regeneration of variety than to the way that heterogeneity persists and reinforces itself.

Finally, in the feedback and increasing returns group, the definition of the economy as a complex adaptive system is based on the existence of heterogeneous agents interacting locally in a decentralized way, even though many of the models assume homogeneous agents.

The contributions of this group support the idea that complex systems can create order. The dynamics of complex systems are essentially 'open-ended'. Therefore, the idea of a global optimum is useless in itself (Arthur, 1989). For these contributions, complex systems can generate order from interactions between decentralized and dispersed agents. In this direction, the notion of steady state should be replaced by evolution. 'New niches, new potentials, new possibilities are continually being created, the economy operates far from any optimum or global equilibrium. The improvements are always possible and in fact they occur regularly' (Arthur *et al.*, 1997: 66) The positive feedbacks generate phase transitions that lead from one attractor to another and take the form of increasing returns, network economies, and externalities of different types.

> An agent's actions generate a feedback to the agent through the choices of other network members, thereby multiplying the effect of any initial stimulus to the agent...
>
> These interactions are of primary importance to firms and policy-makers because they allow a stimulus to one individual to be magnified by its dispersion through the network.
>
> (Hartman *et al.*, 2008: 2)

The location of the firms determines the connection and the network architecture; therefore, no global controller exists. In turn, interactions –which firms can access through specific linkages – are a key factor. The network economies and increasing returns prevailing in this approach are examples of the significance of global information. As in the previous group, some contributions use SNA methodology (Blume *et al.*, 2010) to handle these interactions. There are both hierarchical and multiple scales of analysis. In this group, the emergent property refers to order, defined as an attractor of the system between different multiple attractors. This group of contributions differs from the mainstream because the attractor that the system reaches does not guarantee global optimality. Specifically in the field of technology, a dominant design emerges.

6 Policy implications

Although there is room for heterogeneity under the umbrella of complexity, the historical roots of the different evolutionary neo-Schumpeterian groups lead to very different policy prescriptions. In this section, we will briefly discuss the policy prescriptions of each group and how they are related to both their historical roots and the complexity dimensions that they stress (see Figure 9.1).

As we have pointed out, each of the evolutionary groups fits, albeit loosely, into one of the two paths of complexity in the history of economic thought. The self-organization/self-transformation group is the closest to the first historical tradition. This is because the authors are mainly interested in coordination issue and competition processes inside population. Meanwhile, habits and routines is

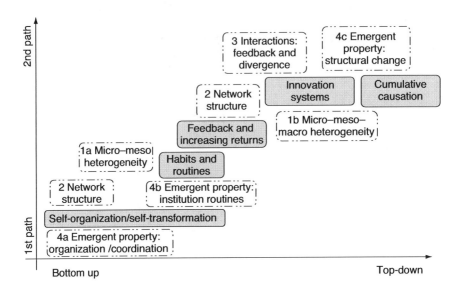

Figure 9.1 The relationship between the two traditions of complexity in the economic
history and the five evolutionary groups (source: own elaboration).

related also to this tradition, although with less strength. It is concerned with the
micro dimension of the competition process and therefore in the competition
between habits and routines and with divergence between populations.

The innovation systems and cumulative causation groups are closer to divergence, stressed by the second tradition. In these groups, divergence and transformation are combined. The innovation systems group emphasizes system
divergence and recognizes the work of the development school as a predecessor.
Contributions in this group also take great effort to explain the mechanisms
through which systems at different aggregation levels diverge. Furthermore,
interactions between firms and their environment lead to different dynamics of
economics aggregates. Backgrounds for such work include a range of contributions from development theory to structuralist and post-Keynesian approach. In
this sense, they argue that economic systems are affected by time and space and
as such are not aligned with the idea of monoeconomics. The proximity of the
cumulative causation group to the second historical tradition is explained in
terms of its special interest in understanding long-term growth processes based
on interactions generated by an expansion of demand. Smith's idea that market
expansion is an engine of economic diversification, creating opportunities for
innovation, is the key link between Keynesian and Schumpeterian dynamics of
growth.

Finally, the feedback and increasing returns group occupies an intermediate
position, although it is closer to the second tradition, because the presence of
divergence and heterogeneity between systems is stressed.

In all evolutionary groups, 'the operational imperfections identified in the neoclassical market failure approach are considered necessary aspects of the dynamics of the generation and the dissemination of knowledge, and not distortion that need to be eliminated by policy' (Bleda and del Rio, 2013: 1050).

Nevertheless, there are differences of policy implications between groups according to the dimensions of complexity they stress. First, to consider heterogeneity as a key ontological dimension leads to a public policy design aimed at increasing variety. In this regard, from a microeconomic perspective, the habits and routines and self-organization groups emphasize the relevance of heterogeneity as the fuel of selection process. Therefore, these groups promote public policies designed to improve individual skills that lead to an increase in innovation, which means an increase in variety. The dynamic capabilities that allow agents to learn are the key determinants of both generic coordination and endogenous generation of knowledge in markets. From this evolutionary perspective, the goal of innovation policy is to enhance agents' dynamics capabilities and their learning processes so that novelty and variety is continuously created. The policies promoted by these groups can mainly be labelled as bottom-up policies.

Second, from a theoretical perspective, the structure of the network and its impact on innovation and economic development has been deeply analysed. The studies have distinguished between different morphologies and types of network and have analysed their impact on knowledge generation and circulation (Watts, 2006; Giuliani and Bell, 2005). Nevertheless, the public policy instruments that emerge from such theoretical developments are still in the experimental stage. In this direction, the policy recommendations basically lead to deepening linkages between organizations regardless of the quality and the kind of resulting structure. The differential stress that each group places on the relevance of the network structure leads to differences in the policy related to this issue. As mentioned before, the self-organization group has been characterized by emphasizing that linkages are more relevant than components in explaining the global dynamics of the system (Potts, 2000). Under this perspective, public policy should aim to encourage

> dynamic coordination among the variety of heterogeneous players involved in the generation of knowledge as a complex and collective process. The state can favor the activity of interface bodies that have the specific mission to increase the dissemination of scientific knowledge and its communication to potential users. The creation of such interface agencies can increase the efficiency of the workings of the knowledge governance systems.
>
> (Antonelli, 2010: 179)

Lee (2013) criticizes this view of innovation policy focused on solving systems failures. He considers that systems failures are derived from previous problems in the capabilities of organizations and networks and linkages should be promoted instead. According to Lee (2013), the contributions of Nelson and Winter, which we included in the habits and routines group, recognize that capacity failures can be more harmful than system failures.

Third, the dimension of complexity 'disequilibrium, interactions, and divergence' gives rise to a set of public policies aimed either at (i) promoting the positive feedbacks associated with virtuous dynamics, or (ii) unlocking blockades in order to reverse divergence phenomena. In this regard, the innovation systems group has emphasized the divergence between systems caused by feedback processes derived from capabilities and interactions between components. As stated by Boschma and Martin (2010: 25):

> region-specific contexts provide opportunities but also set limits to what can be achieved by public policy. Consequently, policy action should avoid 'one-size-fits-all' and 'picking-the-winner' policies. Instead of copying best practices or selecting winners, policy should take the history of a region as a starting point, and identify regional potentials and bottlenecks accordingly. To avoid the problem of regional lock-in, Nooteboom and Stam (2008), among others, have argued that public policy should stimulate the entry of newcomers, encourage new policy experiments, and enhance the establishment of extra-regional linkages.

Meanwhile, the cumulative causation group has emphasized divergence processes arising from the feedback dynamics between productivity and demand. In this regard, Dosi *et al.* state that there is a 'strong complementarity between Schumpeterian policies addressing innovative activities and Keynesian demand-management policies. Both types of policies seem to be necessary to put the economy into a long-run sustained growth path' (Dosi *et al.*, 2010a: 1750). Finally, in the last group, the presences of increasing returns are considered the cause of the divergence phenomena, derived from interactions. 'Interactions are causal in nature and have implications for policy in terms of magnifying the effect of agent-level policy interventions' (Hartman *et al.*, 2008: 3). In these cases, the policy should recognize the presence of divergence and act accordingly in order to generate catch-up processes and unlock the lock-in phenomena.

Fourth, emergent properties considered by each group should be the aim of their policy. As shown in Tables 9.2 and 9.3, the different groups identify emergent properties as specific phenomena. In the self-organization/self-transformation group, the emergent property of the system is organization and coordination. Therefore, public policy should aim to smooth out the way for this emergence to occur. 'Innovation policy must centre on assisting the development and the evolution of the underlying knowledge structure that generates operation outcomes in a market, and not on the operational outcomes themselves.' This means it is important to develop capacities and:

> intervene at the level of constitutional rules in order to provide the adequate underlying structure of regulations, financial institutions, and public infrastructure, and allow flexibility of the legal framework to facilitate adaptation process and accommodate novel forms of transformation and transactions.
>
> (Bleda and Rio, 2013: 1050)

In this regard, the self-organization group is close to the habits and routines group in conceiving institutions as an emergent property as well. However, in the latter group, the emergence of institutions is not given on the basis of a set of elementary constitutional rules, but on the habits that govern the behaviour of agents. According to Nelson and Winter, policy should focus on the creation of micro- and even intra-organizational conditions that ensure the emergence of routines.

Contrary to these mainly bottom-up policy types, public policies derived from the innovation systems and cumulative causation groups aim to recognize that the emergent structure may not be conducive to an economic development process. Therefore, intervention should take into account not only bottom-up aspects but mainly top-down policies, focused on both defining the specialization pattern and choosing the driver-sectors for economic development. The last aspect leads to a discussion on how to identify such sectors and involves various perspectives, ranging from finding windows of opportunity (Peréz, 2009; Dosi, 1982), choosing sectors with increasing returns (Dosi *et al.*, 1990; Reinert, 2007), focusing on short cycle technologies (Lee, 2013), and prioritizing the manufacture and production of capital goods (Rosenberg, 1963; Pisano and Shih, 2009) among others.

In sum, those groups that are closer to the second historical tradition focus on the need to discuss the productive specialization profile (top-down policies), but, nevertheless, see space for evolutionary dynamics in structural change. As Cimoli *et al.* (2010) have pointed out:

> structural change is, by definition, a process of qualitative change, which does not emerge spontaneously from the smooth accumulation of factors of production. In this sense the evidence confirms what the literature on comparative development has already pointed out, namely the key role played by the industrial and technological policies in picking up a dynamic growth path among the various alternative paths.

In the same direction, Freeman (1995: 5) has noticed that:

> the policies promoted by List on his development of the concept of National System of Innovation advocated not only for protection of infant industries but a broad range of policies designed to accelerate, or to make possible, industrialisation and economic growth.

Therefore, he proposed that policies should be 'concerned with learning about new technology and applying it'.

On the contrary, the groups that are more closely linked to the first tradition stress that the specialization profile is naturally an emergent property of the system. In this case, the regulations that have been derived from the theory refer to the need for bottom-up-type intervention that focuses on improving market selection processes (as a set of socially established norms), and raising the minimum capacity thresholds of firms and institutions that fit variety, on which selection process works. In fact, Metcalfe *et al.* (2006: 29) have stressed that 'policy would follow from a bottom-up rather than an aggregate economy-down perspective; that they would depend on the stimulation of enterprise and entrepreneurship; and that they would depend upon the open, unbiased operation of market institutions'.

In this context, there is a contrast between the two forms of conceiving state-based intervention, which are in line with historical precedents and especially with the idea that each group has about development and structural change.

Regardless of the economic dynamic that has arisen from the complexity perspective, it reveals emergent properties that are the consequence of simultaneous bottom-up and top-down processes. In other words, the evolutionary dynamics are built through individual actions, but they are also affected by macro and meso structural conditions, including institutions, which limit their behaviours, choices, and possibilities for learning. In this sense, the complexity approach is coherent with regulatory recommendations in which both types of intervention are justified. For example, intervention is necessary to change commercial specialization in order to avoid lock-in situations while simultaneously developing capacities to increase the generation of variety, which in turn improves the innovative capacity of the system.

In this context, the different dimensions of the complexity approach reveal not only the differences in each group of contributions' policy recommendations but also the need to articulate them. In this way, bottom-up and top-down approaches are not mutually exclusive options but complementary ones. As such, the structural change policy promoted by the different contributions would be enriched because it would not only focus on improving the competitive process in firm populations – as has been suggested by the self-organization/self-transformation and habits and routines groups – but would also, through the selection of technologically progressive sectors, provide more space for the application of bottom-up policies for improving productive, technological, commercial, and organizational capacities.

7 Conclusions

In this chapter, we have discussed the general idea of complexity from a trans-disciplinary perspective by proposing an integrative ontology including different definitions proposed in the literature (Section 2). We have then examined (in Section 3) the background of the idea of complexity which can be found throughout the history of economic theory in two great traditions: one that focuses on order and single economic system and another on transformation and divergence. In Section 4, we have identified a typology of several groups of evolutionary contributions based on their core research questions and on the main concerns they address. We have then analysed how the main dimensions of the ontology of complexity are manifested in the conceptual elaborations of each of these groups (Section 5). In Section 6, we have discussed how belonging to traditions and the connection with different dimensions of complexity affect the goal of policies.

There are similarities and differences between the five evolutionary groups of contributions in terms of the ontological dimensions of complex systems that they stress and how they are linked to the two traditions in the history of economics that are linked to complexity. Regarding the similarities, the presence of heterogeneity in the characteristics of organizations – firms and institutions – is a feature that applies to virtually all the groups. In particular, in many of these contributions, micro-heterogeneity refers to the variety of capabilities, at the level of organizations (firms and institutions) belonging to the complex system, where micro-scale variability is consistent with the macro order. That is, the core features of the system can be described without having information on each of its components. In the evolutionary theory of innovation, the heterogeneity of the system components refers to the diversity of firms in terms of (i) technological, productive, commercial, and organizational skills, (ii) linkages and loci in the network architecture, and (iii) behaviour and productive performance. In this context, they discard an approximation based on methodological individualism and use the idea of population.

But while the habits and routines and self-organization groups use the term heterogeneity mainly to refer to firms, in the feedback and increasing returns group, and especially in the innovation systems and cumulative causation groups, it refers mainly to differences between systems. Therefore, from the perspective of heterogeneity, while the former are closer to the first historical tradition (ending in Hayek), the latter are more linked to the second (ending in the development school).

In terms of the importance of disequilibrium and divergence, all the groups stress disequilibrium but they define divergence differently. While for the habits and routines and self-organization groups, divergence refers mainly to firms belonging to the same population, for the other groups, the divergence between systems is derived from feedbacks. So, once again, we see the same two historical economic traditions of complexity: the first in habits and routines and self-organization and the second in the remaining three groups.

In the remaining two dimensions, we have identified some differences and greater heterogeneity among the evolutionary groups considered. In the habits and routines group, the network architecture takes the form of modularization of routines and interactions with the environment for capability building are also present, even though the information that is appropriated through this interaction is partial. The interaction and the importance of networking groups are central to the innovation systems and self-organization/self-transformation and feedback and increasing returns groups. In all three cases, the emphasis is placed on local interactions. In turn, hierarchy and modularization are also manifested differently. In the habits and routines group, modularization applies to routines and hierarchy does not play a strong role, or at most appears within a micro–meso analysis. The innovation systems group, in turn, is hierarchical, whereas in the cumulative causation group, there is hierarchy but no modularization. In the self-organization/self-transformation group, both dimensions are present, and in the feedback and increasing returns group, hierarchy with multiple attractors for each phase transition prevails.

Finally, while emergence is a key ontological dimension of complexity, what emerges in each of the groups is different: routines, habits, and institutions in the first group, innovation and systems at different scales in the second group, structural change in the third, order and structure in the fourth, and an attractor that is not a global optimum in the fifth.

This implies that each group exhibits a different link with each tradition within the history of economic thought, and therefore also different ways of conceiving public intervention.

The complementarities between all these groups of contributions would enrich the perspective of divergence and transformation in contributions that place more emphasis on the issue of coordination and prioritize competition processes in microeconomic analyses of divergence between systems. Therefore, the groups that have emphasized coordination (habits and routines, and self-organization) would be enriched by the perspective of divergence and transformation. Meanwhile, the groups where divergence is relevant would be enriched by deepening their microeconomic analysis of competition processes.

Notes

1 We appreciate the comments received from Gabriel Porcile, Cristiano Antonelli, Mark Setterfield, Pablo Lavarello, Rasigan Maharaj, Graciela Gutman, Jorge Niosi, Mary Morgan, Tomasso Ciarli, Paolo Saviotti, and Martin Hilbert to previous versions of this chapter. Any errors or omissions are the responsibility of the authors.
2 Hayek (1945) suggests that both the economy and human knowledge are restless.
3 It is well known that in *Theory of Economic Development* (1912), Schumpeter appeals to the idea of equilibrium but, as has been suggested by Langlois (2007), he uses it just as a starting point for his pedagogical explanation of a process of continuous disequilibrium in which the position of the incumbents in the circular economy is challenged by new entrants that introduce novelty into the system.
4 According to Myrdal (1957), economic growth was generated in receiving areas and de-growth in areas that lose population. These dynamics produced additional disparities in wages and employment, and led to new migration processes and circular and cumulative causes of migration.
5 In some cases, more than one contribution was considered for each author.
6 For their part, the groups associated with the first historic stream (habits and routines, and self-organization/self-transformation) account for around 41 per cent of all citations and the remaining groups, which are associated with the second stream, account for 59 per cent.
7 Econlit was also used by Silva and Texeira (2008) in their bibliometric studies of evolutionary papers.
8 The presence of persistent heterogeneity in preferences, endowments, and world views and the immanent possibility of novelty are derived from these assumptions and is also connected with the possibility of generating capabilities along the firm's evolutionary path.
9 The background of these contributions includes the development school of the 1950s.
10 For example, in Saviotti and Pyka's TVCOM model, it remains as an assumption but is not included in the analysis.
11 These contributions can be found in Dosi *et al.* (1990), which follows Thirwall, Perroux, and Kaldor perspectives.

Bibliography

Andersen, E.S., 2004. Population thinking, Price's equation and the analysis of economic evolution. *Evolutionary and Institutional Economics Review* 1, 127–148.

Antonelli, C., 1999. The evolution of the industrial organisation of the production of knowledge. *Cambridge Journal of Economics* 23, 243–260.

Antonelli, C., 2008. *Localised Technological Change: Towards the Economics of Complexity*, London: Taylor & Francis.

Antonelli, C., 2008. Pecuniary knowledge externalities: the convergence of directed technological change and the emergence of innovation systems. *Industrial and Corporate Change* 17(5), 1049–1070.

Antonelli, C., 2010. Pecuniary externalities and the localized generation of technological knowledge, in Ron Boschma & Ron Martin (eds) *The Handbook of Evolutionary Economic Geography*, Cheltenham: Edward Elgar, pp. 162–181.

Antonelli, C., 2011. *Handbook on the Economic Complexity of Technological Change*, Cheltenham: Edward Elgar Publishing.

Arthur, W.B., 1989. Competing technologies, increasing returns, and lock-in by historical events. *The Economic Journal* 394, 116–131.

Arthur, W.B., 1990. 'Silicon Valley' locational clusters: when do increasing returns imply monopoly? *Mathematical Social Sciences* 3, 235–251.

Arthur, W.B., 1994. Positive feedbacks in the economy. *McKinsey Quarterly* 1, 81–95.

Arthur, W.B., 2009. *The Nature of Technology: What It Is and How It Evolves*, London: Penguin.

Arthur, W.B., Durlauf, S.N. and Lane, D.A., 1997. *The Economy as an Evolving Complex System II*, London: Addison-Wesley.

Asheim, B.T. and Coenen, L., 2005. Knowledge bases and regional innovation systems: comparing Nordic clusters. *Research Policy* 34, 1173–1190.

Audretsch, D.B. and Feldman, M.P., 1996. R&D spillovers and the geography of innovation and production. *The American Economic Review* 86, 630–640.

Bleda, M. and del Rio, P., 2013. The market failure and the systemic failure rationales in technological innovation systems. *Research Policy* 42, 1039–1052.

Blume, L.E. and Durlauf, S.N., 2005. *Identifying Social Interactions: A Review*. Wisconsin Madison Working Paper no. 12.

Blume, L. and Durlauf, Steven N., 2006. *Economy as an Evolving Complex System, III*, Oxford: Oxford University Press.

Boschma, R., 2005. Proximity and innovation: a critical assessment. *Regional Studies* 39, 61–74.

Boschma, R.A. and Frenken, K., 2006. Why is economic geography not an evolutionary science? Towards an evolutionary economic geography. *Journal of Economic Geography* 3, 273–302.

Boschma, R.A. and Lambooy, J.G., 1999. Evolutionary economics and economic geography. *Journal of Evolutionary Economics* 9, 411–429.

Boschma, R. and Martin, R.L., 2010. *The Handbook of Evolutionary Economic Geography*, Cheltenham, UK: Edward Elgar Publishing.

Boschma, R.A. and Ter Wal, A.L.J., 2006. Knowledge networks and innovative performance in an industrial district: the case of a footwear district in the south of Italy. *Papers in Evolutionary Economic Geography* 6, 1–23.

Bottazzi, G., Dosi, G., Jacoby, N., Secchi, A., and Tamagni, F., 2010. Corporate performances and market selection: some comparative evidence. *Industrial and Corporate Change* 19(6), 1953–1996.

Bowles, S., Durlauf, S.N., and Hoff, K., eds, 2006. *Poverty traps*, Princeton: Princeton University Press.

Breschi, S. and Lissoni, F., 2001. Knowledge spillovers and local innovation systems: a critical survey. *Industrial and Corporate Change* 4, 975–1005.

Bricmont, J., 1995. Science of chaos or chaos in science? *Annals of the New York Academy of Sciences* 775, 131–175.

Brock, W.A. and Durlauf, S.N., 2007. Identification of binary choice models with social interactions. *Journal of Econometrics* 1, 52–75.

Buenstorf, G. and Klepper, S., 2009. Heritage and agglomeration: The Akron Tyre Cluster revisited. *The Economic Journal* 119, 705–733.

Cantner, U. and Pyka, A., 2001. Classifying technology policy from an evolutionary perspective. *Research Policy* 30, 759–775.

Cantner, U., Hanusch, H., and Klepper, S., 2000. *Economic Evolution, Learning, and Complexity*, New York: Springer.

Carlsson, B. and Stankiewicz, R., 1991. On the nature, function and composition of technological systems. *Journal of Evolutionary Economics* 1, 93–118.

Cimoli, M. and Porcile, G., 2013. Technology, structural change and BOP-constrained growth: a structuralist toolbox. *Cambridge Journal of Economics* bet020.

Cimoli, M., Porcile, G., and Rovira, S., 2010. Structural change and the BOP-constraint: why did Latin America fail to converge? *Cambridge Journal of Economics* 2, 389–411.

Cohen, W.M. and Levinthal, D.A., 1989. Innovation and learning: the two faces of R&D. *The Economic Journal* 99, 569–596.

Cohendet, P. and Llerena, P., 2003. Routines and incentives: the role of communities in the firm. *ICC* 12, 271–297.

Cooke, P., 2001. Regional innovation systems, clusters, and the knowledge economy. *ICC* 10, 945–974.

Cowan, R. and Foray, D., 1997. The economics of codification and the diffusion of knowledge. *ICC* 6, 595–622.

David, P.A., 1985. Clio and the economics of QWERTY. *The American Economic Review* 75, 332–337.

Day, R.H., 1994. *Complex Economic Dynamics. An Introduction to Dynamical Systems and Market Mechanisms*, vol. 1, Cambridge: MIT Press.

Dopfer, K., 2004. The economic agent as rule maker and rule user: Homo Sapiens Oeconomicus. *Journal of Evolutionary Economics* 14, 177–195.

Dopfer, K., 2005. *The Evolutionary Foundations of Economics*, Cambridge: Cambridge University Press.

Dopfer, K., 2006. The origins of meso economics: Schumpeter's legacy. *The Papers on Economics and Evolution*, #0610.

Dopfer, K. and Potts, J., 2004. Evolutionary realism: a new ontology for economics. *Journal of Economic Methodology* 2, 195–212.

Dopfer, K., Foster, J., and Potts, J., 2004. Micro–meso–macro. *Journal of Evolutionary Economics* 14, 263–279.

Dosi, G., 1982. Technological paradigms and technological trajectories: a suggested interpretation of the determinants and directions of technical change. *Research Policy* 3, 147–162.

Dosi, G., 1988. *Technical Change and Economic Theory*, London: Pinter Publishers.

Dosi, G., 2014. Dinámica y coordinación económica. Algunos elementos para un paradigma alternativo 'evolucionista'. Tópicos de la teoría evolucionista neoschumpeteriana de la innovación y el cambio tecnológico.

Dosi, G. and Kaniovski, Y., 1994. On 'badly behaved' dynamics. *Journal of Evolutionary Economics* 2, 93–123.

Dosi, G. and Nelson, R.R., 1994. An introduction to evolutionary theories in economics. *Journal of Evolutionary Economics* 4, 153–172.

Dosi, G., Fagiolo, G., and Roventini, A., 2010a. Schumpeter meeting Keynes: a policy-friendly model of endogenous growth and business cycles. *Journal of Economic Dynamics and Control* 34(9), 1748–1767.

Dosi, G., Lechevalier, S., and Secchi, A., 2010b. Introduction: interfirm heterogeneity – nature, sources and consequences for industrial dynamics. *Industrial and Corporate Change* 6, 1867–1890.

Dosi, G., Pavitt, K., and Soete, L., 1990. *The Economics of Technical Change and International Trade*, London: Harvester Wheatsheaf.

Durlauf, S.N, 1993. Nonergodic economic growth. *Review of Economic Studies* 60(2), 349–366.

Durlauf, S.N., 2005. Complexity and empirical economics. *The Economic Journal* 115(504), F225–F243.

Edquist, C., 1997. *Systems of Innovation: Technologies, Institutions, and Organizations*, London: Psychology Press.

Edquist, C. and Hommen, L., 1999. Systems of innovation: theory and policy for the demand side. *Technology in Society* 21, 63–79.

Edquist, C., Hommen, L., and McKelvey, M.D., 2001. *Innovation and Employment: Process Versus Product Innovation*, Cheltenham: Edward Elgar Publishing.

Foss, N.J., 2003. Bounded rationality and tacit knowledge in the organizational capabilities approach: an assessment and a re-evaluation. *ICC* 12, 185–201.

Foster, J., 2005. From simplistic to complex systems in economics. *Cambridge Journal of Economics* 29(6), 873–892.

Freeman, C., 1995. The 'National System of Innovation' in historical perspective. *Cambridge Journal of Economics* 19, 5–24.

Frenken, K., 2006. Technological innovation and complexity theory. *Economics of Innovation and New Technology* 15, 137–155.

Giuliani, E. and Bell, M., 2005. The micro-determinants of meso-level learning and innovation: evidence from a Chilean wine cluster. *Research Policy* 34, 47–68.

Glaeser, E.L. and Scheinkman, J., 2000. Non-market interactions. *National Bureau of Economic Research Working Paper Series*, No. 8053. Available at: www.nber.org/papers/w8053 (accessed 6 October 2011).

Hartmann, W.R., Manchanda, P., Nair, H., Bothner, M., Dodds, P., Godes, D., Hosanagra, K., and Tucker, C., 2008. Modeling social interactions: identification, empirical methods and policy implications. *Marketing Letters* 19, 287–304.

Hayek, F.A., 1945. The use of knowledge in society. *The American Economic Review* 35(4), 519–530.

Hayek, F.A., 1948. *Individualism and Economic Order*, Chicago: University of Chicago Press.

Helbing, D. and Kirman, A., 2013. *Rethinking Economics Using Complexity Theory*, New York: Social Science Research Network, Rochester.

Hirschman, A., 1958. *The Strategy of Development*, New Haven, CN: Yale University Press.

Hodgson, G.M., 1998. Competence and contract in the theory of the firm. *Journal of Economic Behavior & Organization* 35, 179–201.

Hodgson, G., 2004. *The Evolution of Institutional Economics*, London: Routledge.

Hodgson, G.M., 2009. Choice, habit and evolution. *Journal of Evolutionary Economics* 20, 1–18.

Hoff, K.R., Sen, A., and Team, W.B.D.R.G.G. and I., 2005. *The Kin System as a Poverty Trap?*, World Bank, Development Research Group, Growth and Investment Team.

Kirman, A., 2010. *Complex Economics: Individual and Collective Rationality*, London: Routledge.

Klaes, M., 2004. Ontological issues in evolutionary economics: introduction. *Journal of Economic Methodology* 11(2), 121–124.

Knudsen, T., 2004. General selection theory and economic evolution: the price equation and the replicator/interactor distinction. *Journal of Economic Methodology* 11(2), 147–173.

Krugman, P., 1991. Increasing returns and economic geography. *Journal of Political Economy* 99, 483–499.

Krugman, P.R., 1996. *The Self-Organizing Economy*, London: Blackwell Publishers.

Kwapieńa, J. and Drożdż, S., 2012. Physical approach to complex systems. *Physics Reports* 515, 115–226.

Lane, D.A. and Maxfield, R.R., 2005. Ontological uncertainty and innovation. *Journal of Evolutionary Economics* 15, 3–50.

Langlois, R.N., 2007. *Dynamics of Industrial Capitalism: Schumpeter, Chandler, and the New Economy*, London: Taylor & Francis.

Lee, K., 2013. *Schumpeterian Analysis of Economic Catch-up: Knowledge, Path-Creation, and the Middle-Income Trap*, Cambridge: Cambridge University Press.

Lewin, R., 2002. *Complejidad: el caos como generador del orden*, Barcelona: Tusquets Editores.

Loasby, B.J., 1998. The organisation of capabilities. *Journal of Economic Behavior & Organization* 35, 139–160.

Lundvall, B.-Å., Johnson, B., Andersen, E.S., and Dalum, B., 2002. National systems of production, innovation and competence building. *Research Policy* 31, 213–231.

Malerba, F., 2002. Sectoral systems of innovation and production. *Research Policy* 31, 247–264.

Marshall, A., 1920. *Principles of Economics*, 8th ed., London: Macmillan and Co., Ltd.

Martin, R. and Sunley, P., 2007. Complexity thinking and evolutionary economic geography. *Journal of Economic Geography* 7, 573–601.

Maskell, P. and Malmberg, A., 1999. Localised learning and industrial competitiveness. *Cambridge Journal of Economics* 23, 167–185.

Mathews, J.A., 2003. A resource-based view of Schumpeterian economic dynamics, in P.J.S. Metcalfe and P.D.U. Cantner (eds) *Change, Transformation and Development*. Heidelberg: Physica-Verlag HD, pp 71–96

Metcalfe, J.S., 1994. Competition, Fisher's Principle and increasing returns in the selection process. *Journal of Evolutionary Economics* 4, 327–346.

Metcalfe, J.S., 1995. Technology systems and technology policy in an evolutionary framework. *Cambridge Journal of Economics* 19, 25–46.

Metcalfe J.S., 1998. *Evolutionary Economics and Creative Destruction*, London: Psychology Press

Metcalfe, J.S., 2002. Knowledge of growth and the growth of knowledge. *Journal of Evolutionary Economics* 12, 3–15.

Metcalfe, J.S., 2007. Alfred Marshall's Mecca: reconciling the theories of value and development, *The Economic Record* 83, s1–s22.

Metcalfe, J.S., 2010a. Complexity and emergence in economics: the road map from Smith to Hayek (via Marshall and Schumpeter). *History of Economic Ideas* XVIII(2), 45–75.

Metcalfe, J. Stanley, 2010b. Dancing in the dark: la disputa sobre el concepto de competencia. *Desarrollo Económico, Revista de Ciencias Sociales* 50(197), 59–79.

Metcalfe, J.S. and Foster, J., 2007. *Evolution and Economic Complexity*, Cheltenham: Edward Elgar Publishing.

Metcalfe, J.S., Foster, J., and Ramlogan, R., 2006. Adaptive economic growth. *Cambridge Journal of Economics* 30(1), 7–32.

Myrdal, G., 1957. The principle of circular and cumulative causation; The drift towards regional economic inequalities in a country, in *Economic Theory and Underdeveloped Regions*, New York: Harper, pp. 11–38.

Nekola, J.C. and Brown, J.H., 2007. The wealth of species: ecological communities, complex systems and the legacy of Frank Preston. *Ecology Letters* 10, 188–196.

Nelson, R.R., 1981. Research on productivity growth and productivity differences: dead ends and new departures. *Journal of Economic Literature* 19(3), 1029–1064.

Nelson, R.R., 1991. Why do firms differ, and how does it matter? *Strategic Management Journal* 12, 61–74.

Nelson, R.R., 1993. *National Innovation Systems: A Comparative Analysis*, Oxford: Oxford University Press.

Nelson, R.R. and Winter, S.G., 1977. In search of useful theory of innovation. *Research Policy* 6(1), 36–76.

Nelson, R.R. and Winter, S.G., 1982. *An Evolutionary Theory of Economic Change*, Cambridge, MA: Harvard University Press.

Nelson, R.R. and Winter, S.G., 2002. Evolutionary theorizing in economics. *The Journal of Economic Perspectives* 16, 23–46.

Niosi, J., 2002. National systems of innovations are 'x-efficient' (and x-effective): why some are slow learners. *Research Policy* 31, 291–302.

Pavitt, K., 1984. Sectoral patterns of technical change: towards a taxonomy and a theory. *Research Policy* 13, 343–373.

Pavitt, K., 2002. Innovating routines in the business firm: what corporate tasks should they be accomplishing? *ICC* 11, 117–133.

Peréz, C., 2009. Technological revolutions and techno-economic paradigms. *Cambridge Journal of Economics* 34(1), 185–202.

Pisano, G. and Shih, W., 2009. Restoring American competitiveness. *Harvard Business Review*, July–August.

Porcile, G., Holland, M., Cimoli, M., and Rosas, L., 2006. Especialización, tecnología y crecimiento en el modelo Ricardiano. *Nova Economia* 16(3), 483–506.

Potts, J., 2000. *The New Evolutionary Microeconomics: Complexity, Competence and Adaptive Behaviour*, Cheltenham: Edward Elgar Publishing.

Prebisch, R., 1959. The role of commercial policies in underdeveloped countries. *American Economic Review* 49, 215–273.

Prigogine, I. and Stengers, I., 2002. *La nueva alianza: metamorfosis de la ciencia*, Spain: Alianza.

Reinert, E., 2007. *How Rich Countries Got Rich … and Why Poor Countries Stay Poor*, New York: Public Affairs Press.

Robert, V. and Yoguel, G., 2011. The complex dynamics of economic development, in C. Antonelli (ed.) *Handbook on the Economic Complexity of Technological Change*, Cheltenham: Edward Elgar Publishing, pp. 417–447.

Rosenberg, N., 1963. Technological change in the machine tool industry, 1840–1910. *The Journal of Economic History* 23, 414–443.

Rosenstein-Rodan, P.N., 1943. Problems of industrialisation of eastern and south-eastern Europe. *The Economic Journal* 210/211, 202–211.

Rosser, J.B., 2007. Computational and dynamic complexity in economics. Available at: http://cob.jmu.edu/rosserjb/.

Saviotti, P.P., 2001. Variety, growth and demand. *Journal of Evolutionary Economics* 11, 119–142.

Saviotti, P.P. and Pyka, A., 2004. Economic development by the creation of new sectors. *Journal of Evolutionary Economics* 14, 1–35.

Schumpeter, J., 1912. *The Theory of Economic Development*, Cambridge, MA: Harvard University Press.

Schumpeter, J.A., 1947. The creative response in economic history. *The Journal of Economic History* 2, 149–159.

Schumpeter, J.A., 1978. *Teoría del desenvolvimiento económico. Una investigación sobre ganancias, capital, interés y ciclo económico*, México: Fondo de Cultura Económica.

Schumpeter, J.A., 1994. *Capitalism, Socialism and Democracy*, London: Routledge.

Setterfield, M., 1997. 'History versus equilibrium' and the theory of economic growth. *Cambridge Journal of Economics* 21, 365–378.

Silva, S.T. and Teixeira, A.A.C., 2008. On the divergence of evolutionary research paths in the past 50 years: a comprehensive bibliometric account. *Journal of Evolutionary Economics* 19, 605–642.

Silverberg, G., Dosi. G., and Orsenigo, L., 1988. Innovation, diversity and diffusion: a self-organisation model. *The Economic Journal* 98, 1032–1054.

Simon, H.A., 1969. *The Science of the Artificial*, Cambridge, MA: MIT Press.

Simon, H., 1972. Theories of bounded rationality, in C.B. McGuire and R. Radner (eds) *Decision and Organization*, Amsterdam: North-Holland Publishing Company, pp. 361–376.

Teece, D. and Pisano, G., 1994. The dynamic capabilities of firms: an introduction. *ICC* 3, 537–556.

Thirlwall, A., 1979. The balance of payments constraint as an explanation of international growth rate differences. *BNL Quarterly Review* 128, 45–53.

Vromen, J., 2004. Conjectural revisionary economic ontology: outline of an ambitious research agenda for evolutionary economics. *Journal of Economic Methodology* 2, 213–247.

Watts, D.J., 2006. *Seis grados de separación: la ciencia de las redes en la era del acceso*, Barcelona: Editorial Paidós.

Witt, U., 1997. Self-organization and economics – what is new? *Structural Change and Economic Dynamics* 8, 489–507.

Witt, U., 2004. On the proper interpretation of 'evolution' in economics and its implications for production theory. *Journal of Economic Methodology* 2, 125–146.

Witt, U., 2008. What is specific about evolutionary economics? *Journal of Evolutionary Economics* 5, 547–575.

Young, A.A., 1928. Increasing returns and economic progress. *The Economic Journal* 152, 527–542.

10 The multi-dimensional additionality of innovation policies

A multi-level application to Italy and Spain[1]

Alberto Marzucchi and Sandro Montresor

1 Introduction

Two contrasting forces currently characterize innovation policy in EU countries. On the one hand, public support of innovation is needed to reach the targets of the Europe 2020 strategy (European Commission, 2010). On the other hand, the recent economic crisis spurs governments to control their public debts and increase the effectiveness and efficiency of their economic policy actions, including support for innovation. In this scenario, the evaluation of innovation policies is of great importance: by taking stock of the outcomes of previous supporting schemes, policy makers can better calibrate current actions and plan future ones.

This paper contributes to the empirical analysis of the impact of innovation policy. Its main aim is to investigate the so-called 'additionality' of public support of firms' innovation with three elements of originality not present in the extant literature.[2] First, we adopt a *multi-dimensional* approach and analyse the effects that the policy can have regarding three dimensions of the innovative process: that is, innovative efforts (input), results (output) and behaviours. Second, we follow a *multi-level* perspective and consider the interplay between the effects of innovation policies devised at two levels: national and regional ones. Third, we use a *comparative* methodology and provide more systematic evidence than that emerging from individual case studies.

The empirical application of the paper refers to two European countries, Italy and Spain, which are increasingly often compared in terms of economic-innovation performance and policy-governance. Indeed, the two countries show interesting similarities in terms of industrial structure and innovation processes as well as in the policy interplay between national and regional level. Any evidence of differences in the additionality of innovation policies between these two countries would thus make the exercise that we propose even more compelling for two dissimilar countries.

A set of propensity score matching (PSM) techniques is applied to microdata on manufacturing firms from the fourth wave (2002–2004) of the Community Innovation Survey, exploiting the possibility offered by PSM to control for the presence of a selection bias on the observables.

The rest of the paper is organized as follows. Section 2 reviews the additionality concept and illustrates the three dimensions along which innovation policy will be evaluated. Section 3 discusses the multi-level features of innovation policies and the implications that the existence of a national and regional level of policy has for its additionality evaluation. Section 4 illustrates the empirical application and Section 5 discusses its results. Section 6 concludes.

2 The multi-dimensional additionality of innovation policy

In the standard neoclassical approach, public policy is called to remedy underinvestment by firms in innovation, namely in R&D, generated by market failures.[3] According to the linear model of innovation, which also characterizes the neoclassical approach (Edquist, 1999), underinvestment in R&D would result in an underproduction of innovation. Hence, public interventions should be eventually directed also to increasing the innovation performance of firms.

Following this perspective, innovation policy can be evaluated by simply assessing its 'additionality' in terms of innovative inputs and outputs. Input additionality concerns the amount of resources (for example, R&D investments) that firms would not have allocated to the innovation process in the absence of policy (Georghiou, 2004; Clarysse *et al.*, 2004; Cerulli, 2010). Output additionality concerns the innovative outcomes that firms would not have achieved without public support (Georghiou and Clarysse, 2006), that is, the additional amount of private, innovative outputs brought about by the policy. These outputs can be both the direct result of the innovative projects supported by public intervention (for example, new products, processes and patents) and their economic outcomes (that is, improved business performances, resulting from the introduction of new products or processes) (Georghiou, 2002).

Although quite straightforward, the sole evaluation of the input and output additionality of a policy is affected by an important conceptual limitation: firms which benefit from the policy are treated as 'black boxes'. The process through which they transform innovative inputs into outputs is considered automatic and not explored. However, as the evolutionary theory (e.g. Nelson and Winter, 1982) and the related innovation system perspective to innovation (e.g. Edquist, 1999) have shown for a long time, this is not the case. Firms innovate by adopting a set of learning behaviours that affect, first of all, their internal organization (e.g. their training of human capital). Furthermore, they innovate by interacting with other organizations (public and private). These behaviours can be exposed to additional failures, which have been called system failures (Metcalfe, 1995; Smith, 2000). For example, firms may not be able to develop the internal competencies needed to adapt to new technological developments. They could lack proper hard (e.g. regulations and legal systems) and soft (e.g. social values and culture) institutions for effective innovation cooperation (for a review of these failures, see Woolthuis *et al.*, 2005).

System failures are also in need of policy intervention, although of a possibly different kind (Edquist, 2011). Accordingly, an evaluation of innovation policies should be integrated with an assessment of its additionality in terms of innovative behaviours. Behavioural additionality is defined by Buisseret *et al.* (1995) as 'the change in a company's way of undertaking R&D which can be attributed to policy actions' (p. 590). In other words, an evaluation of behavioural additionality considers whether the policy intervention induces significant changes both in the internal organization of the beneficiaries' innovation process and in their relationships with external sources of knowledge. More precisely, these changes concern the following aspects of the policy-beneficiary firm: improvement of its technological capabilities, enhancement of its networking and interactions with other organizations and acquisition of new and diverse knowledge which can mitigate its lock-in in inefficient technologies[4] (e.g. Georghiou and Clarysse, 2006; Hall and Maffioli, 2008; Breschi *et al.*, 2009; Antonioli and Marzucchi, 2012; Marzucchi *et al.*, 2013; Antonioli *et al.*, 2014).

It should be stressed that, with regard to each of the three dimensions, the actual detection of the additionality of the policy is just a possible outcome of its assessment. As we will see, the nil hypothesis of the relative test is that the policy does not bring about any significant additional effect (with respect to similar, non-treated firms). However, the policy impact could even be significantly negative when public support reduces one (or more) of the investigated firm's innovation dimensions. Also in the innovation realm, by remedying private failures, policy makers could generate public failures, which can *crowd-out* the firms' inputs, outputs and behaviours (Edquist *et al.*, 2004: 430–431; Hommen and Equist, 2008; Tamm, 2010).

With regard to each of these three dimensions, an additionality assessment can be used to measure the depth of policy impact. An additional evaluation can be made by scrutinising whether the policy has a widespread effect on the supported firms or a focused one.[5] A first explorative insight can be obtained, for example, by looking at the combination of additionality effects the policy has along the three dimensions. In this respect, the additionality of the policy can have different degrees of multi-dimensionality. For the three additionality dimensions that we are considering (input, output and behaviour), we could have one of the following five scenarios:

1   *Full multi-dimensionality.* The policy is able to add simultaneously innovative inputs, outputs and behaviours to those of the supported firms. The action of the policy makers has widespread effects on the innovation process and can be considered, *ex-post*, an actual 'system' kind of policy.
2   *Bi-dimensionality.* Some additionality is detected for only two of the three dimensions, with no significant effect on the third one. The policy makers have a partial impact on the innovative process, while one dimension of it remains out of their control.
3   *Mono-dimensionality.* The additionality of the policy is focused and limited to only one of the three dimensions, while the remaining two are unaffected.
4   *Partial cross-dimensional crowding-out.* This is a qualification that the policy gets when a negative additionality outcome emerges along one or two

dimensions. However, the policy is still able to show positive additionality with regard to two, or at least one of them. In this kind of scenario, the policy turns out to suffer from some trade-offs between the dimensions of its effects. Because of these trade-offs, although it could be effective to a certain extent, the policy will inevitably have only a second-best kind of outcome, in terms of the breadth of its effects.

5   *Full cross-dimensional crowding-out.* The policy does not have any positive and significant impact, but one or even more negative additionality effects. The case is one of public failure in innovation. The public sector not only lacks the capacity to solve the problems firms face in innovating, it even exacerbates them, by making firms unable to stick to the counterfactual levels of their innovative efforts, outcomes, or behaviours.

3 The multi-level system of policy

As in other fields, also in innovation, policy actions are undertaken at different levels of government: local, regional, national and super-national (for example, the EU level). Their coordination is thus of crucial importance in making public support of innovation effective. Duplications of efforts need to be avoided as well as action gaps in the search for the most appropriate level of intervention.

At the EU level, policy coordination is managed through the 'subsidiarity principle'. The Union intervenes only when a certain action cannot be achieved by the Member States, either at the national, or at the regional and local level. Economies of scale and externalities are the main elements that support this choice (European Commission, 2009).

Looking at innovation, further elements need to be considered, especially in the relationship between the national and the regional level. The question is not simply which is the best level of government to support innovation, as it was in the early studies on regional innovation systems (RIS). The regional policy maker was considered to be in a better position, compared with the national one, to implement context-specific innovation strategies. In particular, regional policy was recognized as being able to promote network-type of instruments to exploit those agglomeration advantages that are available in territorial clusters (Uyarra, 2010).

However, this viewpoint fails to consider that, in innovation, different levels of public support interact with each other. As noted by Laranja *et al.* (2008), evolutionary processes of selection, generation of novelty and path-dependency occur at multiple geographical scales. Hence, there is not a unique optimal level in which innovation policy should be designed and delivered. Furthermore, innovation is a phenomenon that is shaped by institutional aspects pertaining to different scales (Howells, 1999; Boschma, 2005). In synthesis, public interventions should be seen as part of a multi-level system of policy or governance (Cooke, 2002; Kaiser, 2003) in which different support schemes are initiated at different levels.

This aspect of innovation policy is a crucial one and must also be considered when evaluating its impact. This is particularly so if we follow a multi-dimensional perspective to additionality. It is important to determine whether regional and national interventions overlap in the effects they produce along the different additionality dimensions we have considered. In other words, the evaluation process should look at whether the two levels of policy are capable of inducing firms to 'move towards the same direction' in terms of additionality effects.

For each of the three dimensions we are considering – input, output and behavioural – we can first of all analyse the additionality effects (either positive or negative) generated by both regional and national schemes. The input, output and behavioural additionality of the policy could thus have the following five characterizations:

1   *Full cross-level additionality.* The policy operates in an actual multi-level manner with regard to the relevant additionality dimension. Both regional and national policy makers are able to simultaneously affect it.

2   *Partial cross-level additionality.* The relevant dimension shows additionality only at one of the two levels of government (national or regional) since the other level is incapable of adding anything. This scenario would signal the existence of an 'exclusive' policy-zone which matches the characteristics of the actions undertaken by only one kind (national or regional) of policy makers.

3   *Partial cross-level crowding-out.* Along a certain dimension, one policy level only has an impact, but this is negative, pointing to an innovation sphere in which one level of intervention can only do harm in the absence of the other.

4   *Cross-level mismatch.* The two levels of policy making generate contrasting effects: positive on one level and negative on the other. The relative dimension thus represents a policy-zone where the two levels appear misaligned and actually clash with each other.

5   *Full cross-level crowding-out.* Both levels of government generate a negative impact, making the firms reduce their involvement along the relevant dimension. The public failure in dealing with the correspondent innovation realm thus appears general.[6]

By pooling together the evaluations obtained for each and every dimension, their average can give us a multi-level assessment at the country level. Its multi-level system of policy can therefore also be characterized with regard to the five specifications mentioned above.

A final piece of analysis can be carried out by simultaneously considering the multi-level and the multi-dimensional specification of policy additionality. This can be done by retaining the whole set of effects that regional and national policies have along the three dimensions and keeping the five cross-dimensional configurations illustrated in Section 2 as a reference. This can give us an insight into what can be considered the total cross-level additionality of innovation policy in a certain country.

4 Empirical application

The empirical application of the paper refers to Italian and Spanish innovation policies. Specifically, we focus on the effects of public funding of firms' innovation in the two countries.

The reason for choosing these two countries is twofold. First of all, Italy and Spain are usually considered as relatively similar in the European scenario, when their industrial structure and innovation performance is considered. In addition to what official statistics at the aggregate level reveal,[7] some descriptive statistics from the Fourth Community Innovation Survey (2002–2004), on which we build our empirical application, actually confirm some techno-economic similarity between Italy and Spain (Table A.10.1). Looking at the manufacturing sample of the CIS4, the two countries show a similar distribution of firms in terms of size. A similar dominance of small firms with respect to medium and large ones is associated with a larger share of medium-size companies in Spain when compared with Italy, where the share of small and large companies is slightly higher. The distribution of manufacturing firms among sectors is also similar, with appreciable shares in the notable specialization sectors of the two countries, in particular, low-tech ones. Still, some differences also emerge, with a higher frequency of Italian (Spanish) firms in textiles and fabricated metal products (food, beverages and tobacco, and leather). In the same snapshot, Italian and Spanish firms are not very diverse in innovative terms either (Table A.10.1). The share of CIS4 firms that reported investments in R&D and product innovations is higher in Spain than in Italy, being in the case of Spain slightly more than one third of the total sample.

The previous elements of similarity would make any evidence of heterogeneity in the additionality of innovation policies of the two countries particularly interesting to explain. The second reason that makes the comparison interesting is that both countries are characterized by regional policies that are implemented following different targets and means from the national ones. Italian policies initiated at the sub-national level are generally characterized by a lower public contribution that those at the central level. The former are largely targeted at SMEs and aim to support less formalized innovation activities than the latter (Cefis and Evangelista, 2007; Barbieri *et al.*, 2010). Although with differences, the same occurs in Spain (Garcia-Quevedo and Afcha-Chávez, 2009; Afcha-Chávez, 2011).

The empirical investigation of the additionality generated by innovation policies in these two contexts is not new. Several studies have already addressed it.[8] However, all these studies do not lead to unambiguous results. Furthermore, proper comparisons – even among the studies that are focused on the same country/programme – are not allowed, due to the differences in considered effects and time spans, as well as in employed data and methodologies.

Some general insights can only be made about the input additionality of the overall system of policy of the two countries. The evidence (Parisi and Sembenelli, 2003; Cefis and Evangelista, 2007; González and Pazó, 2008;

Garcia-Quevedo and Afcha-Chávez, 2009; Hall *et al.*, 2009; Cerulli and Potì, 2012b) points to a general presence of positive effects of the policy on the firms' investments in R&D, even if with some differences. In Italy, this result shows several specificities, depending on the kind of policy instrument (for example, direct grants vs. tax incentives) and funding schemes (for example, those named FAR/FSRA vs. FIT) (Barbieri *et al.*, 2010; De Blasio *et al.*, 2011; Carboni, 2011; Cerulli and Potì, 2012c). In Spain, the evidence of input additionality finds an exception in the case of regional policies which are found to be ineffective in stimulating private investment in R&D (Garcia-Quevedo and Afcha-Chávez, 2009).

As for the other additionality dimensions, a comparison between Italian and Spanish public interventions is hardly possible. Some evidence on output additionality, although mixed, is available for the Italian policies only (Cefis and Evangelista, 2007; Merito *et al.*, 2010; Colombo *et al.*, 2011; Cerulli and Potì, 2012b, 2012c). As for behavioural additionality, the only available investigations are mainly focused on the capacity of Spanish policy programmes to stimulate funded firms' interactions with other companies and research organizations (Busom and Fernández-Ribas, 2008; Fernández-Ribas and Shapira, 2009; Magro *et al.*, 2010; Afcha-Chávez, 2011).

All in all, the picture emerging from a review of the extant literature is blurry. For this reason, while representing a test of our methodology, the empirical application will also fill a knowledge gap about the effectiveness of innovation policies in these two countries.

4.1 Econometric strategy

The econometric estimation of the additionality of innovation policies is based on what is called the 'average treatment effect on the treated' (ATT). Let us consider the policy as a treatment, whose status is denoted by D ($D=1$: treated; $D=0$: untreated). If we denote its outcome, in the presence and absence of the treatment (policy), with Y_1 and Y_0, respectively, the ATT can be defined as:

$$ATT = E(Y_1 - Y_0 | D = 1) = E(Y_1 | D = 1) - E(Y_0 | D = 1) \tag{1}$$

In Eq. (1), $E(Y_1 | D=1)$ can be estimated with the average outcome of the treated firms. $E(Y_0 | D=1)$, instead, cannot be observed. For the treated firms, it is not possible to detect the outcome that would have been reached in the absence of public funding. Accordingly, a suitable counterfactual of non-funded firms has to be chosen. Given the non-randomized nature of the policy support, it is important to take into account that treated and non-treated firms can be systematically different, because of either self-selection mechanisms or deliberate strategies followed by the policy makers (e.g. 'picking the winner' or 'aiding the poor') (e.g. Cerulli, 2010). Estimating the counterfactual with the simple average outcome of the non-participants to the policy would thus imply a selection bias.

In order to control for this selection bias (on observables), we use the 'propensity score matching' (PSM) estimation of the ATT (Rosenbaum and Rubin, 1983). This is essentially aimed at pairing treated firms with 'twin' non-treated ones, so that the difference in the outcome is only due to the treatment. More specifically, PSM reduces the dimension of conditioning, matching funded firms with non-funded ones on the basis of their propensity score ($\Pr(D=1|X)$ or $P(X)$). This represents the probability of being treated, given a set of covariates, X. In so doing, the PSM estimation of the ATT is given by:[9]

$$ATT_{PSM} = E_{P(X)|D=1}\left\{E\left[Y_1 \mid D=1, P(X)\right] - E\left[Y_0 \mid D=0, P(X)\right]\right\} \qquad (2)$$

In operational terms, the PSM estimation of the ATT is obtained by applying the multi-step protocol proposed by Caliendo and Kopeinig (2008). At first, the propensity score is estimated with a probit model, which includes as covariates all the variables that are expected to affect the outcome and the treatment status. As a second step, a set of different matching algorithms is chosen. These basically differ in the way non-treated firms used as matches are selected and weighted. The use of additional matching procedures provides us with information on the stability and reliability of the emerging evidence. In particular, three types of algorithm developed in the literature (e.g. Becker and Ichino, 2002; Cameron and Trivedi, 2005; Smith and Todd, 2005; Caliendo and Kopeinig, 2008) are implemented: five nearest neighbours (5NN), calliper and kernel.[10]

The third step in the estimation protocol consists of imposing the common support condition to the matching algorithms. In what follows, a 'minima-maxima comparison' is applied. In addition to this, a 5 per cent 'trim' is also imposed to the 5NN algorithm (Leuven and Sianesi, 2003; Caliendo and Kopeinig, 2008).

Finally, the quality of the matching is assessed by checking that treated firms and matched controls are correctly aligned with respect to the vector of covariates, X. Four tests are employed: a regression-based t-test on differences in the covariates means, a log-likelihood ratio test, a pseudo R^2 test and a standardized bias test (Caliendo and Kopeinig, 2008).

4.2 Dataset, variables and indicators

4.2.1 Dataset

The empirical application of the paper employs data coming from the fourth wave of the Community Innovation Survey (CIS4) (2002–2004). Like all the CIS waves, this is based on a harmonized questionnaire which is the same for all the European countries, thus allowing for comparable analyses.

The two datasets originally consisted of 18,946 observations for Spain and 21,854 for Italy. Nevertheless, in order to provide a proper additionality evaluation of the regional and national policy interventions, their size has been reduced. First, the analysis is limited to manufacturing firms. Second, in order to have the complete range of variables for all the observations, firms with unexpected missing values and firms that did not have to complete the entire questionnaire[11] are dropped. Finally, in order to provide a proper additionality evaluation of the regional (national) policies, the working datasets are limited to have: among the treated units, only firms that obtained regional (national) funding; among the control units, only firms that did not receive any type of public support.

4.2.2 Variables

The first set of variables that we need for our econometric approach should account for the firm's treatment in terms of policy. To this purpose, we considered whether the firm received some funding from the regional/local (*FUNLOC*), national (*FUNGMT*) or European (*FUNEU*) levels of government. Furthermore, we looked at whether the European support was granted within the fifth or sixth European Framework Programme for Research and Technical Development (*FUNRTD*). These dummy variables allow us to identify, on the one hand, the firms that were supported by regional or national funding schemes and, on the other, the ones that were not funded at all.

The second set of variables refers to the covariates, X, to be included in the probit estimation of the propensity score specification (see Table A.10.1 in the Appendix). These are identified by drawing on, and extending, recent studies that use a similar methodology (e.g. Czarnitzki and Licht, 2006; Aerts and Schmidt, 2008; Busom and Fernández-Ribas, 2008). First, the size of the firms and their economic sector are controlled through the logarithm of their turnover (*ln_TURN02*) and a set of size (*SMALL, MEDIUM* and *LARGE*) and sector-dummies (*SEC_DA-SEC_DN*).[12] The firm's belonging to a business group (*GP*), its affiliation to a multinational corporation (*MNCGROUP*) and its engagement in foreign markets (*EXPORT*) are also considered.[13]

Three other aspects are considered to explain the firms' participation in the investigated policy schemes: their engagement in R&D, their financial constraints and their capacity to gather relevant information on the funding schemes. As for the first one, *RDENG* and *RDCONT* capture whether the firm engages in R&D and whether it does so in a continuous way, respectively. As for the second one, *HFENT1, HFENT2* and *HFENT3* are three dummies that capture whether the firm faces a 'nil or low', 'medium' or 'high' lack of internal funding, respectively. Similarly, *HFOUT1, HFOUT2* and *HFOUT3* capture whether the firm faces a 'nil or low', 'medium' or 'high' level of problems in accessing external funding, respectively. Finally, three dummies (*SMGT1, SGMT2* and *SGMT3*) indicate the relevance ('nil or low', 'medium', 'high') that firms attach to governmental sources of information for their innovative activities. Similarly, another three dummies indicate the relevance of innovative information coming from professional and industry associations (*SPRO1, SPRO2* and *SPRO3*).[14]

The last group of variables that we consider is the set of outcome variables[15] which capture input, output and behavioural additionality. As far as input additionality is concerned, two variables are considered, that is: (i) the expenditure in intramural R&D, in the year 2004 (*RDEXP*); (ii) the intensity of the intramural R&D investment (*RDINT*) on the turnover, in the year 2004. As for the output dimension, six outcome variables are considered: (i) a dummy for product innovation (*PRODINNO*); (ii) a dummy for process innovation (*PROC-INNO*); (iii) the percentage of turnover in the year 2004, due to product innovations introduced in 2002–2004 that were new to the market (*TURNMAR*); (iv) the percentage of turnover in the year 2004, due to product innovations introduced in 2002–2004 that were new to the firm (*TURNIN*); (v) the sum of *TURNIN* and *TURNMAR* (i.e. *TURNINNO*);[16] (vi) a dummy for the presence of patent applications (*PROPAT*). Concerning the behavioural dimension, two types of impact are considered with five further dummies. On the one side, the internal behavioural additionality of the policies is addressed by considering, with the dummy *TRAINENG*, the presence in the firm of training programmes to upgrade the competencies of its employees. On the other hand, the external behavioural additionality of the policy is captured by four dummy variables which refer to the cooperation agreements of the beneficiaries – *COOPFIRM* and *COOPORG*[17] – and to their interactions for information sourcing – *INFOFIRM* and *INFOORG*[18] – with other firms and research organizations, respectively.

4.2.3 Indicators for multi-additionality and multi-level analysis

As we have illustrated in Section 4.1, the additionality of the investigated policy schemes is revealed by the significance, sign and size of the ATT with regard to the three groups of outcome variables capturing the input (two variables), the output (six variables) and the behavioural (five variables) dimensions. Whereas an analysis of the ATTs can be used to look at the depth of the policy effects, simple indicators created upon the ATTs themselves can be used to investigate the multi-dimensional and multi-level aspects that we have illustrated in Sections 2 and 3.

As for the multi-dimensionality of innovation policies, the identification of the relevant scenario – out of the five described in Section 2 – is carried out as follows. We first define, for each type of intervention (regional and national, Italian and Spanish), an indicator of how widespread the effect of the policy across the different aspects (outcome variables) of a given additionality dimension (i.e. input, output or behavioural) is. For each additionality dimension, this is calculated by attaching value +1, to positive and significant effects, −1 to negative and significant effects, and 0 to non-significant effects of the policy at work. Summing up these values and dividing them by the number of aspects (outcome variables) of each dimension gives us a dimension-specific indicator, which ranges between +1 and −1. The rationale of this indicator is the following. Gaining additionality (of any size) on more aspects makes the policy more extensively additional along a certain dimension, possibly to the maximum extent (+1). Conversely, registering crowding-out on some aspects counterbalances the fact of having additionality on some others, or even fully dominates the dimension (–1).[19] Finally, we calculate a synthetic multi-additionality measure for each and every policy intervention. This is a combined analysis of the indicators obtained for each of the three additionality dimensions and should lead us to ascertain, for each and every policy, what we call its full multi-dimensionality, bi- or mono-dimensionality, rather than partial or full, cross-dimensional crowding-out.

As for the multi-level additionality of the policy, in order to ascertain which is the most relevant characterization – out of the five described in Section 3 – we proceed as follows. First of all, for each additionality dimension (i.e. input, output and behavioural), we count the number of cases in which the ATT of a certain outcome variable is significantly positive at both the regional and national level and, then, we divide it by the number of outcome variables. For each additionality dimension, this gives us an indicator – ranging between 0 and 1 – that can be used to grasp the extent (or degree) to which the regional and national innovation policies show full cross-level additionality. *Mutatis mutandis*, with a similar procedure – that is, calculating the average number of cases in which, for each dimension, we have additionality or crowding-out at only one of the two levels, contrasting effects at the two levels and crowding-out at both of them – we can have an indication of what we called, respectively: partial cross-level additionality; partial cross-level crowding-out; cross-level mismatch; full cross-level crowding-out. In synthesis, for each dimension, we are able to have a measurement of the five cross-level characterizations of Section 3 and see which is the most relevant.

We then calculate the average, across the three dimensions (input, output and behaviour), for each of these five indicators, in order to have a country-level specification for each of them. In so doing, we can have an indication, again on a scale of between 0 and 1, of the extent to which the country displays, overall, one of the same specifications (i.e. full cross-level additionality, partial cross-level additionality, partial cross-level crowding-out, cross-level mismatch and full cross-level crowding-out).

As far as the last part of our analysis is concerned, the total cross-level additionality that innovation policies show in a certain country can be investigated by amending the procedure to calculate the indicators we described above in order to analyse their multi-dimensionality. More precisely, we simply need to re-run the first step of the relative procedure by counting and averaging up algebraically all the effects that, along a certain dimension, have been brought about by *both* regional and national policies. By combining these additionality indicators by dimension and calculating their average, we can determine whether a certain policy-system shows – this time with a 'total' specification: full multi-dimensionality, bi- or mono-dimensionality, rather than partial or full cross-dimensional crowding-out (see Section 2).

5 Results

In what follows, we present the evidence emerging from our empirical investigation. First, we comment on the ATT results emerging from the PSM estimation and look at the intensity of the additionality of the investigated policies. Second, we examine the extension of the ATT results and consider the multi-dimensional and multi-level nature of policy additionality.

5.1 *The additionality of Italian policies*

Looking at Table 10.1, Italian regional and national policies appear to have quite a different impact on the investigated dimensions. Starting with the regional ones, the absence of input additionality is a first important result. Consistently with other empirical investigations (e.g. Cefis and Evangelista, 2007; Barbieri *et al.*, 2010), this is possibly explained by their greater attention for small-scale innovation projects where activities have a more exploitative than explorative nature.

In terms of output additionality, regional policies give us the impression of inducing Italian firms to adopt a sort of shift in their innovation outcomes. With regard to similar non-funded firms, funded ones are more likely (from +11.1 per cent to +13.3 per cent, depending on the adopted matching procedure) to achieve process innovation, but less likely to introduce a new or improved product (from –4.7 per cent to –6.3 per cent). This lower propensity is also reflected in the proportion of turnover due to incremental product innovations which is found to be negatively affected by public support (from –1.6 per cent to –2.5 per cent). This is an interesting result which suggests that regional policies in the country help firms deepening, rather than reversing, the innovative patterns that Italian firms show in their local systems of production (industrial districts, in particular), whose sectoral specialization (for example, in textiles, ceramics, machinery, and the like) actually rely more on a process rather than a product kind of innovation (Boix and Galletto, 2009).

The evidence regarding the behavioural additionality of Italian regional policies is generally quite gloomy. The likelihood of being engaged in training programmes is lower for supported firms than for similar non-funded companies (from –4.3 per cent to –5.2 per cent). In their cooperation agreements, funded firms are generally not statistically different from non-funded ones. In addition, funded firms are less engaged in information sourcing than similar non-funded ones (from –4.3 per cent to –6.5 per cent). All in all, regional policies not only seem unable to tackle system failures in the RISs, but they even appear to pose firms further public failures which may diminish their pre-policy innovative behaviours. The only significant exception is represented by their positive effect on the firms' propensity to acquire relevant information from research organizations (from +9.5 per cent to +10.1 per cent). Given the role that this information sourcing has for innovation at the regional level (Varis and Littunen, 2010), although somewhat isolated, such a result should be welcomed as an extremely positive one.

Looking at the national interventions (Table 10.1), unlike the regional ones, Italian policies show a significant input additionality. In terms of R&D investments, the policy effect on the supported firms ranges from +427,914.1 euros to

+447,613.6 euros. This is reflected in the increased intensity of firms' R&D investment, from +0.6 per cent to +0.7 per cent. National policies in Italy are actually able to tackle the most typical market failures in innovation. However, the higher investment in formal innovation activities induced by the policy does not translate into an increased capacity to introduce product and patentable innovations. Funded firms, with respect to similar non-supported ones, only have a higher propensity to introduce new or improved processes (from +8.3 per cent to +9.6 per cent). No significant effect is instead found for all the other output additionality indicators. Once more, the production structure of the country can provide an explanation for this result. Furthermore, the same result suggests that public interventions devised at central level are not able to display their effect along the whole linear model in innovation and remain somewhat blocked at the input level.

When we consider the results in terms of behavioural additionality, positive results emerge, unlike the regional level, pointing to a size effect in stimulating an open innovation mode. Italian national policies are found to increase the propensity of funded firms to engage in R&D cooperation with both other firms (from +4.9 per cent to +5.2 per cent) and, to a larger extent, with research partners (from +10.3 per cent to 11.6 per cent). Furthermore, national funding schemes induce increased information sourcing from universities and private R&D institutes (from +10.8 per cent to +11.3 per cent).

5.2 The additionality of Spanish policies

Table 10.2 shows the additionality of the Spanish policies at the regional and national level.

As much as in Italy, regional policies lack significant effects on private investment in R&D in Spain too. Similar arguments – in terms of size and scope of the funding schemes – can be put forward, still consistently with the extant literature (e.g. Garcia-Quevedo and Afcha-Chávez, 2009; Afcha-Chávez, 2011).

In this case, however, unlike the Italian one, regional support schemes enhance the probability of introducing product innovations (from +3.8 per cent to +3.9 per cent), in particular radical and commercially valuable ones. With respect to similar non-funded firms, funded ones are characterized by a higher percentage of turnover due to radical product innovations (from +1.5 per cent to +1.8 per cent). Finally, this higher innovation performance is coupled with a higher propensity to file patent applications (from +6.0 per cent to +7.2 per cent). In brief, Spanish regional policies appear able to induce local firms to adopt a higher level of innovative outcomes than Italian ones. Furthermore, unlike in Italy, this radical-product additionality does not occur at the expense of other lower level innovative outcomes (e.g. process and incremental like).

The presence of this output additionality, in the absence of the input one, may appear difficult to explain. However, an interpretation can be given by looking at the behavioural additionality of Spanish regional policies. On the one hand, they enhance the learning process of the beneficiary firms, increasing their propensity

Table 10.1 Additionality of Italian policies

Regional policies	5NN		Caliper		Kernel		5NN Trim	
	ATT	S.E.	ATT	S.E.	ATT	S.E.	ATT	S.E.
Input add.								
RDEXP	42,295.320	67,483.270	43,382.720	67,180.760	23,791.990	47,706.630	45,794.740	71,086.020
RDINT	0.003	0.002	0.003	0.002	0.002	0.002	0.003	0.002
Output add.								
PRODINNO	−0.047*	0.028	−0.058**	0.029	−0.050**	0.023	−0.063**	0.031
PROCINNO	0.122***	0.031	0.118***	0.029	0.111***	0.023	0.133***	0.033
TURNMAR	0.002	0.013	−0.003	0.012	−0.002	0.010	0.002	0.013
TURNIN	−0.021**	0.010	−0.025**	0.010	−0.016*	0.009	−0.022*	0.012
TURNINNO	−0.019	0.017	−0.028*	0.016	−0.017	0.013	−0.019	0.015
PROPAT	−0.023	0.026	−0.019	0.025	−0.007	0.020	−0.021	0.025
Behavioural add.								
TRAINENG	−0.046*	0.025	−0.046*	0.027	−0.043*	0.022	−0.052*	0.027
COOPFIRM	−0.028	0.020	−0.028	0.018	−0.015	0.013	−0.040**	0.019
COOPORG	−0.019	0.016	−0.019	0.016	−0.012	0.013	−0.028*	0.017
INFOFIRM	−0.059***	0.022	−0.065***	0.024	−0.043**	0.020	−0.065***	0.023
INFOORG	0.097***	0.029	0.101***	0.028	0.097***	0.027	0.095***	0.031
N treat. on support	598		598		598		570	
N treated total	599		599		599		599	
N non-treated	1407		1407		1407		1407	

National policies	5NN		Caliper		Kernel		5NN Trim	
	ATT	S.E.	ATT	S.E.	ATT	S.E.	ATT	S.E.
Input add.								
RDEXP	429,066.1*	238,670.7	427,914.1*	228,623.0	447,613.6**	218,544.8	313,001	261,069.2
RDINT	0.007**	0.003	0.007**	0.003	0.006**	0.003	0.007**	0.003
Output add.								
PRODINNO	0.004	0.034	0.005	0.034	0.006	0.025	0.000	0.033
PROCINNO	0.086**	0.036	0.086**	0.035	0.096***	0.027	0.083**	0.037
TURNMAR	−0.002	0.013	−0.001	0.015	−0.005	0.010	−0.002	0.013
TURNIN	0.016	0.012	0.016	0.014	0.013	0.011	0.015	0.012
TURNINNO	0.014	0.018	0.014	0.017	0.007	0.014	0.013	0.018
PROPAT	0.047	0.030	0.048	0.031	0.061***	0.024	0.041	0.030
Behavioural add.								
TRAINENG	0.007	0.032	0.005	0.033	0.010	0.029	−0.002	0.032
COOPFIRM	0.051**	0.026	0.050*	0.026	0.052***	0.019	0.049**	0.023
COOPORG	0.104***	0.027	0.103***	0.025	0.116***	0.022	0.108***	0.024
INFOFIRM	−0.010	0.025	−0.009	0.027	−0.015	0.022	−0.014	0.026
INFOORG	0.113***	0.035	0.112***	0.036	0.108***	0.027	0.111***	0.038
N treat. on support	433		433		433		417	
N treated total	438		438		438		438	
N non-treated	1407		1407		1407		1407	

Source: own elaboration, based on data from the Fourth Community Innovation Survey.

Notes

***, **, * indicate a significance level of 1 per cent, 5 per cent, 10 per cent. Standard errors are calculated with a 200-replication bootstrap procedure.

to implement formal training programmes (from +4.8 per cent to +6.1 per cent). On the other hand, they also trigger the firms' attitude to cooperate with both other firms (from +7.3 per cent to +7.5 per cent) and research organizations (from +9.6 per cent to +10.3 per cent), and acquire relevant knowledge from research partners (from +10.5 per cent to 12.1 per cent). On this basis, we could argue that regional policies help firms to innovate more, by helping them to resort more to an open innovation mode, in which external knowledge is a crucial innovative input.[20]

Looking at the Spanish national policies (Table 10.2), as for the Italian ones, their input additionality is evident. Innovation supporting schemes devised at the central level are found to stimulate an additional investment in intramural R&D (from + 354,036.2 Euros to + 371,922.7 Euros). However, unlike the Italian case, a similar positive effect is not found for the intensity of the R&D investment. In other words, it seems like the national policies are not able to increase the relative incidence of R&D investments on the business scale of the treated firms.

In terms of output additionality, national policies also show important effects. With respect to similar non-funded companies, supported firms are characterized by a higher percentage of turnover due to radical product innovations (from +3.7 per cent to +4.0 per cent) and a higher propensity to file patent applications (from + 5.9 per cent to +7.3 per cent). Unlike Italy, national interventions impact on the most valuable kind of innovative outcomes. This difference emerges even if the two countries do not have radically dissimilar production structures.

Given the important impact that national policies show in terms of input, this result suggests their capacity to spread their effects along the whole innovation chain. This is supported by the significant number of behavioural changes induced by public support at the same level. National policies enhance the propensity to cooperate with both research organizations (from +10.5 per cent to +11.3 per cent) and other firms (from +8.1 per cent to +8.6 per cent). Treated firms show a higher propensity to acquire relevant information from both other firms (from +5.0 per cent to +7.0 per cent) and research organizations (from +10.0 per cent to +11.6 per cent). Last, but not least, funded firms are more likely to implement training programmes (from +5.1 per cent to +6.0 per cent), a result which was missing in the Italian national policies.

In synthesis, the two countries show a great deal of differences in the effects that their innovation policies have.[21] As we suggest, some of these differences have to do with the different way in which the ATTs combine across the different additionality dimensions, and across the levels of government. This is an aspect that the analysis of the following two sections will try to illustrate in a more explicit way.

5.3 The multi-dimensional additionality of innovation policies

As we have implicitly acknowledged in the previous two sections, in both the investigated countries, full multi-dimensionality is exclusive of the additionality of national policies (Figure 10.1).[22] In both Italy and Spain, the national policy schemes have a widespread impact on the innovation process of the targeted firms. In other words, they generally serve to cure, although to different extents, a large array of failures that firms face in their innovation system.

The average multi-dimensionality indicator for the national policies of the two countries yields very similar values: 0.59 in Italy and 0.61 in Spain. The overall pictures would seem to point to innovation programmes characterized by full multi-dimensionality (see Section 2). However, rather interestingly, Italian and Spanish national supporting schemes are characterized by different and somewhat symmetric multi-dimensionality profiles. Diagrammatically, this is reflected by the quasi-perfect mirroring of the two corresponding rhombs (Figure 10.1). The number of aspects (outcome variables) along which the policy significantly adds something is maximum for the input dimension in Italy, and for the behavioural one in Spain. Conversely, net additionality has approximately half of the value for the behavioural dimension in Italy, and for the input one in

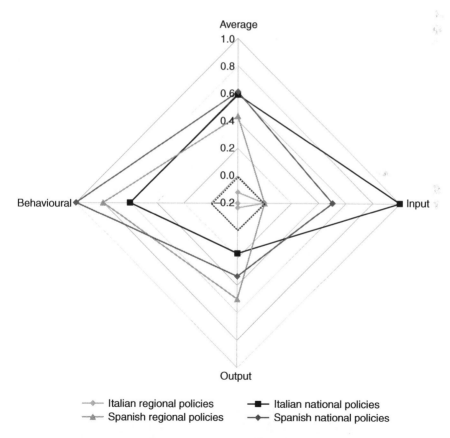

Figure 10.1 The multi-dimensional additionality of innovation policies (source: own elaboration, based on the Fourth Community Innovation Survey).

Table 10.2 Additionality of Spanish policies

Regional policies	5NN		Caliper		Kernel		5NN Trim	
	ATT	S.E.	ATT	S.E.	ATT	S.E.	ATT	S.E.
Input add.								
RDEXP	-5305.556	34,001.730	-5352.441	34,923.640	17,351.620	20,613.090	-7059.569	35,644.120
RDINT	0.154	0.151	0.154	0.147	0.156	0.139	0.161	0.147
Output add.								
PRODINNO	0.038*	0.022	0.039*	0.023	0.039*	0.021	0.038	0.025
PROCINNO	0.022	0.023	0.023	0.025	0.042**	0.019	0.023	0.026
TURNMAR	0.017*	0.009	0.017*	0.009	0.015***	0.007	0.018**	0.008
TURNIN	0.002	0.014	0.001	0.013	0.001	0.011	-0.001	0.013
TURNINNO	0.019	0.016	0.019	0.014	0.016	0.013	0.017	0.015
PROPAT	0.068***	0.020	0.068***	0.020	0.060***	0.016	0.072***	0.021
Behavioural add.								
TRAINENG	0.048**	0.023	0.048**	0.022	0.061***	0.018	0.048**	0.024
COOPFIRM	0.073***	0.021	0.075***	0.020	0.073***	0.015	0.073***	0.019
COOPORG	0.099***	0.018	0.099***	0.016	0.103***	0.013	0.096***	0.017
INFOFIRM	0.019	0.018	0.021	0.020	0.020	0.013	0.017	0.020
INFOORG	0.105***	0.021	0.105***	0.022	0.121***	0.019	0.115***	0.023
N treat. on support	876		874		876		836	
N treated total	879		879		879		879	
N non-treated	3231		3231		3231		3231	

National policies	5NN		Caliper		Kernel		5NN Trim	
	ATT	S.E.	ATT	S.E.	ATT	S.E.	ATT	S.E.
Input add.								
RDEXP	367,677.1**	162,523.3	371,922.7**	164,501.7	359,347.8***	132,797.8	354,036.2**	156,419.1
RDINT	0.071	0.049	0.072	0.046	0.075	0.054	0.074	0.050
Output add.								
PRODINNO	0.001	0.027	0.001	0.028	0.014	0.022	0.015	0.030
PROCINNO	0.022	0.030	0.026	0.028	0.037	0.023	0.012	0.029
TURNMAR	0.037***	0.011	0.038***	0.012	0.040***	0.010	0.040***	0.011
TURNIN	−0.013	0.015	−0.012	0.016	−0.018	0.013	−0.009	0.015
TURNINNO	0.024	0.019	0.026	0.018	0.022	0.015	0.032*	0.019
PROPAT	0.059**	0.025	0.062***	0.023	0.064***	0.020	0.073***	0.025
Behavioural add.								
TRAINENG	0.060**	0.030	0.061**	0.031	0.051**	0.026	0.060*	0.032
COOPFIRM	0.086***	0.026	0.086***	0.029	0.081***	0.020	0.081***	0.025
COOPORG	0.111***	0.021	0.113***	0.023	0.110***	0.019	0.105***	0.023
INFOFIRM	0.061***	0.024	0.061***	0.023	0.050***	0.018	0.070***	0.024
INFOORG	0.100***	0.026	0.100***	0.028	0.116***	0.021	0.101***	0.028
N treat. on support	564		564		564		536	
N treated total	564		564		564		564	
N non-treated	3231		3231		3231		3231	

Source: own elaboration, based on data from the Fourth Community Innovation Survey.

Notes

***, **, * indicate a significance level of 1 per cent, 5 per cent, 10 per cent. Standard errors are calculated with a 200-replication bootstrap procedure.

Spain. The higher net degree of Spanish additionality in the output dimensions concludes this multi-additionality comparison at the national level. In light of these results, it would be interesting to investigate whether Italian and Spanish firms attach a different (perhaps opposite) strategic value to their innovative inputs and behaviours when using a national policy support.

Regional innovation policies do not cover such a wide set of failures as the national ones in both countries, but with different characterizations. Italian regional policies show what we call full cross-dimensional crowding-out. This emerges as the combination of small negative net impacts, in terms of output and behavioural additionality, which the absence of any significant input additionality does not compensate for. In Figure 10.1, the relative contour is fully inscribed into the zero-values rhomb (dotted line). Although, as we have seen in Section 5.1, some positive insights have emerged from the inspection of specific outcome variables, this result represents a serious concern about the effectiveness of local innovation policies in Italy.

The 'twin' policy schemes in Spain seem to work much better across the considered dimensions. The Spanish result suggests, like the Italian one, the general difficulty of regional innovation policies in stimulating additional R&D investments: the relative contour shares the correspondent vertex of the zero-values rhomb. However, the Spanish regional policies appear to have remarkable bi-dimensionality in terms of behavioural and output additionality. To be sure, the Spanish net effect in terms of behavioural and output additionality shows how regional policies can get closer to, or even forge ahead (in terms of output) of, national ones. In the case of Spanish regional policies, the average multi-dimensionality indicator has a value (0.43) not that far away from that of the national ones (0.61). In this respect, it seems plausible that Spanish regional policies, by targeting (with success) the achievement of important behavioural changes, overcome the lack of input additionality and increase the capacity of funded firms to obtain more radical product innovations and patents (see also Table 10.2). Hence, at least with respect to this specific case, it seems that the lack of input additionality, per se, does not completely hamper the effect of public support on the outputs of the innovation process, especially when significant behavioural changes are stimulated by the policy.

5.4 The multi-level additionality of innovation policies

Figure 10.2 reports the cross-level (c.l.) characterization of policy additionality in Italy and Spain, following the taxonomy of Section 3. Overall, the two levels of policy do not concur in crowding out pre-policy engagement of the firms in any of the three dimensions. They also do not clash in the 'sign' of the effect they produce, pointing to a minimum degree of coherence of the policy systems of the two countries (full cross-level crowding-out and cross-level mismatches are never observed).

The input dimension is the only one along which, in both countries, the unique possible cross-level pattern is of partial additionality, with only one effective policy level: the national one. This is more so in Italy than in Spain. However, in both countries, regional and national polices seem to follow a labour division in this realm. This result can also be explained by the way in which the policy systems are implemented in the two countries. In both Italy and Spain, regional policies, when compared with national ones, are characterized by lower public support and higher attention to less formalized innovation activities

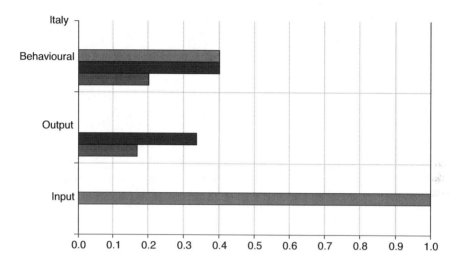

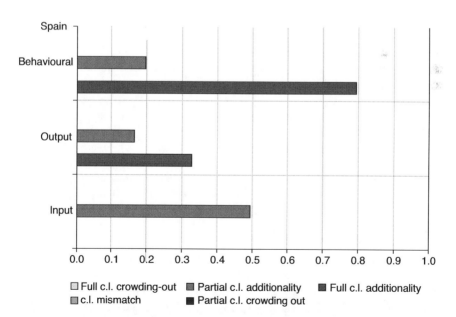

Figure 10.2 Multi-level additionality of innovation policies (source: own elaboration, based on the Fourth Community Innovation Survey).

(Cefis and Evangelista, 2007; Barbieri *et al.*, 2010; Garcia-Quevedo and Afcha-Chávez, 2009; Afcha-Chávez, 2011). Hence, our result could also suggest that input additionality is not an automatic effect of public support of firms' innovation activities. It rather emerges when policies are characterized by a sufficiently large scale and scope.

When considering the output dimension, a certain degree of full cross-level additionality can be detected in both countries. However, this is twice as high in Spain (0.33) as in Italy (0.17). Furthermore, in Italy this is more than counterbalanced by the evidence of partial cross-level crowding-out. In a higher number of cases (outcome variables) than that of full cross-level additionality, Italian regional policies have a negative impact on the innovative output of the treated firms, while the national level does not add anything. Although in a limited number of cases, this suggests that the output dimension is a critical one in Italy to foster when both national and regional policies are at work. In Spain, on the other hand, a remarkable extent of full cross-level additionality is accompanied by lower partial cross-level additionality. The number of cases in which the two levels simultaneously add to the firms' innovative output is higher than those in which it occurs individually. Overall, the two levels of government show a higher capability to act together and spur the firms' innovative outcomes in Spain than in Italy.

With regard to the behavioural dimension, Spain shows a picture which is similar to that of the output dimension, though with different degrees. Even with a slightly higher partial cross-level additionality, the extent to which regional and national policies both add to the firms' innovative behaviours (full cross-level additionality) in Spain is nearly maximum (0.8 out of 1). The two policy levels look very effective in combining their efforts to solve the system failures by which innovation can be affected. The picture is quite different in Italy where partial cross-level additionality and partial cross-level crowding-out are the most observed. In the majority of cases, Italian national and regional policies work somehow in isolation, subtracting or adding something, to the same extent, from the pre-policy innovative behaviours of the treated firms.[23]

The resulting average picture is illustrated in Figure 10.3. Overall, Spain has a much higher extent of full cross-level additionality. On the other hand, Italy dominates in the partial cross-level crowding-out and, above all, partial cross-level additionality of its two levels of government. On this basis, we can conclude that the multi-level system of policy has worked more extensively in Spain than in Italy.

To conclude, let us consider the total cross-level additionality of the innovation policies. It should be noted that this analysis is substantially different from the 'simple' cross-level one in Figures 10.2 and 10.3. In what follows, the effects of the two levels of government are pooled together along each dimension, irrespective of their matching, according to their simple existence and their actual sign. Figure 10.4 shows that, in terms of total cross-level effects, Spanish innovation policies exhibit full multi-dimensionality. With the same specification,

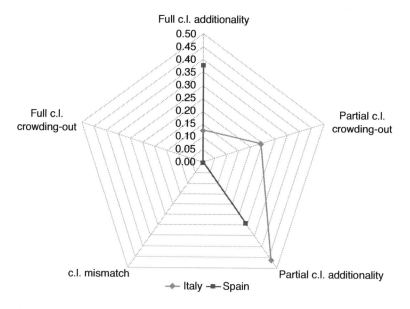

Figure 10.3 The multi-level additionality of innovation policies, cross-dimensional aver-
ages (source: own elaboration, based on the Fourth Community Innovation
Survey).

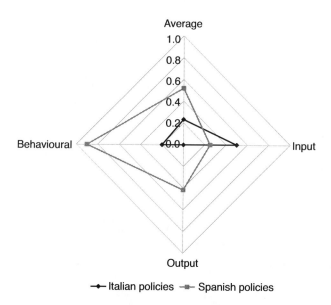

Figure 10.4 The multi-dimensional additionality of innovation policies, total cross-level
effects (source: own elaboration, based on the Fourth Community Innovation Survey).

instead, Italian ones appear only bi-dimensional in their additionality. In other words, in aggregated terms, the considered innovation policies have more extensive additionality effects in Spain than in Italy.

When we consider the single additionality dimensions, Italian policies appear unable to obtain a total significant effect on the firms' innovative outputs, confirming a critical aspect we identified in the cross-level analysis. The convergence of regional and national support schemes appears to make the treated firms face a picture of conflicting trade-offs which, in the end, do not substantially increase the firms' innovativeness in extensive terms.

All in all, Italian policies display a greater capacity than Spanish ones to tackle the most standard underinvestment in R&D due to the market failures in innovation. Conversely, the set of Spanish regional and national interventions that significantly impact on the aspects of the firms' behavioural (higher in Spain than in Italy) and output additionality suggests that Spanish policies have a greater capacity to tackle system-type failures.

6 Conclusions

Evaluating the impact of innovation policies is a complex task. On the one hand, failures can be of a different nature and pertain not only to the firm's innovative efforts and outcomes, but also to its innovative behaviours. On the other hand, the public interventions that aim to cure these failures are devised at different levels of government, raising the issue of their possible combined effects. For these reasons, evaluation needs to be multi-dimensional and cross-level.

In this paper, we have shown that, by looking at the additionality of innovation policies, this complex evaluation can be effectively undertaken. Furthermore, it can be carried out on a systematic basis, with the possibility of recovering the lack of comparability from which policy evaluations generally suffer. Using the propensity score matching (PSM) estimation of the average treatment effect on the treated (ATT), a multi-dimensional analysis can be carried out by looking at outcome variables pertaining to different realms. Their multi-level analysis is also possible by using as treatment variables policy schemes initiated at different levels of government: in particular, regional and national. Finally, some simple indicators can be built up in order to express the results of these analyses in a synthetic way.

The empirical application we have carried out for Italy and Spain has served as a test for this complex evaluation procedure. First, it has provided us with interesting results for the single dimensions along which additionality has been investigated and the single aspects which refer to each dimension. For example, consistently with previous evidence, regional policies do not show input additionality in the two countries: a result which appears to be explained by the nature of the innovative projects that regional policies target. However, unlike Italy, Spanish regional policies also have remarkable output additionality impacts. The behavioural additionality that, again unlike Italy, they show in this context can provide one explanation for this.[24] Spanish regional policies stimulate firms' innovation by enabling them to rely more on external knowledge. This is an interesting piece of evidence which contrasts the predictions of the standard linear innovation model.

Another illustrative result concerns the output additionality that national policies reveal in the two countries. In Italy, their impact is limited to process innovation, whereas in Spain it reaches product innovation, even of a radical nature. Given the relatively similar production structure of these two countries – and also their not very dissimilar innovation profile – this result is somewhat surprising. The different behavioural additionality that the two policies schemes present in the two countries could provide one explanation of this result.

The empirical application has also given us useful insights into classifying and comparing the policy schemes in the two countries, in terms of extension of their impact, across the considered dimensions and levels. For example, only national policies appear to show full multi-dimensionality in the two countries and are able to tackle the whole array of failures to which firms are exposed. Regional policies generally appear to have a narrow impact, but have a different nature in Spain and in Italy. In the former case, their additionality is bi-dimensional (behavioural and output). In the latter, instead, it is even negative across the different dimensions, showing a full crowding-out impact, which hints at the presence of public failures in the relevant level of government.

Interesting results also emerge by looking at cross-level additionality. For example, a sort of labour division seems to emerge, in both countries, between the two levels of governments in the input-additionality realm, which appears to be a sort of exclusive national sphere of intervention. Equally interesting is the evidence regarding the absence of full cross-level crowding-out and mismatch across the two levels in the two countries, pointing to a minimum degree of coherence of the respective policy-systems, which is however accompanied by important cases of partial crowding-out in Italy.

By pooling together all the additionality effects that the policies have, only the Spanish multi-level system of policy exhibits full multi-dimensionality. With the same specification, on the other hand, the Italian one appears only bi-dimensional.

This work also opens up further lines of research. These particularly concern the investigation of the likely interactions that may emerge between the three additionality dimensions. Further analysis should be devoted to investigating this 'system of relationships' (e.g. Antonioli and Marzucchi, 2012). This may clarify whether input additionality affects the output and behavioural impacts of the policy and whether policy-induced changes in the innovation behaviours affect the additional R&D investment and innovation outputs.

Appendix

Table A.10.1 Italy and Spain in the CIS4: descriptive statistics

	Italy %	Spain %
Firms by size		
Small	65.45	62.16
Medium	25.24	28.84
Large	9.31	9.00
Firms by sector		
Food products, beverages and tobacco	9.03	12.46
Textiles and textile products	12.42	6.92
Leather and leather products	2.81	2.43
Wood and wood products; pulp, paper and paper products	7.51	6.07
Publishing, printing and reproduction of recorded media	4.52	4.36
Coke, refined petroleum products and nuclear fuel; chemicals, chemical products and man-made fibres	6.18	8.71
Rubber and plastic products	4.50	5.35
Other non-metallic mineral products	7.15	7.79
Basic metals	4.19	3.24
Fabricated metal products, except machinery and equipment	14.27	10.26
Machinery and equipment n.e.c.	8.33	9.96
Electrical and optical equipment	9.15	8.99
Transport equipment	5.27	5.88
Manufacturing n.e.c.	4.68	7.58
Firms by innovative effort and performance		
R&D	27.60	38.21
PRODINNO	21.01	33.32
Total manufacturing firms in the sample	**7206**	**9916**

Source: own elaboration based on Fourth Community Innovation Survey.

Table A.10.2 Probit estimation of propensity scores

	FUNLOC – Italy		FUNGMT – Italy		FUNLOC – Spain		FUNGMT – Spain	
	Coeff.	S.E.	Coeff.	S.E.	Coeff.	S.E.	Coeff.	S.E.
SMALL	0.185	0.159	-0.234	0.164	0.535***	0.101	-0.325***	0.095
MEDIUM	0.330***	0.123	-0.119	0.116	0.381***	0.096	-0.271***	0.086
lnTURN02	-0.029	0.034	0.066*	0.038	0.009	0.006	-0.018***	0.006
GP	-0.250***	0.085	-0.002	0.088	-0.008	0.064	0.288***	0.067
MNC	-0.295**	0.125	-0.346***	0.116	-0.203**	0.093	-0.419***	0.093
EXPORT	-0.005	0.075	-0.004	0.088	0.011	0.055	0.053	0.070
RDENG	0.125	0.082	-0.035	0.096	0.215***	0.065	0.280***	0.086
RDCONT	0.295***	0.077	0.397***	0.089	0.069	0.063	0.357***	0.076
HFENT2	0.036	0.083	0.079	0.091	0.147**	0.063	-0.014	0.072
HFENT3	0.083	0.100	-0.148	0.117	0.057	0.073	-0.079	0.087
HFOUT2	0.104	0.085	0.196**	0.094	0.076	0.063	0.074	0.074
HFOUT3	-0.311***	0.099	-0.059	0.111	-0.035	0.071	-0.037	0.086
SPRO2	0.255***	0.085	0.106	0.093	0.116	0.060	-0.062	0.073
SPRO3	0.551***	0.134	0.117	0.159	-0.069	0.116	0.077	0.126
SGMT2	-0.056	0.192	0.667***	0.161	0.374***	0.093	0.496***	0.100
SGMT3	0.294	0.249	0.148	0.271	0.702***	0.197	0.576***	0.218
CONST.	-0.346	0.640	-1.603***	0.715	-1.494***	0.194	-1.174***	0.219
Sectoral dummies	Included		Included		Included		Included	
N	2006		1845		4110		3795	
Prob>χ^2	0.000		0.000		0.000		0.000	
Pseudo R^2	0.059		0.077		0.039		0.098	

Source: own elaboration, based on data from the Fourth Community Innovation Survey.

Notes
***, **, * indicate a significance level of 1 per cent, 5 per cent, 10 per cent. A VIF test leads to exclude the multicollinearity of the covariates (all the VIF values are lower than 10).

Notes

1 A previous version of this paper was presented at the SPRU Freeman Centre Friday Seminars at the University of Sussex, Brighton (UK), 19 October 2012. The authors are grateful to the participants for their useful comments. The usual caveats apply.

2 See Cerulli and Potì (2012a) for other recent developments in the literature.

3 The semi-public good nature of technological knowledge and the information asymmetries that emerge in the relative transactions are the most important of these failures (Arrow, 1962).

4 Given the lack of proper data, this third type of effect is not considered in the following analysis. For an investigation of the capacity of the policy to stimulate the acquisition of diverse competencies, see Marzucchi *et al.* (2013).

5 This kind of analysis could be considered introductory to the search for a specific kind of relationship (for example, complementarity and substitutability) between the different dimensions. This is an issue which recent research is concentrating on, with different approaches and results (e.g. Czarnitzki and Licht, 2006; Autio *et al.*, 2008; Clarysse *et al.*, 2009; Antonioli and Marzucchi, 2012).

6 A final case, which we could consider as a benchmark to identify the others, would be represented by a situation in which both levels of governments do not have any effect on the dimension at stake.

7 To use the most conventional proxy, the R&D intensities of Italy and Spain in 2010 differed by only 0.13 percentage points and were among the lowest in the distribution of the OECD countries (1.26 per cent and 1.39 per cent, respectively, compared with the OECD average of 2.40 per cent) (OECD Factbook 2013: Economic, Environmental and Social Statistics).

8 For an extensive review of these works, see Marzucchi (2012).

9 This relies on two important assumptions (i.e. the conditional independence assumption, *CIA*, and the stable unit-treatment value assumption, *SUTVA*) and on the common support condition. See, among others, Rubin (1986), Cameron and Trivedi (2005), Smith and Todd (2005) and Caliendo and Kopeinig (2008).

10 Caliper matching is implemented with a maximum tolerance of 0.02 and kernel matching by using an Epanechnikov kernel function.

11 These are the companies that in the period 2002–2004 did not introduce any product or process innovation and did not carry out any innovation activities.

12 Since *FUNLOC* and *FUNGMT* refer to the 2002–2004 period, to avoid endogeneity problems, whenever possible, the propensity scores specification includes variables referred to the first year of the period (2002). This can be done for *ln_TURN02*, *SMALL*, *MEDIUM* and *LARGE*.

13 Italian firms belonging to NACE rev. 1.1 19 (i.e. secDC in the CIS4 sectoral classification), 20 (belonging to sec20–21) and 23 (belonging to secDF-DG) are dropped from the working sample: for these sectors the anonymization process, carried out by the Italian National Statistical Institute, resulted in the aggregation of medium and large firms into a unique dimensional class. Firms belonging to NACE rev. 1.1 30 (belonging to secDL) and 37 (belonging to secDN) are dropped too: for these sectors the anonymization process resulted in the aggregation of small, medium and large firms into a unique dimensional class.

14 *LARGE, HFENT1, HFOUT1, SGMT1, SPRO1, SEC27* (i.e. NACE rev 1.1 sector 27) are used as reference terms in the probit estimation of the propensity score.

15 Unless stated differently, the variables defined below refer to the period 2002–2004.

16 *TURNMAR, TURNIN* and *TURNINNO* are rescaled from 0 to 1.

17 *COOPFIRM* captures cooperation agreements in existence with: national (*COOPGP-NAT*) and foreign firms belonging to the same group (*COOPGPFOR*); national (*COOPSUPNAT*) and foreign suppliers (*COOPSUPFOR*); national (*COOPCUSNAT*) and foreign customers (*COOPCUSFOR*); national (*COOPCOMNAT*) and foreign

competitors (*COOPCOMFOR*). Similarly, *COOPORG* accounts for the presence of cooperation agreements with: national (*COOPINSNAT*) and foreign private R&D institutes and commercial labs (*COOPINSFOR*); national (*COOPUNINAT*) and foreign universities (*COOPUNIFOR*); national (*COOPPUBNAT*) and foreign governmental agencies or public research institutes (*COOPPUBFOR*).

18 These latter two dummies are created from the four-point Likert scales, included in the CIS4 dataset, through which firms indicate the importance of different sources of information for their innovation activities. The dummies take value *1* if the relevance of the information is 'medium' or 'high', and *0* otherwise. *INFOFIRM* captures information coming from suppliers (*INFOSUP*), customers (*INFOCUS*) and competitors (*INFOCOM*). *INFOORG*, instead, includes information sourcing from universities (*INFOUNI*) and private research institutes (*INFOINS*).

19 Values of this indicator close to zero could be equally due to compensating aspects or to non-significant ones and would require careful inspection at the single aspect level (outcome variables).

20 When considering this effect on the firms' networking, it is important to recognize the likelihood spillover effect that this impact may generate. By increasing funded firms' interactions, the policy may indirectly affect the innovation activities of the non-beneficiaries. This would imply a bias in the matching estimates (e.g. through a violation of the *SUTVA*), which available data and current techniques do not unfortunately allow us to control.

21 It should be stressed that, although not reported, the results of the tests (available upon request) largely support the quality of all the employed matching procedures of Tables 10.1 and 10.2.

22 The following analysis is based on the most used of the matching procedure in the PSM, that is the 5NN. However, like those in the previous section, the results are robust across the other procedures.

23 As can be seen in Table 10.1, Italian national policies outperform regional ones in terms of impact on firms' interactions. This might be due to two possible factors. On the one hand, a higher support, which can also take the form of explicit requirement, to collaborate with research organizations or (also through temporary consortia) with other firms. On the other hand, the larger scale, scope and aim of the projects funded by the Italian national policies (Cefis and Evangelista, 2007; Barbieri *et al.* 2010) may induce firms to look for necessary assets, both tangible and intangible, which are located outside their boundaries.

24 Of course, this is not exclusive. The reason why Italian regional innovation policies are so weak deserves deeper investigation. On the one hand, we should consider the heterogeneity of the regional policies, and thus their effects. On the other hand, we should bear in mind that the period considered in this analysis (2002–2004) is only immediately subsequent to the 2001 reform of the Italian Constitution, which gave regions substantial autonomy in terms of innovation policy.

References

Aerts, K. and Schmidt, T. (2008), 'Two for the price of one? Additionality effects of R&D subsidies: a comparison between Flanders and Germany', *Research Policy* 37(5), 806–822.

Afcha-Chávez, S.M. (2011), 'Behavioural additionality in the context of regional innovation policy in Spain', *Innovation: Management, Policy & Practice* 13(1), 95–110.

Antonioli, D. and Marzucchi, A. (2012). 'Evaluating the additionality of innovation policy. A review focused on the behavioural dimension', *World Review of Science, Technology and Sustainable Development* 9(2–4), 124–148.

Antonioli, D., Marzucchi, A. and Montresor, S. (2014), 'Regional innovation policy and innovative behaviour: looking for additional effects', *European Planning Studies*, 22(1), 64–83.

Arrow, K. (1962), 'Economic welfare and the allocation of resources for invention', in Nelson, R. (ed.), *The Rate and Direction of Inventive Activity: Economic and Social Factors*, pp. 609–626, Washington: NBER.

Autio, E., Kanninen, S. and Gustafsson, R. (2008), 'First-and second-order additionality and learning outcomes in collaborative R&D programs', *Research Policy* 37(1), 59–76.

Barbieri, E., Iorio, R. and Lubrano Lavadera, G. (2010), 'Incentivi alla Ricerca and Sviluppo in Italia: un'indagine sugli effetti della legge 46/82' ['Italian R&D policy schemes. An analysis on the effects of the law 46/82'], *L'Industria* 31(2), 335–366.

Becker, S.O. and Ichino, A. (2002), 'Estimation of average treatment effects based on propensity scores', *The Stata Journal* 2(4), 358–377.

Boix, R. and Galletto, V. (2009), 'Innovation and industrial districts: a first approach to the measurement and determinants of the I-district effect', *Regional Studies* 43(9), 1117–1133.

Boschma, R. (2005), 'Rethinking regional innovation policy', in Fuchs, G. and Shapira P. (eds), *Rethinking Regional Innovation and Change*, pp. 249–271, New York: Springer.

Breschi, S., Cassi, L., Malerba, F. and Vonortas, N. (2009), 'Networked research: European policy intervention in ICTs', *Technology Analysis and Strategic Management* 21(7), 833–857.

Buisseret, T., Cameron, H.M. and Georghiou, L. (1995), 'What difference does it make? Additionality in the public support of R&D in large firms', *International Journal of Technology Management* 10(4–5–6), 587–600.

Busom, I. and Fernández-Ribas, A. (2008), 'The impact of firm participation in R&D programmes on R&D partnership', *Research Policy* 37(2), 240–257.

Caliendo, M. and Kopeinig, S. (2008), 'Some practical guidance for the implementation of the propensity score matching', *Journal of Economic Surveys* 22(1), 31–72.

Cameron, A.C. and Trivedi, P.K. (2005), *Microeconometrics. Methods and Applications*, Cambridge: Cambridge University Press.

Carboni, O.A. (2011), 'R&D subsidies and private R&D expenditures: evidence from Italian manufacturing data', *International Review of Applied Economics* 25(4), 419–439.

Cefis, E. And Evangelista, R. (2007), 'La valutazione delle politiche per l'innovazione. Un confronto tra Italia e Paesi Bassi' ['The evaluation of innovation policies. A comparison between Italy and Netherlands'], *L'Industria* 27(2), 243–264.

Cerulli, G. (2010), 'Modelling and measuring the effect of public subsidies on business R&D: a critical review of the econometric literature', *Economic Record* 86(274), 421–449.

Cerulli, G. and Potì, B. (2012a), (eds), 'Evaluating the effect of public policies on corporate R&D and innovation: processes and behaviours, measurement methods and indicators', Special Issue of *World Review of Science, Technology and Sustainable Development* 9, 2/3/4.

Cerulli, G. and Potì, B. (2012b), 'Evaluating the robustness of the effect of public subsidies on firm R&D and innovation: an application to Italy', *Journal of Applied Economics* 15, 2.

Cerulli, G. and Potì, B. (2012c), 'The differential impact of privately and publicly funded R&D on R&D investment and innovation: the Italian case', *Prometheus. Critical Studies in Innovation* 30, 1.

Clarysse, B., Bilsen, V., Steurs, G. and Larosse, J. (2004), 'Measuring additionality of R&D subsides with surveys: towards an evaluation methodology for IWT Flanders', *Innovation Science Technology IWT-Observatory* 48, 23–56.

Clarysse, B., Wright, M. and Mustar, P. (2009), 'Behavioural additionality of R&D subsidies: a learning perspective', *Research Policy*, 38(10), 1517–1533.

Colombo, M.G., Grilli, L. and Murtinu, S. (2011), 'R&D subsidies and the performance of high-tech start-ups', *Economic Letters* 112(1), 97–99.

Cooke, P. (2002), 'Regional innovation systems: general findings and some evidence from the biotechnology clusters', *Journal of Technology Transfer* 27(1), 133–145.

Czarnitzki, D. and Licht, G. (2006), 'Additionality of public R&D grants in a transition economy', *Economics of Transition* 14(1), 101–131.

De Blasio, G., Fantino, D. and Pellegrini, G. (2011), 'Evaluating the impact of innovation incentives: evidence from an unexpected shortage of funds', *Bank of Italy Working Papers* n. 792.

Edquist, C. (1999), 'Systems of innovation: theory and policy for the demand side', *Technology in Society* 21(1), 63–79.

Edquist, C. (2011), 'Design of innovation policy through diagnostic analysis: identification of systemic problems (or failures)', *Industrial and Corporate Change* 20(6), 1637–1643.

Edquist, C., Malerba, F., Metcalfe, J.S., Montobbio, F. and Steinmueller, W.E. (2004), 'Sectoral systems: implication for European innovation policy', in Malerba, F. (ed.), *Sectoral Systems of Innovation*, pp. 427–461, Cambridge: Cambridge University Press.

European Commission (2009), 'Making public support for innovation in the EU more effective. Lessons learned from a public consultation for action at Community level', *Commission Staff Working Document* SEC(2009)1197, 9 September 2009.

European Commission (2010), 'EUROPE 2020. A strategy for smart, sustainable and inclusive growth', Communication from the Commission Com(2010) 2020, Brussels.

Fernández-Ribas, A. and Shapira, P. (2009), 'The role of national and regional innovation programmes in stimulating international cooperation in innovation', *International Journal of Technology Management* 48(4), 473–498.

Garcia-Quevedo, J. and Afcha-Chávez, S. (2009), 'El impacto del apoyo público a la I+D empresarial: un análisis comparativo entre las subvenciones estatales y regionales' ['The impact of public funding to firms' R&D: a comparative analysis of national and regional subsidies'], *Investigaciones Regionales* 15, 277–294.

Georghiou, L. (2002), 'Impact and additionality of innovation policy', *Innovation Science and Technology IWT Observatory* 40, 57–65.

Georghiou, L. (2004), 'Evaluation of behavioural additionality. Concept paper', *Innovation Science and Technology IWT Observatory* 48, 7–22.

Georghiou, L. and Clarysse, B. (2006), 'Introduction and synthesis', in OECD (ed.), *Government R&D Funding and Company Behaviour: Measuring Behavioural Additionality*, pp. 9–38, Paris: OECD.

González, X. and Pazó, G. (2008), 'Do public subsidies stimulate R&D spending?', *Research Policy* 37(3), 371–389.

Hall, B.H. and Maffioli, A. (2008), 'Evaluating the impact of technology development funds in emerging economies: evidence from Latin America', *European Journal of Development Research* 20(2), 172–198.

Hall, B.H., Lotti, F. and Mairesse, J. (2009), 'Innovation and productivity in SMEs: empirical evidence for Italy', *Small Business Economics* 33(1), 13–33.

Hommen, L. and Edquist, C. (2008), 'Globalization and innovation policy', in Edquist, C. and Hommen, L. (eds) *Small Country Innovation Systems: Globalization, Change and Policy in Asia and Europe*, pp. 442–484, Cheltenham, UK: Edward Elgar.

Howells, J. (1999), 'Regional systems of innovation?', in Howells, J., Archibugi, D. and Michie, J. (eds), *Innovation Policy in a Global Economy*, pp. 67–93, Cambridge: Cambridge University Press.

Kaiser, R. (2003), 'Multi-level science policy and regional innovation: the case of Munich Cluster for Pharmaceutical Biotechnology', *European Planning Studies* 11(7), 841–857.

Laranja, M., Uyarra, E. and Flanagan, K. (2008), 'Policies for science, technology and innovation: translating rationales into regional policies in a multi-level setting', *Research Policy* 37(5), 823–835.

Leuven, E. and Sianesi, B. (2003), 'PSMATCH2: stata module to perform full Mahalanobis and propensity score matching, common support graphing and covariate imbalance testing' Available at: http://ideas.repec.org/c/boc/bocode/s432001.html.

Magro, E., Aranguren, M.J. and Navarro, M. (2010), 'Does regional S&T policy affect firms' behaviour?', Paper presented for the *Regional Studies Association Annual International Conference 2010*, Pécs, Hungary. Available at: http://citeseerx.ist.psu.edu/viewdoc/download?doi=10.1.1.169.7827&rep=rep1&type=pdf

Marzucchi, A. (2012), *Evaluating the Additionality of Innovation Policy: An Investigation at Different Levels of Analysis*, PhD thesis, University of Trento.

Marzucchi, A., Antonioli, D. and Montresor, S. (2013), 'Industry–research cooperation within and across regional boundaries. What does innovation policy add?', *Papers in Regional Science* (Early View), doi: 10.1111/pirs.12079.

Merito, M., Giannangeli, S. and Bonaccorsi, A. (2010), 'Do incentives to industrial R&D enhance research productivity and firm growth? Evidence from the Italian case', *International Journal of Technology Management* 49(1–2–3), 25–48.

Metcalfe, J.S. (1995), 'The economic foundations of economic policy: equilibrium and evolutionary perspectives', in Stoneman, P. (ed.), *Handbook of the Economics of Innovation and Technological Change*, pp. 409–512, Hoboken, NJ: Blackwell Handbooks in Economics.

Nelson, R. and Winter, S. (1982), *An Evolutionary Theory of Economic Change*, Cambridge, MA: The Belknap Press of Harvard University Press.

Parisi, M.L. and Sembenelli, A. (2003), 'Is private R&D spending sensitive to its price? Empirical evidence on panel data for Italy', *Empirica* 30(4), 357–377.

Rosenbaum, P. and Rubin, D. (1983), 'The central role of the propensity score in observational studies for causal effect', *Biometrika* 70(1), 41–55.

Rubin, D. (1986), 'Comment: which ifs have causal answers', *Journal of the American Statistical Association* 81(396), 961–962.

Smith, J.A. and Todd, P.E. (2005), 'Does matching overcome LaLonde's critique of non-experimental estimators?', *Journal of Econometrics* 125(1–2), 305–353.

Smith, K. (2000), 'Innovation as a systemic phenomenon: rethinking the role of policy', *Enterprise & Innovation Management Studies* 1(1), 73–102.

Tamm, D. (2010), 'System failures in public sector innovation support measures: the case of Estonian innovation system and dairy industry', *Diskurs* 2010–07.

Uyarra, E. (2010), 'What is evolutionary about "regional systems of innovation"? Implications for regional policy', *Journal of Evolutionary Economics* 20(1), 115–137.

Varis, M. and Littunen, H. (2010), 'Types of innovation, sources of information and performance in entrepreneurial SMEs', *European Journal of Innovation Management* 13(2), 128–154.

Woolthuis, K., Lankhuizen, M. and Gilsing, V. (2005), 'A system failure framework for innovation policy design', *Technovation* 25(6), 609–619.

11 Innovation policies as engines of economic growth

Standard lessons and systemic insights for Bulgaria

Sorin M.S. Krammer[1]

1 Introduction

Given the impressive amount of attention devoted to this topic, it is difficult to ignore the contribution of innovation and new technologies in determining the patterns of economic growth and competitiveness (Cameron, 1996; Hall and Jones, 1999; Freeman, 2002; Rosenberg, 2004; Wang *et al.*, 2007; Gibson and Naquin, 2011). Beyond the theoretical calls for more innovation, the current global crisis has exposed significant weaknesses of anchoring growth to non-tradables (e.g. financial sector, real estate and construction), and research and technological innovation have been proposed as sustainable economic alternatives for the future. As a result, both science and technology are nowadays more integrated in the economic rationale, and the Innovation Systems (IS) paradigm dominates the policy arena. However, despite a strong consensus on pursuing innovation through both public and private vehicles, the practical implementation of growth-enhancing policies is often difficult and idiosyncratic (Mowery and Oxley, 1995; Gu, 1999; Hadjimanolisa and Dickson, 2001; Wang *et al.*, 2007). Therefore, implementing a certain 'recipe' which has proved to work for innovation-driven growth in a given country is a common fallacy of innovation policies worldwide. Beyond the well-known economic failure of free-markets to produce an optimum amount of innovation (Nelson, 1959; Arrow, 1962), allocation conundrums are particularly salient for latecomer countries (Furman *et al.*, 2002; Hu and Matthews, 2005; Dodgson, 2009; Krammer, 2009) where private firms lack resources to innovate and rely heavily on public and foreign knowledge. In these cases, the supporting infrastructure and policies, conceptualized within the systemic NIS (Lundvall, 1992; Nelson, 1993) or STIG – science, technology, innovation and growth – frameworks (Aghion *et al.*, 2009), become essential to long-term competitiveness and economic success.

The approach I undertake in this study is to analyse in depth the components of these systems, identify the 'problems' or 'failures' of each component and the overall system, and provide policy avenues for future development, based on their structure and existing linkages. These aspects will be captured at the country level using a wide range of proxies from primary and secondary data. My assessment of international competitiveness draws upon recent findings in the literature on industrial production, exports and economic growth (Feenstra and Rose, 1997; Imbs and Wacziarg, 2003; Klinger and Lederman, 2004). According to these studies, countries climb the ladder of export sophistication and competitiveness over time first, by diversifying, and later by specializing in upper echelons of products with high value-added (Cadot *et al.*, 2007). This process is fuelled both by *internal* (e.g. in-house R&D and scientific production, existing human capital) and *external* sources of innovation (e.g. licensing, foreign direct investment, technological alliances, learning by exporting, spillovers) that jointly contribute to the development and success of new products.

Combining theoretical arguments from the innovation systems literature and export-led growth theory, I provide a detailed systemic analysis of economic competitiveness and STI performance in Bulgaria, a laggard in both economic and innovation terms within the enlarged European Union. Moreover, throughout these diagnostics, Bulgaria is assessed against a set of six benchmark countries which have been chosen to represent both more advanced EU countries (Finland, Italy), as well as similar neighbours (Romania, Hungary) and non-EU fast-growing economies (Turkey and Croatia). The first diagnostic assesses Bulgarian competitiveness using detailed (four-digit) export data and identifies possible niches for future export-led development (Hausmann and Klinger, 2008). The second analysis provides a comprehensive analysis of both 'new-to-the-market' and 'new-to-the-world' innovative output using international and domestic patent data (Acs *et al.*, 2002; Grupp and Mogee, 2004). In the third analysis, I close the STI circle by analysing the current scientific system in Bulgaria using bibliometric data (Weingart, 2005) and identify opportunities for future capability development (D'Este and Patel, 2007) based on the linkages between industrial and technological systems. These diagnostics are supplemented with microeconomic insights on firm innovation from the 2013 Business Environment and Enterprise Performance Survey (BEEPS).

Following these analyses, the remainder of the paper develops concrete policy recommendations which aim to enhance Bulgaria's competitive advantage through a more efficient utilization of its STI assets. This part addresses structural weaknesses that impede productivity and export-oriented growth. Furthermore, it promotes actions to bring 'science, higher education, and business closer together' as a governmental priority to both achieve the innovation targets of the EU agenda and spur a faster economic recovery.

My findings suggest that the challenges identified in this study should be addressed immediately through a mix of policy measures that tackle both 'standard' innovation issues as well as 'systemic' deficiencies associated with Bulgarian STI. In the short and medium run, it is imperative for Bulgaria to support product innovation and upgrades in potential export-champion sectors through national funding instruments. Better incentives and finance for these activities are required to stimulate the domestic knowledge creation as a base for export-driven growth. In terms of science and innovation, international collaboration remains a critical source of comparative advantage for laggards such as Bulgaria, given its role in foreign knowledge absorption and building of a critical

STI mass, which can subsequently spur, through innovation, product diversity and export performance. Another priority involves harmonizing the links between academia and business through new policies in tertiary education and R&D legislation. Finally, as one of the 'new' EU members, Bulgaria needs to take better advantage of the existing European opportunities by accessing structural funds, eliminating bottlenecks in the absorption of these resources and redesigning instruments to promote commercialization of public-sector research. In the long run, Bulgaria needs to make significant changes to its STI systems to address the systemic issues identified in this study. Improving innovation funding instruments and coordination mechanisms between governmental agencies and ministries is one example of these difficult tasks ahead. This will also involve the restructuring of the Bulgarian Academy of Science (BAS), the main hub for scientific knowledge creation in the country, which still exhibits significant organizational deficiencies. Furthermore, there is a need to encourage and support regional scientific specialization outside the capital city, aiming to create specialized centres of excellence that are meant to support and reinforce innovation in regional industries. In terms of commercial innovation, a revision of the regulatory elements pertaining to IP is necessary to accommodate for joint public–private research and applied knowledge creation in universities. Moreover, the creation and support of specialized training and skill-building programmes in higher education is required to provide the necessary human capital for rising industries such as IT where 'brain drain' remains an important challenge. Finally, policymakers should incorporate the lessons and experience of other countries regarding the implementation of monitoring and evaluation practices for the use of funds and resources, and a better dissemination of their domestic STI outputs throughout the economy.

The rest of this chapter is structured as follows. Section 2 provides an overview of the literature on competitiveness and its links with exports and innovation. Section 3 presents the analyses for Bulgarian export competitiveness, innovation and scientific performance. Based on these results, Section 4 proposes a mix of standard and systemic policy measures to address some of these issues, while Section 5 concludes with final reflections and potential applications of this kind of analysis for other countries seeking to improve their systemic efficiency and better utilize their STI capabilities for economic growth.

2 Competitiveness, growth and the knowledge economy

2.1 Defining competitiveness

Despite its apparent simplicity and conspicuous appeal to policymakers and mass media, competitiveness remains a complex concept that is often misunderstood and difficult to quantify. Most definitions refer to competitiveness in a multidimensional setting as the success of an entity (a firm, sector, country or group of countries) in competing with peers. However, this multidimensional complexity induces significant difficulties in identifying what being competitive means exactly and at which level this should be measured. Thus, major criticisms refer to issues such as the arbitrary nature of measures employed (Reichel, 2002), sector and country aggregation problems (Jenkins, 1998) and strong overlap with productivity metrics (Krugman, 1994). However, competitive advantage is viewed as a way of improving the performance of firms, sectors and economies (Porter, 1990), and as a result, competitiveness indexes have become extremely popular in policy and media circles (Thomson, 2004).

From a pure economic perspective, the competitiveness of a country is synonymous with superior productivity. Both concepts are deeply rooted in the country's microeconomic success (Porter, 1990) driven by national systems of innovation (R&D investments, product quality and innovation, human capital) and quality of institutions.[2] Theory and empirics likewise posit a strong two-way link between competitiveness and trade (Alcalá and Ciccone, 2004). Thus, the most common way to analyse international competitiveness is to look at either conventional trade indicators such as Balassa, Michaely and Lafay indices and other 'modified' export and import ratios of a country (Zaghini, 2005; Damijan *et al.*, 2008), or more recent trade indices taken from the export-led growth literature (i.e. export sophistication, unit value distance, open forest) described in the work of Hausmann and Klinger (2008), Imbs and Warcziag (2003) or Klinger and Lederman (2004).

Identifying systemic capabilities that drive competitiveness and their interactions is an important target for economic policy in terms of future growth perspectives. As a result, many studies attempt to capture one or multiple facets of competitiveness using narrow or broad indicators. The latter encompass a large variety of aspects such as economic factors (e.g. the ability to attract investment, employment rate, cost of living), business factors (e.g. management efficiency, corporate governance, finance), infrastructure (e.g. basic infrastructure, scientific and technological infrastructure, education, research and development) and governmental efficiency (fiscal policy, institutional quality, public spending, business environment), all of which shape a country's ability to compete internationally (IMD, 2010; Schwab, 2010).[3] However, by going broad one loses focus in terms of what these indexes actually measure (institutions, economic development, or really competitiveness). Therefore, in this paper, I emphasize one distinct and important aspect of competitiveness (i.e. export competitiveness) since this is considered a significant growth source in the broader economics literature. Moreover, by considering a finer grained measure of competitiveness than commonly used 'generic' indicators (e.g. IMD and WEF), I am able to draw better links between the components of the STI systems and the resulting economic output, which is my main line of inquiry in this research.

2.2 Innovation, exports, competitiveness and growth: a self-enforcing relationship

Since the 1980s, academic research on growth and competitiveness has shifted its focus from classical price- and cost-related factors to a more Schumpeterian view which emphasizes the role of technology and innovation in the international performance of firms, sectors or countries (Hall and Jones, 1999). Surveys on the relationship between technology and trade reveal a self-enforcing relationship between them through learning-by-doing and spillovers from investments in research and development (R&D), which in turn also affects the evolution of technology (Grossman and Helpman, 1994). The new-growth theory (Romer, 1991; Grossman and Helpman, 1991; Aghion and Howitt, 1992) proposes increasing returns and positive spillovers from R&D efforts across multiple levels: firm, industry or country (Coe and Helpman, 1995; Keller, 2004; Lumenga-Neso *et al.*, 2005). However, trade models are still based on a set of assumptions that warrant both tractability and consistency with established doctrines in the field, and moreover often fail to replicate stylized facts such as skewed distributions of innovation and labour productivity across countries or sectoral specificity (Dosi *et al.*, 1990). The evolutionary branch of economics provides similar answers by focusing on the sector-specific nature of innovation and investigating its impact on the competitiveness of these systems (Nelson and Winter, 1977; Dosi, 1988). While extremely different in their approaches (e.g. theoretical foundations, empirical implementation and policy prescriptions), these two strains of literature strongly agree upon the existence of robust linkages between innovation and economic competitiveness (Mulder *et al.*, 2001).

Likewise, the industrial organization literature documents the link between growth differentials and trade patterns with both theoretical and empirical evidence (Lankhuizen, 2000). Export performance and competitiveness share a selection mechanism: countries that become competitive in a certain sector also manage to secure a higher export share in that domain and vice versa. Moreover, the recent export-growth studies suggest two stylized facts: first, there is a U-shaped relationship between export specialization and income per capita and, second, developing countries that produce 'sophisticated' goods tend to grow faster (Feenstra and Rose, 1997; Imbs and Wacziarg, 2003; Klinger and Lederman, 2004; Lee, 2011). The quality or sophistication level of products is contingent on a country's internal technological capabilities. Thus, developing economies tend to specialize in narrow niches of production and exports, usually low-tech industries. In dynamics, a rise in income triggers diversification and the introduction of new and more sophisticated products. Finally, at high levels of income (i.e. developed nations) specialization occurs again: certain export lines close down and there is again an overall tendency for concentration, especially towards the upper value added echelons of products. Through this process, countries advance their production and export patterns and secure a more competitive position in the global economic system.

Production diversification is also important for industrial policy, especially when countries are looking to overcome export instability or reduce negative impacts from terms of trade in primary products. Cadot *et al.* (2007) find that industrial diversification precedes export diversification: while the turning point for the former is around US$16,500 (PPP), export diversification remains positive up to levels of US$22,500 (PPP).[4] This is consistent with the view that, in order to be competitive internationally, one must first develop production capabilities. Through this structural transformation, countries move from 'poor-country goods' to 'rich country ones' mediated by diversification. Finally, diversified economies are better equipped to take advantage of the export opportunities in the global market and harness them to accelerate growth.

To close the circle, both trade and growth theories predict a strong relationship between exports and innovation. Product life-cycle models predict that innovation is emerging from a well-technologically endowed North to be imitated and then slowly adopted later on in the production of Southern goods (Vernon, 1966; Krugman, 1979; Dollar, 1986), while more recent strains manage to endogenize this process and replicate the distribution of exporters within an economy based on a selection process that makes use of superior technologies and know-how (Melitz, 2003; Melitz and Ottaviano, 2005). Moreover, empirical findings associate economic success with innovation (Cassiman and Golovko, 2007; Lachenmaier and Wößmann, 2006) and learning-by-exporting effects (Clerides *et al.*, 1998; Damijan and Kostevc, 2010), although causality remains debatable across this literature (Bernard and Jensen, 1999; Damijan *et al.*, 2008). Lastly, countries are structurally interlinked with each other, and the interplay between trade flows and technological change (i.e. innovation) dictates growth performance across all countries. As a result, one way to improve growth perspectives is to stimulate the diffusion of technology across borders and liberalized trade as a valuable carrier for structural change that will reduce sectoral disparities, raise productivity levels and allow for beneficial specialization patterns across countries and sectors (Cimoli and Porcile, 2011).

Further away from the mainstream economic reasoning, the integration between S, T and I in the innovation systems literature employs different complex concepts such as the triple helix (Leydesdorff and Etzkowitz, 1998), innovation ecosystems (Aulet, 2008) or knowledge triangles (Soriano and Mulatero, 2010). All these frameworks draw attention to the systemic nature of innovation, the actors involved and the existing feedback loops that challenge conventional linear models of innovation. Within such ecosystems, the emphasis is put on multiple drivers of innovation (e.g. research, financial support, entrepreneurs, culture, education, etc.) that interact and stimulate each other through self-enforcing mechanisms and spillovers. Moreover, empirical evidence strongly supports the existence of multiple non-linear interactions between STI components and subsequent economic success. Thus, the systemic context, either at the national or at the regional level in the form or national/regional STI systems, exhibits numerous and intricate connections between different actors involved in the creation of new knowledge (i.e. R&D and basic science performing firms, universities, laboratories, governmental agencies, etc.) and firms who employ it in the final production sector of the economy (Castelacci, 2008). As a result of these links, national and regional STI systems provide the basis for developing knowledge-based activities in the form of basic and applied research moderated by the quality of existing infrastructure and existence of different technological competences which further downstream translate into patterns of firm productivity, which are closely linked to trade specialization and the competitiveness of regions and countries (Freeman, 2004).

Given the critical role of STI systems in shaping productivity and special-ization patterns across regions and countries, it is important to analyse these systems in detail and use the results to improve/optimize the overall system via policy measures rather that 'fix' specific components of it. While today's dominant paradigm of 'laissez-faire' preserves its appeal and political conven-ience, it can be a 'convenient fiction, but worse, a self-delusion on the part of those who embrace it as a requirement for policy design' (Aghion *et al.*, 2009). Building on these arguments, I aim to provide policymakers with policy recom-mendations to improve the functionality of STI systems and subsequently harness the latter to improve a country's export competitiveness. These analyses will be carried out for Bulgaria, with a potentially larger base of application to other EU member and developing economies that are facing significant chal-lenges in harnessing their STI systems to improve their economic wellbeing.

3 Bulgarian competitiveness and STI performance

After the 1990 shift from a centralized economic system to a free-market one, Bulgarian competitiveness has steadily improved, but not enough to catch up with its European peers or with other emerging markets. Bulgaria ranks seventy-fourth out of 133 countries in the Global Competitiveness Report 2012–2013 and sixty-sixth out of 183 economies in the Doing Business Report 2013. These statistics consistently provide a bleak picture of its performance, suggesting that severe institutional problems (i.e. financial barriers, corruption and bureaucracy) should be tackled immediately to make the country more competitive and pros-perous. Furthermore, in these turbulent times of macroeconomic volatility and high risks of double-dip recessions occurring all over the world, there is strong consensus in Bulgaria that 'business as usual' is unlikely to generate sufficient economic growth to dent unemployment and achieve economic convergence with the core of the EU.

3.1 Export competitiveness: past, present and future

Following the recent crisis, Bulgarian policymakers have subscribed to the idea that exports need to play a more central role in the country's growth to strengthen the current recovery and insulate it from future boom–bust cycles. Prior to the crisis, Bulgaria benefited from large inflows of FDI (about 30 per cent of GDP in 2008), which have returned now to their pre-boom levels (i.e. 4 per cent of GDP in 2010). In the context of weak domestic demand, as house-holds and firms deleverage and continue fiscal adjustment, exports present a viable alternative for sustaining growth. The experience of Germany and other emerging countries shows that, when growth is anchored on exports, it is pos-sible for the economy to achieve a faster (i.e. V-shaped) recovery after a signi-ficant macroeconomic downturn.

In this section, I will provide a detailed analysis of Bulgarian exports vis-à-vis several benchmark countries by examining their aggregate historical evolution, geographic distribution, composition of the export basket and sophistication of the top export products. Exports remain an important component of the Bulgarian economy, representing nearly 60 per cent of its GDP, with important increases over the last decade. However, this performance puts Bulgaria in the middle of the Eastern European group of countries, but behind regional export champions (such as Hungary), despite similar export levels in the early 1990s. In 2008, Bulgaria had exports of US$3,958 per capita, more than Romania (US$2,781) and Turkey (US$2,378), but below Croatia (US$6,553), Hungary (US$12,549), Italy (US$11,100) and Finland (US$22,664). Moreover, the country's trade balance is still negative for most of its top exports, raising doubts as to its long-term sustainability. To assess the Bulgarian export performance, I will focus on its main exports at two and four-digit granulation compared with the rest of the world.

Geographically, most exports target the EU common market (Greece, Germany, Italy and Romania), neighbouring countries (Turkey and Serbia) and other large markets (e.g. Russia, USA, China, Saudi Arabia, India and Pakistan) (see Table 11.1). Export growth to neighbouring EU markets, particularly Greece and Romania, is expected to be low given the recent macroeconomic turbulences in this region as a result of the financial and fiscal crises. Consequently, market openings will occur in regions experiencing robust domestic demand such as China, Russia and other CIS states, Turkey and the Gulf countries. Throughout this period, labour- and resource-intensive manufacturing industries that benefited from global increase in commodity price mostly drove Bulgaria's export growth. Thus, petroleum products, metals and derivatives, chemicals, cereals and apparel, all with double-digit growth rates in this period, accurately synthesize the structure of Bulgarian exports, one that is heavily oriented towards mature industries with declining margins in terms of labour and energy costs.

Figure 11.1 shows that the main products in which Bulgaria has a relative high market share (above 0.5 per cent) are resource-based (copper), agricultural products (cereals, oil seeds) and garments (knitted and not-knitted apparel). Moreover, except for copper, cereals and garments, its trade balance is negative in all its top exports. The average growth rate of the top ten exported products is 22.5 per cent per year between 2004 and 2008. The second tier of exported products (ranked 10–20) includes more sophisticated goods, such as glassware, optical apparatus, pharmaceuticals, chemicals and plastics, which also record higher growth rates worldwide (averaging 32.5 per cent between 2004 and 2008). Over time, garments, organic chemicals, plastic products and other commodities have diminished their importance in the Bulgarian export basket, while agricultural products, aluminium, organic chemicals and optical/medical apparatus have gained in these rankings. This heavy reliance on natural resources, characterized by a low or intermediate degree of processing, is even clearer upon examination of net Bulgarian exports. Here, products like refined copper and petroleum oils account for about a quarter of the total net exports of Bulgaria (see Figure A.11.1, Appendix).

Table 11.1 Main export destinations for Bulgaria

Country	Trade indicators				
	Exports US$ mil.	Trade balance US$ mil.	Share in Bulgaria's exports (%)	Growth 2004–2008 (%)	Growth partner's imports 2004–2008 (%)
Greece	2,230	272	9.90	23	15
Germany	2,045	-2,361	9.10	21	14
Turkey	1,979	-80	8.80	21	20
Italy	1,887	-1,058	8.40	11	12
Romania	1,631	-448	7.30	43	27
Belgium	1,327	657	5.90	24	13
Serbia	1,045	764	4.70	0	31
France	921	-323	4.10	19	13
Russian Fed.	610	-1,471	2.70	53	38
FYR Macedonia	507	87	2.30	26	21
World	22,478	-11,295	100.00	23	15

Source: own calculations, based on UN COMTRADE, 2010.

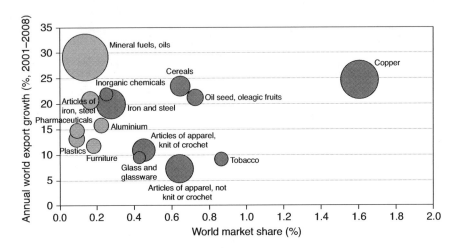

Figure 11.1 Dynamic export profile of Bulgaria (source: own calculations for the period 2001–2008 based on UN COMTRADE, 2010).

Note
The area of the circles corresponds to the export size in US$ mil.; only the top 15 exports are represented.

To further assess the competitiveness of Bulgarian exports, I compute the aggregated unit value which captures performance in terms of prices and quality comparative to the 'frontier' (i.e. the most proficient country in terms of exporting a given product):

$$UVD_{c,t} = \sum_i \log(P\max_{i,t} - P_{i,t}) \frac{xval_{i,c,t}}{x_{c,t}}$$

where c refers to country, t is the time period, P_i is the price of product i, $P\max_{i,t}$ is the highest priced export for good i worldwide, $xval$ and X are the total exports of i, and respectively of country c.[5] The *unit value distance* reveals that Bulgaria's export basket has made virtually no progress between 1990 and 2008. Bulgaria's rankings (seventy-first in 1990; eighty-sixth in 2000; sixty-seventh in 2008) remained unchanged as opposed to countries like Hungary and Turkey, suggesting that Bulgaria has stalled on both technology and efficiency improvements regarding its exports. Next, I construct a sophistication measure for the export basket of a country (EXPY) following Hausmann *et al.* (2007). This measure equals the weighted average of the sophistication of each of its exported goods (PRODY):

$$EXPY_{c,t} = \sum_i \left(\frac{xval_{i,c,t}}{X_{c,t}} \right) PRODY_{i,t}$$

Where $Y_{c,t}$ is the GDP per capita, $xval_{i,c,t}/X_{c,t}$ is the value-added share of the commodity in the country's overall export basket of a country c. Superior or sophisticated products (higher PRODY) are the home turf of developed nations, while a countries' EXPY is a good predictor for their future economic performance (Figure 11.2). Likewise, previous studies have established significant links between EXPY and other more standard proxies of competitiveness, such as total factor productivity, high-tech exports and profitability (World Bank, 2008; Jarreau and Poncet, 2012). Therefore, subscribing to these views, I will examine Bulgarian performance in terms of EXPY both across time and in comparison with its benchmarked peers.

Overall, Bulgaria holds an average position in EXPY, with moderate improvements over time that are in line with Turkey, Romania or Serbia, but below Central European nations and global top exporters. This finding is consistent with previous studies that have examined the evolution of trade patterns and specialization of other transition countries using Lafay indexes (Zaghini, 2005). In fact, for Bulgaria, only six of its top 15 exports have sophistication levels above the global average (see Table A.11.1 in the Appendix), supporting the call for trade reorientation and high-sophistication niche targeting (i.e. electric current, copper and derivatives, etc.) as feasible export-led growth strategies for the future. A leading cause for this low level of export sophistication is the limited contribution (3 per cent) of high-tech exports to the Bulgarian basket, substantially below the EU-27 average (16 per cent). Even among their top ten exported goods, only electrical equipment and boilers and machinery possess a high-tech component.[6] Bulgarian sophisticated products (glassware, optical apparatus, pharmaceuticals, chemicals and plastics) are currently in a second tier of performance (ranked 10–20) and have very small market shares.

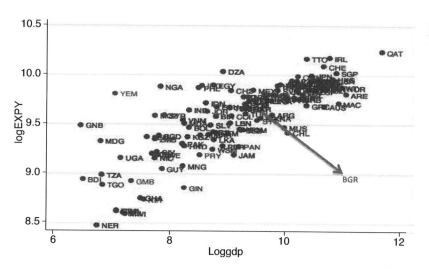

Figure 11.2 Export sophistication and GDP per capita (source: own calculations for year 2008, based on UN COMTRADE, 2010).

There are several policy measures which can facilitate the growth and sophistication of Bulgarian exports. For example, to reverse this trend towards lower product sophistication of exports, the government and industry need to collaborate in promoting aggressively medium- and high-tech product exports. Prior studies suggest that industrial diversification precedes export diversification (Cadot *et al.*, 2007) because diversified economies are better equipped to take advantage of export opportunities in the global market. In practice, the experience of export champions such as Korea and Malaysia suggests that diversification and exporting opportunities were significantly advanced through technology absorption and innovation, but this process is neither automatic nor costless. In such long-term endeavours, governmental intervention plays a catalytic role by attracting foreign sources of technologies through targeted FDI measures and by addressing market failures that depress private innovation (Girma *et al.*, 2004; Keller and Yeaple, 2009; Aghion *et al.*, 2009).

Besides horizontal measures to spur export-oriented FDI, the government should consider introducing innovation policies and instruments targeting sectors with high export potential. Attracting export-oriented FDI (e.g. ideally FDI that is R&D intensive and can support Bulgaria's efforts to meet one of Europe 2020's strategic targets of reaching the 3 per cent of GDP for R&D investments) would be a good avenue to increase the share of medium- and high-tech exports.[7] However, in addition to offering horizontal measures such as tax incentives, there is a need to remove specific bottlenecks faced by high-potential industries whether skills or infrastructures, etc. A sector-focused approach that sets specific policies for each industry, including reforms and public investments to resolve bottlenecks, could anchor the medium-to-long-term expectations of foreign (and local) investors and tip the balance in favour of Bulgaria as a destination for R&D-intensive FDI.

3.2 Bulgarian STI systems: micro- and macroeconomic insights

3.2.1 Technological and scientific profile of Bulgaria

In this subsection, I focus on capturing the technological and scientific profile of Bulgaria both in historical terms and vis-à-vis the benchmark countries to provide an overview of the 'knowledge-creating' activities in the country and their match with the economic performers identified in the previous section. To measure the innovative capacity of a country, I turn to patents and publications statistics as common yardsticks of policy analysis and, by now, standard indicators for innovative performance. Bearing in mind the caveats associated with these measures, I employ US patent (USPTO) and European patent (EPO) datasets to obtain an overview of existing Bulgarian technologies and their impact worldwide.[8] To check the robustness of the results and get a broader perspective on these issues, I compare the results with data on domestic inventions from the Bulgarian patent office (BPO).[9] Finally, I employ several bibliometric tools to track scientific production over time within specific disciplines and organizations. The results of these analyses are presented below.

Overall, Bulgaria has a relatively weak track record in terms of patenting (averaging 0.85 US patents per million inhabitants), surpassing Romania (0.24) and Turkey (0.19), but below advanced transition countries such as Hungary (5.16) and Croatia (3.08) and far from Western European nations (Italy, 27.81; Finland, 137.11). Similar results and rankings emerge from the European Patent Office data on patent applications. These results confirm previous country-level findings in the literature regarding the downfall of innovation in transition countries after 1990 and the rebound after 2000 as a result of improved macro-economic conditions in the region (Krammer, 2009).

Compared with the pre-transition period (i.e. before 1990), fewer Bulgarian individuals, research institutes or firms are patenting today. Moreover, upon distinguishing the distribution of patents across the different technological classes described by Hall *et al.* (2001), the historical data show a massive drop in the usual Bulgarian patenting fields (e.g. mechanical, electrical and electronics, chemical) driven both by a reduction in investments and by a lack of technology upgrades. Moreover, I can identify a clear shift between technical specialization before and after 2000, which unofficially marks the end of the transition period. Thus, before 2000, Bulgaria's top-performing patenting classes were connected to traditional industries with mature technologies, such as metallurgy, chemicals, industrial heating and medicaments, all stemming from the industrial heritage of the communist period. Today, Bulgarian companies prefer to upgrade product lines with foreign capital goods rather than develop indigenous technologies and devote resources to internal R&D. As a result of this and the fact that these are mature industries with a slow technological pace, the previous technological champions of past decades have lost their spotlight in the Bulgarian innovation profile. On the other hand, a novel and positive trend has developed since 2000 with new patents coming from high-tech industries, driven by significant R&D efforts by multinationals, especially in IT-related industries (Table 11.2).While this portfolio is small in absolute terms, it is concentrated entirely on emerging technological fields: communication and navigation technology, data processing, computers, software and memory and miscellaneous others (defence, engines).[10] Such diversification into new technological areas that are more relevant in the current global economic environment is an important development and should be nurtured in the future through careful policy support.

The other significant trend of Bulgarian patenting is the rapid internationalization of innovation. Prior to 1990, most patents were generated by 'all Bulgarian' teams of inventors, either in public R&D institutes or in large institutes. Collaboration with foreign researchers and firms rose in the late 1990s and has increased ever since, allowing them to produce more and 'better' innovations (Figure 11.3). Today, these co-inventions count for about half of the country's patents at USPTO, resonating with findings at the regional level (Goldberg *et al.*, 2008). Most of these collaborations occur with researchers and firms from Western Europe (Germany, Sweden, Belgium), the USA and Japan. As a rule, the emergence of new players, some of them important multinationals with a global presence (GE, Samsung, Sun, Nokia), as assignees of Eastern European patents is

Table 11.2 The structural shift and rebirth of Bulgarian international patenting

Top five patent classes	1963–2000
Metal founding	18
Organic compounds	15
Electrolysis: process, composition, etc.	14
Electric heating	14
Drug, bio-affecting and body treating	13

Top five patent classes	2001–2010
DP: database and file management or data structures (data processing)	26
Multicomputer data transferring	22
Inter-programme/inter-process communication	11
DP: software development, installation and management (data processing)	11
DP: presentation processing of document, operator interface processing	9

Source: data from USPTO online search patent database (accessed March 2012).

not surprising (Krammer, 2009). However, there is almost no collaboration with Eastern Europe, except for a few patents co-authored with Russian inventors.

The catalytic role of scientific research in nurturing innovation is widely acknowledged in the literature (Rosenberg, 1990; Pavitt, 1991). Regardless of its mechanisms (e.g. a simple linear relationship or complex 'chain-linked' models à la Kline and Rosenberg, 1986, with different feedback loops), basic research is the main contributor to knowledge, and an indirect driver of innovation, production and productivity. Furthermore, scientific education is reflected directly by the available human capital and absorptive capacity of firms (Cohen and Levinthal, 1990) that feeds back into their capacity to develop new products and services and assimilate outside knowledge. Thus, strengthening the scientific base becomes a critical issue for maintaining a steady flow of new knowledge and skilled personnel into the economy.

To capture the Bulgarian position in the global scientific landscape, I employ several bibliometric indicators based on data from several specialized databases, namely *Web of Science*, *Essential Science Indicators* and *SCOPUS* from Elsevier.[11] Overall, Bulgarian scientific production has proved more resilient than the patenting of new technologies, but still not enough for Bulgaria to retain its pre-transition position relative to its peers. Measured on a per capita basis, Bulgaria's scientific production is on a par with Romania, Turkey and Croatia but lags behind the leaders (Finland and Italy) and Central Eastern countries (Croatia and Hungary) in our comparison group. Between 2001 and 2009, Bulgarians published over 21,000 papers compared to 18,685 (1991–2000) and 14,839 (1981–1990) in the past. This translates into an 8 per cent annual growth, similar to Finland (4 per cent), Italy (7 per cent), Hungary (8 per cent) and Poland (5 per cent), but below Romania (29 per cent), Croatia (18 per cent) and Turkey (14 per cent). In fact, the growth of Bulgarian publications lags behind the world's average and, consequently, Bulgaria's

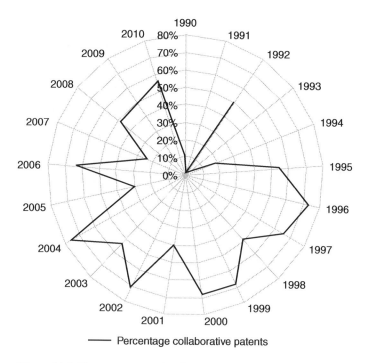

Figure 11.3 The percentage of Bulgarian patents with international co-inventors (source: own computations based on utility patents granted at USPTO).

contribution to the global pool of publications decreased from 0.19 per cent in 1996 to 0.14 per cent in 2008. Another challenge Bulgaria faces is improving the quality of this output, namely achieving greater impacts in its specialities. Looking at the H-index,[12] Bulgaria has a score of 97 (it has 97 papers with at least 97 citations between 1996 and 2008), similar to Romania and Croatia, but below Turkey, Hungary or Poland (Table A.11.2, Appendix).

The scientific strengths of Bulgarian publications reside in the fields of physics (optics, applied, condensed matter and multidisciplinary), chemistry and engineering (materials science, electrical and electronics). The largest increases are in optics and electrical and electronic engineering, while the most notable decrease occurred in multidisciplinary sciences (see Figure 11.4). Overall, Bulgaria's pure science and engineering remain the main source of international publications. The specialization patterns are shown in Table 11.3, based on an index that measures the ratio of the country's world share of publications in a discipline to the world share in all disciplines.[13] Similar to patenting, three quarters of Bulgaria's scientific production occurs around Sofia (Academy of Science, University of Sofia and University of Chemistry, Technology and Manufacturing are the most prolific institutions), while other regions (Varna, Plovdiv, Pavlikeni) are far less visible (Table A.11.4, Appendix).

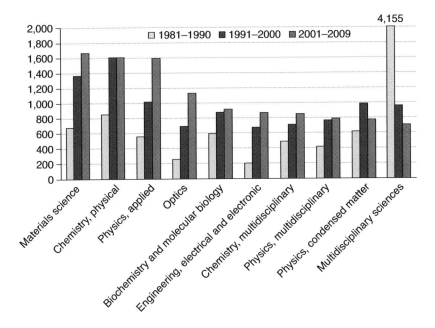

Figure 11.4 Distribution of Bulgarian scientific publications (source: own calculations based on SCOPUS database, accessed March 2012).

Overall, the impact of Bulgarian science remains far below European comparators. Its global share of scientific publications is 0.14 per cent, similar to Romania (0.22 per cent) and Croatia (0.18 per cent), but behind bigger countries such as Turkey (1.17 per cent) or more prolific ones, such as Hungary (0.38 per cent), Finland (0.65 per cent) or Italy (3.27 per cent). Moreover, when controlling for scientific output quality, the situation does not improve (see Figure 11.5). New

Table 11.3 Scientific specialization index for Bulgaria

Disciplines	1996	2008
Agricultural and biological sciences	0.77	1.22
Biochemistry, genetics and molecular biology	1.03	1.10
Chemical engineering	2.02	1.52
Chemistry	1.96	1.98
Computer science	0.63	0.65
Engineering	0.59	0.69
Materials science	2.07	1.40
Mathematics	2.12	1.56
Medicine	0.76	0.59
Physics and astronomy	1.84	2.17

Source: own calculations based on SCOPUS data (2012).

funding policies could narrow this gap if fresh resources were allocated to institutions that demonstrate measurable increases in the impact of their research. This will create a more competitive environment in which management of research institutes is encouraged to increase the quality of research, and not just the head-count of full-time researchers.

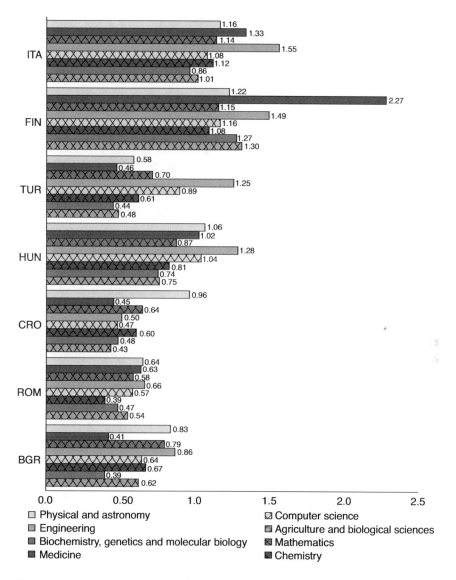

Figure 11.5 Relative impact index in selected disciplines for Bulgaria and comparators (source: own calculations for the period 1996–2008 based on SCOPUS database, accessed March 2012).

The literature on the economics of science (Partha and David, 1994; Stephan, 1996) underlines the importance of micro-level incentives in stimulating publishing in high-impact and peer-reviewed journals. But the incentive framework operating in Bulgaria tends to reward the length of time that researchers have been employed rather than the quality of scientific outputs. In the US Ivy League universities or R&D institutes such as the National Institutes of Health (NIH), the 'tenure track' process provides a useful filtering function for junior faculty on their way to be promoted to tenured faculty (i.e. associate and later on full professors). This includes a stringent review of the number of publications in peer-reviewed journals, the teaching record, evaluations, etc.

Note that the relative scientific impact index is computed as the ratio of the world share of citations for a country A between 1996 and 2008 to the world share of A's publications in a certain year. A value above 1 indicates that country A received more citations per paper (thus is more visible) than the global average.

Finally, a look at the most influential scholarly articles with a Bulgarian author using the 'New Hot Papers' section of ISI Thomson reveals that these stem from, in this order, the fields of physics, clinical medicine, chemistry and engineering[14] (Table A.11.3, Appendix). Moreover, like patenting, most of these articles are co-authored and more often with researchers from abroad. While this identifies the existence of a couple of 'star' scientists, it suggests that Bulgaria needs to strive for more external collaborations as an avenue to enrich its scientific perspectives.

The share of co-authored publications with foreign scientists has increased tremendously, from 16 per cent in the communist period (1981–1990) to 35 per cent in the 1990s, and over 50 per cent in the present day (Table A.11.5, Appendix). Most foreign collaborators come from Germany, France Italy and the USA, although recent trends record an increase in partnerships with scientists from other EU countries (Belgium, Spain and Poland) and Russia.[15] These are very positive developments since bibliometric studies find that papers with international co-authors have significantly more visibility and impact (measured by citations) than is otherwise the case (Figg *et al.*, 2006; Ma and Guan, 2005; Inzelt *et al.*, 2009).

3.2.2 Innovation and exports: firm-level insights

In this section, I will focus on one important set of actors in the national STI systems – namely, the group of innovating firms – try to understand what distinguishes innovating from non-innovating firms and cross-tabulate these characteristics with their export status. Business or private R&D is commonly regarded as a country's main driver of innovation in the literature (Furman *et al.*, 2002). To capture different aspects of business innovation in Bulgaria, I will rely on recent firm-level surveys that provide interesting insights into the differences between innovating and non-innovating firms, and the relative importance of several factors in both stimulating and dampening innovation in Bulgaria.

The results of these enterprise surveys suggest that Bulgarian firms are actively upgrading their product lines, but a minority diversifies via new products, and only few actually finance long-term R&D projects (see Table 11.4). This finding is consistent with the low level of private R&D for the country (0.15 per cent of GDP), which is way below the European average. Moreover, such low participation corresponds to a lack of entrepreneurial spirit from Bulgarian firms, which prefer to limit themselves to improvements and upgrades of their existing processes/products rather than diversifying company portfolios of products and exports. Finally, it matches the strategic direction of exports focused on traditional low-tech products with relative stable market shares and less uncertainty from competitors or technological shifts.

BEEPS data for 2013 shows that, in the last three years, almost 25 per cent of companies have introduced a new product line or service, 17 per cent have developed process innovations and 30 per cent have introduced managerial and logistical innovations. However, only 8.3 per cent of firms declare that they have invested in R&D in the same period. An analysis of Bulgarian companies grouped according to their innovation and exporting propensities shows that companies that perform innovative activities are larger than average, with innovating firms that export being even larger, suggesting possible benefits from industrial policies that support economies of scale and several large producers in the market. Moreover, the results highlight the importance of clusters since most innovating companies are located near Sofia, even more so for innovating exporters. Finally, affiliation with foreign companies or multinationals significantly increases the chances of innovating and exporting: one in four firms in the exporting innovating cluster has significant FDI, compared to one in fifteen firms in the non-exporting innovating cluster. These results highlight the importance of firm size, location and FDI on domestic firms' success in terms of innovation and exports. These effects are more obvious when splitting the sample into innovative versus non-innovative exporters: the former have a great impact on growth and job creation through increased sales and new personnel hired at about one and a half times the growth rate for the latter.

These findings are in line with the Schumpeterian perspective whereby large firms that are internationally connected via FDI deploy resources to increase their innovative capacity, leading to a technological comparative advantage that opens up export opportunities (Cohen *et al.*, 1987). Moreover, they mirror to a large extent the distribution of firms in the latest Community Innovation Survey (CIS) concerning innovators' size, profile and export propensity. Firms that innovate and export tend to have, on average, more advanced internal capabilities, although there are nuanced differences between the categories (see Table 11.4).

These results also document the importance of competitive pressures for innovation with straightforward policy implications. In Bulgaria, most managers identify domestic competition as an important factor that affects the firms' decision to develop new products, services and markets. An important aspect, salient in emerging economies such as Bulgaria, is informal competition, which is strongly supported by both innovators and non-innovators that cater to the domestic market (see Table 11.5). Moreover, financing is a significant barrier: about one in five innovative companies face constraints in their access to finance. Similarly, the

Table 11.4 Firm internal capabilities development across innovators and exporters

Firm internal capabilities	Non-innovators	Innovators	Non-exporters	Exporters
Percentage of companies that have conducted R&D	2.27	27.4	6.85	13.51
Percentage of companies with an online presence (website)	58.2	64.38	53.88	77.03
Percentage of companies with internationally recognized quality certification (ISO 9000/9002/14000)	22.27	37.00	20.55	44.59
Average percentage of employees with university degree	21.83	25.65	22.56	23.45
Percentage of firms that allow employees to explore new ideas	10.85	34.29	16.59	16.90
Percentage of firms using licensed technology (excepting software)	7.27	24.66	9.13	18.92
Percentage of firms where an inadequately educated workforce is a major or important obstacle to current operations	9.54	20.55	12.87	13.51
Number of firms	73	220	74	219

Source: own estimates based on BEEPS 2013 data.

Note
The definition of innovating firms is based on their performance in terms of new product innovations (both to the market and to the firm), while exporting firms are those that export both directly and indirectly.

Table 11.5 External drivers and obstacles for firm innovation and exports

External factors	Non-innovators	Innovators	Non-exporters	Exporters
Percentage of companies for which pressure from informal competitors affects its operations	42.01	56.16	49.08	35.14
Percentage of companies for which corruption is a major obstacle that affects its operations	18.27	35.25	33.41	18.92
Percentage of companies that export their production	24.20	28.77	–	–
Percentage of companies that received subsidies from the government or EU over the last three years	6.85	10.96	6.42	12.16
Percentage of companies for which access to finance is an obstacle to its operations	18.63	23.29	18.35	16.11
Top three elements in the business environment which represent the biggest obstacle faced by the firm	• Access to finance • Access to land • Business licenses and permits	• Access to finance • Corruption • Courts	• Access to finance • Access to land • Business licenses and permits	• Access to finance • Business licenses and permits • Corruption
Number of companies	73	220	74	219

Source: own estimates based on BEEPS 2013 data.

Note
The definition of innovating firms is based on their performance in terms of new product innovations (both to the market and to the firm), while exporting firms are those that export both directly and indirectly.

Bulgarian CIS data highlight that these finance-related aspects are severely impacted by current macroeconomic conditions (Correa and Iootty, 2011).[16]

In terms of incentives, few Bulgarian firms (around 10 per cent) have received a grant from the state or the EU, which suggests that demand-side innovation measures need to be scaled up to have an impact. To strengthen their impact, the demand side of innovation policies must be expanded through various measures documented in the literature: matching grants and venture capital (VC) funds to co-finance private R&D and technology commercialization, promote entrepreneurial innovation and adopt international quality certification and ICT technology. Implementation of some of these instruments may prove to be difficult and therefore a clear prior understanding of what is feasible for Bulgaria is crucial.

Understanding the drivers and suppressing factors of firm innovation is critical to policy design, in particular for selecting the appropriate support instruments. These insights can help tailor and structure innovation support from the government: for example, tax credits are more suitable for large companies, whereas business incubators and matching grants are better at incentivizing start-ups and SMEs. Section 4 offers recommendations to improve existing support instruments in the present national and European context. Among them, a critical policy design issue is concerned with the selection criteria for awarding public financing programmes. The selection criteria is a major challenge since a poor selection of beneficiaries of financial instruments will significantly reduce the impact of the subsidies provided. The factors that are associated with innovation point to criteria that could help to filter companies based on their track record of investments so that the firms with the greatest capacity are supported.

4 Policy implications: complementing standard lessons with systemic provisions

As a laggard within the EU, Bulgaria is subject to some standard policy recipes regarding both industrial and STI development. However, the purpose of this exercise was to identify and complement these standard responses with systemic insights that usually escape the eye of policymakers, given their long-term orientation. Hence, following these analyses, I propose several recommendations to address some of the issues identified in the previous sections. Overall, I group these recommendations into two major areas of interest.

4.1 'Standard' policy measures which help address obvious deficiencies in the area of export promotion and STI

(a) Stimulate exports of products with increased sophistication and technological intensity in line with scientific capabilities and specialization

Diversification into higher value-added goods and services in the mid-term to long-term is an indispensable ingredient for sustaining export growth and international competitiveness. Bulgaria retains a mediocre position in this regard, with only 3 per cent high-tech exports. There is a great need to support these high-potential areas via both domestic and FDI-driven innovation as well as stimulation of linkages with correspondent scientific bodies in forms of technical parks and business incubators. Moreover, bottlenecks faced by firms in these high-potential industries, whether skills, infrastructure or other issues, should be removed through concerted policy measures.

(b) Encourage long-term private R&D investment and increase the overall funding for R&D and science as an engine of long-term growth

Enterprise surveys suggest that, as well as lacking the necessary skills, firms are not encouraged to undertake their own R&D projects. In fact, the financing of innovation projects is very problematic (20 per cent) and the number of available grants is insufficient. These results in significant losses for the Bulgarian economy, given the clear differences in terms of value and job creation between exporters and non-exporters, especially those that also innovate. In order to meet its proposed target (1.5 per cent of GDP for R&D), the government needs to increase the absorption of EU funds, lift public spending and raise efficiency of its national funding instruments. Estimates point out that this will require the absorption of €539.2 million from the Operational Programme 'Development of the Competitiveness of the Bulgarian Economy' funds by 2015 (World Bank, 2012). So far, the absorption of European funds has been very slow due to a multitude of factors (low administrative capacity, excessive red tape and restrictive eligibility criteria, poor awareness of the programmes, lack of pre-finance activities). Bulgaria could also benefit more from fostering participation in other European initiatives, such as Eurostars, JEREMIE and CIP.[17] Public spending needs a boost as well as its efficiency levels, so that each €1 spent on innovation and R&D finds the best utilization.[18] National instruments need to play a crucial role as project pipelines for EU support since they are the only source available for funding early-stage R&D. While these instruments grew substantially after 2005, they suffered significant cuts due to greater fiscal discipline and budget constraints in the wake of the global crisis.

(c) Stimulate international STI cooperation and target productivity and international impact through new funding schemes.

In terms of innovation, after a severe plunge throughout the 1990s, the Bulgarian supply of new technologies is slowly picking up, driven mostly by foreign sources of technologies. Most of these new patents granted to Bulgarians by USPTO come from high-tech industries, especially computers and communications, as a result of the R&D efforts of multinationals in Bulgaria. These developments emphasize the crucial aspect of supporting and encouraging inward 'high-tech' FDI into the country as a gateway to world-class innovators and corporate R&D. The present performance of Bulgarian science calls for similar measures to support international collaboration and flows of knowledge via people and projects. Moreover, scientific productivity needs to be incentivized through funding increases to research institutions conditional on measurable improvements in impact metrics. This would create a more competitive environment in which research institute management is encouraged to increase the quality of research undertaken.

(d) Develop targeted innovation policies and instruments for selected priority sectors

There is an urgent need to develop targeted innovation policies and instruments for priority sectors. My analysis suggests that there are several viable options (i.e. pharmaceuticals and IT) for future export champions that can be fuelled by FDI inflows and a strong domestic scientific base. However, both of these industries face specific challenges and require tailored policy interventions from the government. Specific obstacles for the development of the pharmaceuticals industry include administrative hurdles that delay entry by generic drug producers, informal market competition from countries outside the EU and limited uptake of funding instruments for innovation. Similarly, the development of the IT industry could be facilitated by a strategic orientation in funding and resource availability for firms, broadband infrastructure development, leaner legislative burden, the development of education curricula in schools and universities and stronger IPR laws.

4.2 Measures to target the systemic issues identified in this study

Besides these standard policy recommendations for spurring innovation, Bulgaria could benefit significantly by implementing several measures to target the systemic issues identified in this study. These systemic policy measures will address issues that hinder the development of successful STI systems across four main structural dimensions (Chaminade and Edquist, 2010)

(e) Actors' problems

A salient issue identified in this study regarding the issues faced by one of the main actors of STI systems (firms) remains the low level of private R&D which is the main engine of innovation in developed nations (Furman *et al.*, 2002). Overall, the R&D intensity of the country (0.15 per cent of GDP) mirrors its low overall innovative and entrepreneurial rate of domestic activities. While there are Bulgarian firms that perform R&D and employ it in production, thus improving their export figures and performance, this percentage remains relatively small (28 per cent) compared with developed Western economies. Moreover, geographically speaking, these firms are heavily concentrated around the capital city (Sofia), which poses difficulties for sustainable growth across all other regions. Policy measures should seek to create an environment that stimulates innovation through effective funding schemes (i.e. operational programmes, national instruments, venture capital, foreign investors), stronger links between research and business and a functional system for commercialization of technologies. Therefore, initial exercises to diagnose and map potential trajectories for different industries are required, complemented by significant measures (streamlining, transparency, early support schemes, rigorous evaluation measures) to improve the funding of innovation and the protection of intellectual property (IP) resulting from this process.

Likewise, for universities, public labs and other entities involved in the creation of applied and basic science, the analysis has revealed significant challenges that boil down to developing and sustaining a globally relevant STI system that is driven by excellence in certain core areas. The Bulgarian Academy of Sciences, as well as supporting universities and research institutes, needs a restructured system of distribution of research funds, one that is more transparent and equitable vis-à-vis the performance and relevance of the research conducted in these institutions. The introduction of policy measures that encourage collaboration with private firms as well as foreign researchers within consortia is greatly needed, complemented by measures that facilitate the disclosure and monetization of IP.

Finally, highly skilled human capital is crucial to STI development. Therefore, competitive funding schemes should be introduced based on individual and institutional merits with the aim of retaining and repatriating top Bulgarian scientists. In the medium and long term, the emphasis should also be placed on human capital formation by providing additional incentives for young people to study science and technical subjects, and tie up the links with the needs of the industry (through development of joint courses, research programmes or scholarships).

(f) Institutional deficiencies

The Bulgarian STI system suffers from numerous institutional deficiencies. First, it lacks coherence across actors and across time. With numerous actors involved in these systems, it is important to ensure that there is a long-term common vision and goals that all the parties are involved in. The current institutional arrangements of Bulgaria regarding STI span across multiple levels and responsible entities (*strategy/priority setting* – Council of Ministers; *policy formulation and evaluation* – different Ministries; *advisory* – National Council for Innovation and National Council for Scientific Research; *implementation* – National Funds for Science and, respectively, Innovation; *STI activities* – universities, firms, labs, institutes, etc.), which makes coordination difficult. Moreover, these entities often have different strategies to develop separate components of the STI systems (e.g. human capital formation, scientific excellence, etc.) in isolation from the other levels of the system.

Aiming for vertical integration of governance mechanisms or at least coherence of existing policies and tasks would improve the speed of the policy measures and warrant better results for the system as a whole. Moreover, streamlining the institutional framework that spans innovation and R&D would help Bulgaria to fully exploit the opportunities provided by EU funds that support competitiveness and human resource development. There are two separate Operational Programmes (OP) supporting scientific research and innovation in Bulgaria – OP Competitiveness and OP Human Resources. These programmes are not well coordinated and they have different implementation authorities and instruments to foster R&D. To maximize the impact from public investments, it would be useful to strengthen the links between the support instruments and consolidate the implementing bodies in the subsequent programming period.

(g) Infrastructure

Broadly speaking, infrastructure can refer to the physical, financial and knowledge infrastructure of a country. In terms of infrastructural problems, they can refer to absence of a specific type of infrastructure or inadequate or lower quality when it is available but not functioning properly. For physical infrastructure (e.g. roads, railways), one aspect that is relevant to STI is connectedness with the rest of the world. IT penetration has increased substantially in Bulgaria over the past decade and about 48.8 per cent of its population has access to the internet. However, this is still substantially lower than the European average (71 per cent), impeding access to information and resources that are critical for the development of STI systems. Therefore, investments in IT infrastructure should be a priority for the Bulgarian government. In the case of financial infrastructure, the BEEPS data highlights the fact that most Bulgarian firms perceive 'access to finance' to be a significant barrier to innovation and about 20 per cent describe it as an obstacle for their daily operations. This fact has become even more salient now after the crisis, when financial resources have become even harder to secure, and appears to affect both innovating and exporting firms alike. Therefore, a number of procedures to further support business innovation could be implemented: increasing the transparency of funding (clear guidelines, reducing the number of requirements to only the most relevant ones) and redesigning scoring criteria for funding proposals so that experts are able to evaluate them easily. Moreover, when designing different support programmes (e.g. business incubators, mobile application labs, technology transfer offices, innovation vouchers, etc.), the government should distinguish between existing firms and startups so that they can be supported with different instruments (World Bank, 2012). Finally, as depicted in previous sections, the quality of the existing basic and applied knowledge infrastructure of Bulgaria is still low, both in terms of absolute numbers (number of patents or publications per capita) and in terms of impact (few patents and articles retain good positions in terms of citations vis-à-vis of their international peers). This is partly a result of path dependency given the skewed specialization of STI towards mature and low-tech fields and partly a result of the obvious complementarity problem existing between various components of the STI system, which will be analysed in the next sub-section. Only a small number of research organizations are able to conduct research on a par with international peers, and among these the Bulgarian Academy of Sciences retains the central role, although only half of the research institutes in it have international visibility in their areas of expertise (World Bank, 2012).

(h) Interactions

Lastly, my analysis has revealed significant interaction problems between various actors in the STI systems. These can be broadly classified as complementarity issues or lack of interactions between actors due to weak networks (Chaminade and Edquist, 2010). The analysis of STI systems shows a significant gap between the research (basic science, measured using bibliometric data) branch and the applied one (commercial innovation, measured using patent data). Medical and chemical fields are well under-represented in terms of applied science where the bulk of international patents are in the broad field of IT and deal with database and file management. Moreover, there are also weak connections with the production and export side of the economy, in line with the weak participation of firms in STI activities and their specialization in low-tech and resource-intensive products for global markets. Both mineral-based products and electronics lack a strong scientific and patent base to support a related-diversification strategy that would allow Bulgaria to branch out into higher value-added products with a high technological content. Thus, there is a stringent need to bridge the gap between STI components and the economic realities and needs of the Bulgarian economy (producing and exporting firms). This can be done through specific support instruments, such as collaborative research grants between private firms and public institutions and universities aimed at spurring excellence in research and fast commercialization strategies, or consortia programmes meant to develop STI and E networks and partnerships. These measures should combine both demand-pull (i.e. governmental contracts) and supply-push (i.e. incentives to innovate, IP benefits and protection, etc.) instruments that will deepen the connections between these actors and make innovation and research a much more fruitful avenue for future endeavours.

5 Conclusions and future agenda

STI policies are regarded today as important tools for enhancing the competitiveness and welfare of nations. These actions seek to optimize the interrelations between actors and components of these systems and must account for a multitude of factors. Competitiveness involves high STI dynamism, being able to change and adapt fast to a new environment and taking advantage of the existing knowledge and technologies. This dynamism is improved through multiple measures that target and incentivize various components in STI systems, such as industrial cluster policies, R&D and science support, taxation and education policies, to name a few, with a clear objective of improving the long-term competitiveness at the national (regional) level. Moreover, in many cases, supra-national bodies are involved in this coordination (e.g. European Research Area for the EU, the MERCOSUR for Latin America or the ASEAN in South-East Asia) and are initiating multiple avenues for advancement.

In this study, I have provided a systemic analysis of a country's international competitiveness, using export data, and its qualitative links with domestic STI capabilities, as proxied by its scientific and innovation performance. As a case study, I have applied this framework to Bulgaria using a set of quantitative and qualitative data to obtain a comprehensive picture of its STI and economic systems. Bulgaria was chosen as a representative case both for transition economies from Eastern Europe and for other developing nations that aim to improve their international export competitiveness and use it as a growth-enhancing tool in the post-crisis period. The results of these analyses supplemented with information on Bulgarian STI from surveys and secondary data yield several stringent (short-term) policy recommendations, as well as lessons and advice for the long and medium term to tackle both 'standard'(i.e. market-failures) and 'systemic' issues (i.e. pertaining to the well-functioning of STI systems) that plague the future development of Bulgarian STI systems. The proposed solutions call for a comprehensive and harmonized response across STI systems and account for both Bulgarian (National Reform Programme 2011–2015) and European realities (Europe 2020 agenda).

Overall, Bulgaria has made significant improvements over the last decade in terms of living standards. However, the recent crisis has revealed, as for many other countries, that this growth was built on unsustainable grounds by being rooted in financial and real estate bubbles. Its competitive position in terms of trade is based on low-tech and low-value added products that lack sophistication and diversification opportunities. This is a direct result of poor technological performance that still depends heavily on mature sectors from the historical lock-in that was set-up during the previous regime. As a consequence, the socialist legacy still weighs down on the scientific Bulgarian profile and the decouple between R&D and production remains significant. Most researchers are employed in higher education and public research institutes around the country, which severely limits the absorptive capacity of domestic firms. Businesses lack incentives and financial resources to undertake innovation, which in turn dictates their chances of success, both domestic and international. The scientific and technological competences accumulated are quite narrow and rapidly moving towards obsolescence, while the shift towards current relevant and rewarding areas of research battles with systemic inertia, a lack of skilled human capital and financial restraints.

So what opportunities does Bulgaria have to harness STI for competitiveness and growth? Throughout the sections of this analysis, I have provided several indications of what needs to be done now and in the near future. In Section 4, I provide a synthesis of these recommendations grouped into 'standard' innovation policy advice (i.e. increase overall R&D intensity, incentivize private firms to undertake innovation, etc.) and potential solutions to 'systemic' issues (i.e. the disconnect between STI components, the streamlining of the national innovation system, etc.) identified by this study. It is clear that Bulgaria needs a good dosage of both in order to rekindle its innovation capabilities and it must harness them more efficiently to boost its STI and economic performance.

Bulgarian STI systems need to be restructured in a way that addresses some of the systemic fallacies identified in this study. Channels for communication among actors within these systems (firms, universities, Academy of Sciences) need to be streamlined so that the exchange of knowledge and alignment of interests and cross-incentives goes smoothly. Enterprises themselves need to change as well: they should adopt R&D as a vehicle for future success and pursue it internally as well as externally through alliances and collaboration with universities or institutes. Finally, despite significant institutional change since 1990, much remains to be improved in this area. To meet its EU targets, Bulgaria will need to considerably increase its absorption of EU funds for competitiveness and human resource development, lift public spending, target priority sectors, streamline the institutional STI framework and raise the efficiency of its national instruments. The latter plays a crucial role in creating a project pipeline for EU support programmes, as the only funding source for early-stage R&D. Moreover, there is a need for policy integration and harmonization that stems from both the systemic nature of STI and lessons of current failures, such as the achievement of 'knowledge-based' status for the EU as a whole. Blindly following a strategy to increase certain innovative inputs (e.g. targeting R&D expenditures of x per cent, giving out tax breaks) does not guarantee success in the absence of other factors that are related to a country's factor endowments and institutional characteristics (e.g. qualified workforce, efficient patent system, etc.). Thus, continuous adjustments and a systemic approach towards tailoring Bulgarian STI systems will be required in order to achieve technology-induced international competitiveness.

Appendix

Table A.11.1 Top 15 products contributing to Bulgarian export sophistication (EXPY)

Code	Short product description	PRODY (PPP)	Contribution to EXPY (%)	Exports, $US mil.	RCA	UVD
6821	Copper and copper alloys refined	12,822	6.12	1,920	20.69	0.45
5417	Medicaments (including veterinary)	28,535	2.20	530	0.67	0.08
0412	Other wheat and meslin, unmilled	18,566	2.05	311	7.31	0.05
6744	Sheet, plates, rolled of thick iron	18,933	1.66	446	5.83	0.02
7492	Cocks, valves and similar appliances	26,543	1.42	355	2.04	0.05
6732	Bars, rods (not wire rod)	15,586	1.37	216	3.97	0.12
6842	Aluminium and aluminium alloys	19,884	1.30	355	2.82	0.03
6822	Copper and copper alloys, worked	13,582	1.27	265	4.37	0.05
2820	Waste and scrap metal of iron	13,049	1.00	211	4.06	0.02
8439	Women, girls, infants outerwear	17,819	0.97	198	3.34	0.05
7781	Batteries and electric accumulators	20,364	0.84	565	2.92	0.04
8745	Measuring, controlling instruments	24,670	0.79	310	10.47	0.04
8451	Outerwear knitted or crocheted	20,962	0.76	220	2.29	0.02
0484	Bakery products	17,913	0.72	166	4.82	0.01
7752	Domestic refrigerators	17,138	0.72	129	6.15	0.06

Source: own calculations for 2008 based on UN COMTRADE, 2010. Product codes are SITC Rev. 2 at four digits.

Notes

RCA is computed using the Balassa method; UVD (unit value distance) is computed for each product as the log difference between unit values in the highest-price country for an exported product and Bulgaria's exports at SITC four-digit level.

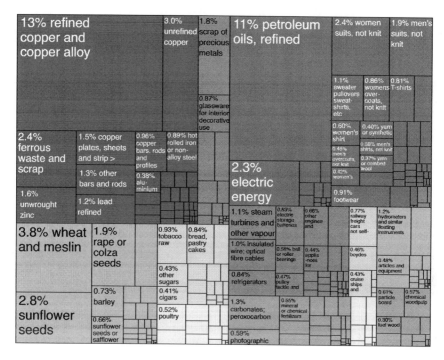

Figure A.11.1 Composition of net exports for Bulgaria, 2010 (source: adapted from the
Observatory of Economic Activity, http://atlas.media.mit.edu/, accessed
December 2012).

Note
Net exports are defined as the value of a country's total exports minus the value of its total imports in
a given product class.

Table A.11.2 Scientific publications and citation totals

Country	Citable documents	Citations	Citations per document	Scientific impact (H index)
Italy	581,455	6,809,577	12.29	432
Finland	121,358	1,714,200	15.10	273
Hungary	70,330	633,534	9.37	183
Turkey	162,296	821,820	6.03	139
Bulgaria	29,342	165,992	5.92	97
Romania	41,408	175,079	5.00	96
Croatia	30,886	136,669	4.90	92

Source: own calculations based on data for the period 1996–2008 obtained from SCIMAGO and
SCOPUS (accessed March 2012).

Table A.11.3 Top five Bulgarian 'hot' scientific papers in terms of citations

Rank	Title	Field	Bulgarian author	No. co-authors	Institution	Citations	Year
1	Predicting cardiovascular risk...	Clinical medicine	Nachev, C.	13	Alexandrovs Univ. Hosp., Dept of Internal Med., Sofia	554	1999
2	Global positioning system constraints on plate kinematics....	Geosciences	Georgiev, I.	28	National Acad. of Science, Geodesy Dept, Sofia	494	2000
3	Antiphospholipid syndrome – clinical and immunologic manifestations...	Clinical medicine	Baleva, M.	22	Medical University of Sofia	418	2002
4	Shaped-pulse optimization of coherent emission...	Physics	Kapteyn, H.C.	8	Univ. of Sofia, Dept of Physics	346	2000
5	Identification of neutral and charged nxoy surface species...	Chemistry	Hadjivanov, K.I.	0	Bulgarian Acad. Sci., Inst. Gen. & Inorgan. Chemistry	319	2000

Source: own calculations based on Essential Science Indicators for the period 1996–2008 (accessed March 2012).

Table A.11.4 Top Bulgarian institutions in terms of scientific publications

Main institutional contributors	1981–1990			1991–2000			2001–2009		
	Rank	*Total*	*%*	*Rank*	*Total*	*%*	*Rank*	*Total*	*%*
Bulgarian Academy of Sciences	1	7,977	53.76	1	9,744	52.15	1	10,473	49.08
University of Sofia	2	2,062	13.90	2	3,052	16.33	2	2,737	12.83
Medical University, Sofia	3	1,058	7.13	4	351	1.88	3	1,076	5.04
Univ. Chem. Tech. and Metallurgy	4	514	3.46	9	236	1.26	4	846	3.96
Medical Academy, Sofia	7	156	1.05	6	275	1.47	5	595	2.79
Total	14,839			18,685			21,340		

Source: author's own calculations based on Web of Science data (accessed March 2012).

Table A.11.5 Top scientific partners in Bulgarian publications

International collaborations	1981–1990			1991–2000			2001–2009		
	Rank	*Total*	*%*	*Rank*	*Total*	*%*	*Rank*	*Total*	*%*
Germany	2	590	3.97	1	1,694	9.07	1	2,845	13.33
USA	3	225	1.52	2	1,061	5.68	2	1,759	8.24
France	5	201	1.35	3	896	4.80	3	1,452	6.80
Italy	8	120	0.81	4	715	3.83	4	1,320	6.19
England	7	120	0.81	7	392	2.10	5	964	4.52
Spain	27	15	0.10	6	486	2.60	6	866	4.06
Russian Federation	1	874	5.89	5	622	3.33	7	836	3.92
Belgium	22	25	0.17	13	240	1.28	8	800	3.75
Poland	6	146	0.98	13	240	1.28	9	767	3.59
Switzerland	18	37	0.25	10	293	1.57	10	608	2.85
Total		14,839			18,685			21,340	

Source: author's own calculations based on Web of Science data (accessed March 2012).

Notes

1 The author would like to thank participants at the EU-SPRI 2013 (Madrid) and Globelics 2012 (Hangzhou, China), Gabriel J. Goddard and Adelheid Holl for useful comments and suggestions. The author acknowledges financial support for this research, as part of the World Bank technical assistance project 'Enhancing Bulgaria's Competitiveness and Exports through Technology Absorption and Innovation' (2010–2012).

2 In Porter's model, all four main determinants of competitiveness (firm strategy, structure and rivalry; demand conditions; supporting industries; factor conditions) are subject to policy stimuli from the government.

3 The two most popular measures are the ones prepared by the International Institute for Management Development (IMD) and the World Economic Forum (WEF). However, all these constructs lack a strong theoretical backbone.

4 For example, Bulgaria's GDP per capita in PPP terms is still below this point, averaging US$13,000 in 2009.

5 The main weakness of these measures lies in the data quality and availability and harmonization across countries and time.

6 Aerospace, computers, office machinery, electronics, instruments, pharmaceuticals, electrical machinery and armament are considered high-technology sectors according to OECD classifications.

7 Europe 2020 is a ten-year strategy proposed by the European Commission in 2010 aiming for 'smart, sustainable and inclusive, growth', which follows the Lisbon EU strategy (2000–2010). Among the elements of this strategy, smart specialization is a policy framework that suggests countries should specialize and promote innovation in areas where they have comparative advantage, regardless of whether they are high-tech or low-tech ones.

8 The two sources of data we draw on have the advantage of providing comparable data across countries. Due to the significant costs involved and the perceived future value of the invention, only the best Bulgarian innovations will apply for a patent abroad. As a result, there is a downward bias for developing countries when analysing their international patenting rates.

9 The latter provides a broader picture of the technologies that are developed in the Bulgarian economy; however, national patenting rates tend to be noisier measures and not useful for cross-country comparisons.

10 Patents granted to Bulgarian inventors declined substantially post-1990, but there has been a surge since 2000, mostly due to the activity of SAP labs, a German IT company.

11 As a well-known limitation, both Web of Science and Essential Science Indicators do not monitor any Bulgarian language journals; however, SCOPUS covers several such publications.

12 This measure was developed by Jorge Hirsch and equals h if a country publishes h papers each of which has been cited by others at least h times in the considered time frame.

13 The performance and specialization of comparator countries reveals both similarities and differences with Bulgaria. Romania's scientific strengths are very similar and lie mainly in chemical engineering (2.55), chemistry (2.03) and mathematics (2.61). Croatia tends to do well in social sciences (2.68), agricultural and biosciences (1.52) and environmental sciences (1.34). Hungary has a larger pool of strong fields, ranging from arts and humanities (1.21) to neuroscience (2.56), mathematics (2.17) and veterinary medicine (1.66). Turkey is very strong in dentistry (2.92), energy (1.58) and veterinary (2.23). Finland has an advantage in neuroscience (1.22), business and management (1.36), economics (1.15), environmental science (1.90), computer science (1.50) and decision science (1.69). Italy tends to do better in decision science (1.33) and dentistry (1.34).

14 This list is based on the number of citations received, corrected by field propensities. The top five 'hot' Bulgarian papers come from medicine, physics, chemistry and geosciences (March 2010), and most of them are co-authored and international.

15 According to SCOPUS data, increases in terms of international cooperation have been similar for Finland (from 33 per cent to 49 per cent) and Italy (30 to 41 per cent), while the rest of the comparator countries have been less impressive in this respect (on average 1 to 5 per cent between 1996 and 2008).

16 The CIS asks companies to classify the factors that hamper enterprise innovation activities according to their importance. The main obstacles to the enterprise operations reported by the CIS in Bulgaria are the high cost of innovations (4.8 per cent of firms), the lack of funds within the enterprise (4 per cent), the lack of sources outside the company (3.1 per cent), market power of the established companies (2.4 per cent) and lack of qualified workforce (2.2 per cent).

17 Eurostars is a European Joint Programme dedicated to R&D performing SMEs; JEREMIE is the Joint European Resources for Micro to Medium Enterprises; CIP stands for Competitiveness and Innovation Framework Programme, run by the European Commission.

18 In 2011, 0.8 per cent of the planned total budgetary expenditures were allocated to science, 2.8 per cent of which are capital expenditures.

References

Acs, Z.J., L. Anselin and A. Varga. 2002. Patents and innovation counts as measures of regional production of new knowledge. *Research Policy* 31(7): 1069–1085.

Aghion, P. and P. Howitt. 1992. A model of growth through creative destruction. *Econometrica* 60(2): 323–351.

Aghion, P., A. David and D. Foray. 2009. Science, technology and innovation for economic growth: towards linking policy research and practice in 'STIG systems'. *Research Policy* 38: 681–693.

Alcalá, F. and A. Ciccone. 2004. Trade and productivity. *The Quarterly Journal of Economics* 119(2): 612–645.

Arrow, K.J. 1962. Economic welfare and the allocation of resources for inventions, in Nelson, R.R. (ed.), *The Rate and Direction of Inventive Activity: Economic and Social Factors*. Princeton: Princeton University Press.

Aulet, B. 2008. *How to Build a Successful Innovation Ecosystem*. Sloan: MIT Press.

Bernard, A.B. and J.B. Jensen. 1999. Exceptional exporter performance: cause, effect, or both? *Journal of International Economics* 47(1): 1–25.

Cadot, O., C. Carrare and V. Strauss-Kahn. 2007. Export diversification: what's behind the Hump? *CEPR Discussion Papers*, 6590. http://ideas.repec.org/p/cpr/ceprdp/6590.html.

Cameron, G. 1996. Innovation and economic growth, Centre for Economic Performance, London School of Economics and Political Science.

Cassiman, B. and E. Golovko. 2007. Innovation and the export–productivity link. *SSRN eLibrary* (April). http://papers.ssrn.com/sol3/papers.cfm?abstract_id=1003366.

Castelacci, F. 2008. Innovation and competitiveness of industries: comparing the mainstream and evolutionary approaches. *Technological Forecasting and Social Change* 75: 984–1006.

Chaminade, C. and C. Edquist. 2010. Rationales for public intervention in the innovation process: a systems of innovation approach, in Smits, R., Kuhlmann, S. and Shapira, P. (eds), *The Theory and Practice of Innovation Policy: An International Research Handbook*. Cheltenham: Edward Elgar.

Cimoli, M. and G. Porcile. 2011. Global growth and international cooperation: a structuralist perspective. *Cambridge Journal of Economics* 35(2): 383–400.

Clerides, S.K., S. Lach and J.R. Tybout. 1998. Is learning by exporting important? Microdynamic evidence from Colombia, Mexico, and Morocco. *Quarterly Journal of Economics* 113(3): 903–947.

Coe, D.T. and E. Helpman. 1995. International R&D spillovers. *European Economic Review* 39(5): 859–887.

Cohen, W.M. and D.A. Levinthal. 1990. Absorptive capacity: a new perspective on learning and innovation. *Administrative Science Quarterly* 35: 128–152.

Cohen, W.M., R.C. Levin and D.C. Mowery. 1987. Firm size and R&D intensity: a reexamination. *Journal of Industrial Economics* 35(4): 543–565.

Correa P. and M. Iootty. 2011. R&D decisions during the crisis: firm-level evidence for selected eastern countries. *World Bank Group Enterprise Note No. 21*.

Damijan, J.P. and R. Kostevc. 2010. Learning from trade through innovation: causal link between imports, exports and innovation in Spanish microdata, *SSRN eLibrary* (August). http://papers.ssrn.com/sol3/papers.cfm?abstract_id=1658389

Damijan J.P., M. Rojec and M. Ferjancic. 2008. Growing export performance of transition economies: EU market access versus supply capacity factors. *LICOS Discussion Paper*, 20208.

D'Este, P. and P. Patel. 2007. University–industry linkages in the UK: what are the factors underlying the variety of interactions with industry? *Research Policy* 36(9): 1295–1313.

Dodgson, M. 2009. Asia's national innovation systems: institutional adaptability and rigidity in the face of global innovation challenges, in *Conference on Varieties of Asian Capitalism*, Brisbane, QLD, Australia, 10–12 December 2007.

Dollar, D. 1986. Technological innovations, capital mobility, and the product cycle in north–south trade. *American Economic Review* 76(1): 177–190.

Dosi, G. 1988. Sources, procedures, and microeconomic effects of innovation. *Journal of Economic Literature* 26(3): 1120–1171.

Dosi, G., K. Pavitt and L. Soete. 1990. *The Economics of Technical Change and International Trade*. LEM Book Series. Laboratory of Economics and Management (LEM), Sant'Anna School of Advanced Studies, Pisa, Italy. Available at: http://econpapers. repec.org/bookchap/ssalembks/dosietal-1990.htm.

Feenstra R.C. and A.K. Rose. 1997. *Putting Things in Order: Patterns of Trade Dynamics and Growth*. Cambridge, MA: National Bureau of Economic Research, Inc.

Figg, W., L. Dunn, D. Liewehr, S. Steinberg, P. Thurman, C. Barrett and J. Birkinshaw. 2006. Scientific collaboration results in higher citation rates of published articles. *Pharmacotherapy* 26(6): 759–767.

Freeman, C. 2002. Continental, national and sub-national innovation systems – complementarity and economic growth. *Research Policy* 31(2): 191–211.

Freeman, C. 2004. Technological infrastructure and international competitiveness. *Industrial and Corporate Change* 13(3): 541–569.

Furman, J., M. Porter and S. Stern. 2002. The determinants of national innovative capacity. *Research Policy* 31: 899–933.

Gibson, D.V. and H. Naquin. 2011. Investing in innovation to enable global competitiveness: the case of Portugal. *Technological Forecasting and Social Change* 78: 1299–1309.

Girma, S., D. Greenaway and R. Kneller. 2004. Does exporting increase productivity? A microeconometric analysis of matched firms. *Review of International Economics* 12(5): 855–866.

Goldberg I., L. Branstetter, J.G. Goddard and S. Kuriakose. 2008. Globalization and technology absorption in Europe and Central Asia: the role of trade, FDI, and cross-border knowledge flows. *World Bank Working Papers*, no. 150.

Grossman, G.M. and E. Helpman. 1991. Trade, knowledge spillovers, and growth. *European Economic Review* 35(2): 517–526.

Grossman, G.M. and E. Helpman. 1994. Technology and trade. *Working Paper 4926*. National Bureau of Economic Research. Available at: www.nber.org/papers/w4926.

Grupp, H. and M.E. Mogee. 2004. Indicators for national science and technology policy: how robust are composite indicators? *Research Policy* 33(9): 1373–1384.

Gu, S. 1999. *Implications of National Innovation Systems for Developing Countries: Managing Change and Complexity in Economic Development*. Tokyo: United Nations University, Institute for New Technologies.

Hadjimanolis, A. and K. Dickson. 2001. Development of national innovation policy in small developing countries: the case of Cyprus. *Research Policy* 30(5): 805–817.

Hall, R.E. and C.I. Jones. 1999. Why do some countries produce so much more output per worker than others? *The Quarterly Journal of Economics* 114(1): 83–116.

Hall, B.H., A.B. Jaffe and M. Trajtenberg. 2001. The NBER Patent Citation Data File: lessons, insights and methodological tools. *National Bureau of Economic Research Working Paper Series*, No. 8498.

Hausmann, R. and B. Klinger. 2008. *Achieving Export-Led Growth in Colombia*. Cambridge, MA: Center for International Development at Harvard University.

Hausmann, R., J. Hwang and D. Rodrik. 2007. What you export matters. *Journal of Economic Growth* 12(1): 1–25.

Hu, M.C. and J.A. Mathews. 2005. National innovative capacity in East Asia. *Research Policy* 34: 1322–1349.

Imbs, J. and R. Wacziarg. 2003. Stages of diversification. *American Economic Review* 93(1): 63–86.

IMD World Competitiveness Yearbook 1995–2010. Accessed at: www.worldcompetitiveness.com/ (September 2011).

Inzelt, A., A. Schubert and M. Schubert. 2009. Incremental citation impact due to international co-authorship in Hungarian higher education institutions. *Scientometrics* 78(1): 37–43.

Jarreau, J. and S. Poncet. 2012. Export sophistication and economic growth: evidence from China. *Journal of Development Economics* 97(2): 281–292.

Jenkins, R. 1998. Environmental regulation and international competitiveness: a review of the literature and some European evidence. *Discussion paper no. 9801*, UN INTECH, Maastricht.

Keller, W. 2004. International technology diffusion. *Journal of Economic Literature* 42(3): 752–782.

Keller, W. and S.R. Yeaple. 2009. Multinational enterprises, international trade, and productivity growth: firm-level evidence from the United States. *The Review of Economics and Statistics* 91(4): 821–831.

Kline, S.J. and N. Rosenberg. 1986. An overview of innovation, in Landau, R. and Rosenberg, N. (eds), *The Positive Sum Strategy: Harnessing Technology for Economic Growth*. Washington DC: National Academy Press.

Klinger, B. and D. Lederman. 2004. Discovery and development: an empirical exploration of new products. SSRN eLibrary (November). http://papers.ssrn.com/sol3/papers.cfm?abstract_id=625328.

Krammer, S.M.S. 2009. Drivers of national innovation in transition: evidence from a panel of Eastern European countries. *Research Policy* 38(5): 845–860.

Krugman, P. 1979. A model of innovation, technology transfer, and the world distribution of income. *Journal of Political Economy* 87(2): 253–266.

Krugman, P.R. 1994. Competitiveness: a dangerous obsession. *Foreign Affairs* 73(2): 1–17.

Lachenmaier, S. and L. Wößmann. 2006. Does innovation cause exports? Evidence from exogenous innovation impulses and obstacles using German micro data. *Oxford Economic Papers* 58(2): 317–350.

Lankhuizen, M. 2000. Shifts in foreign-trade, competitiveness and growth potential: from Baltics to 'Bal-techs'? *Research Policy* 29: 9–29.

Lee, J. 2011. Export specialization and economic growth around the world. *Economic Systems* 35: 45–63.

Leydesdorff, L. and H. Etzkowitz. 1998. The triple helix as a model for innovation studies. *Science and Public Policy* 25(3): 195–203.

Lumenga-Neso, O., M. Olarreaga and M. Schiff. 2005. On 'indirect' trade-related R&D spillovers. *European Economic Review* 49(7): 1785–1798.

Lundvall, B.A.1992. Introduction, in *National Systems of Innovation: Towards a Theory of Innovation and Interactive Learning*. London: Pinter Publishers.

Ma, N. and J. Guan. 2005. An exploratory study on collaboration profiles of Chinese publications in Molecular Biology. *Scientometrics* 65(3): 343–355.

Melitz, M.J. 2003. The impact of trade on intra-industry reallocations and aggregate industry productivity. *Econometrica* 71(6): 1695–1725.

Melitz, M.J. and G.I.P. Ottaviano. 2005. Market size, trade, and productivity. *National Bureau of Economic Research Working Paper Series*, No. 11393. Available at: http://ideas.repec.org/p/nbr/nberwo/11393.html.

Mowery, D.C. and J.E. Oxley. 1995. Inward technology transfer and competitiveness: the role of national innovation systems. *Cambridge Journal of Economics* 19(1): 67–93.

Mulder P., H. De Groot and M.W. Hofkes. 2001. Economic growth and technological change: a comparison of insights from a neoclassical and an evolutionary perspective. *Technological Forecasting and Social Change* 68(2): 151–171.

Nelson, R.R. 1993. *National Innovation Systems: A Comparative Analysis*. New York, Oxford: Oxford University Press.

Nelson R.R. 1959. The simple economics of basic scientific research. *Journal of Political Economy* 67: 297–306.

Nelson, R.R. and S.G. Winter. 1977. In search of useful theory of innovation. *Research Policy* 6(1): 36–76.

Partha, D. and P.A. David. 1994. Toward a new economics of science. *Research Policy* 23(5): 487–521.

Pavitt, K. 1991. What makes basic research economically useful? *Research Policy* 20: 109–119.

Porter, M.E. 1990. *The Competitive Advantage of Nations*. London: Macmillan.

Reichel, R. 2002. *Ökonomische Theorie der internationalen Wettbewerbsfähigkeit von Volkswirtschaften*. Wiesbaden: Deutscher Universitätsverlag.

Romer, P. 1991. Endogenous technological change. *National Bureau of Economic Research Working Paper Series*, No. 3210. Available at: http://ideas.repec.org/p/nbr/nberwo/3210.html.

Rosenberg, N. 1990. Why do firms do basic research (with their own money)?, *Research Policy* 19: 165–174.

Rosenberg, N. 2004. *Innovation and Economic Growth*. Paris: OECD. Available at: www.oecd.org/dataoecd/55/49/34267902.pdf.

Schwab, K., ed. 2010. *The Global Competitiveness Report 2010–2011*. Geneva: World Economic Forum.

Soriano, F. and F. Mulatero. 2010. Knowledge policy in the EU: from the Lisbon Strategy to Europe 2020. *Journal of the Knowledge Economy* 1(4): 289–302.

Stephan, P.E. 1996. The economics of science. *Journal of Economic Literature* 34(3): 1199–1235.

Thomson, E.R. 2004. National competitiveness: a question of cost conditions or institutional circumstances? *British Journal of Management* 15: 197–218.

Vernon, R. 1966. International investment and international trade in the product cycle. *The Quarterly Journal of Economics* 80(2): 190–207.

Wang, T.Y, C. Shih-Chien and C. Kao. 2007. The role of technology development in national competitiveness – evidence from Southeast Asian countries. *Technological Forecasting and Social Change* 74: 1357–1373.

Weingart, P. 2005. Impact of bibliometrics upon the science system: inadvertent consequences? *Scientometrics* 62(1): 117–131.

World Bank. 2008. *Unleashing Prosperity: Productivity Growth in Eastern Europe and Former Soviet Union.* Washington, DC: World Bank Publications.

World Bank. 2012. Going for smart growth: making research and innovation work for Bulgaria. Policy Note, no. 66263. Available: http://documents.worldbank.org/curated/en/2012/06/16373409/going-smart-growth-making-research-innovation-work-bulgaria.

Zaghini, A. 2005. Evolution of trade patterns in the new EU member states. *Economics of Transition* 13(4): 629–658.

12 The emergence of wind energy in Spain

A review of the policy mix

Cristian Matti and Davide Consoli

1 Introduction

The European Community (EC) has proactively promoted the development of renewable energy for over 20 years by means of standards and regulation designed to align incentives and opportunities. These actions have spurred a variety of responses and modes of implementation of a distinctively local character among member states. The diffusion of wind energy in Spain is a good case in point to illustrate how coordinated multi-level environmental policy can successfully promote the emergence of new sectors. Building on a wide platform of supranational and national directives, Spanish regional governments have designed and implemented development strategies based on the mobilization of locally available assets. This has resulted in differential growth of industrial, research and policy capacities across regions, and a rich spectrum of development trajectories that leverage on and feed back into regional-specific tangible and intangible assets.

This chapter outlines the intertwining of technological, industrial and institutional developments that have allowed Spain to become an active pole of innovation and growth in the wind energy sector. The chapter is divided into five sections. Section 2 describes the general trajectory of the wind sector in Spain and its regional dimension and Section 3 analyses the policy mix related to the development of this new sector in the search for market deployment and technology development. Section 4 discusses the Spanish case and considers the synergies in a multi-level and multi-sectoral context and Section 5 offers some conclusions.

2 Emergence of the wind energy sector in Spain

This section outlines the long-term trajectory of the Spanish wind energy sector in two parts. The first provides a broad overview while the second provides an analysis of the key developments observed at regional level.

2.1 Main trajectories and cross-sectoral linkages

Accumulated world capacity in wind energy production has grown fourfold during the first decade of the 2000s. Against this global backdrop, Spain has kept pace with Germany and India, is ranked fourth among the world's wind energy producers (Figure 12.1) and is widely recognized as a world leader in the global energy industry. At domestic level, wind power capacity has expanded at an impressive pace: wind farms by 207 per cent and wind turbines by 108 per cent between 2003 and 2010 (Figure 12.2).

This remarkable acceleration is due to the intersection of various factors. On the one hand, the regulatory framework of the European Union (EU) provided a

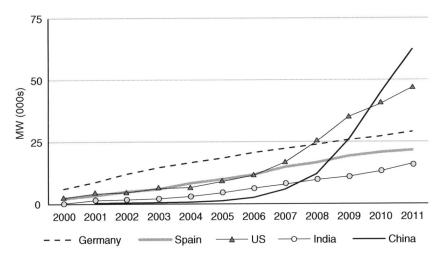

Figure 12.1 Wind energy cumulated capacity (selected countries) (source: own elaboration based on OECD, 2013, DE, 2013 and EWEA, 2013).

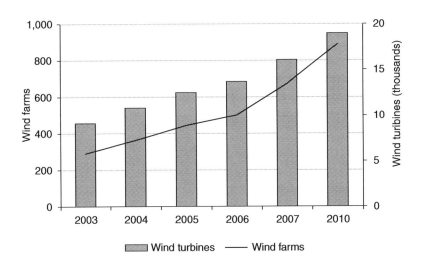

Figure 12.2 Total wind farms and wind turbines in Spain, 2003–2010 (source: own elaboration based on IAEST, 2013).

solid platform for harmonizing incentives and opening up opportunities. On the other hand, the demand for alternative forms of energy has grown significantly, thus engendering significant transformations in the structure of supply due also to the emergence of new peripheral markets.

2.1.1 The organizational ecology of the wind energy value chain

The European wind energy value chain includes utilities, independent power producers (IPPs) and developers.

Utilities are traditional players in the energy sector involved throughout the value chain from generation and transmission to distribution of electricity. Utilities operate under various organizational forms, such as investor-owned, publicly owned, cooperatives or nationalized companies, depending on the attendant competitive forces and the regulatory framework. As a result of increased market liberalization and growing cost advantage of delocalization, some utility companies have moved away from the established vertically integrated structure towards mixed forms that entail limited participation in specific segments of the value chain. In some cases, utilities operate as brokers that buy and sell rather than produce electricity.

Independent power producers (IPPs) are also important actors in the renewable energy market, often operating as small facilities, large corporations or cooperatives. Their business is regulated by long-term price guarantee schemes such as feed-in tariffs or power purchase agreements. The emergence of IPPs is a reflection of organizational adaptation following the wave of deregulation that sought to reduce the market power of the incumbent utilities in the early 1980s. Once IPPs were active players in the game, the logic of competition changed. These organizations are extremely adaptive and compete by developing, owning or operating wind farms. IPPs are often early adopters of new technology and early entrants in niche markets, and they promote the mobilization of local competences and the conversion of existing industrial capacity. This is especially relevant in the case of Spain where wind energy IPPs have drawn heavily on the installed base of skills in the construction and other large-scale industries. There are two main types of IPP in Europe: integrated IPPs with competences across the entire value chain, which retain high control over all operations in their portfolio, and wind project buyers, with no direct involvement in the development of wind plants, but acting as coordinators of platforms of part producers. This strategic route has brought about significant variety in wind energy production since the relevant knowledge is no longer limited to technical expertise related to the construction of turbines but also includes managerial expertise and financial literacy.

The last group of key actors in the value chain is the developers – that is, companies involved in the deployment of wind farms, purchasing or leasing land, installing equipment to quantify wind currents, and securing transmission, power sales, turbine supply, construction and financing agreements. Some large developers operate entire wind farms or evolve into IPPs, although most lack the operational capacity and necessary financing and limit their activities to developing parts of a project before selling them on to larger companies.

2.1.2 Evolution of value chain

In less than ten years, the wind energy value chain has shifted from being vertically integrated towards the distributed asset ownership and production model shown in Figure 12.3. As a result, there is no longer a stark distinction between wind turbine assemblers and service providers since turbine manufacturers are now involved in service activities such as operation and management while at the same time wind farm operators often experiment with turbines. Utility companies also acquire an increasingly global outlook and attract financial investors and foreign direct investment activity. This fragmented value chain is more efficient with regard to the goal of capturing emergent markets and more competitive in increasingly contested markets. In both cases, local specialized suppliers are crucial for facilitating access to specialized competences, technical expertise and financial capacity that otherwise would be costly to retrieve.

Spanish firms have become prominent actors in both the domestic and the international arenas owing to appropriate strategic choices concerning the reconversion of established competences from metallurgy, electronics and construction to wind energy. Large firms have sought technology transfer by means of joint ventures with foreign giants: this is the case of Gamesa, a specialist in robotics and materials, and its ally Vestas, a Danish developer of agriculture machinery, electronics and hydraulic cranes, and the merger between Ecotecnia and Alstom, a French firm with experience in train and boat construction.

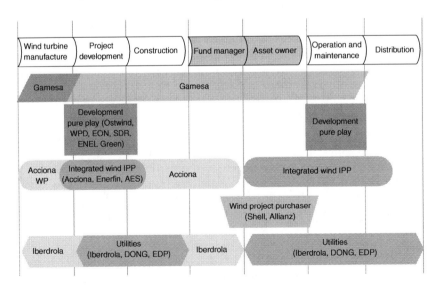

Figure 12.3 Wind farm technologies and forms of know-how (source: own elaboration, adapted from EWEA, 2009).

Interestingly, global players such as General Electric (US) and Siemens (Germany) followed similar paths and entered the wind energy industry via the acquisition of specialized companies. Spanish actors have achieved leading positions in the global markets for energy production (i.e. Iberdrola, Acciona) and technology manufacturing (i.e. Gamesa, MTorres, Acciona, Almstom-Ecotecnia) over a relatively short time span. Table 12.1 provides a snapshot of their role in the global market. A distinctive feature among these actors is the high strategic flexibility which allows them to be both leading global manufacturers and 'smart developers' at the local level. This is the case of Gamesa and Acciona, which are actively involved in different parts of the value chain and play different roles depending on the demands and the opportunities of the local context. The structure and composition of the Spanish wind energy market varies across developers and technology manufacturers. Table 12.2 shows the market share evolution over three critical years: 2004, the inception of the new special regime; 2008, the shift to the special regime/feed-in tariff; and 2012, a recent year characterized by the generalized slowdown in regime incentives due to the economic crisis.

As far as developers are concerned, big utilities are the main players in wind energy generation, mainly as a consequence of liberalization.[1] Moreover, mergers and acquisitions have changed the ownership of installed capacity over time, so that, for example, early leader Iberdrola saw its share rapidly eroded in favour of other actors, either Spanish (i.e. Acciona) or international (i.e. ENEL [Italy], EDP [Portugal] and EON [Germany]). As for technology manufacturers, the data show significant concentration, with four companies accounting for more than 85 per cent of installed wind capacity in 2008 and 2012. During this period, Gamesa accounted for half of the market, supported by early cooperation with Vestas[2] and acquisition of MADE in 2003. Vestas has increased its participation significantly, Alstom's position has remained stable and Acciona WP's participation has slightly decreased. Since 2012, new actors have entered the arena, mostly international companies such as Sinovel (China, ranked second in the world market), Suzlon (India, ranked fifth in the world market), Nordex (US) and Kenetech (US). The latter two, together with GE, signal a growing presence of firms from the US, currently the major foreign investor in Spain after Vestas (Denmark).

The evolution of market concentration differs in these sectors due to two forces. First, the share of 'other' developers has grown compared with that of utilities and big IPPs (i.e. Acciona), while manufacturing has moved towards higher levels of concentration. Second, the links between developers and manufacturers have grown mostly at local level, so that, for example, regions maintain competences of implementation of wind plans as well as industry, environmental and land use policy, while other actors hold dominant positions and own the rights to exploit their technologies and services. On the whole, the structure of regional markets varies according to policy strategies and industrial concentration, with increased independence enjoyed by autonomous communities. The next section discusses the main ingredients of the very rich industry setting, its knowledge resources and policy framework.

Table 12.1 Global market shares – main wind turbine manufacturers

	2008		2009		2010		2012
Vestas (Den)	19.8	Vestas (Den)	12.5	GE Energy (USA)	14.7	GE Energy (USA)	15.5
GE Energy (USA)	18.6	Sinovel (CHI)	12.4	Vestas (Den)	11.1	Vestas (Den)	14
Gamesa (SP)	12	GE Energy (USA)	9.2	Siemens (GER)	9.5	Siemens (GER)	9.5
Enercon (GER)	10	Goldwind (CHI)	8.5	Enercon (GER)	9.4	Enercon (GER)	8.2
Suzlon (IND)	9	Enercon (GER)	7.2	Suzlon (IND)	7.2	Suzlon (IND)	7.4
Siemens (GER)	6.9	Suzlon (IND)	6.7	Gamesa (SP)	6.8	Gamesa (SP)	6.1
Sinovel (CHI)	5	Dongfang (CHI)	6.5	Goldwind (CHI)	6.6	Goldwind (CHI)	6
Acciona (SP)	4.6	Gamesa (SP)	6.4	United Power(CHI)	6.6	United Power(CHI)	4.7
Goldwind (CHI)	4	Siemens (GER)	5.9	Sinovel (CHI)	6	Sinovel (CHI)	3.2
Dongfang (CHI)	4	Guodian Utd Power (CHI)	3.4	Mingyang (CHI)	4.2	Mingyang (CHI)	2.7

Source: own elaboration based on Deloitte (2011) and Navigant (2013).

Table 12.2 National market share of wind power capacity – developers and wind turbine manufacturers

Main developers	2004	2008	2012	Main wind turbine manufacturers	2004	2008	2012
IBERDROLA	34.51	28.03	24.2	GAMESA	51.63	48.63	52.3
NEO ENERGIA		8.08		*MADE*	12.23	8.43	
ACCIONA ENERGIA	10.8	17.68	18.8	VESTAS	2.89	14.66	17.9
CESA	4.49			ALSTOM			7.6
EDPR			9.2	*ECOTECNIA*	7.79	7.32	
GENESA	3.88			*ACCIONA WP*		8.21	7.3
ENEL GREEN POWER ESPAÑA			6.2	GE	7.13	5.93	6.2
ENDESA	10.78			SIEMENS			3.4
*ENEL UNION FENOSA**		1.97		*NAVATINA-SIEMENS*		4.03	
ECYR		8.36		ENERCO			2.3
UF ENEL	3.67			SUZLON			1
GAS NATURAL FENOSA RREE			4.2	NORDEX		0.56	0.8
GAS NATURAL		2.53		DESA	0.67	0.67	0.4
ENEL UNION FENOSA		1.97		KENETECH		0.2	0.2
Other	31.9	31.3	37.6	Other	17.8	1.4	0.8

Source: own elaboration based on AEE (2005–2013).

Note

* The partnership between Gas Natural Fenosa and Enel in renewable energy was dissolved in 2010. These two companies each own 50 per cent of ENEL now.

2.2 The regional dimension

The distribution of wind energy production varies across regions depending on the location and availability of land for wind farm deployment.[3] Figure 12.4 shows that the largest Spanish Autonomous Communities (CCAA) in terms of land extension are also leaders in installed capacity measured in mega watts (MW): Castilla y León, 5,233 MW; Castilla-La Mancha, 3,736 MW; Galicia, 3,272 MW; and Andalucía, 3,066 MW. Different patterns of local development emerge from this aggregate picture whereby each region has developed 'innovative capacities' based on the articulation of public and private competences that would best suit the goal of exploiting the existing patterns of industry and policy specialization.

Figure 12.5 provides a snapshot of industry capacity captured by the relative density of industrial centres by type of activity across regions.[4] Up to 2007, four autonomous communities accounted for 83 per cent of industry sites: Galicia[5] (40 per cent), Castilla y León (17 per cent), Navarra (15 per cent) and Castilla-La Mancha (10 per cent). However, an expanding supply chain has changed this distribution and reduced these shares to Galicia (19 per cent), Castilla y León

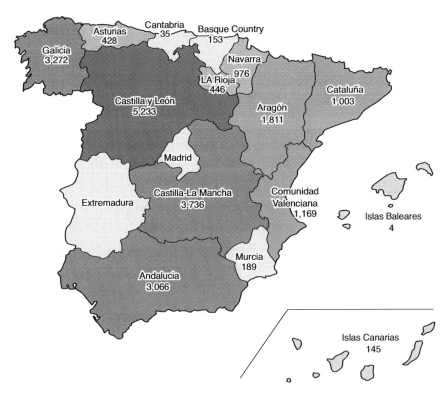

Figure 12.4 Wind power installed capacity (MW), Spanish regions, 2011 (source: own elaboration, based on AEE, 2012).

(13 per cent) and the Basque Country (12 per cent). This trajectory reflects the patterns of industry specialization in 2013. Since 2006, regional industrial capacity increased in terms of both local involvement in wind energy-related activities as well as in the variety of actors within the supply chain (see Table 12.3). Interestingly, the rate of expansion of industry sites (IS) has not been affected by the economic downturn in the second half of the 2000s. Rather, the number of actors has outgrown the expansion of activities, thus suggesting a move towards higher levels of specialization, and activities have become more geographically spread, with regions that were formerly peripheral becoming active in wind energy, although the leadership of Galicia and the Basque Country has not been undermined. This pattern of evolution is common in mature stages of a technology life cycle when non-production activities – for example, maintenance – acquire bigger shares.

Organizational capacity among developers and technology manufacturers relies on regional competences to deliver long-term plans related to energy and the industry (i.e. wind plans, renewable technology sectoral plans), and the location of dominant actors in the region. Appropriate regional policy strategies can promote the operations of IPPs, which may or may not be involved in the development of wind farms. Thus, even if a non-developer holds the dominant share in the national renewable energy market,[6] the distribution of shares at the regional level may be significantly different (Figure 12.6). For example, in Castilla-La Mancha, Iberdrola and Acciona account for more than 50 per cent of the market, and Acciona also owns 62 per cent, 29 per cent and 27 per cent of markets in Navarra, Valencia and Galicia. However, Andalucía, Castilla y León and Galicia are leaders in power capacity with a market mostly controlled by small and individual developers. Small IPPs and developers dominate the markets in Aragón, Cataluña, Valencia and other smaller regions. This distribution resonates with the territorial distribution of market competences among utility companies, which makes wind farm ownership profitable for the companies that traditionally operated in those regions. At the same time, lower entry barriers encourage the participation of small developers/IPPs. Among wind turbine manufacturers (WTM), Gamesa is dominant nationally, but shows different cross-regional performance: it is a leader in large regions such as Castilla y León, Castilla-La Mancha, Andalucía and Galicia but holds lower, still

Table 12.3 Industrial sites specialized in wind energy technologies: Spain, 2006–2013

	2006	*2007*	*2008*	*2009*	*2010*	*2011*	*2012*	*2013*
Total industrial sites	35	52	76	90	102	115	142	175
Number of Spanish regions with IS	5	6	7	10	10	10	10	12
Total firms owning at least one IS	9	19	40	52	53	58	70	82
Number of activities/categories involved	10	14	20	26	27	28	29	30

Source: own elaboration based on AEE (2007–2013).

significant, shares in other regions. Overall, Gamesa and Vestas account for 67 per cent of the Spanish market and hold dominant positions in most leading regions (see Figure 12.6). Small manufacturers have higher shares in the smaller regions due partly to the experimental nature of many wind farms that local governments own in less developed market, such as the Canary Islands and the Balearic Islands.

Performance among regions shows significant concentrations of WTM and developers/utilities. However, there are different patterns among regions; for example, leading regions Castilla y León and Andalucía present high levels of concentration in WTM, but lower concentration in the developers sector. This may be due to the significant number of developers that own a wind farm. Galicia and Castilla-La Mancha show high presence of both types of actors. Finally, the pattern of concentration in wind power capacity – estimated by

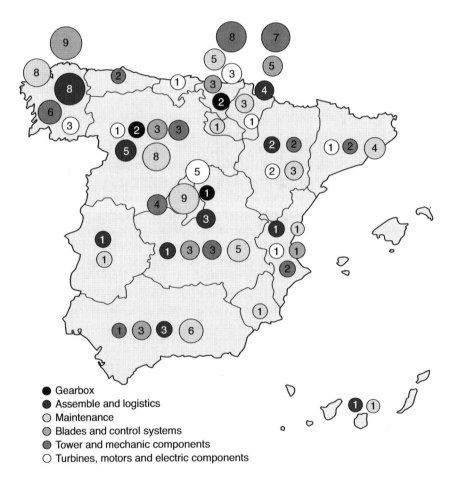

● Gearbox
● Assemble and logistics
○ Maintenance
◐ Blades and control systems
◑ Tower and mechanic components
○ Turbines, motors and electric components

Figure 12.5 Wind power industrial sites, 2013 (source: own elaboration, based on AEE, 2013).

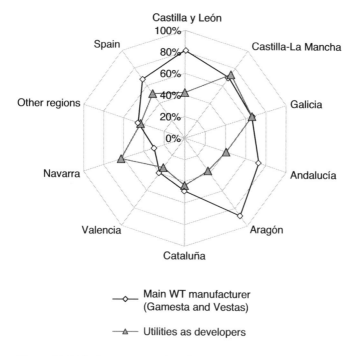

Figure 12.6 Market concentrations in the Spanish wind energy market: main actors (source: own elaboration).

Herfindahl–Hirschman Index based on regional ownership of wind farms – confirms the results for the leading regions (Figure 12.7). However, note that Navarra is the region with the highest concentration of wind power capacity, which can be explained by the fact that most wind farms are owned by the local firm Acciona. Its lower concentration index for Spain (national index) may be explained by the predominance of small developers and IPPs, which hold around 49 per cent of national wind power capacity.

Research capacity depends on the presence of a specialized regional R&D infrastructure. Despite the maturity of wind energy technologies, research plays a fundamental role in enabling better interoperability across wind farm components and greater efficiency. Four Spanish regions account for the majority of the research infrastructure (63 per cent), namely Madrid, the Basque Country, Castilla y León and Andalucía. The Basque Country hosts most of the country's technology centres; the other three regions show more variety in their research infrastructures. Basic research data show inter-annual increase in the number of projects in renewable energy related areas during the period 2004–2012, the main actors being universities in Madrid, Andalucía and the Basque Country. The Basque Country and Navarra show the best performance in applied R&D through intensive collaboration with universities (41 per cent) and technology

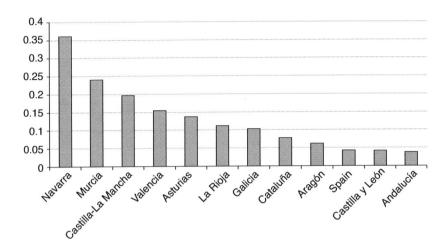

Figure 12.7 Concentration of wind power capacity at regional level (source: own elaboration based on AEE, 2013b).

Note
HHI concentration index based in ownership of wind farms. Herfindahl–Hirschman Index is estimated
using

$$HHI = \frac{\left(\sum_{i=1}^{N} S_i^2 - \frac{1}{N}\right)}{1 - \frac{?}{N}}$$

where *si* is the market share of firm *i* in the market, and *N* is the number of firms.

centres (36 per cent). Strong industry leadership easily translates into strong
market deployment (Galicia and Castilla y León), while a strong R&D orientation, such as that exhibited by the Basque Country, Navarra and Madrid, opens
up global market opportunities. Thus, industry strengths and specialization are
complements and act as facilitators (Figure 12.8).

Policy capacity refers to the linkages between the transfer of competences and
management of regional resources, which has been crucial in the case of Spain.
As Table 12.4 shows, this particular dimension accelerated significantly between
2000 and 2005 and coincided with the introduction of the special regime.[7] In
2010, 50 per cent of renewable energy-related regional policy was related to
industry regulation, with the remainder focused on the environment and land
use. The most heavily regulated regions are Galicia, Navarra, Castilla y León,
Cataluña and the Basque Country. Policy in Cataluña, Galicia and the Basque
Country includes implementation of renewable sector regulation, although the
first regions to formulate wind energy plans were Galicia, Navarra and Aragón.

A bird's-eye view of these dimensions suggests a rather rich ecology of
regional development patterns, which are summarized in Table 12.5. Here we

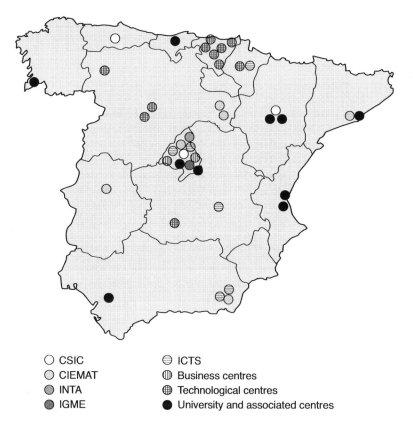

Figure 12.8 Distribution of energy research infrastructure, 2012 (source: own elaboration based on López & Moliner, 2012).

propose the main region archetypes that emerge from the foregoing analysis as well as their relative comparative advantage in intensity and composition of technology, policy and organizational capacities.

Galicia can be described as an early mover due to its early developments in wind energy capacity and industry infrastructure. Galicia's regional policy prioritized the national market for energy and manufacture of components. Castilla y León can be described as a smart implementer based on its remarkable performance in building wind capacity and industry infrastructure through a decentralized approach mechanism, despite its late entry into the sector. Finally two regions can be considered smart followers due to significantly increased wind capacity and the implementation of basic supporting infrastructure (maintenance and logistics). Other regions focused more on R&D activities, such as the Basque Country, which shows weak performance in the energy market but has achieved outstanding results in technology development and penetration in

Table 12.4 Distribution of policy instruments among regions by category

Region	Main areas			Coding categories				Total
	Industry	Environment	Land use	EE	RREE	Wind energy	Other	
Cataluña	11	9	4	2	2	3	17	24
Baleares	9	4	7	3	2		15	20
Galicia	9	6	5	4		3	13	20
Basque Country	10	5	4	1	2	2	14	19
Aragón	9	5	2	4	2	3	7	16
Madrid	12	1	3	4	1		11	16
Navarra	8	3	5	1	1	5	9	16
Valencia	6	5	5	1	4	1	10	16
Castilla y León	6	4	4	3	1	6	4	14
Extremadura	8	4	2	2	3	2	7	14
Canarias	6	3	4	3		1	9	13
Castilla-La Mancha	7	3	3	2	2	1	8	13
Andalucía	8	2	2		6		6	12
Asturias	1	5	4			2	8	10
La Rioja	4	3	3	1	1	2	6	10
Cantabria	5	2	2	2	1	1	5	9
Murcia	5	2	2	3	1		5	9
Total	124	66	61	36	29	32	154	251

Source: own elaboration based on MIETUR (2005).

Notes
EE is energy efficiency; RREE is renewable energy.

Table 12.5 Main archetypes of regions and their relative comparative advantage

Region	Wind potential	Infrastructure	Policy measures	Industry position	Value chain positioning	Market orientation	Energy balance/wind specialization*	
Galicia	Medium (6°)	Strong (3°)	Market	Strong (1°)	Upstream/all	Home	Medium	Early mover
Castilla y León	Strong (1°)	Strong (1°)	Market R&D	Strong (2°)	Upstream/all	Home	High	Smart implementer
Castilla-La Mancha	Strong (2°)	Strong (2°)	Market	Medium (6°)	Components	Home	High	Follower
Andalucía	Strong (3°)	Strong (4ª)	Market	Medium (7°)	Services	Home	Low	Follower
Basque Country	Weak (13°)	Weak (12°)	Industry R&D	Strong (3°)	Whole	Home/external	None	Knowledge creator
Navarra	Medium (9°)	Medium (8°)	Market R&D	Strong (5°)	Whole	Home/external	High	Early mover/ Knowledge creator
Madrid	Weak (12°)	None	Industry R&D	Strong (4°)	Components	Home/external	None	Knowledge service

Source: own elaboration.

Note

* These differences emerge from a comparison of wind energy shares under the special regime, in 2001 and 2012, and from the Balassa index of revealed comparative advantage.

external markets, or Navarra, which had a head start driven by abundant wind capacity and the R&D performance of two key actors such as CENER and Acciona. Finally, the capital region Madrid can be considered a knowledge hub based on intense R&D activity and other activities crucial for wind technology development.

3 The evolution of policies in the development of renewable energy in Spain

Spain has had policy instruments in place to foster the renewable energy sector since the second energy crisis (1979). Early initiatives were aimed at reducing dependence on an external supply of fossil fuel resources through the gradual introduction of alternative technologies for the production of electricity and to achieve energy efficiency. Subsequently the energy market in Spain has undergone major transformations, most of which have been driven by the coupling of higher level energy policy and environmental commitments (i.e. EU Directives, international climate change deals) and the emergence of European energy markets.

Taken together, dependence on imported resources and response to international commitments have made Spain one of the most active countries for the introduction of energy policy instruments. Indeed, the country currently ranks seventh in Europe and among OECD countries for the introduction of renewable energy policy (see Table 12.6). The chronological evolution of policy shows a turning point in 1999 when the number of initiatives increased significantly to promote a trend that lasted nearly ten years. However, the most intense period of policy implementation was 2007–2012 when Spain was ranked first for wind energy sector policy.

The most important policy instruments for fostering production from renewable energy sources (RES-E) are tariff schemes, namely the Premium tariff (PT) and the Feed-in tariff (FIT). The PT is a fixed sum (the premium) which is applied to the market price; the FIT is a fixed price for commercialization (Del Río González, 2008). The FIT benefits energy generators and increases profits compared with the standard electricity market[8] price. The PT is more beneficial if the market price increases more than forecast. Both schemes are updated annually in combination with a set of national targets (i.e. energy consumption) to increase the share of RES-E in the energy balance. This set of financial instruments aims at improving the economic conditions of RES-E by reducing risk and providing stability via long-term support. In addition, R&D support programmes for technology developments and a variety of regional strategies have been introduced to increase technological capabilities related to deployment in the RES-E market. Those strategies involve measures affecting the energy sector and renewable energy technologies combined with environmental and planning regulations. Figure 12.9 (see Section 3.3.4) provides a chronology of energy policy and the main dimensions of research policy in Spain (i.e. R&D EU and national programmes).

Table 12.6 Performance of EU/OECD countries in the introduction of renewables*

Renewable energy

Country	1974–1995	1996	1997	1998	1999	2000	2001	2002	2003	2004	2005	2006	2007	2008	2009	2010	2011	2012	2013	Total
Total	60	10	17	10	34	30	37	35	26	42	47	38	76	68	68	53	36	21	15	723
US	13	1	1		2		2	6	2	4	8	4	11	17	7	3	2			78
Australia	1		1	2	2	5	1	2	2	9	1	3	3	8	9	3	2	1		55
Germany	8	1	1	1	4	2	1	2		1	2	3	3	4	4	2	2	4		41
Canada	2	1	2	1	4		4	2	5		1	2	7	3	2	2	2			35
France	2	1			6	3	3	2	1	4	1	1	4	2	4	2	2			35
UK						3		7	3						4	3	6		1	35
Spain	4		1			1		1		1	1	3	4	1	4	3	3	3	1	32
Denmark	5			3	2	1	3			2			1	1	4	1	2	2	1	26
Japan	4	1	4	1		1				2	2	2	6	2	2	2	1	1	1	24
EU Dir.			1				2		1	1	2	2	2	2	2	2	1	1	1	18
Other EU	21	5	5	2	14	14	21	13	14	18	30	21	36	24	27	36	20	10	13	344

Wind energy

Country	1974–1995	1996	1997	1998	1999	2000	2001	2002	2003	2004	2005	2006	2007	2008	2009	2010	2011	2012	2013	Total
Total	9	2	5	0	1	3	3	3	2	5	5	3	9	9	14	3	4	3	4	87
Spain	2		1			1	1	1		1	1		1		2	1	1	1	1	14
UK						1		1	1			1	1	1	3	1				9
Luxembourg	2	1					1			1	1			1						8
Canada	1	1	1		1								2							6
Germany	1	1	1			1							1	1	1					6
Hungary							1			1			1	1						5
Italy										1		1				1	1	1		5
US	1					1							1	2		1			1	5
Other	2		2				1	2		2	3	1	3	3	4	1	2	1	2	29

Source: own elaboration based on IEA (2013).

Note

* The data include policies, measures and various instruments. Updates are indicated as new events allowing more detailed tracking of policy performance. Spain's ranking is based on its main policy introductions and is maintained if updates are included.

3.1 The policy stages

The trajectory of EU policy in support of RES-E begins in the second half of the 1990s when new legislation sought to increase competition while guaranteeing security of supply. The promotion of renewable energy in the early 2000s was based on the establishment of targets for energy production, criteria for participation and emission regimes (De Alegría Mancisidor *et al.*, 2009; Del Río González, 2008; Montes *et al.*, 2007; Río & Burguillo, 2009). More recent instruments include energy consumption standards, decentralization of energy production, mechanisms for energy trade and developments led by regions and small and medium-sized enterprises (SMEs). Security of supply being a crucial ingredient in support for emergent renewable energy (RREE) sectors, Spain has a dynamic (RES-E) environment compared with the rest of Europe, at least up to 2009, punctuated by various shifts in the organizational configuration of the energy sector (Del Río González, 2008). Spain's domestic energy market emerged in the 1990s and developed along the ethos of a renewables market and mechanisms related to trade in energy (2000–2010). Since then, cross-country cooperation has increased with a view to greater energy exchange and achievement of EU-wide objectives.

The significant expansion in the renewable energy sector generally came to a halt in 2009 with the onset of the economic crisis, resulting in a reduction in tariff deficit associated with the special regime and, after 2012, reduction in subsidies. In addition, the barriers to entry to the renewable energy market have increased.

Wind energy sector development in Spain consists of three stages:

1   Creation of an energy market
2   Creation of a RREE market
3   Financial crisis and tariff deficit

In what follows, we discuss European policies as a background to an analysis of Spanish national policy. We provide an overview of performance and policy implementation at Spanish regional level. Early policy implications are highlighted in relation to market deployment and technology developments. Specific research programmes and R&D support are investigated in more detail as part of the regional dimension to wind energy development.

3.2 European level

EU policy on RREE was introduced in the second half of the 1990s with the goal of increasing competition and guaranteeing security of supply. European policy and regulation contributed to the identification of key actors, such as energy producers, energy transporters and energy distributors, and their roles. At the same time, national governments formulated security of supply rules and supported liberalization through subsidies and regulation. The promotion of a renewable energy market started with Directive 2001/77/EC, which imposed common norms and targets[9] on member states and defined long-term strategy for the exploration of external market opportunities. At this stage, the EU was not considering a harmonized system but only a coordination of schemes to support cooperation among countries. Subsequent directives defined complementary aspects such as specific support for renewable energies for transport and biofuels (2003/30/EC), regulation of internal energy markets and definition of main activities (i.e. generation, transport, distribution), actors and networks (2003/54/EC) and the establishment of a trading rights regime related to greenhouse gas emissions with limits set on the basis of the Kyoto protocol and the new emissions market (2003/87/EC).

Directive 2009/28/EC modified Directive 2001/77/EC by setting general binding objectives for renewable energy production in Europe by 2020.[10] This Directive defines the criteria for achieving gross final energy consumption standards and includes a new calculus mechanism for imported energy and the relevance of development led by regions and SMEs. It provides explicit support for decentralization of energy production and defines independent quotas for renewable energy related to transportation.

3.3 National level

The Spanish national renewable energy policy portfolio provides a broad framework for appreciating the implementation mechanisms put in place by regional governments. Two key principles underlie these actions: the transfer of energy competencies and the design of specific regulations for the management of natural resources, land and environmental impacts governed by means of industry policy (incentives and regulation), environment (control and monitoring) and urban planning (land use). The evolution of national policy followed different stages, which will now be reviewed in detail.

3.3.1 1990–2000: creation of an internal energy market

Energy market liberalization in Spain was defined by the Energy National Plan (PEN 1991–2000) and, although no specific reference to renewable energy was made, it emphasized the issue of security of supply. Improvements in the national energy balance and efficiency and market internationalization were introduced in line with the creation of a common European Energy Market. In 1994, additional regulation (RD 2366/1994 and National law 40/1994) provided better conditions for renewables through a special regime (tariff scheme) to support electricity generation from renewables and cogeneration technologies. Subsequently, the energy price was determined by government and energy supply defined as a public good.

Law 54/97 started the process of liberalization where the energy price was defined by market mechanisms. In line with EU Directive 96/92/CE, it introduced competition in energy supply and vertical segmentation in the market while at the same time distinguishing between traditional and renewable energy producers through the introduction of a FIT scheme (RD 21818/1998). The special regime includes new technologies and allowed RES-E producers to participate in the energy market aimed at achieving 12 per cent production from renewables by 2010. Under the special regime, RES-E producers received a premium (sum cost), associated with production capacity, in the form of an additional subsidy.

3.3.2   2000–2010: creation of renewable energy market and support for opportunities in external markets

In the early 2000s, energy market liberalization progressed thanks to a set of initiatives that enhanced competition in the different energy sector areas. The main advances included decentralization of activities through the introduction of new actors such as the system operator (Law 53/2002) and energy trading companies (RD 485/2009). Improvements to the productivity and efficiency of the whole system (Law 24/2005) and transposition of EU regulation were emphasized in order to increase competition and avoid dominance in transport and distribution network operations (Law 17/2007).

Specific renewable energy measures included a sequence of long-term plans to guide the promotion of RREE and emphasize specific targets. The Plan for the Promotion of Renewable Energy (PFER 2000–2010) was the first long-term policy which guaranteed subsidies and funding, and set priorities for renewable energy technologies to achieve the 12 per cent target. A series of Action Plans for Renewable Energy (PANER 2005–2010, 2008–2012) were introduced in line with EU regulation (Directives 2001/77/CE and 2003/87/CE), which included procurement mechanisms, R&D programmes and decentralization of energy production and a more significant role for regional developments and SMEs.

Accordingly, the FIT scheme underwent a series of reforms. A long-term perspective was introduced to provide market stability (RD 1432/2002) along with a new regulatory framework and conditions related to different technologies and categories (RD 436/2004). Critical changes to the 2004 regulation included introduction of improved mechanisms for annual tariff adjustments via the price index, removal of barriers for RES-E generators participating directly in the electricity market and explicit support for photovoltaic and hydropower within a 15 to 25-year time horizon. RD 661/2007 updated the 2004 special regime by introducing new prime and tariff schemes based on a cap and floor system.[11] This system was aimed at reducing the costs for consumers by putting a limit (cap) on prices and profits, while guaranteeing a certain level of revenues and reducing the risks for investors (floor value – lower limit). It included differing compensation according to the technology and the average electricity price (AET), but decreasing over the lifetime of the installation. The introduction of RD 6/2009 changed conditions: thermosolar and Aeolian projects had significantly exceeded the goals set by PNER 2005–2010, and this new law decreed closure of the producer register and imposed a new system of annual quotas.

3.3.3 2010–present: economic crisis and new policy set

Since 2009, the FIT scheme has undergone repeated reforms shaped by the reduction of public subsidies and the need to identify a new, and stable, regulatory framework. In the attempt to revert to the conditions of 2007, RD 1614/2010 sought to reduce the tariff deficit. A series of important changes also occurred in 2012: first, economic incentives were withdrawn for new installations (RD 1/2012); second, cost–benefit deviations were corrected; third, limits were imposed on the construction of new infrastructures (13/2012). Finally, new schemes of network tolls, taxes and subsidies were added to both ordinary and special regimes (RD law 20/2012, law 15/2012 and law 17/2012). On the whole, these changes reduced the scope of the special regime of economic incentives, which had a major impact in the early days. Although the special regime remains in place, new installations had to compete on the basis of the market price rather than a regulated price.

RD law 2/2013 contains the latest modification to the special regime for renewable energy and established two procedures for the energy market: (1) transfer of electricity under a regulated tariff and (2) sale of electricity for electric power production with no additional premium. Conversely, RD law 9/2013 seeks to provide a more sustainable solution to the tariff deficit by imposing a new remuneration regime for renewable energy. Accordingly, firms receive an investment cost plus remuneration based on the specific technology (i.e. less and more risky investment).[12]

The Renewable Energy Plan 2011–2020 (PFNER 2011–2020) forecasts a future in which Spain will achieve a 22.7 per cent share of the renewable energy market and a 42.3 per cent share of electricity generation. The surplus can be transferred to other countries under the EU mechanism. However, the changes in regulation since 2012 had an impact on production and energy substitution (self-consumption/auto-producers of energy) costs as well as on the market price spread. Long-term investments in infrastructure are affected retroactively through the impact on operating installations (i.e. premium originally assigned) and market foresight since application processes for new energy producers are temporally eliminated.

3.3.4 Key performance indicators for policy instruments

The energy balance in Spain has changed significantly since the introduction of the special regime for renewable energy production in 1997. The latter was modified twice in 2004 and 2007, and in 2007, the energy balance peaked, with energy delivered by the special regime increasing to 239 per cent (see Figure 12.9). Subsequently, total energy production slowed based on the slowdown of energy generated by technologies under the ordinary regime. However, the electricity production under the special regime kept increasing until 2012. Performance under the special regime based on the FIT scheme has been outstanding for energy production,[13] as has corresponding development of power capacity in RES-E (see Figure 12.10). Capacity under the normal regime increased 42 per cent, while capacity under the

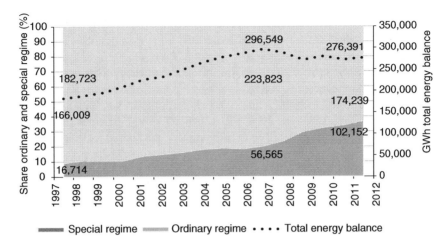

Figure 12.9 Evolution of energy balance in Spain: ordinary and special regime, 1997–2012 (source: own elaboration).

special regime reached 522 per cent and total wind power capacity rose by 3,820 per cent in the period 1997–2008. Overall, in the period 1997–2012, subsidies in the wind energy sector based on the FIT scheme increased by 4,336 per cent, while the RES-E produced from wind increased by 3,436 per cent (Figure 12.11). Finally, special regime accounts for 37 per cent of the energy balance, and wind energy was the main contributor to the special regime (46.6 per cent) in 2012. These results confirm that implementation of the FIT scheme and the targets for RES-E have achieved more than the expected 12 per cent target of RES-E for 2010 and even the 2020 target of 20 per cent.

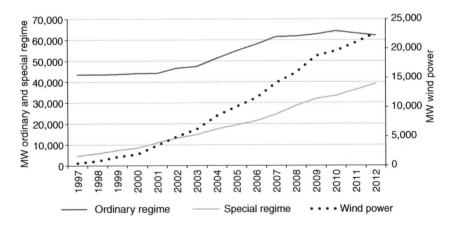

Figure 12.10 Evolution of power capacity in Spanish electricity system: wind power, ordinary and special regime, 1997–2012 (source: own elaboration).

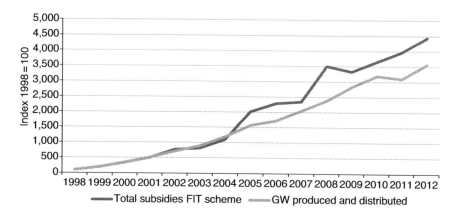

Figure 12.11 Evolution of total subsidies granted by FIT scheme and RES-E produced with wind resources, 1998–2012. Index 1998 = 100 (source: own elaboration based on REE, 1997–2012).

The different contribution of each technology to national performance can be analysed in terms of power capacity trajectory and cost–benefit related to implementation of the FIT scheme. Different and decreasing (since 2007) price compensation has affected the performance (productivity and efficiency) of RES-E technologies. Solar energy has enjoyed significantly larger subsidies than wind energy, but represents a small share of energy produced. The disparity in price compensation (see Figure 12.12) and contribution to the energy balance over time had a significant impact on the tariff deficit. The price of wind energy increased from 6.8 cents to 25.1 cents/kW, while the price of solar has risen from 7 cents to 32 cents/kW. The average price of solar energy was 59 cents in

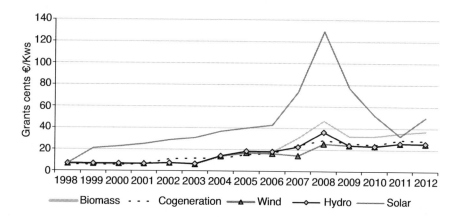

Figure 12.12 Evolution of average price compensation, 1998–2012 (source: own elaboration).

2004–2012 with a peak of 128 cents in 2008. In 2004–2012, grants for solar energy increased considerably and relatively more than the energy produced (see Figure 12.13). In the case of wind energy, production increased more than the grants.

To sum up, the implementation of the FIT scheme in Spain tilted the energy balance mix towards RES-E technologies. Subsequent reforms to FIT improved market conditions and competition over a wide spectrum of different energy sources under both the ordinary and the special regimes. In this context, under the FIT scheme (1997–2012), wind energy emerged as the leading RES-E and as one of the main contributors to the total energy balance. At the same time, the implementation of the FIT tightly depended on the conditions related to the development of the energy infrastructure and industry capacity for renewable energy technologies in the regions. The main aspects of regional policy are presented below.

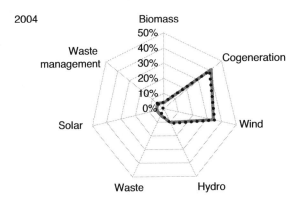

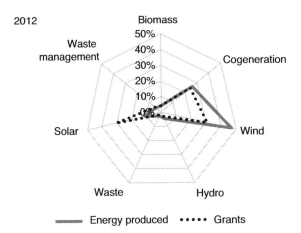

Figure 12.13 Grants and energy produced as part of the total, 2004 and 2012 (source: own elaboration based on CNE, 2013).

3.4 Regional level

The FIT scheme is the national policy instrument supporting renewable energy that set the foundations for the development of RES-E capacity. Under this broad umbrella, a variety of implementation schemes have flourished across regions driven by two forces:

- *Transfer of competences.* Following decentralization to CCAAs in the 1980s, regions became responsible for energy consumed within the CCAA in which it was produced, with the result that it did not enter the national electricity network. This required a set of regulations for regional energy production.
- *Management of natural resources, land use and environmental impact* related to the design, authorization, implementation and control of the energy infrastructure managed by three types of regional policy: industry policy (incentives and regulation), environmental policy (control and monitoring) and urban planning (land use).

Since the mid-1990s, regions have had frameworks in place for managing RES-E related policies that were designed at higher levels of jurisdiction. After the inception of the FIT scheme, regional regulation on industry, the environment and the urban landscape established new conditions for the development of the energy sector and the manufacture of renewable energy technologies. Figure 12.14 depicts these developments since the beginning of the 1990s, showing high levels of growth in 2000 and 2005, which coincide with the national special regime. The evolution of regional frameworks differs across regions. Galicia, Navarra, Castilla y León, Cataluña and the Basque Country are policy leaders

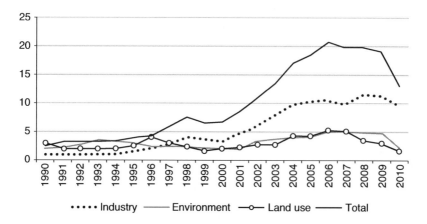

Figure 12.14 Evolution of regional normative related to renewable energy in CCAA, 1990–2010 (four-year moving average) (source: own elaboration based on MIETUR, 2005).

with established regional strategies for market deployment and industrial development based on support to R&D, experimental programmes, mandatory purchase of domestically produced components and government participation in wind farm ownership. The most important instrument is the territorial wind plan, which implies specific actions to identify suitable areas and includes procedures and conditions for exploiting natural resources.

3.4.1 Wind plans

Wind plans are instruments consisting of actions for the development of wind farms, including land expropriation for wind farm developments and agreements with utilities and manufacturers of energy technologies. The features of the regional governance system regarding the level and types of interaction between government and private actors differ depending on whether they are related to home market deployment or industrial development. Wind plans include formal long-term agreements including commitments and rights related to the exploitation of wind resources and set the basis for coordination among regional governments, utilities and manufacturers of renewable energy technologies. Regional governments can adopt a centralized or a decentralized approach to the management of resources and decision-making. For example, the business model for exploitation of regional resources can be designed to favour the participation of the main regional companies (i.e. the utilities) or entrepreneurial initiatives such as IPPs and local public–private management of wind farms. In the first option, a set of industry measures (e.g. long-term policies supporting manufacturing related sectors) promotes stronger developer–manufacturer linkages and a broader variety of size of industry actors and position in the supply chain.

In contrast, the decentralization of decision-making on the implementation of wind plans to the local (i.e. provincial) level may be aimed at actions related to the environmental impact of the wind infrastructure on other economic activities competing for the same resources (i.e. forestry, tourism) and the options of local actors, such as local government and citizens, regarding co-ownership and management of wind farms to satisfy local demand. These different objectives can lead to different positions related to the economic and administrative conditions associated with land expropriation and local resources management.

4 Reflections on the Spanish case

RES-E policy includes a range of mechanisms linking energy and industry policy to foster innovation in emergent sectors. This set of instruments for application at different levels may belong to specific energy policy categories or be part of supply and demand-side measures to support industry more generally. In what follows, we reflect on the policy actions that have supported the development of renewable energy and innovation in Spain through the lenses of the existing literature.

4.1 Matching policy instruments

The most common instruments in support of renewable energy sectors are demand-pull policies (Barradale, 2010; Enzensberger *et al.*, 2002; Jacobsson & Lauber, 2006; Lewis & Wiser, 2007; Lund, 2009; Meyer, 2007; Nemet, 2009) that are part of a broader set of supply and demand-oriented instruments, but act as direct and indirect mechanisms to foster the developments of new sectors. These instruments include both direct and indirect instruments with accompanying regulation and technical standards where implementation can occur in two directions. First, new market creation is pursued through rules and frameworks for competitive conditions (i.e. definition of actors and activities) and target-setting for energy production (quotas) and the emissions regime. Second, technology development is supported by basic R&D programmes with dedicated funding for RREE sector initiatives to support market penetration, R&D assessment, market evaluation, technology transfer, diffusion and commercialization.

Enzensberger *et al.* (2002) highlight a divide in the legislative background/ support. They focus on legislative support instruments, which include:

- *Demand and control*: regulation and standards that establish limits on and ways to achieve particular objectives and control particular quantitative (types of energy, technical specifications, environmental indicators) and qualitative (techniques, materials) variables. Technical specifications and 'mandate fuel off-take' as a type of regulation will be a main part of the analysis.
- *Market-based instruments*: these fall into two groups. First, supply-push measures oriented towards construction or production incentives that include financial stimuli (incentives, tax exemptions, grants). These are aimed at internalizing some externalities and setting appropriate prices. FIT and primes as direct subsidies are analysed. Second, demand-push measures that influence energy demand.

These two types of instruments are associated with most measures that form demand-driven innovation policies related to public intervention to improve articulation of demand in order to facilitate innovation and allow diffusion in new markets. Edler and Georghiou (2007) define them as follows: 'Demand side innovation policies are defined as all public measures to induce innovation and/ or speed up the diffusion of innovation through increasing the demand for innovation, defining new functional requirements for products and services or better articulating demand.' Demand-side policy can take various forms, but typically they are sector specific and address the specific barriers affecting market introduction and diffusion of innovations. Table 12.7 presents a general overview of policy considered by OECD in the broad category of demand-driven innovation.

In the specific case of the RES-E sector, public procurement can be considered a strategic instrument for influencing demand for certain technologies

Table 12.7 Taxonomy of demand-side policy and instruments

Policy type	Detail
Public procurement	Different types: Buy ready-made products for which no R&D is required Innovation-oriented procurement – purchasing not-yet-existing product Pre-commercial public procurement of R&D (PCP): no guarantee the public sector will buy the good or service) Catalytic procurement: state buys to support private purchases in the decision to buy. Ice-breakers. Applied in energy-efficient technologies
Innovation-oriented regulations and standards	Standards setting for technical specifications (e.g. energy efficiency eco-labelling)
Regulations	Rules to influence behaviours (e.g. renewables policy based on tariff scheme and quotas for Germany and California)
Standards	Rules, practices, metrics or conventions used in technology trade and society (e.g. ICT-internet and biometrics in the UK)
Lead markets	Aimed at diffusing innovation from one market to another (e.g. GMS telephone in Europe, combined supply–demand-side policy for green innovation in Japan, EU LM initiative: eHealth, protective textiles, sustainable construction, recycling, bio-based products and renewable energies)
Consumer policies	Education and awareness (e.g. generic and specific consumer skills in the UK)

Source: own elaboration adapted from OECD (2011).

and stimulating their market deployment. However, this instrument can also be part of a specific policy mix in which regulation and standards combine to provide a form of guaranteed tariff and specific purchasing power purchase instruments. These instruments affect both sides of the market (i.e. supply and demand) by creating better economic and institutional conditions for the sector. The analysis of RES-E policies to promote the wind energy sector in Spain considers commonalities among the instruments.

4.2 The RES-E policy setting in Spain

Since the EU introduced new norms for regulation of the energy sector in 1996, the competences and variety of actors and operation of the system have evolved into a more complex energy matrix. Some of the changes introduced were structural and based on radical liberalization and creation of a market. Other changes, linked to a sequence of different environmental objectives and commitments, have been introduced more gradually.

In Spain, security of supply has been a crucial ingredient in support of emergent RES-E sectors. Early policies were implemented to increase efficiency by considering vertical segmentation and introduction of new technologies (i.e. renewables) to improve the energy matrix. Spanish regulation has been strongly linked to the EU framework through two interconnected processes: market liberalization and the introduction of environmental regulation. Specific sectoral regulation promoted the introduction of new technologies based on technical standards related to efficiency, productivity and CO_2 reductions. While financial stimuli (FIT), RREE targets and R&D programmes were designed at national level, their implementation and accompanying environmental, energy and industry policies rely on local assets, including natural resources, and organizational and regulatory competences. Local policy created employment and market opportunities on the back of existing R&D and industrial capacity. The policy portfolio encompasses 'direct' support, such as mandatory purchase of regionally produced components, financial and tax incentives (manufacturing components), export assistance, R&D and instruments to facilitate commercialization (i.e. pilots, demonstration, trade missions).

'Indirect' mechanisms favour market pull to induce demand via FIT and mandatory renewable energy grants (Renewable Portfolio Standard-RPS quotas) explicitly included in long-term energy plans and the FIT scheme. The RPS quotas fall into the broad category of public procurement since its implementation requires coordination between the national and regional levels to provide permits and allowances for the development of new energy capacity (e.g. wind, thermal, solar, photovoltaic). This action includes technical requirements related to the scale, type and category of the technology. The regulatory framework has also redefined the activities and roles of actors in energy networks and removed the barriers to electricity market access.

These measures were introduced in the regional wind plans based on competitive government tenders. This common normative framework resulted in a range of responses across Spanish regions with some favouring public procurement oriented instruments (i.e. government tendering and local content requirements) and others keen to improve the competitiveness of their domestic industries (i.e. R&D support and commercialization and internationalization tools). The leading regions adopted the strategy of coupling wind energy plans with sectoral industry plans for the manufacture of renewable energy technologies. This strategy implies a series of regional agreements between the energy producers (i.e. utilities, large and small IPPs) and the manufacturers of the technology. As part of the strategy to increase the variety of business models for RES-E, some regional regulatory frameworks have allowed public–private partnerships between developers, local manufacturers and local government. Thus, these regional instruments have linked the actors in the local industrial setting to a stable and clear implementation processes. This has reduced the risks for investors by proposing a long-term scenario for market deployment and local technology development.

Table 12.8 summarizes these policy instruments. The shading of policies indicates the level of their implementation (i.e. national or regional). Specific features of regional governance regarding both the level and the structure of interaction among local government, the utilities and manufacturers are important determinants of domestic market expansion, deployment and industrial development. The strategic plans for wind energy include instruments aimed at flexible management to adapt decision-making to the local context. For example, the model for natural resources exploitation encourages the participation of regional companies and local entrepreneurial ventures such as IPPs, and local public–private management of wind farms. In relation to regional companies, the existence of a simultaneous set of industry policies (e.g. long-term policies supporting manufacturing-related sectors) allows for tighter developer–manufacturer linkages and a greater variety of size and position in the supply chain of industry actors. Decentralized implementation of wind plans at the provincial level responds to the competition for resources, for example, by minimizing the environmental impact of wind energy infrastructures on local activities such as forestry or tourism.

The portfolio of instruments presented in Table 12.8 is aimed at security of energy supply and development of the wind energy sector. Support for the creation of a renewable energy market has been expanding in relation to the European market and technologies (renewable industry and transport). In Spain, the energy market created ensures self-sufficiency by emphasizing renewable energy. The application of regulation in the form of financial stimuli (i.e. FIT scheme) has improved the economic conditions for investment in RES-E power capacity and industry developments related to renewables manufacturing. The provision of long-term targets encouraging industrial sectors in the process of market deployment, which was facilitated by additional regulation, aimed to remove barriers to access to the electricity market.

The role of regional policy has been critical for the implementation process of RES-E policy set through the introduction of government tendering as a form of public procurement. Public procurement has introduced a temporal horizon to the deployment of new markets and reorganized RES-E value chain operations in relation to the importance of local components and relations between electricity generators and manufacturers. The leading regions followed different paths towards home market deployment and technology development. Learning and technological improvements may take place in regions where public procurement (i.e. government tendering, wind plans and industry plans) are part of the policy mix, including R&D support, commercialization and internationalization strategies. This wider set of policies benefits not only the RES-E generators and the manufacturing sector but also the set of services, operations, maintenance and other activities involved in RES-E.

5 Concluding remarks

This chapter has outlined key steps in the emergence of the wind energy sector in Spain. The policy mix in support of renewable energy has encompassed a broad spectrum of instruments with cross-level and cross-sectoral links. Accordingly, synergies among different levels of government have been achieved by means division of roles and of activities. The general framework was set by the national government in relation to financial stimuli (FIT) and long-term objectives (Spanish–EU commitment to targets for RES-E); regional governments have been responsible for implementation through government tendering (i.e. wind plans), promotion of manufacture of local components and facilitation of agreements between key actors such as utilities, developers and technology manufacturers.

The reorganization of new roles and agreements in the sector has been coupled with liberalization of the electricity market in which new emerging IPPs play a significant role in a more favourable institutional and industrial setting. The links between energy production and the manufacture of RES-E technologies have been strengthened by identifying complementarities between the supply and demand sides in combination with instruments supporting demand by setting targets for market shares, and financial and regulatory instruments to improve economic (FIT) and technological (R&D support) production conditions.

Based on the identification of widely applied, but distinctively oriented instruments to foster the wind energy sector (e.g. FIT, targets, government tendering, regional agreements), this chapter has drawn attention to the broad variety of demand-driven innovation policies that were prominent in the Spanish case. Public procurement instruments, regulation and standards, and promotion of lead markets have been combined in a multi-level framework that considers a wide spectrum of activities along a complex value chain. As a result, in less than ten years, Spain has developed a new sector which is exploiting local market deployments and technological developments.

Table 12.8 Typologies of policy instruments for renewable energy

Demand-driven innovation polices by OECD	Policy instruments fostering wind energy			
	Legislative	Market-based (economic)/Market deployment		Non-legislative
	Demand and control (regulatory)	Supply push (prices, costs)/financial stimulus	Demand pull (amount)	Information, administrative and resource mapping
Public procurement	Government (competitive) tendering for wind projects and resources Regional wind plans Industrial sectoral plans (manufacturing sector/renewable energy technologies)			
Ready-made products NO R&D	Participation/ownership of local government in wind farms			
Pre-commercial public procurement of R&D		R&D, market deployment and other support programmes for demonstrations and experiments		
Innovation-oriented regulation and standards	Mandatory purchase of regional components **Mandated fuel off-take RREE**			

Policy matrix (read as figure):

Policy category	Column 1	Column 2	Column 3
Regulations	CO₂ and efficiency environmental standards	Direct access to electricity market (barriers removal)	National energy plans (NEP) EU directives on RREE and CO₂ emissions
	Renewable portfolio standards (RPS-Quotas) NEP/EU targets: 12 per cent for 2010 and 20 per cent for 2020	Retribution scheme based on treasure bones (substitution of feed-in tariff scheme since 2013) **Special regime – feed-in tariff scheme**	Administrative procedures (R&NI)
	Environmental, energy and industrial regional policy	Land expropriation for wind farms development	
Standards	Normative setting wind energy specifications (type and scale)		
Lead markets	WE farms and new business models by independent power producers		Commercialization and internationalization support programmes
	Regional coordination/agreements with utilities and manufacturers		Aeolian map
Consumer policies			Information and awareness campaign

Source: own elaboration.

Note

Cell shading identifies the policy level – National , Regional and Regional and national (R&N)

Annex

Key aspects of the technology and industry

The basic operating principle of wind turbine technology is the capturing of kinetic energy generated by the propulsion of air currents and its transformation into mechanical energy, which, in turn, generates electric power. The dominant technological design is a horizontal three-blade turbine that was first conceived in the early 1900s (Figure 12.15). The core technological principle involved, mechanical optimization, entails an efficiency trade-off between size and weight in turbine design. Conversely, the chief economic concern is the balance between capital investments in infrastructure and the variable costs involved in the operation and maintenance of turbines.

While improving turbine design was the main goal of early inventive efforts, the pursuit of higher efficiency has in recent times been linked to the exploration of new materials and of interoperability across mechanical, electric and electronic systems. In fact, the economically efficient way to generate energy from air currents is the deployment of wind farms (or wind farms), that is, installations of several individual turbines that can extend for up to several hundred square miles. Wind farms are energy systems that accrue economies of density due to co-location while at the same time entailing technical and organizational challenges that differ from those related to designing, managing and operating individual turbines. Wind farms entail generation, storage and distribution issues that call for the integration of complementary technological components. In addition to the functionally mechanical parts of individual turbines, smooth electricity generation requires electronic systems to manage remote monitoring and traffic control (see Box 12.1).

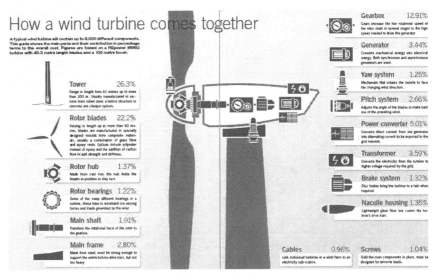

Figure 12.15 Main technological components of a wind turbine (source: EWEA, 2007).

Box 12.1 The knowledge grid

Wind farms are not just grids of interconnected technologies; they are also systems of integrated know-how. The main components of a wind turbine, i.e. generator, blades and gearbox, are sourced from established sectors such as hydroelectric, naval and aircraft industries. The relevant knowledge base comes from traditional basic science in the metal-mechanics industry sectors and mechanical engineering. However, in the wind farm context, other domains of expertise are needed (Figure 12.16): informatics and telecommunication for remote operation and control; logistics and civil engineering for efficient management of land; energy system management for efficient storage and distribution.

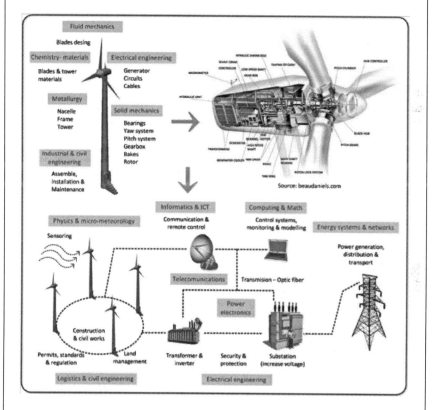

Figure 12.16 Wind farm technologies and forms of know-how (source: own elaboration).

Notes

1 According to a 2006 resolution of the National Commission of Energy, the major operators in the Spanish electricity market are: Endesa; Iberdrola; Union Fenosa; HC Energia (acquired by EDP in 2005) and Viesgogeneracion (acquired by EON in 2008). www.cne.es/cne/doc/legislacion/cne02_06.pdf.

2 Gamesa Wind was established in 1994 with 51 per cent of the capital held by Gamesa and 40 per cent by its Danish partner Vestas Wind Systems, with which it has a technology agreement. Vestas sold its 40 per cent share to Gamesa in 2001.

3 The study developed by IDAE (2013) indicates that the threshold for optimal operation is speed >6 metres per second at a height of 8 metres.

4 The shaded circles denote different types of industrial activity; the figures in the circles denote the total number of industrial sites per region with size adjusting accordingly.

5 In 2007, Galicia had industry sites focused on each of the different categories.

6 Electricity from renewable energy sources (RES-E) in the wind sector is concentrated 51 per cent in the big utilities (Iberdrola, EDPR, Enel Green Power and Union Fenosa) (Acciona is the leading IPP) and 49 per cent in other/small developers.

7 A detailed description of the regional policy mix is provided in Section 3.

8 The normal electricity generation regime/market uses traditional energy sources such as hydroelectric, nuclear and fossil-based thermal plants (i.e. coal, oil, gas).

9 Directive 2001/77/EC outlined: (1) national goals for achieving 12 per cent coverage of electricity demand by renewable energy by 2010; (2) energy production from renewables should be 22.1 per cent of total EU energy production (29.4 per cent for Spain); (3) member countries could develop their own strategies within the common framework.

10 Directive 2009/28/EC stated that the Spanish target for the share of energy from renewable sources should be 20 per cent of gross final energy consumption by 2020.

11 The cap and floor system affected the FIT by introducing a variable payment adjusted to the wholesale electricity market price and the cap and floor values.

12 The new scheme seeks to guarantee a 'reasonable' profit based on treasure bones interest rate (ten years issued) plus a spread (+300 pts) which is equivalent to 7.5 per cent profitability.

13 The share of the special regime in the energy balance increased from 9 per cent in 1997 to 37 per cent in 2012, while the share of wind power increased from 1 per cent to 22 per cent in the same period.

References

AEE. (2005–2013). *Eólica*. Annual report on Spanish wind energy sector (several years).

AEE. (2013b). Wind map. Available at: www.aeeolica.org/es/sobre-la-eolica/la-eolica-en-espana/mapa-eolico/.

Barradale, M.J. (2010). Impact of public policy uncertainty on renewable energy investment: wind power and the production tax credit. *Energy Policy*, 38(12), pp. 7698–7709.

CNE. (2013). Informe mensual de ventas de energía del régimen especial – August 2013. Available at: www.cne.es/cne/Publicaciones?id_nodo=143&accion=1&soloUltimo=si&sIdCat=10&keyword=&auditoria=F.

DE. (2013). *Wind Power Capacity*. Washington: US Department of Energy. Available from DE dataset.

De Alegría Mancisidor, I.M., Díaz de Basurto Uraga, P., Martínez de Alegría Mancisidor, I. and Ruiz de Arbulo López, P. (2009). European Union's renewable energy sources and energy efficiency policy review: the Spanish perspective. *Renewable and Sustainable Energy Reviews*, 13(1), pp. 100–114.

Del Río González, P. (2008). Ten years of renewable electricity policies in Spain: an analysis of successive feed-in tariff reforms. *Energy Policy*, 36(8), pp. 2917–2929.

Deloitte. (2011). *Estudio Macroeconómico del Impacto del Sector Eólico en España*. Madrid: Elaborado por Deloitte para AEE.

Edler, J. and Georghiou, L. (2007). Public procurement and innovation – resurrecting the demand side. *Research Policy*, 36(7), pp. 949–963.

Enzensberger, N., Wietschel, M. and Rentz, O. (2002). Policy instruments fostering wind energy projects – a multi-perspective evaluation approach. *Energy Policy*, 30(9), pp. 793–801.

EWEA. (2007). Focus on supply chain. *Wind Directions*, January/February.

EWEA. (2009). *Wind Energy – The Facts: A Guide to the Technology, Economics and Future of Wind Power*. London: Earthscan for the European Wind Energy Association.

EWEA. (2013). *Wind in Power: 2013 European Statistics*. Brussels: European Wind Energy Association.

IAEST, Instituto Aragonés de Estadística. (2013). *Wind Turbines and Wind Farms, 2003 to 2010*. Zaragoza: IAEST. Available from IAEST dataset.

IDEA. (2013). *Spanish Wind Atlas*. Available at http://atlaseolico.idae.es/index.php?idioma=EN.

IEA, International Energy Agency. (2013). *Policy and Measures Dataset*. Paris: International Energy Agency. Available from IEA datasets.

Jacobsson, S. and Lauber, V. (2006). The politics and policy of energy system transformation – explaining the German diffusion of renewable energy technology. *Energy Policy*, 34(3), pp. 256–276.

Lewis, J.I. and Wiser, R.H. (2007). Fostering a renewable energy technology industry: an international comparison of wind industry policy support mechanisms. *Energy Policy*, 35(3), pp. 1844–1857.

López, R.M.M. and Moliner, R. (2012). Energía sin CO2. *Química e industria: QeI*, 600, pp. 32–35.

Lund, P.D. (2009). Effects of energy policies on industry expansion in renewable energy. *Renewable Energy*, 34(1), pp. 53–64.

Meyer, N.I. (2007). Learning from wind energy policy in the EU: lessons from Denmark, Sweden and Spain. *European Environment*, 17(5), pp. 347–362.

MIETUR. (2005). *Plan de Acción Nacional de Energías Renovables de España (PANER)*. Ministerio de Industria, Energia y Turismo, Gobierno de España.

Montes, G.M., Martín, E.P. and García, J.O. (2007). The current situation of wind energy in Spain. *Renewable and Sustainable Energy Reviews*, 11(3), pp. 467–481.

Navigant. (2013). *International Wind Energy Development: World Market Update 2012*, BTM wind report. Boulder, CO: Navigant Research.

Nemet, G.F. (2009). Demand-pull, technology-push, and government-led incentives for non-incremental technical change. *Research Policy*, 38(5), pp. 700–709.

OECD. (2011). *Demand-side Innovation Policies*. Paris: Organisation for Economic Co-operation and Development.

OECD. (2013). *Stat Extracts. Wind Power Capacity*. Paris: Organisation for Economic Co-operation and Development. Available from OECD dataset.

REE Red Eléctrica Española. (1997–2012). *Balance energético* (several years).

Río, P. del and Burguillo, M. (2009). An empirical analysis of the impact of renewable energy deployment on local sustainability. *Renewable and Sustainable Energy Reviews*, 13(6), pp. 1314–1325.

13 The role of environmental policy for eco-innovation

Theoretical background and empirical results for different countries

Jens Horbach

1 Introduction

Eco-innovations leading to reduced environmental impacts or a reduction in material and energy use are being focused on by politicians because of both positive environmental and even economic effects. Eco-innovations help to remedy the negative external environmental effects of economic activities. Following the respective theoretical literature, in most cases, these negative external effects have to be internalized by regulation measures and the role of regulation as a determinant of eco-innovation is therefore crucial. The famous Porter hypothesis even goes a step further and postulates positive effects of environmental regulation on the innovation behaviour of the whole firm.

This chapter summarizes the main determinants of eco-innovations from a theoretical perspective (Section 2.1) with a special focus on the role of environmental policy (Section 2.2). In a second step, the recent empirical literature on the drivers of eco-innovation is summarized and aims to provide some common 'stylized facts' (Section 3.1). In Section 3.2, empirical analyses on the role of environmental policy in the development of eco-innovation are considered. The section includes a discussion of the problems of measuring the impacts of environmental policy on eco-innovation and different approaches to finding empirical evidence for the Porter hypothesis.

2 Determinants of eco-innovation from a theoretical perspective

2.1 Overview of different eco-innovation determinants

In an EU-funded research project called 'Measuring Eco-Innovation' (MEI), eco-innovation has been defined as follows (Kemp and Pearson, 2008):

> Eco-innovation is the production, application or exploitation of a good, service, production process, organizational structure, or management or business method that is novel to the firm or user and which results, throughout its life cycle, in a reduction of environmental risk, pollution and the negative impacts of resource use (including energy use) compared to relevant alternatives.

This definition is based on the outcomes of innovation activities. If innovations lead to positive environmental effects, they are defined as eco-innovations. The MEI definition also defines innovations as 'green' if the underlying innovation activities were not intended to improve the environment. Therefore,

> it does not matter if environmental improvements have been the primary goal of a new product or process, or came about as a by-product or simply by chance. Eco-innovations can thus be the result of other economic rationales such as increasing market share or reducing costs.
>
> (Horbach *et al.*, 2012: 113)

The general innovation theory accentuates the importance of technology push and market or demand-pull factors in an explanation of innovation activities (Hemmelskamp, 1999; see Table 13.1 for an overview). These factors are of course also important for eco-innovations. However, as most environmental problems represent negative external effects, there may be no clear economic incentives to develop new environmentally benign products and processes. Therefore, (environmental) policy measures and institutional factors may play an important role in the development of eco-innovations. In Section 2.2, the special importance of environmental policies will be discussed in detail.

Do eco-innovations have specific determinants compared with 'other' innovations? Eco-innovations may be dependent on the environmental consciousness of consumers and firms, which may be interpreted as an environmentally oriented demand-pull effect. Furthermore, cost savings, especially those caused by the reduction of material and energy use, may also be more important for eco-innovations than other innovations because, in many cases, they are linked to reduced environmental impacts – for example, less material consumption signifies a reduction in waste and energy savings are normally accompanied by reductions in CO_2 emissions (Horbach *et al.*, 2013).

Furthermore, there are also regional and location conditions favouring eco-innovations (Cainelli *et al.*, 2011; Horbach, 2014). Many eco-innovations fields are relatively new (e.g. renewable energies, electro mobility) and they are therefore more dependent on external sources of information and on basic research activities compared with more established innovation fields. Therefore, the existence of universities and other research institutions seems to be especially relevant to eco-innovation. These institutions contribute to the regional availability of high-skilled employees who have a 'fresh' education in new research fields such as new energy technologies. As information flows seem to be particularly important for young technologies, local cooperation networks may also especially promote eco-innovation. On the other hand, sunk costs and path dependencies are not so important to new eco-innovation fields and the production of eco-innovative products may therefore also offer chances for regions with an underdeveloped or old industry structure.

Table 13.1 Determinants of eco-innovation

Supply side	• Technological capabilities
	• Appropriation problem and market characteristics
Demand side	• (Expected) market demand (demand-pull hypothesis)
	• Social awareness of the need for clean production; environmental consciousness and preference for environmentally friendly products
Institutional and political influences	• Environmental policy (incentive-based instruments or regulatory approaches)
	• Institutional structure: e.g. political opportunities of environmentally oriented groups, organization of information flow, existence of innovation networks

Source: own elaboration, adapted from Horbach (2008).

2.2 Specific role of environmental policy

From a traditional point of view, environmental policy imposes additional production costs and therefore reduces the international competitiveness of a firm (Ambec *et al.*, 2013). For end-of-pipe pollution abatement technologies requiring additional and 'unproductive' equipment in particular, this argumentation seems to be really justified. 'In this static world, where firms have already made their cost-minimizing choices, environmental regulation inevitably raises costs and will tend to reduce the market share of domestic companies on global markets' (Porter and van der Linde, 1995: 97). But, contrary to that view, Porter and van der Linde (1995) point to possible innovation offsets: a better environmental performance caused by regulation may be accompanied by material and energy savings, leading to an increase in competitiveness so that the additional production costs may be even overcompensated.

Porter and van der Linde (1995: 99–100) give six reasons for the positive effects of environmental regulation on firm performance:

•   Regulation provides signals that reduce information deficits about the incomplete utilization of resources or the minimizing of discharges.
•   Regulation promoting environmentally related information gathering may raise corporate awareness of environmental problems leading to a reduction in resource use.
•   Regulation reduces the uncertainty of environmentally related investments leading to cost savings at least in the long run.
•   Regulation creates pressure to motivate innovation activities by replacing pressure coming from competitors. Especially in totally new research fields, this additional pressure from regulations may be fruitful.
•   Regulation 'levels the transitional playing field' by ensuring 'that one company cannot opportunistically gain position by avoiding environmental investments' (Porter and van der Linde, 1995: 100).
•   Regulation is needed when innovation is not able to offset compliance costs in the short term.

In fact, the Porter hypothesis assuming imperfect information, organizational problems and market failures questions the ability of firms to maximize profit. This has been criticized by many economists (see, e.g. Palmer *et al.*, 1995) but at least in the short run it seems plausible that managers may fail to recognize cost-saving potentials. The newer organizational and behavioural literature tries to explain low incentives to invest in environmental technologies. One argument consists in the fact that the success of managers is predominantly measured by their short-run profit so that these 'present-biased managers' (Ambec *et al.*, 2013) will postpone environmental innovations because their costs have to be paid now, but the benefits will only appear in the long run. Another strand of literature (see, e.g. Mohr, 2002) argues that environmental regulation may reduce underinvestment in R&D stemming from technology spillovers as market failure.

The Porter hypothesis that all types of environmental regulations automatically lead to innovation offsets should not be misinterpreted (Ambec *et al.*, 2013) – for example, regulations explicitly requiring the implementation of specific end-of-pipe technologies such as filters seem to have little or no innovation effects, whereas flexible instruments such as eco-taxes seem to be preferable (Jaffe *et al.*, 2002).

Some authors make the distinction between a weak and a strong version of the Porter hypothesis (see Jaffe and Palmer, 1997; Lanoie *et al.*, 2011 for an empirical analysis). The weak version only postulates that regulation induces eco-innovations without claiming that these innovations are socially benign, whereas the strong version assumes that the regulation-induced innovations overcompensate for the cost of compliance, thus leading to an increase in the competitiveness of the firm.

In the end, the question of whether the Porter hypothesis can be confirmed or not remains an empirical problem. Section 3.2 summarizes the main recent empirical analyses of the determinants of eco-innovation with a special focus on the role of environmental policy measures.

3 Empirical analyses of eco-innovation

3.1 'Stylized facts' of eco-innovation drivers – an overview

Besides case studies, which are not the focus of this chapter, many empirical analyses of the driving forces of eco-innovation using econometric methods already exist. In most cases, these analyses are based on survey or patent data. In the following, the aim is to detect some 'stylized facts' based on this literature (also see Table 13.2 for an overview).

In the survey by Bartolomeo *et al.* (2003), the three most cited reasons for introducing an environmental innovation to Germany were to improve the firm's image, to comply with environmental regulation and to reduce costs. Furthermore, organizational innovations are also important because they trigger product and process innovations. 'An organizational innovation is the implementation of

Table 13.2 Main determinants of eco-innovations from an empirical perspective

Supply side
- Cost savings (Johnstone, 2007; Bartolomeo *et al.*, 2003; Horbach *et al.*, 2012; Demirel and Kesidou, 2012; Kesidou and Demirel, 2012; Triguero *et al.*, 2013)
- Resource prices (Grupp, 1999)
- Improvement of the firm's image (Bartolomeo *et al.*, 2003; Del Rio Gonzalez, 2005)
- Environmental impacts (Johnstone, 2007)
- Existence of a specialized R&D department (Rennings *et al.*, 2006; Johnstone, 2007)
- Network activities and external cooperation (Mazzanti and Zoboli, 2006; Coenen and Díaz López, 2010; de Marchi, 2012)
- Person explicitly responsible for environmental concerns (Johnstone, 2007)
- Influence of environmental management systems (Rennings *et al.*, 2006; Johnstone, 2007; Horbach, 2008; Rehfeld *et al.*, 2007; Ziegler and Nogareda, 2009)
- Path dependencies – 'innovation breeds innovation': positive influence of past firm performance (Mazzanti and Zoboli, 2006; Horbach, 2008)

Demand side
- Market demand (Horbach, 2008)
- Customer benefits (Kammerer, 2009)

Policy measures
- Complying with environmental regulation, strictness of environmental policy (e.g. Jaffe and Palmer, 1997; Cleff and Rennings, 1999; Bartolomeo *et al.*, 2003; Brunnermeier and Cohen, 2003; Johnstone, 2007; Horbach *et al.*, 2012; Demirel and Kesidou, 2012)

Source: own elaboration

a new organizational method in the firm's business practices, workplace organisation or external relations' (OECD and Eurostat, 2005: 51). Environmental management systems (EMS) can be understood as environmental organizational innovations (see Rennings *et al.*, 2006). The importance of EMS for eco-process and eco-product innovations has been shown by Rennings *et al.* (2006), Rehfeld *et al.* (2007), Wagner (2008) and Khanna *et al.* (2009). EMS seem to be very important, especially for the introduction of cost-saving cleaner technologies because they help to overcome incomplete information within a firm (see also Sections 2.2 and 3.2). Cost savings are not achieved because firms do not have the necessary information. Khanna *et al.* (2009) illustrate the important role of EMS in their theoretical and empirical analysis:

> senior management commitment, team-work, empowerment of employees at all levels, and techniques such as process mapping, root cause analysis and environmental accounting can enable the firm to become aware of inefficiencies that were not recognized previously and to find new ways to increase efficiency and reduce the costs of pollution control.
>
> (Khanna *et al.*, 2009: 90)

Rennings *et al.* (2006) use German survey data to analyse the influence of environmental management systems (especially EMAS) on environmentally related organizational, process and product innovations. Other than the positive influences of environmental management tools, the authors show that the existence of a specialized R&D department as an input variable triggers environmental innovation. A paper written by Rehfeld *et al.* (2007) detects a positive relationship between the certification of environmental management systems and environmental product innovations for German manufacturing.

Horbach (2008) uses two German panel data bases, the establishment panel of the Institute for Employment Research (IAB) and the Mannheim Innovation Panel (MIP) of the Centre for European Economic Research (ZEW), to explore the determinants of environmental innovations. The econometric estimations show that an improvement in technological capabilities ('knowledge capital') by R&D or further education measures triggers environmental innovations. Environmental regulation, environmental management tools and general organizational changes also encourage environmental innovation. The hypothesis that 'innovation breeds innovation' is confirmed by an analysis of the MIP data. General and environmental innovative firms in the past are also more likely to innovate in the present. The demand-pull hypothesis is confirmed in both models. Kammerer (2009) finds empirical evidence that customer benefits are crucial to eco-innovations as soon as a product is connected with added value for the customer. While it may be difficult to get added value from green electricity, there are environmental product innovations with substantial customer benefits, such as food or baby clothes (Horbach *et al.*, 2012). Consequently, consumers are more likely to pay more for organic food or organic baby clothes but not for green electricity.

Using a panel data set of Italian firms in 2002 and 2004, Mazzanti and Zoboli (2006) stress the positive influence of network activities and R&D as an input for environmental innovation. Cainelli *et al.* (2011) confirm the important role of networking with other firms in the adoption of eco-innovations. Furthermore, the authors point out that strategic relationships within regions and at the international level are crucial. Systemic and evolutionary approaches (van den Bergh *et al.*, 2007; Coenen and Díaz López, 2010) strongly support these findings. Following Coenen and Díaz López (2010: 1150), 'innovations are iteratively enacted through networks of social relations, rather than through singular events by isolated individuals or organisations'. Also with regard to regional and location factors, Horbach (2014) shows that eco-innovations seem to be a chance for underdeveloped regions looking for new business activities because they are more likely in regions characterized by high poverty rates. Furthermore, they seem to be less dependent on urbanization advantages. The pre-condition for such regions attracting eco-innovations is a good infrastructure concerning research institutions.

For Spain, de Marchi finds out that cooperation with external partners, especially suppliers, universities and knowledge-intensive business services, is more important for eco-innovations than other innovations (de Marchi, 2012).

Del Rio Gonzalez (2005) analyses the drivers of adopting cleaner technology in the Spanish pulp and paper industry. He found that most of the environmental technologies introduced were end-of-pipe (i.e. waste water treatment plants) or incremental clean technologies. Regulatory pressure and corporate image were the main drivers for adopting green technologies. In contrast with other survey results where cost savings are one of the main drivers of cleaner technologies, costs are often seen as an obstacle, especially for firms that do not develop innovations themselves but have to buy them from suppliers. For a sample of Spanish firms, Canon de Francia *et al.* (2007: 307) find that the 'availability of greater technical knowledge within a company moderates its vulnerability in the face of the demands of new environmental regulations'.

In another recent analysis for Great Britain, Demirel and Kesidou (2012) confirm the important role of environmental regulations for end-of-pipe technologies. Furthermore, the authors show that market factors, such as cost savings, are important for the development of environmental R&D. Their results also show a positive role of environmental management systems in the introduction of eco-innovations. Further survey results for the determinants of the introduction of environmental R&D and cleaner technologies are available from an OECD project in 2003 on Public Environmental Policy and the Private Firm, covering seven OECD countries (Canada, France, Germany, Hungary, Japan, Norway and the USA) (see Arimura *et al.*, 2007; Frondel *et al.*, 2007; Johnstone, 2007). The whole data set includes more than 4,000 observations originating from manufacturing facilities with at least 50 employees. Around 74 per cent (3,100) of the sample facilities took significant technical measures to reduce the environmental impacts associated with their activities (Frondel *et al.*, 2007). Econometric results exploiting the OECD database show that a strict environmental policy measured by the perceived policy stringency of the questioned firm, environmental accounting systems and flexible environmental instruments stimulates environmental R&D. Environmental management tools and the possibility of cost savings are very important for the introduction of cleaner technologies (Frondel *et al.*, 2007) but not for end-of-pipe measures.

Triguero *et al.* (2013) analyse eco-innovation drivers in European SMEs based on Eurobarometer data for a survey on managers in 27 European countries. The authors show that supply-side factors such as cost savings seem to be especially important for eco-process innovations, whereas existing regulations are more important for eco-product and eco-organizational innovations.

Finally, firm-specific factors also influence the innovation decision, such as knowledge transfer mechanisms and involvement in networks (Wagner, 2009). From the perspective of a resource-based view of a firm, 'green capabilities' play an important role (Hart, 1995; Kammerer, 2009).

3.2 *The impact of environmental policy instruments*

As already mentioned in Section 3.1, environmental regulation plays a crucial role in triggering eco-innovations. In this section, the corresponding empirical results in the literature will be discussed in more detail. In fact, all these studies have to solve the problem of measuring the impact of policy measures using adequate indicators. Direct indicators of policy measures describe, for example, the introduction of a policy measure at a certain time point by a dummy variable. An analysis of the causal effects of regulation requires time series, and patent data are therefore often used. One caveat lies in the fact that patents only partly cover the broad range of eco-innovations because many eco-innovations, such as organizational changes in the production process, are not recorded by patents. Further problems occur because the lag structure is not easy to recognize and/or the lack of data may cause difficulties in analysing long-term effects of environmental policy. Furthermore, these indicators do not allow the analysis of anticipated future policy measures.

In some empirical analyses, pollution abatement or compliance expenditures also serve as regulation indicators. Besides the advantage of good availability of data, this indicator only measures policy stringency indirectly. Furthermore, treating this indicator as an exogenous policy measure is problematic. Other indicators are monitoring activities but they only capture one aspect of the regulation process. In many survey analyses, self-perceived stringency measures are used. It is easy to include respective questions in surveys, but the answers may be biased because the questioned firms may give strategic responses. All in all, there seems to be no ideal indicator for policy measures.

In many empirical studies, regulation has been identified as an important determinant of eco-innovation (e.g. early studies from Green *et al.*, 1994; Cleff and Rennings, 1999; Rennings and Zwick, 2002; Brunnermeier and Cohen, 2003) and is known as the 'regulatory push/pull effect' (Rennings, 2000; recent overview in Del Rio Gonzalez, 2009). Popp (2006) found evidence in a study based on patent data from the United States, Japan and Germany that companies' innovation decisions were mainly driven by national regulation. Del Rio Gonzalez (2005) identified regulation pressure and corporate image as the main drivers of adopting cleaner technology in a survey in the Spanish pulp and paper industry. Frondel *et al.* (2007) find that policy stringency is generally an increasingly important driving force for eco-innovation rather than the choice of single policy instruments – a similar result was found by Arimura *et al.* (2007) for the effect of regulation on green R&D. Facilities facing very stringent environmental regulation are more likely to conduct environmental R&D. Frondel *et al.* (2007) point out that the effects of regulation may differ with regard to different environmental technology fields: whereas end-of-pipe technologies are triggered by regulation in particular, cost savings and environmental management systems seem to be more important for the introduction of cleaner technologies. Horbach (2008) analyses panel data and finds influence from regulation and the cost-saving motivation to be main determinants. A recent paper from Khanna *et al.* (2009) also distinguishes between present and anticipated environmental regulation. Using a sample of S&P 500 firms, the authors find that 'anticipated regulation and the presence of "complementary assets" is important for creating incentives and the internal capacity to undertake incremental adoption of pollution prevention techniques' (Khanna *et al.*, 2009: 85). Using German CIS data for 2008, Horbach *et al.* (2012) show that the influence of regulation varies for different environmental technology fields. Whereas current and expected government regulations particularly trigger air, water or noise emissions, hazardous substances and the recyclability of products, they are less important for material and energy savings. Rennings and Rexhäuser (2011) analyse the long-term effects of regulation for eco-innovation using the same German database. They find that command-and-control regulations trigger eco-innovations in the long run – a somewhat surprising result because the theoretical literature has doubts about the positive dynamic effects of this type of environmental policy instruments. The results are not supported for all environmental innovation fields because the long-term effects could not be observed for material use and energy efficiency or for compensation of dangerous inputs and improvement of recycling possibilities.

Rexhäuser and Rammer (2014) confirm the Porter hypothesis (see Section 2.2) but only for eco-innovations improving resource efficiency, whereas innovations that only reduce environmental externalities tend to reduce firm profitability. Following the theoretical work of Jaffe and Palmer (1997), Lanoie *et al.* (2011) test different variants of the Porter hypothesis based on an OECD database for seven countries. The so-called weak version that environmental regulation is able to stimulate environmental innovations is strongly supported by their econometric results. The strong version, which postulates that regulation-induced cost savings have to overcompensate the compliance costs, is not fully supported because the authors only find partial offsets of the compliance costs.

Johnstone *et al.* (2010b) point out that policy stringency is important for eco-innovation because it leads to higher prices for resource use. However, efficient environmental policy measures have to have additional characteristics. The stability and predictability of a policy especially matters because firms will only invest if the future returns are stable. Patent-based empirical evidence over the period 2001–2006 supports this hypothesis. Furthermore, a high flexibility of policy measures that allow investors to find the best way to reduce environmental impacts is very important.

Johnstone *et al.* (2010a) analyse the effects of different policy instruments on the development of renewable energy technologies. Their patent analysis reveals a high importance of feed-in-tariffs for solar energy, whereas more cost-competitive technologies such as wind power are not triggered by this policy instrument.

Vona *et al.* (2012) find out that liberalization of the highly concentrated energy market is important for the development of renewable energies. Environmental policy measures are more efficient if they are combined with lower entry barriers in the energy market. Their patent analysis for different OECD countries also accounts for the endogeneity of environmental policy. Veugelers (2012) uses the Flemish CIS to explore the influence of different drivers of eco-innovation. She points out that 'policy interventions are shown to be more powerful to induce the adoption and development of new clean technologies when designed in policy mix and time consistently, affecting future expectations' (Veugelers, 2012: 1770).

All in all, the studies confirm the decisive role of present and anticipated regulations for the introduction of eco-innovations, but empirical evidence for the strong version of the Porter hypothesis still remains weak.

4 Summary and research needs

Eco-innovations help to reduce the negative environmental effects of production and consumption activities. The theoretical literature stresses the role of environmental policy in the internalization of negative external effects. In a traditional perspective, environmental policy measures led to higher production costs thus decreasing firms' competitiveness. Since the introduction of the Porter hypothesis, this traditional view on the effects of environmental policy has changed. Porter and van der Linde (1995) point to possible innovation offsets: a better environmental performance due to regulation may be accompanied by material and energy savings leading to an increase in competitiveness so that the additional production costs may be even overcompensated. Whether this hypothesis is true or not remains an empirical question. In the meantime, there is considerable empirical literature on the determinants of eco-innovation. Most of these analyses for different countries and different data sources confirm the positive role of environmental policy for the development of eco-innovations, thus supporting the so-called weak version of the Porter hypothesis. In fact, the strong version of this hypothesis denoting an overcompensation of regulation-induced production costs is only partially confirmed and strongly depends on the nature of the analysed eco-innovation. Eco-innovations also leading to energy or material savings are naturally more likely to lead to innovations offsets compared with end-of-pipe innovations, such as the development of a new catalytic converter.

In addition to environmental regulation and cost savings as motivations for eco-innovation, further determinants have been empirically observed. Environmental management systems play a crucial role because they improve the information basis within firms to overcome organizational and coordination problems. Furthermore, network activities and external cooperation lead to synergy effects that are especially important for young environmental research fields such as renewable energy. Market demand and customer benefits are also essential for the development of eco-innovations.

Limitations to current eco-innovation research are mainly due to data restrictions. An analysis of the effects of environmental regulation on eco-innovation, in particular, would require time series data. Patent data partially fill this gap but they only partially capture the broad range of eco-innovations. An extension of the Community Innovation Survey regarding a permanent eco-innovation filter question in each wave would be very helpful for this field of research.

References

Ambec, S., Cohen, M.A., Elgie, S. and Lanoie, P. (2013): The Porter hypothesis at 20: can environmental regulation enhance innovation and competitiveness? *Review of environmental economics and policy*, Vol. 7, No. 1, 2–22.

Arimura, T., Hibiki, A. and Johnstone, N. (2007): An empirical study of environmental R&D: what encourages facilities to be environmentally innovative? In: Johnstone, N. (ed.) *Environmental Policy and Corporate Behaviour*. Cheltenham: Edward Elgar.

Bartolomeo, M., Kemp, R., Rennings, K. and Zwick, T. (2003): Employment impacts of cleaner production: theory, methodology and results. In: Rennings, K. and Zwick, T. (eds) *Employment Impacts of Cleaner Production. ZEW Economic Studies 21*, Heidelberg: Physica Verlag.

Brunnermeier, S.B. and Cohen, M.A. (2003): Determinants of environmental innovation in US manufacturing industries. *Journal of Environmental Economics and Management*, Vol. 45, No. 2, 278–293.

Cainelli, G., Mazzanti, M. and Zoboli, R. (2011): Environmental innovations, complementarity and local/global cooperation: evidence from North-East Italian industry. *International Journal of Technology, Policy and Management*, Vol. 11, Nos. 3/4, 328–268.

Canon de Francia, J., Garcés-Ayerbe, C. and Ramírez-Alesón, M. (2007): Are more innovative firms less vulnerable to new environmental regulation? *Environmental & Resource Economics* Vol. 36, 295–311.

Cleff, T. and Rennings, K. (1999): Determinants of environmental product and process innovation – evidence from the Mannheim innovation panel and a follow-up telephone survey. *European Environment*, Vol. 9, No. 5, 191–201.

Coenen, L. and Díaz López, F.J. (2010): Comparing systems approaches to innovation and technological change for sustainable and competitive economies: an explorative study into conceptual commonalities, differences and complementarities. *Journal of Cleaner Production*, Vol. 18, 1149–1160.

de Marchi, V. (2012): Environmental innovation and R&D cooperation: empirical evidence from Spanish manufacturing firms. *Research Policy*, Vol. 41, 614–623.

Del Rio Gonzalez, P. (2005): Analysing the factors influencing clean technology adoption: a study of the Spanish pulp and paper industry. *Business Strategy and the Environment*, Vol. 14, 20–37.

Del Rio Gonzalez, P. (2009): The empirical analysis of the determinants for environmental technological change: a research agenda. *Ecological Economics*, Vol. 68, 861–878.

Demirel, P. and Kesidou, E. (2012): Stimulating different types of eco-innovation in the UK: government policies and firm motivations. *Ecological Economics*, Vol. 70, No. 8, 1546–1557.

Frondel, M., Horbach, J. and Rennings, K. (2007): End-of-pipe or cleaner production? An empirical comparison of environmental innovation decisions across OECD countries. *Business Strategy and the Environment*, Vol. 16, No. 8, 571–584.

Green, K., McMeekin, A. and Irwin, A. (1994): Technological trajectories and R&D for environmental innovation in UK firms. *Futures*, Vol. 26, 1047–1059.

Grupp, H. (1999): Umweltfreundliche Innovation durch Preissignale oder Regulation? – Eine empirische Untersuchung für Deutschland. *Jahrbücher für Nationalökonomie und Statistik*, Vol. 219, Nos 5/6, 611–631.

Hart, S.L. (1995): A natural resource-based view of the firm. *The Academy of Management Review*, Vol. 20, No. 4, 986–1014.

Hemmelskamp, J. (1999): *Umweltpolitik und technischer Fortschritt*, Schriftenreihe des Zentrums für Europäische Wirtschaftsforschung. Heidelberg, New York: Physica.

Horbach, J. (2008): Determinants of environmental innovation – new evidence from German panel data sources. *Research Policy*, Vol. 37, 163–173.

Horbach, J. (2014): Do eco-innovations need specific regional characteristics? An econometric analysis for Germany. *Review of Regional Research*, Vol. 34, Issue 1, 23–38.

Horbach, J., Oltra, V. and Belin, J. (2013): Determinants and specificities of eco-innovations – an econometric analysis for France and Germany based on the Community Innovation Survey. *Industry and Innovation*, Vol. 20, No. 6, 523–543.

Horbach, J., Rammer, C. and Rennings, K. (2012): Determinants of eco-innovations by type of environmental impact – the role of regulatory push/pull, technology push and market pull. *Ecological Economics*, Vol. 78, 112–122.

Jaffe, A. and Palmer, K. (1997): Environmental regulation and innovation: a panel study. *The Review of Economics and Statistics*, Vol. X, 610–619.

Jaffe, A.B., Newell, R.G. and Stavins, R.N. (2002): Environmental policy and technological change. *Environmental and Resource Economics*, Vol. 22, 41–69.

Johnstone, N. (ed.) (2007): *Environmental Policy and Corporate Behaviour*. Cheltenham: Edward Elgar.

Johnstone, N., Haščič, I. and Popp, D. (2010a): Renewable energy policies and technological innovation: evidence based on patent counts. *Environmental and Resource Economics*, Vol. 45, 133–155.

Johnstone, N., Haščič, I. and Kalamova, M. (2010b): Environmental policy characteristics and technological innovation. *Economia Politica: Journal of Analytical and Institutional Economics*, Vol. XXVII, No. 2, 277–301.

Kammerer, D. (2009): The effects of customer benefit and regulation on environmental product innovation. Empirical evidence from appliance manufacturers in Germany. *Ecological Economics*, Vol. 68, 2285–2295.

Kemp, R. and Pearson, P. (2008): Final report MEI project about measuring eco-innovation, Maastricht, www.merit.unu.edu\MEI.

Kesidou, E. and Demirel, P. (2012): On the drivers of eco-innovations: empirical evidence from the UK. *Research Policy*, Vol. 41, 862–870.

Khanna, M., Deltas, G. and Harrington, D. R. (2009): Adoption of pollution prevention techniques: the role of management systems and regulatory pressures. *Environmental and Resource Economics*, Vol. 44, 85–106.

Lanoie, P., Laurent-Lucchetti, J., Johnstone, N. and Ambec, S. (2011): Environmental policy, innovation and performance: new insights on the Porter hypothesis. *Journal of Economics and Management Strategy*, Vol. 20, No. 3, 803–842.

Mazzanti, M. and Zoboli, R. (2006): Examining the factors influencing environmental innovations. *FEEM Working Paper Series*, No. 20, Milano.

Mohr, R.D. (2002): *Technical change, external economies, and the Porter hypothesis. Journal of Environmental Economics and Management*, Vol. 43, 158–168.

OECD and Eurostat (2005): *Oslo Manual Guidelines for Collecting and Interpreting Innovation Data*, 3rd edn. Paris, Luxemburg: OECD, Eurostat.

Palmer, K., Oates, W.E. and Portney, P.P. (1995): Tightening environmental standards: the benefit–cost or the no-cost paradigm? *Journal of Economic Perspectives*, Vol. 9, No. 4, 119–132.

Popp, D. (2006): International innovation and diffusion of air pollution control technologies: the effects of NOx and SO2 regulation in the US, Japan, and Germany. *Journal of Environmental Economics and Management*, Vol. 51 No. 1, 46–71.

Porter, M.E. and van der Linde, C. (1995): Toward a new conception of the environment–competitiveness relationship. *Journal of Economic Perspectives*, Vol. 9, No. 4, 97–118.

Rehfeld, K., Rennings, K. and Ziegler, A. (2007): Determinants of environmental product innovations and the role of integrated product policy – an empirical analysis. *Ecological Economics*, Vol. 61, 91–100.

Rennings, K. (2000): Redefining innovation – eco-innovation research and the contribution from ecological economics. *Ecological Economics*, Vol. 32, 319–332.

Rennings, K. and Rexhäuser, S. (2011): Long-term impacts of environmental policy and eco-innovative activities of firms. *International Journal of Technology, Policy and Management*, Vol. 11, Nos 3/4, 274–290.

Rennings, K. and Zwick, T. (2002): The employment impact of cleaner production on the firm level – empirical evidence from a survey in five European countries. *International Journal of Innovation Management (IJIM)*, Special Issue on 'The management of innovation for environmental sustainability', Vol. 6, No. 3, 319–342.

Rennings, K., Ziegler, A., Ankele, K. and Hoffmann, E. (2006): The influence of different characteristics of the EU environmental management and auditing scheme on technical environmental innovations and economic performance. *Ecological Economics*, Vol. 57, No. 1, 45–59.

Rexhäuser, S. and Rammer, C. (2014): Environmental innovations and firm profitability: unmasking the Porter hypothesis. *Environmental and Resource Economics*, Vol. 57, No. 1, 145–167.

Triguero, A., Moreno-Mondéjar, L. and Davia, M.A. (2013): Drivers of different types of eco-innovation in European SMEs. *Ecological Economics*, Vol. 92, 25–33.

Van den Bergh, J.C.J.M., Faber, A., Idenburg, A. and Osterhuis, F. (2007): *Evolutionary Economics and Environmental Policy: Survival of the Greenest*. Cheltenham: Edward Elgar.

Veugelers, R. (2012): Which policy instruments to induce clean innovating? *Research Policy*, Vol. 41, 1770–1778.

Vona, F., Nicolli, F. and Nesta, N. (2012): Determinants of renewable energy innovation: environmental policies versus market regulation, OFCE documents de travail 2012–05, Paris.

Wagner, M. (2008): Empirical influence of environmental management on innovation: evidence from Europe. *Ecological Economics*, Vol. 66, Nos 2–3, 392–402.

Wagner, M. (2009): Erfolgsfaktoren für Nachhaltigkeitsinnovationen: qualitative und quantitative Befunde. *Zeitschrift für Umweltpolitik und Umweltrecht (ZfU)*, Vol. 2, 179–198.

Ziegler, A. and Nogareda, S. (2009): Environmental management systems and technological environmental innovations: exploring the causal relationship. *Research Policy*, Vol. 38, No. 5, 885–893.

14 Innovation policy for knowledge production and R&D

The investment portfolio approach

Susana Borrás and Charles Edquist

1 Introduction

Who produces scientific and technical knowledge these days? What type of knowledge is being produced and for what purposes? Why are firms and governments funding research and development? This chapter studies these questions by looking at the role of knowledge production (and especially R&D activities) in the innovation process from an innovation system perspective. There are in fact several possible answers due to the fact that societies and economies organize the production of knowledge and R&D activities in different ways. Naturally, not all of these are equally successful when it comes to attaining the various general goals of economic growth, environmental sustainability, public health, consumer protection, etc. This chapter begins by acknowledging this diversity in terms of socio-economic organization and in terms of these diverse goals of innovation policy. The chapter aims to provide a consistent conceptual and theoretical framework based on the innovation systems approach, which will serve to capture and analyse these systemic differences as well as the most relevant recent trends in innovation policy.

Innovations can be defined as new creations of economic or societal significance. Following most of the literature in these matters, innovation is related to the emergence, diffusion and combination of knowledge and their transformation into new products or processes. Seen from this perspective, innovation and innovative activities are intrinsically related to knowledge, which can be either entirely new knowledge or old/existing knowledge which is being combined and used in new ways. For this reason, the production of knowledge and its development is a fundamental activity in any innovation system, albeit not the only one (Edquist 2011).

This chapter proceeds as follows. The next section discusses the role of knowledge production in the innovation process from a perspective of innovation systems. It pays special attention to 'research and development' (R&D) as a specific and crucial activity related to knowledge production. In so doing, this section examines who produces R&D and what types of R&D. The chapter then examines one of the most crucial issues for innovation policy-makers from the perspective of investment portfolio[1] in an innovation system as well as its respective returns. Knowledge production in innovation systems has been experiencing important transformations over the past two decades. In this chapter, we focus on two specific themes – namely, the transformations in direct and indirect public funding to knowledge production and the rapid transformations in the governance of research universities (here mainly the autonomy of universities – or lack thereof, and the measurement of research universities' outputs).

The following section examines the critical and most important issues at stake from the point of view of innovation policy, looking particularly at the unresolved tensions and systemic imbalances related to knowledge production in the system. Finally, the concluding section elaborates a set of overall criteria for the selection and design of relevant policy instruments and addresses those tensions and unbalances.

2 Knowledge and R&D in the innovation system

The innovation system approach sees the production of knowledge (and R&D in particular) as a crucial element in any innovation system, economy and society. It is crucial but not as the 'linear view' suggests. In contrast to the automatic, direct, mono-causal link between the 'amount' of knowledge and R&D activities and the innovativeness of that economy suggested by the linear model, the innovation system perspective argues that this relationship is much more complex and not necessarily direct.

From the current perspective on innovation systems, we can distinguish between a broad definition of knowledge and a more specific definition of R&D. Box 14.1 conceptually clarifies 'knowledge production', 'research' and 'development'.

Box 14.1 Knowledge production, research and development – concepts

Knowledge production refers to the creation of new knowledge. This is the widest concept and does not necessarily refer to scientific and technical knowledge but all sorts of new knowledge.

   Research refers to the production of knowledge by using scientific and technical methods.

   Development refers to the production and the adaptation of new knowledge in its use context, typically related to processes of prototyping, demonstration, testing, certification, modelling, scale modelling, proof of concept and clinical trials.

Source: own elaboration

As Box 14.1 indicates, 'knowledge' is the widest notion. Hence, knowledge is not the same as R&D, which refers to the type of knowledge produced by scientific and technical methods. An example of this is a patient organization that produces relevant knowledge by collecting information about certain observed secondary effects of a specific drug. This knowledge is relevant for the patients themselves, as well as for authorities and the producing firm. The patient organization may decide to send that knowledge to the firm and to the relevant authorities for further analysis but, as such, the knowledge of the patient organization may not necessarily be the direct result of R&D activities but simply the collection and desktop interpretation of specific observations.

Admittedly, the borderline between knowledge production and R&D is difficult to trace with exactitude. This is so because, from an innovation system perspective, the production of knowledge and R&D is largely contingent to the wider contextual and social dynamics that are unique to each society. Knowledge and R&D are highly embedded in the social, cultural and political contexts that are unique to each society and time. This is the reason why the specific features and idiosyncrasies of different forms of organizing knowledge production and research and development activities are not replicable elsewhere or at other points in time. This is important when designing innovation policy. Policy initiatives aiming at fostering the production of knowledge, as well as research and development, must take these societal, economic and organizational contexts into account.

But what is knowledge and what type of knowledge exists? This is a very relevant question because there are a multitude of different views on knowledge types. One of the most influential understandings of knowledge and knowledge types was made by ancient Greek philosophers when Plato defined knowledge as 'justified true belief'. The Greeks distinguished between 'episteme', a form of knowledge which is based on disinterested understanding and contemplation (not involving the act of doing manual work) and 'techné', which is the context-based, applied knowledge that derives from manual work and craftsmanship. This ancient distinction is behind the conventional division between basic research and applied research. Although it continues to enjoy wide acceptance in policy-making circles, this division has been contested on the grounds of the complex nature of knowledge (some types of knowledge are both basic and applied) and on the grounds of the particular dynamics of knowledge production (some scientists, such as Louis Pasteur, do basic and applied science simultaneously) (Stokes 1997).

An alternative and perhaps more useful distinction looks at the ultimate purpose of knowledge production. Here the distinction is between curiosity-driven and utility-driven knowledge (Strandburg 2005, van den Hove 2007). Partly overlapping, there is also a distinction between knowledge that is a fundamental discovery and knowledge that is a technical invention. The latter has been quite relevant in the political and legal discussions of patent law when trying to determine the limits on what type of knowledge can be patented.

This latter remark raises another distinction, namely the one between tacit and codified knowledge. The debates surrounding their respective nature and their relative importance in the knowledge-based economy have been quite intense (Cowan *et al.* 2000, Johnson *et al.* 2002). The backdrop of these discussions was the so-called 'patent era', or the increasing trend in knowledge appropriation and commercialization through the issuing of patenting rights (a form of codified knowledge) (Foray 2001).

These discussions evolved towards a different approach, namely the different types of knowledge-bases' in innovation systems. Here, a distinction has been made between STI (science, technology, invention) and DUI (doing, using, interacting) types of knowledge (Jensen *et al.* 2007) or in another version, analytical knowledge base and synthetic knowledge base in local or regional economies (Asheim and Coenen 2006). All innovation systems have both types of knowledge bases but one of the knowledge bases tends to be predominant over the other. The relative presence of these knowledge bases shapes the particular dynamics of innovation in a system.

Naturally, the borderlines between techné/episteme, basic/applied science, curiosity-driven/utility-driven knowledge, fundamental discovery/technical invention, tacit/codified knowledge, synthetic/analytical knowledge bases are very fluid and can always be challenged. However, they are still valid for analytical reasons: they can help us grasp the complex dynamics, processes and purposes of knowledge production and their use, and what is most important, they can help us understand on what grounds innovation policy-makers have made decisions. This is to say that we are not interested in an ontological discussion about the nature and types of knowledge per se, nor in what types of knowledge are more important in the innovation system and for innovation policy. Rather, we are interested in understanding the way in which these distinctions have been influential in innovation policy-making and in crucial decisions regarding the allocation of private and public investments.

This chapter focuses on a specific sub-set of knowledge production, namely the knowledge that is produced through research and development activities (R&D). As seen in Box 14.1, research and development is a very composite and heterogeneous activity. A useful way of studying R&D in an innovation system is to consider the actors that produce it. This can provide a useful analytical tool and a snapshot regarding the 'who' and 'what' of R&D activities at a specific given point in time and its changes through time. Naturally, these are schematic and representative tools that could be combined with indicators and other analytical instruments.

Following from the discussions above regarding the nature of knowledge and the context in which it is produced, and being particularly inspired by Pasteur's Quadrant (Stokes 1997) and its subsequent elaborations (Guinet 2009), we can consider two crucial dimensions for the study of R&D and knowledge production in an innovation system.

The first dimension follows from the discussions above and, in particular, from the distinction between fundamental discovery and technical invention. This distinction has naturally been questioned as it is difficult to draw the line between one and the other. Naturally, the boundaries between them are not at all as clear cut as may seem at first sight. However, it serves here as a heuristic to grasp analytically different logics behind R&D.

The second important dimension looks at the exploration or exploitation of knowledge (March 1991). This is the distinction between R&D that is directed more towards the exploration of new frontiers of knowledge (curiosity-driven;

basic science) and the R&D activities that are geared towards the exploitation of that knowledge with a specific purpose (profit or non-profit). In most South East Asian countries, emphasis on the exploitation and development side of R&D activities was a strategy for a rapid catch-up process in the 1970s and 1980s, combining the imitation and exploitation of existing knowledge with its further development at product level (Kim 1997).

The mapping in Figure 14.1 visualizes the spaces these R&D producers occupy along these two dimensions. The specific cases of organizations located in these two dimensions illustrate a generic example. In analytical terms, mapping the different R&D organizations of an innovation system along these two dimensions allows strengths and weaknesses to be identified in terms of possible duplications, as well as empty spaces of R&D activities in a system. It can also help to compare R&D strengths and weaknesses across countries or regions. This may help to design innovation policy.

3 R&D investment portfolio and its returns

When looking at the R&D that is being generated in an innovation system, two considerations are paramount. First, given its centrality for social as well as for economic development, R&D is to be considered an investment (rather than expenditure).[2] This perspective induces us to look at R&D as an investment

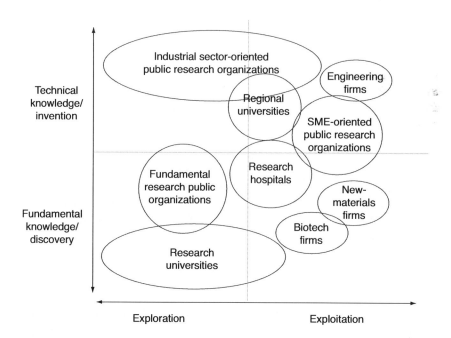

Figure 14.1 Mapping R&D organizations in innovation systems – a generic illustration (source: own elaboration).

portfolio. Following the business literature, by 'investment portfolio' we refer to the set of different investments that public funding agencies and private actors make to produce knowledge and R&D activities in an innovation system. These investments can be different in terms of the time perspective of the investment (long or short term) and in terms of the different levels of expected risks and potential results. From an innovation policy point of view, as we will discuss later in this chapter, it has to do with the overall set of public policy initiatives towards knowledge production and R&D, and their features in terms of time perspective as well as risk and results.

The idea of an investment portfolio approach in the policy initiatives towards knowledge production and R&D has to do with the crucial question of whether the government places the investment well (a balance between risk and yields of returns and a balance between short and long term, and a certain variation across different areas of knowledge) (Jackson 2006). The emergence and use of the portfolio approach allows the construction of complex project portfolios which spread risk and can thus allow the pursuit of a few highly risky projects among several other projects with a much lower risk. Public procurement and public-supported venture capital are two high-risk areas of action in a public investment portfolio. These two are more high-risk oriented than conventional areas of public R&D investment, such as, for example, 'development' activities (see below). Venture capital seems to be particularly high risk since it typically entails a combination of innovative projects with entrepreneurship. For this reason, policy-makers may be inclined to support this type of activity as a form of promoting the creation of new firms with innovative capacity in the system, even if the rates of return may be low.

Second, it is paramount to examine the rate of return of that investment, both the private rates of return as much as the social rates of return. Both considerations are important from the point of view of innovation policy. Any decision regarding public support for R&D activities must have a clear notion of the nature of the (country/region's) public investment portfolio as well as its rates of return. Cost–benefit analysis is a possible analytical tool that public policy-makers may consider using to define the possible outcomes of public investments and to define the composition of the public investment portfolio.

There are roughly three funding sources of R&D investment. These are private-for-profit R&D investment (typically by firms), private-not-for-profit R&D investment conducted/funded by philanthropic or charitable organizations and public R&D investment conducted/funded by public authorities. Thus, one place to start when examining the levels of R&D investment in an innovation system is to look at the relative share of private, philanthropic and public investment. This share varies considerably across countries. A general tendency is that, in countries with high levels of innovativeness in their economies, the share of private-for-profit R&D investment tends to be proportionally higher than the other two.

These three types of funding sources of R&D investment indicate the 'who' and partly the 'how' of R&D activities in an innovation system. However, we may need to take a much closer look at how the overall investment portfolio is distributed across different knowledge areas in the innovation system; in other words, in what type of R&D a particular innovation system tends to be special-ized in. Some of these investments are clearly targeted at some knowledge and industrial areas, whereas others are more generic in nature (i.e. basic research public funding).

From the point of view of innovation policy, policy-makers must also define whether the existing general levels of investment and the investment portfolio are adequate vis-à-vis the collective expectations and societal goals defined (hopefully) democratically by the government and parliament. Decisions on the distribution of funds and strategic areas are naturally political decisions which are (also hopefully) made on the basis of solid knowledge about the existing portfolios as well as on the basis of the sources of strategic intelligence for innovation policy-making.

Innovation policy-makers must examine and determine whether the different sources (public/private/philanthropic) of R&D investment are complementary to each other or not. Complementarity is important because one crucial issue that public R&D investment would like to avoid is a displacement effect on private sources of investment, or the effect by which public funds displace or substitute (crowding out) private investment in R&D (Jaffe 1998). Likewise, policy-makers must consider the question of whether public investment should be prim-arily placed in existing knowledge/industrial sectors where the economy is specialized or, on the contrary, in those sectors where there is virtually no specialization or presence but a wish or need to achieve this.

The second consideration for innovation policy-makers from an innovation system perspective is the rate of private and social returns of R&D investments. The reason for this is quite obvious, namely R&D investment is expensive and it is expected to yield positive returns. Economists have dealt with the question of measuring rates of return for several decades and in different ways, either by looking at specific cases (technologies or public programmes) or by conducting econometric analysis with a more macro-level perspective. The increasing avail-ability of panel data and improved methodologies has gradually made these ana-lyses more sophisticated and comparable; however, large uncertainties remain given that

> the return to R&D is not an invariant parameter but the outcome of a complex interaction between firm strategy, competitor strategy, and stochas-tic macro-economic environment, much of which is unpredictable at the time a firm [or a public policy] chooses its R&D program.
>
> (Hall *et al.* 2010: 4)

The private rate of return to R&D refers to the return that the individual firm gets from its own investment in R&D activities. Several case studies of technologies as well as wider macroeconomic analysis indicate that there are very different rates of private return across cases and across technologies (see Hall *et al.* 2010 for a review). Perhaps the most relevant finding among the widespread studies of private rates of return is that there seems to be a very skewed distribution of private returns (Scherer and Harhoff 2000). By comparing different data sets, the authors find that 'the lion's share of the privately appropriated value through investments in innovation comes from roughly 10 per cent of the technically successful prospects' (Scherer and Harhoff 2000: 561). In other words, very few investments in R&D yield positive returns and they typically yield very large returns. Furthermore, nothing suggests that the skewed distribution of private rates of return may be any different from the social rates of return. In other words, few public R&D investments yield large positive social returns (Scherer and Harhoff 2000).

> All this suggests the need for both nations and firms to pursue a portfolio approach to backing new technology, recognizing that only a few of the projects supported will pay off on a large scale and hoping that the generous returns from the relatively few successes will also cover the cost of the many less successful projects.
>
> (Scherer and Harhoff 2000: 562)

The rates of return may not only benefit the individual firm, they may also benefit the economy and society in a much wider sense. The social rate of return is a notion that includes the private rate of return plus the knowledge and market spillovers of these R&D activities. Hence, the social rate of return to R&D is larger than those of private returns and is closely intertwined with spillovers. Box 14.2 distinguishes between these concepts.

Box 14.2 Rates of returns of R&D and spillovers

Private rate of return of R&D: the firms' rate of return from their own R&D investment.

Social rate of return: the rate of return which includes not only the private rate of return but also the knowledge and market spillovers of R&D activities (see below).

Spillover (general): an unintended transfer of market benefits to other market agents with no payment involved.

Knowledge spillover: knowledge created by one agent which is used by another agent without compensation, or with compensation that is less than the value of the knowledge.

Market spillover: when the market for a new product or process creates benefits to the consumers and to other producers through better products and lower costs.

Technology transfer: 'trade in technology which occurs when an agent sells a piece of technology with a price attached to the transaction' (Hall *et al.* 2010: 25).

Source: own elaboration

As we saw above, policy-makers must place R&D investment in a way that does not displace private R&D investments. In order to do so, a rule of thumb says that policy-makers must fund projects which yield high social rates of return but have low commercial prospects (Jaffe 1998). Determining ex-ante which project will have these two features is however a very difficult task, given the unpredictability of R&D investment results.

In his seminar paper from 1986, David Teece put the returns of R&D investment into a broad context (Teece 1986). He started with the remark that often innovating firms (those inventing and commercializing first) are not those who profit most from the innovation. Teece suggests that there are three factors that determine an individual firm's ability to obtain profits from its own innovation. These are the appropriability regime (the way in which the patent system works for product innovations and the relative irrelevance of patenting process innovations), the complementary assets of the firm (marketing, post-sale services, etc. are crucial for an innovation to be successful) and the dominant design paradigm (what competition the new product faces in the market, whether it is a paradigmatic design or a post-paradigmatic design). Teece's paper puts firms' R&D investments in relation to innovation activities (of the firm itself and of the innovation system). This contextual approach is paramount to understanding the factors behind higher or lower private rates of return, which tend to vary across firms and systems.

A similar contextual approach has been recently emerging when studying the rates of social returns. Coming from the world of research evaluation, these new studies no longer look at the aggregated social returns of privately funded R&D activities. Instead, they look at the social returns of research and science policy programmes. This is an important issue, far more when the goals of public R&D programmes are not just advancing scientific and economic goals but typically other social goals, such as improved public health services, carbon-free and renewable energy sources or consumer protection. Bozeman and Sarewitz study the 'public value' of R&D policy in these latter terms. They conceptualize 'public value' as the overall impact of R&D activities on the public goals stated in the policy documents which are typically other and more than just scientific or economic goals (Bozeman and Sarewitz 2011). This approach is a promising new way to study the impacts of public R&D policies on the self-defined 'grand social challenges'.

4 Research: recent trends in public funding

Continuing with our analysis of R&D investments above, we will now address how the public funding of research activities has been changing in most countries over the past few decades. Before doing that, we need to distinguish between direct and indirect public funding of research activities. Direct public funding refers to government budgetary appropriations for research activities. At first sight, these are relatively easy to identify. However, sometimes research funding is distributed across different levels of government (national, subnational, local) and across different types of public agencies in such a way that finding the exact total figure of governmental investment may not be simple.

Indirect public support, for its part, refers to the tax incentives (or other type of monetary incentives) in the form of depreciations and exemptions to firms (and other taxable organizations) on the research activities they have conducted (Köhler *et al.* 2012). This is an indirect support in the sense that it exempts research activities from some specific taxation obligations, with clear monetary effect for the firms in question. Direct and indirect public funding of research is a vast topic and abundant empirical literature has been dedicated to it. For this reason, this chapter focuses on the first one because it is an area of major reform and changes over the past few decades.

When examining the direct public funding of research under the prism of investment portfolio, two broad trends seem to be worth looking at. The first one has to do with the increase of competitive public funds for research vis-à-vis the traditionally non-competitive public funding. The second trend has to do with the fundamental changes in mission-oriented and diffusion-oriented public funding of research. We will examine these two trends below.

Governments have been supporting research activities since the inception of the modern state. Traditionally, this support has been in the form of direct public endowments to public (or private) universities, as well as the creation and financial support to different types of public research organizations. In their 2007 paper, Lepori and others empirically studied the distribution of public research funding between project and non-project schemes in several European countries (Lepori *et al.* 2007, 2009). Project funding refers to the public funding that is granted on a time-limited basis and typically the outcome of a project application process. Sometimes this project funding is competitive, but sometimes it is not.

Findings by Lepori *et al.* show that over the past few decades the share of project-based funding has increased significantly in all countries. There are, though, important differences across countries in terms of the size of that share and in terms of the distribution among different types of beneficiaries (firms, universities or public research organizations). The time-limited and performance-related allocation of public research funding has had a particularly important impact for universities (Hicks 2012). If this performance measurement is conducted only on the basis of scientific rather than socio-economic performance, these allocation mechanisms may run counter to most governments' intentions to enhance the diffusion and technology transfer of publicly funded research.

The second large trend over the past decades has been the changes in the orientation of public funding. In his work, Henry Ergas distinguished between two types of public research and technology policy styles (Ergas 1987). Mission-oriented research policies are those where 'big science is deployed to meet big problems' (Ergas 1987: 193). This type is when public funding of research is dominated by programmes serving specific government missions and targeted research in some areas (defence, agriculture, health, energy...). In contrast to this, countries with a diffusion-oriented policy style 'seek to provide a broad capacity for adjusting to technological change throughout the industrial structure' (Ergas 1987: 194). In these latter countries, public funding of research is dominated by instruments and schemes of a horizontal nature.

As indicated above, many countries have engaged in significant reforms of their public support policies for research. A rapid examination of some cases such as France, Germany or Denmark tend to indicate that there may be a process where diffusion-oriented countries like Denmark and Germany have introduced important elements of mission-oriented policy. For example, the creation since 2001 of three different strategic research councils (and its recent merger into one) indicates Danish willingness to address more applied-based and targeted public funding. Denmark remains a country with a mainly diffusion-oriented approach but the introduction of these important instruments has introduced a relevant diversity in the Danish public funding compared with earlier. Something similar has happened in Germany, with the first high-tech strategy created in 2006. In contrast, France has experienced the introduction of a significant number of instruments and organizational reorganization geared towards more diffusion-oriented policy, including the creation of National Research Council funding research projects on a competitive basis, or the creation of the Poles de Competitivité and Carnot Institutes. This is quite remarkable for a country which tended to be one of the clearest examples of mission-oriented policies in Europe.

The extent to which these changes are the expression of convergence across some countries (or not) is still a question that remains empirically unanswered. One might expect the extensive exchange of ideas and cross-country comparative analysis at international level, as in the EU, the OECD or the World Bank, to have generated some learning among policy-makers (Borrás 2014).

5 Development: the crucial little brother

So far we have mainly discussed R&D activities focusing on 'research'. However, R&D is quite heterogeneous. For this reason, when examining R&D from an investment portfolio approach, we need to consider other types of activities. Particularly important in this regard is 'Development', which is the 'D' of the R&D acronym. It encompasses a series of different yet crucial and interlinked activities in the innovation process, such as prototyping, demonstration, testing, certification, modelling, scale modelling, proof of concept and clinical trials. Broadly speaking 'development' or 'product development' refers to the modification of an existing product or process adapting it to new needs, or the formulation of an entirely new product or process that addresses specific needs.

By definition, 'development' is application-related, meaning that it encompasses a set of activities whose direct purpose is to design a suitable product or process (suitable in terms of complying with user needs and, depending on the sector, complying with the legal requirements of safety too). Development is also highly sector context-specific, meaning that the precise steps and activities of the development depend to a large extent on the specific features of the industrial/knowledge sector in question. For example, the development of products in the aeronautic sector involves typically different forms of prototyping and scale modelling, whereas the development of products in the pharmaceutical sector involves several steps in clinical trials.

In contrast to the 'R' of R&D, the different set of activities defined here as 'development' have received surprisingly little attention from scholars of innovation processes. Admittedly, the debate on different types of knowledge as well as on investment portfolio and rates of return (see sections above) has involved issues related to 'development' in a very indirect way, without taking into consideration the differences between these (i.e. clinical trials are very different from prototyping). However, there are few relevant studies which analyse the social organization of development activities and their respective design-related challenges (Carlsen *et al.* 2014, Hsu and Fang 2009, Watanabe *et al.* 2011). These studies rarely include generalizable findings that can be used in broader analyses of innovation processes in an innovation system.

Box 14.3 provides our definitions of some of the most important generic types of development activities.

Box 14.3 Some generic types of development activities

Prototyping: an early sample of a product in order to test its design, functionality and/or material components. There are different types/processes of prototyping in various industrial sectors. Prototyping usually involves sequential tests of the design of relatively generic features of the final product.

Computer modelling: this is a prototype designed and tested by computer software, not involving a physical artefact, but digitally simulating the expected features of the product. It is currently a common development activity in several engineering sectors.

Clinical trials: sets of tests in medical research and drug development that prospectively assign human participants to health-related interventions in order to evaluate their health outcomes (typically, drug effects and their safety).

Product certification: the documentation that a specific product has undertaken and successfully passed a series of performance tests indicating that the product in question complies with pre-determined criteria typically defined by regulations and/or (semi-)mandatory technical specifications set up by governments and/or standardizing bodies. Certification is conducted by certifying laboratories/organizations usually of a semi-public nature.

Source: own elaboration

The multiple types of development activities are performed by very diverse organizations. Sometimes these activities are conducted inside firms' own R&D labs, whereas at other times they are outsourced to specialized external organizations/firms of a typically private or semi-public nature. These organizations normally sell their services to companies or to governmental agencies and may sometimes enjoy (generous) state support for some basic costs. Most of the time they are specialized in some sectors (e.g. medical devices development, fire safety testing, or defence-related product development).

Traditionally these organizations have operated in their national/sub-national contexts. However, their activities have become more internationalized over the past decades, probably due to an accelerated internationalization of certification and standardization processes as well as cross-border regulations and trade agreements. These development-related organizations usually constitute crucial organizations that bridge the world of research and new knowledge production with the world of industrial application, commercial use and regulatory compliance. This bridging role must not be underestimated in an innovation system. This is particularly important for small and medium-sized enterprises (SMEs) for whom access to specialized development competences and the necessary laboratory infrastructure and equipment would otherwise not be possible.

Seen from a perspective of innovation policy and an investment portfolio approach, most of these development activities have tended to go under the radar of policy debates. Generally speaking, much emphasis is typically put on the 'research' side of R&D to the detriment of 'development'. The result of this is that this little brother has tended to remain under-examined and under-considered. This is a major paradox since innovation entails, to a great extent, the ability of an innovation system to be able to successfully conduct development activities. Furthermore, development activities form part of the policy-makers' decisions related to the investment portfolio of public support to R&D. Section 7 looks at the deficiencies, tensions and problems of innovation systems in this respect.

6 Research universities: a top-down revolution

Universities are central organizations in any innovation system. There are, however, many different types of universities and many different ways in which national/regional governments interact with, regulate and fund their universities. In this chapter, we focus on universities where there is an important component of research activities and examine two key issues which are having a profound effect on universities, namely, the deep transformation of university roles and organization in some countries and the recent emergence of global university rankings.

The relative presence and weight of universities in innovation systems varies considerably from country to country. In some countries, such as Sweden, the Netherlands and Canada, universities tend to perform between 25 per cent and 30 per cent of the country's overall R&D expenditure, whereas this is much lower in other countries. This depends on the features of the innovation system and on the relative tradition of research universities (Mowery and Sampat 2005). In the USA, the very strong research-based universities grew from the turn of the twentieth century (Geiger 2004) and have recently become an example for developments in this direction in Asia, Latin America (Altbach and Balán 2007) and, not least, Europe (McKelvey and Holmén 2009).

Over the last two decades, research universities have moved from a relatively unnoticed life outside public scrutiny towards being seen as core elements in the innovation performance of a national economy. During this period, universities have been seen as performing a series of different tasks (Uyarra 2010): the production of scientific knowledge (university as 'knowledge factory'), the sharing of knowledge with firms ('relational university'), the commercialization of their research outputs ('entrepreneurial university'), the activities related to boundary spanning in the innovation system ('systemic university') and their active contribution to economic development in their local area ('engaged university'). These tasks and roles largely overlap and most universities have introduced significant organizational changes that meet these external demands and political expectations. These organizational changes are closely linked to the introduction of top-down reforms of university governance and the introduction of more competition-based R&D funding allocations to universities.

Most of the university reforms in Europe, Asia and elsewhere have been guided by a national government's wish to make universities strategic actors in the innovation system. However, their ultimate ability to become so largely depends on the overall framework of university governance in that country (Whitley 2008). More concretely, this refers to the extent to which universities exercise authority over their inputs and outputs (their levels of dependence on state funding, their discretion on resource allocation inside the university, the ability to employ directly or not their scientific staff and their ability to select students), as well as their ability to exercise authority over internal processes (discretion over establishing and closing departments, on promotion of scientific groups inside the university, on establishing research and teaching priorities and on defining their own performance goals and mechanisms to pursue them). In other words, their ability to become a strategic actor in the innovation system depends on their degree of organizational, regulatory and financial framework.

The recent reforms of university governance in some countries show a large degree of variation in scope and focus. This diversity reflects the different roles that research universities have traditionally exercised in innovation systems. However, most of these reforms are somehow linked to the social and political wish that universities are able to compete in a national and international context. This competitive zeitgeist can be observed in the second key feature examined here.

The second key feature of the recent and profound transformation in higher education is the remarkable thrust towards the detailed measurement of the quantity and quality of universities' research outputs. This measurement includes international publication databases, the widespread use of citation analyses, the introduction of university and scientific discipline-level of peer review exercises, and perhaps the most politically visible of them all, the introduction of a large number of university rankings. Different countries have taken very different approaches towards this matter. In any case, the growing attention towards measuring university R&D performance has been equally prominent in developed and developing countries.

Some of these initiatives have been taken by governments in an attempt to make new incentive mechanisms based on performance. This is, for example, the case of public initiatives that aim at measuring cross-university performance. Perhaps one of the most far-reaching (and controversial) initiatives in this regard has been the Research Assessment Exercises (RAE) by the UK government (Hicks 2012). Other initiatives, however, have come from private (or non-governmental) organizations. This is the case, for example, of databases and software tools measuring and analysing scientific citations such as 'google. scholar.com' or 'Hartzing's Publish and Perish' software tools. These new entrants in the market of publishing and citation indexes have been game changers in the field, providing free and easily accessible information to users and challenging incumbents.

Private initiatives in the field of higher education and research in the early 2000s have had a profound impact. This is particularly the case for university rankings. The publication in 2003 of the 'Academic Ranking of World Universities' by Shanghai Jiao Tong University created a true wave of discussions about the quality of higher education worldwide. Since then, the number of university rankings has grown rapidly. Today, the most well-known rankings are produced by a series of private or semi-public organizations, including the Shanghai Ranking Consultancy (SRC), Times Higher Education-Thomson Reuters, Quacqarelli-Symmonds (QS), CWTS Leiden, Taiwan Higher Education Accreditation and Evaluation Council and the Centre for Higher Education Development/*die Zeit*, or Reitor, among others.

The European Commission and the OECD too have launched their own ranking projects, namely, the European Multidimensional University Ranking System (U-Multirank) and the Assessment of Higher Education Learning Outcomes Project (AHELO), respectively. Almost since the creation of all these rankings there have been growing criticism regarding several important aspects. The European University Association pointed to the fact that the rankings tend to be elitist, focusing only on the research-heavy, oldest and largest universities worldwide (European University Association 2011).

More problematic perhaps is the growing view that the methodologies of these rankings are not transparent (methodologies and data not – sufficiently – available) and use disputable data (i.e. self-reported data, lack of normalization of data). Sometimes the methodologies have changed rapidly, rendering virtually incomparable results of the same ranking through time (Hazelkorn 2013). Yet, regardless of these issues, it is obvious that the rankings have had tremendous impact. They have exposed higher education to international comparison and governments and university leaders alike have had to deal with them. It has been virtually impossible to ignore them, most probably because their comparative effects have caught the eye of the media and public debates.

7 Deficiencies, tensions and imbalances in the system and in policy-making

After the previous sections' examination of the R&D investment portfolios and their returns, the recent trends in the public funding on research, the role of 'development' in R&D activities and the organizational change of universities, we need to look at some of the possible deficiencies, tensions and imbalances in the innovation system. As mentioned above, knowledge production (and especially R&D) is performed in specific contexts. 'Context' refers not only to the fact that the production of new scientific-technical knowledge offers new opportunities for innovation activities but also that innovation is highly related to the features and dynamics of the economy and society.

Three general sets of deficiencies, tensions and imbalances in the innovation system in relation to R&D activities seem to come to the fore from the previous sections. The first set has to do with *the insufficient and unbalanced levels of R&D activities in an economy and society*. As mentioned above, determining the levels of R&D is essentially a political (and hopefully also a democratic) process. Societies must explicitly define their own wishes with regard to their aspirations for economic growth and for other socio-political goals. From this point of departure, it can be useful to analyse the extent to which the levels of R&D activities in an innovation system are sufficient in fulfilling those goals.

Since the 1950s and 1960s, economists have argued that there is invariably an underinvestment in R&D activities by firms because knowledge is a public good and hence partly inappropriable (Nelson 1959, Arrow 1959/2002). Without questioning the public nature of knowledge and its associated appropriability problems, our argument is that the overall levels of investment (or underinvestment) in an innovation system are essentially an issue of socio-political goals rather than a one-size-fits-all 'optimum' for all economies. Furthermore, the factors that generate R&D underinvestment may not just be the public nature of knowledge itself but far more complex factors, highly embedded in specific social and economic contexts. For example, if Spanish firms have underinvested in R&D activities in the period 2007–2014, this is most probably associated with a number of problems related to the severe economic and financial crisis (most crucially, the accessibility to capital and the brain drain of highly skilled workers) than with the appropriability of knowledge as such.

The unbalanced level of different types of R&D activities is another important problem. For example, too much emphasis on 'R' (research activities) in relation to 'D' (development activities) may not have a positive effect on overall innovation performance. The overfunding of research (most typically public investment) is observable in some prestige projects where governments have funded research facilities, infrastructures and equipment, without considering the context (geographical, socio-technical and the like) in which that investment is made and without considering how this knowledge will be exploited in relation to 'development' activities.

The notion that the more quantitative investment in research, the more innovation will automatically come out of it is still widespread today. Sometimes, there is an overwhelming focus on increasing the level of public and private funding in research activities without much consideration for the less attractive but no less crucial 'development' activities. Other forms of unbalanced investment levels in an innovation system have to do with differences in big and small science (or big and small research activities). Recent studies suggest that large publicly funded projects are proportionally less productive than small publicly funded projects (Fortin and Currie 2013). A similar issue may emerge between small and large firms' investment in R&D and their respective yields in innovation performance. Knowledge-intensive SMEs have traditionally been seen as relatively weaker compared with large knowledge-intensive firms. This particular concern was behind the creation of the SBRI programme in the USA in the 1980s supporting small business research (Black 2006).

A second set of imbalances and deficiencies of R&D activities in the innovation system has to do with *the undefined goals of public R&D investment*. For many decades, the development of R&D public investment has been conducted within the parameters of very broadly defined political goals. Naturally, this is not a problem in itself. The problem, or more correctly the deficiency, has to do with the lack of a systemic view in terms of the overall expected outcomes of such an investment. In particular, the strong emphasis on the fact that R&D activities' purpose is to contribute to economic growth has somehow tended to put the focus on improving the aggregate level of private rates of return to those firms receiving public funds. We know from the discussions in this chapter that the social rates of return of R&D investment can at times exceed those of private returns due to spill-overs (here including not only market benefits but also knowledge spillovers). However, public investment has not always focused on that. Sometimes it has just focused on increasing the aggregated levels of private returns. An example of the latter is the motto 'from research to bill' ('fra forskning til faktura'), which dominated the Danish research policy in the early 2000s and partly reflected that focus on the aggregate level of private rates of return rather than on the social rates.

Another deficiency in the innovation system has to do with time, or more concretely with the time lag between the decision to invest and the returns of the investment. As we have seen in this chapter, R&D activities require at times heavy investments, both public and private. In some areas, such as space research, biotech or nanotech, the time lag between investment in research activities and their outcomes in terms of innovative outputs is extremely long and extremely uncertain. Moreover, it takes approximately 15–20 years to build up research environments in public research organizations or universities. This important time lag is an issue in terms of finding suitable capital (for private firms) as well as enabling a country to position itself in new emerging scientific and research areas and re-direct or re-orient R&D efforts in other (declining) scientific/knowledge and industrial areas. This time lag can be particularly problematic in times of financial constraints. As the financial and economic crisis since 2008 has clearly shown, some Southern European countries have disregarded the long-term effects of public R&D investments in favour of the short-term needs of cutting public expenditures. This (at times massive) discontinuation in public R&D investment may become very problematic for the future competitiveness of those economies. Furthermore, this will be aggravated by the brain drain of young researchers, which will together represent a net loss of competences (skills and expertise) as well as R&D outputs.

These latest remarks bring to the fore the last, but not least important, set of imbalances of R&D activities in the innovation system, namely, those that have to do with *problems directly related to policy-making.* In our industrialized societies (developed or developing), the role of public action is intrinsically embedded in the innovation system. This means that public action is today a reality and part and parcel of the innovation system as such. Therefore, when examining imbalances or problems in innovation systems, we can also refer to those that are related to the role of public action itself. Two such problems come to the fore. One problem has to do with a certain tendency to traditionalism in public R&D funding. This has to do with the observation that, in spite of political rhetoric, sometimes public R&D support programmes are not designed in a way that promotes the most cutting-edge or novel type of knowledge production. Continuity of research funding lines, logics and targets, may secure stability in the funding of R&D environments (universities, public research organizations or firms). The extent to which that continuity is positive for the overall innovation system depends very much on the ability of these environments to generate R&D outputs that are significant and valuable assets for the innovativeness of the economy. This is what economists have referred to as the 'technological lock-in' in innovation systems, which is not only a matter of firms' own investment decisions but also the inability of public R&D investment to break such negative lock-in dynamics.

The second type of problem associated with public R&D investment in the innovation system has to do with the unbalanced and somehow unsophisticated use of indicators and performance measures of R&D outcomes. The quantitative measurement of R&D and innovation activities has improved dramatically over the past few years (Moed *et al.* 2010). The creation of new databases and new measurement methodologies had revolutionized the fields of research evaluation and the comparative studies of national innovation systems (Schmoch *et al.* 2006). Today we have a much more empirically based analysis of innovation systems, their dynamics and their comparative performance. In spite of this, policy-making tends sometimes to be based on rather simple measurement techniques that do not reflect sufficiently well the complexity of factors that interplay in the performance. This is, for example, the recent case of university rankings. Some of these university rankings use inconsistent methodologies across time (making them unsuitable for comparison across time), use partly self-reported data by universities (with all the reliability problems that this represents) and lack theoretical foundations behind the specific weighting of variables in their aggregate indexes. In spite of these severe problems, university rankings are extensively used today in the public domain as comparative indicators of quality. However, their methodological inconsistency, data unreliability and a theoretical character make them problematic. If taken too seriously, these rankings may induce poorly considered policy action and public R&D investments.

8 Conclusions: criteria for designing R&D funding in innovation policies

The production of knowledge, and in particular R&D activities, is an essential part of an innovation system. After defining on a general level the role of knowledge and of R&D activities in the innovation system and the related conceptual clarification, this chapter has examined four specific areas, namely, R&D investment returns, the recent trends in public research funding, the relevance of 'development' activities in the innovation system and the profound transformations of research universities over the past few years. These considerations have been the backbone for the identification of a series of general types of deficiencies, tensions and imbalances in the system and policy-making in R&D.

This section examines the lessons of these previous issues in relation to the design of innovation policy. In particular, it aims to identify and develop a series of criteria for such design. Traditionally, economic approaches in the 1950s and later have focused on two rationales for public R&D expenditure, namely, the *additionality* of public R&D expenditure vis-à-vis private expenditure (or its non-substitution effect over private expenditure) and the need to introduce public regulation to secure the *appropriability* of knowledge production by firms conducting R&D activities, as a way to overcome the lack of incentives in the market due to the public nature of knowledge. In this chapter, we do not aim to discuss these traditional theoretically deduced rationales. Instead, we aim to put forward a set of criteria for the design of innovation policy that is based on empirical observations and on the analysis of the deficiencies, tensions and imbalances in R&D activities. Hence, our perspective is not so much based on theoretical considerations concerning the nature of knowledge but rather on the real context in which knowledge and R&D are being produced and used. In so doing, we aim to present a more realistic picture of the actual and direct problems associated with R&D activities and the dilemmas and challenges that policy-makers currently face when making decisions regarding the allocation of public budgets and the organization of R&D activities in the system.

As expressed earlier, our point of departure is the understanding that R&D is not an expenditure but an investment and policy-makers must therefore consider the distribution of this investment portfolio according to the different types of investments (long–short term, high–low risk and results). This also means that governments must examine the private and social rates of returns of this public portfolio investment. All in all, the investment portfolio approach means a perspective where policy-makers are able to set targets and goals for what is expected from public investment in R&D. Before setting such targets, policy-makers must take into consideration the current imbalances, deficiencies and tensions in their innovation systems and design their policies accordingly. In particular, they must look carefully at three large sets of issues, namely, the balance between R&D activities in the economy and society, the goals of public R&D investment and the problems directly related to policy-making.

The following criteria emerge from the above discussions:

Innovation policy must secure adequate levels of private and public investment in R&D (according to politically defined goals). Innovation policy must secure the diversity of knowledge production and R&D activities and a certain balance between different types of R&D activities, namely 'research' and 'development' and between knowledge-intensive large and small firms as well as large and small collaborative R&D projects.

Public R&D investment must focus primarily on enhancing the social rates of return in an innovation system. This is because policy-makers must be aware and encourage processes of knowledge spillovers while securing certain levels of appropriability. Since appropriability will invariably be imperfect, policy-makers must be attentive to the positive spillover effects of knowledge production in a system to a point where private incentives to invest in R&D are not undermined.

Public investment in R&D must be risk-taking. We know that the return on investment in R&D is skewed due to the high levels of unpredictability of R&D investments. This gives policy-makers leeway to think strategically, designing policy in a way that takes into account the unavoidable skewness of any such investment return. The risk of public R&D investments, however, must never reach a 'systemic risk level'. That would jeopardize the entire innovation system and its future dynamism.

Public investment must be patient. We know that there is a large time lag between public (and private) decisions to invest and the returns thereof. This is actually part of the risk that public action must be willing to take. However, such patience must not be blind. Policy-makers must define guideposts and milestones regarding the performance of that investment along the way.

Adaptable public funding on R&D. Policy-makers must avoid problems of lock-in in the investment of specific scientific and industrial areas. They must also avoid excessively rapid changes and inconsistent policy targets because it takes at least 15–20 years to build strong research groups. Hence, policies must strike a balance between problems of institutional inertia and interest capture in R&D areas of investment and too rapid a change in focus which results in insufficient public investment.

Last but not least, *R&D investments and organizational public decisions must be based on intelligent and reliable-data based performance measurements of the innovation system*, not least for universities (avoiding the misuse of unreliable university rankings and other simplistic benchmarking exercises).

Notes

1 See definition of 'investment portfolio' in Section 3 below.
2 R&D has traditionally been accounted as 'expenditure' rather than 'investment' in public budgets. Yet, this is currently changing. In spring 2013, the US started to consider R&D in its public budget formally as an investment.

References

Altbach, P. and J. Balán, Eds. (2007). *Transforming Research Universities in Asia and Latin America. World Class Worldwide.* Baltimore, The Johns Hopkins University Press.
Arrow, K.J. (1959/2002). Economic Welfare and the Allocation of Resources for Invention. *Science Bought and Sold. Essays in the Economics of Science.* P. Mirowski and E.-M. Sent. Chicago, University of Chicago: 165–180.

Asheim, B. and L. Coenen (2006). Contextualising Regional Innovation Systems in a Globalising Learning Economy: On Knowledge Bases and Institutional Frameworks. *The Journal of Technology Transfer* 31(1): 163–173.

Black, G.C. (2006). Geography and Spillover. Shaping Innovation Policy through Small Business Research. *Shaping Science and Technology Policy. The Next Generation of Research.* D.H. Guston and D. Sarewitz. Madison, Wisconsin, The University of Wisconsin Press: 77–101.

Borrás, S. (2014). Reforms of National Innovation Policies in Europe. Coordinating Sensemaking across Countries. *Sources of Institutional Competitiveness. Sensemaking and Institutional Change.* S. Borrás and L. Seabrooke. Oxford, Oxford University Press: 60–77.

Bozeman, B. and D. Sarewitz (2011). Public Value Mapping and Science Policy Evaluation. *Minerva* 49(1): 1–23.

Carlsen, H., L. Johansson, P. Wikman-Svahn and K.H. Dreborg (2014). Co-evolutionary Scenarios for Creative Prototyping of Future Robot Systems for Civil Protection. *Technological Forecasting and Social Change* 84: 93–100.

Cowan, R., P.A. David and D. Foray (2000). The Explicit Economics of Knowledge Codification and Tacitness. *Industrial and Corporate Change* 9(2): 211–253.

Edquist, C. (2011). Design of Innovation Policy through Diagnostic Analysis: Identification of Systemic Problems (or Failures). *Industrial and Corporate Change* 20(6): 1725–1753.

Ergas, H. (1987). The Importance of Technology Policy. *Economic Policy and Technological Performance.* P. Dasgupta and P. Stoneman. Cambridge, Cambridge University Press: 51–96.

European University Association (2011). *Global University Rankings and Their Impact.* Brussels, European University Association.

Foray, D. (2001). Intellectual Property and Innovation in the Knowledge-based Economy. *Beleisstudies Technologie Economie* 37(special): 13–43.

Fortin, J.-M. and D.J. Currie (2013). Big Science vs. Little Science: How Scientific Impact Scales with Funding. *PLoS ONE* 8(6): e65263.

Geiger, R.L. (2004). *To Advance Knowledge. The Growth of American Research Universities 1900–1940.* New Brunswick, New Jersey, Transaction.

Guinet, J. (2009). *Boosting Innovation. Some Lessons from the Experience of OECD Countries*, OECD, Paris.

Hall, B., J. Mairesse and P. Mohnen (2010). Measuring the Returns to R&D. *Handbook of the Economics of Innovation.* B. Hall and N. Rosenberg. Amsterdam, Elsevier. 2: 1033–1082.

Hazelkorn, E. (2013). Reflections on a Decade of Global Rankings: What We've Learned and Outstanding Issues. *Beiträge zur Hochschulforschung* 35(2): 8–33.

Hicks, D. (2012). Performance-based University Research Funding Systems. *Research Policy* 41(2): 251–261.

Hsu, Y.-H. and W. Fang (2009). Intellectual Capital and New Product Development Performance: The Mediating Role of Organizational Learning Capability. *Technological Forecasting and Social Change* 76(5): 664–677.

Jackson, B.A. (2006). Federal R&D. Shaping the National Investment Portfolio. *Shaping Science and Technology Policy. The Next Generation of Research.* D.H. Guston and D. Sarewitz. Madison, Wisconsin, The University of Wisconsin Press: 33–54.

Jaffe, A.B. (1998). The Importance of 'Spillovers' in the Policy Mission of the Advanced Technology Program. *Journal of Technology Transfer* 23(2): 11–19.

Jensen, M.B., B. Johnson, E. Lorenz and B.Å. Lundvall (2007). Forms of Knowledge and Modes of Innovation. *Research Policy* 36(5): 680–693.

Johnson, B., E. Lorenz and B.-Å. Lundvall (2002). Why All This Fuss about Codified and Tacit Knowledge? *Industrial and Corporate Change* 11: 245–262.

Kim, L. (1997). *Imitation to Innovation. The Dynamics of Korea's Technological Learning.* Boston, Harvard Business School Press.

Köhler, C., P. Laredo and C. Rammer (2012). *The Impact and Effectiveness of Fiscal Incentives for R&D.* NESTA, London.

Lepori, B., J. Masso, J. Jabłecka, K. Sima and K. Ukrainski (2009). Comparing the Organization of Public Research Funding in Central and Eastern European Countries. *Science and Public Policy* 36(9): 667–681.

Lepori, B., P. van den Besselaar, M. Dinges, B. Potí, E. Reale, S. Slipersaeter, J. Thèves and B. van der Meulen (2007). Comparing the Evolution of National Research Policies: What Patterns of Change? *Science and Public Policy* 34(6): 372–388.

March, J.G. (1991). Exploration and Exploitation in Organizational Learning. *Organization Science* 2(1): 71–87.

McKelvey, M. and M. Holmén (2009). Introduction. *Learning to Compete in European Universities. From Social Institution to Knowledge Business.* M. McKelvey and M. Holmén. Cheltenham, Edward Elgar: 1–18.

Moed, H.F., W. Glänzel and U. Schmoch, Eds. (2010). *Handbook of Quantitative Science and Technology Research: The Use of Publication and Patent Statistics in Studies of S&T Systems* Dordrecht, The Netherlands, Kluwer Academic Publishers.

Mowery, D. and B. Sampat (2005). The Bayh-Dole Act of 1980 and University-Industry Technology Transfer: A Model for Other OECD Governments? *Essays in Honor of Edwin Mansfield.* A.N. Link and F.M. Scherer, Dordrecht, Springer: 233–245.

Nelson, R.R. (1959). The Simple Economics of Basic Scientific Research. *The Journal of Political Economy* 67(3): 297–306.

Scherer, F.M. and D. Harhoff (2000). Technology Policy for a World of Skew-distributed Outcomes. *Research Policy* 29(4–5): 559–566.

Schmoch, U., C. Rammer and C. Legler, Eds. (2006). *National Systems of Innovation in Comparison. Structure and Performance Indicators for the Knowledge Society.* Dordrecht, Springer.

Stokes, D.E. (1997). *Pasteur's Quadrant. Basic Science and Technological Innovation.* Washington DC, The Brookings Institution.

Strandburg, K.J. (2005). Curiosity-Driven Research and University Technology Transfer. *American Law & Economics Association Annual Meetings* 68.

Teece, D.J. (1986). Profiting from Technological Innovation: Implications for Integration, Collaboration, Licensing and Public Policy. *Research Policy* 15(6): 285–305.

Uyarra, E. (2010). Conceptualizing the Regional Roles of Universities, Implications and Contradictions. *European Planning Studies* 18(8): 1227–1246.

van den Hove, S. (2007). A Rationale for Science–Policy Interfaces. *Futures* 39(7): 807–826.

Watanabe, C., J.-H. Shin, J. Heikkinen, W. Zhao and C. Griffy-Brown (2011). New Functionality Development Through Follower Substitution for a Leader in Open Innovation. *Technological Forecasting and Social Change* 78(1): 116–131.

Whitley, R. (2008). Universities as Strategic Actors: Limitations and Variations. *The University in the Market.* L. Engwall and D. Weaire. London, Portland Press Ltd.: 23–37.

15 Conclusions and policy implications

Francesco Crespi and Francesco Quatraro

This book stemmed from the key observation that the increasing complexity in the dynamics of generation of new technological knowledge represents a challenge to policymakers interested in promoting innovation-driven development paths.

Actually, a large body of empirical evidence, including that presented in this text, shows that knowledge creation cannot be viewed as the outcome of research activities conducted randomly across technological space and promoted by untargeted financial support. On the contrary, innovation activities are bounded by path dependency and dynamic irreversibilities. Learning dynamics and the accumulation of competences over time indeed set evident constraints to the technological opportunities that individuals can profitably exploit in their innovation efforts. In this context, a multiplicity of enabling factors, from both the demand and the supply side, act and interact as drivers of knowledge generation, shaping the performance of innovation systems.

The implications for technology policy are relevant, and call for the adoption of an integrated system of policies capable of stimulating all the elements of innovation systems that play a role in the production of new scientific and technological knowledge. This book highlights that a "competent and smart" demand-driven approach is crucial when the relevance of the co-evolution between demand and technological change for economic development is fully appreciated. The "competent demand" hypothesis suggests that demand can pull the introduction and adoption of new superior technologies only if and when it is "competent" (i.e., devised by creative customers). Moreover, it has to be accompanied by qualified user–producer interactions that make the necessary access to external knowledge possible and allow its effective use as an input into the recombinant generation of technological knowledge. The effects of demand pull will be negligible, in terms of total factor productivity, when firms cannot access external knowledge, but rather rely upon flexible inputs, both capital and labor, that make it possible to adjust quickly to the demand levels moving on the existing map of isoquants in equilibrium conditions.

This framework stresses the importance of the types of knowledge interactions that link each sector to the others. An important implication is that the users involved in the system experience productivity increases that are directly related to the innovative activity of the rest of the system. The contribution of the system to the actual levels of technological advancement of each agent consists in the spillovers entering the recombinant generation of technological knowledge and enabling the introduction of technological innovations. The appreciation of the powerful effects of learning by using in the adoption process complements the well-known effect of learning by doing and makes it possible to appreciate both the upstream and the downstream linkages as important vectors of knowledge externalities. As suggested in this book, the quality of local contexts, including the level of social capital and quantity and quality of accumulated knowledge, shapes the dynamics of knowledge spillovers between different actors involved in the generation of new technologies.

Hence, government support should also be "smart," as innovation-based strategies for competitiveness can exert an effective impact on innovation insofar as policymakers and economic agents target new activities and new technologies that show some degree of relatedness with the core competences that individuals and regions have accumulated in their past history. The stimulation of innovation efforts directed towards the implementation of radically new technological trajectories appears to be more risky in that they need the development of new competences and new complementary assets, both tangible and intangible. As the complexity of innovation dynamics is augmented when discontinuities in the local patterns of development are at stake, the role of the public sector in favoring innovation efforts in new technological sectors may be crucial. As shown in this book, part of the EU R&D intensity gap with main competitors is related to the sectoral composition of European economies. Targeted industrial policies, addressing the innovation potential of those sectors that may potentially drive economic growth in the next decades, appear to be necessary. In this respect, the present text discussed the role of public policies for stimulating the emergence and the diffusion of new environmental technologies that have the potential to be the major driver for the transformation of economic systems into environmentally sustainable ones.

As evidenced in this book, complexity issues have to be considered for the identification and the implementation of a balanced and well-structured policy mix, due to the very nature of knowledge characteristics, the great number of policy instruments to be managed within the policy portfolio and the different governance levels at which policies are implemented. This is a very difficult outcome to be achieved for policymakers. Such difficulties clearly emerge in the analysis when a systemic framework is adopted, as it allows us to appreciate how the interactions between agents, institutions and policies shape system performances and how coordination problems arising from these interactive behaviors represent a major issue to be tackled by policy action.

In this framework, innovation systems can be enhanced by building on feedbacks in policymaking processes emerging from different stakeholders and actors involved in knowledge generation processes, as well as on cross-fertilization mechanisms between academic and policy debates that may lead to the introduction of new instruments and models of policy action.

Index

Page numbers in *italics* denote tables, those in **bold** denote figures.